Transfigured Rites
in Seventeenth-Century English Poetry

Transfigured Rites

in Seventeenth-Century English Poetry

A. B. CHAMBERS

University of Missouri Press

Columbia and London

Copyright © 1992 by
The Curators of the University of Missouri
University of Missouri Press, Columbia, Missouri 65201
Printed and bound in the United States of America

5 4 3 2 1   96 95 94 93 92

Library of Congress Cataloging-in-Publication Data

Chambers, A. B. (Alexander B.)
   Transfigured rites in seventeenth-century English poetry / by
A. B. Chambers.
        p.   cm.
   Includes bibliographical references and index.
   ISBN 0–8262–0808–8 (alk. paper)
   1. English poetry—Early modern, 1500–1700—History and criticism.
2. Christian poetry, English—History and criticism. 3. Rites and
ceremonies in literature. 4. Ritual in literature. I. Title.
PR545.R4C434   1992
821′.409382—dc20   91–39864
                                                             CIP

⊗™ This paper meets the requirements of the
American National Standard for Permanence of Paper
for Printed Library Materials, Z39.48, 1984.

Designer: Elizabeth Fett
Typesetter: Connell-Zeko Type & Graphics
Printer: Thomson-Shore, Inc.
Binder: Thomson-Shore, Inc.
Typeface: California

To the memory of my parents

Contents

Acknowledgments

Some of the bits and pieces of this book, now heavily reworked and greatly revised, have appeared before, but I am especially grateful to the editors of *The John Donne Journal* for permission to use a revised version of "'Goodfriday, 1613. Riding Westward': Looking Back," *JDJ* 6 (1987): 185–202. "Crooked Crosses in Donne and Crashaw" first appeared in *New Perspectives on the Life and Art of Richard Crashaw*, ed. John Roberts (Columbia: University of Missouri Press, 1990).

A Note on Bibles and on The Book of Common Prayer

Biblical passages are quoted with very great frequency throughout this book, and since I regularly present them in the context of liturgy, it has been impossible to avoid quoting two different English translations, sometimes in close proximity. The reason is that some biblical lessons are read from the church's Bible(s), but others are read from (and therefore necessarily printed in) the Book of Common Prayer. In 1559, when the first Prayer Book of the reign of Elizabeth I was promulgated, the translation in both cases was the Great Bible, a fact that was not affected when the Prayer Book was slightly revised in 1603. In 1611, however, the "King James" replaced the Great Bible as the "Authorized Version" for church use, and from that point on, those biblical lessons that were to be read from the Bible itself began to be heard in the version often used even today. The Psalter, however, and the Communion Gospels and Epistles (to mention the most significant and recurrent examples) continued to be sung and/or read from the Prayer Book, and they therefore continued to be heard in the earlier translation. In 1645 the Prayer Book was abolished by order of Parliament, and the surrender of all private copies was mandated under penalty of heavy fines. I mention the suppression because the hiatus probably contributed to the feeling that a revision was needed when the Prayer Book was reinstated at the Restoration. The new version first appeared in 1662, and the Psalter, formerly printed as a supplement, was bound up with the Book of Common Prayer but otherwise was not changed. The Authorized Version, however, at that point *did* replace the Great Bible as the translation used in the Prayer Book and, thus, for the first time became the version used for all biblical lessons. The 1662 Book of Common Prayer, I should add, included a number of other significant revisions, some of them far more substantive than the relatively minor changes made in 1603.

It follows that for most of the authors discussed in this book, Prayer Books printed in 1662 or later are not reliable, and the Authorized Version is *not* the one to quote when referring to the Psalter or lessons read from the Prayer Book. Invaluable help in keeping track of modifications up to and including 1662 is supplied by William Keeling, *Liturgiae Bri-*

*tannicae, Or The Several Editions of the Book of Common Prayer . . .
arranged to shew forth their respective variations,* 2d ed. (London, 1851;
repr. 1969), but Keeling, with so much else to present in parallel columns,
simply could not find the space to print either translation of the biblical
lessons. Also invaluable is *The Annotated Book of Common Prayer* (cited
more fully below), but its basic text, understandably enough, is 1662.

For my purposes, therefore, the best compromise in choosing a single
Book of Common Prayer from which to quote appears to be the version
modified in 1603 (and so dated, old-style fashion, on the title page, al-
though first published in 1604). Spelling and punctuation, naturally, are
old-style, and since it seemed sensible to quote from an old-style Autho-
rized Version, a personal copy dating from 1619 was a convenient choice
to make. For these various reasons, then, the Prayer Book, the biblical
lessons printed therein, and the Psalter are quoted from

> The Booke of Common Prayer, and Administration of the Sacraments,
> And other Rites and Ceremonies of the Church of England.
> Imprinted at London by Robert Barker, Printer to the Kings most
> Excellent Maiestie. Anno 1603.

And (separately printed),

> The Psalter or Psalmes of David, after the Translation of the Great
> Bible: *Pointed as it shall be sung or said in Churches.* Imprinted at
> London by *Robert Barker,* Printer to the Kings most Excellent Maiestie.
> Anno 1603.

The Authorized Version is quoted from

> The Holy Bible . . . Imprinted at London by Bonham Norton and
> Iohn Bill, Printers to the Kings most Excellent Maiestie. M.DC.XIX.

Context indicates which translation is being quoted at any given point,
but some of the more familiar passages now sound strange in the lan-
guage of the Great Bible, and I occasionally insert reminders of the rea-
son why.

My references to the Latin Vulgate, the Douai-Rheims translation of
it, the Greek New Testament, and the Hebrew Bible are so infrequent
that printing style is unimportant except in the sense that modern edi-
tions (listed below) are much easier to read than their seventeenth-cen-
tury counterparts. I also include a few references to the Renaissance Lat-
in translation prepared for Protestant use by Tremellius and Junius (Old
Testament) and Beza (New Testament), and since this work has largely
fallen into disuse, I mention here that as a matter of convenience I have
used a personal copy of

> Biblia sacra, sive Testamentvm vetvs . . . et Testamentvm novvm.
> Londini . . . apud Nathanielem Ponder . . . 1680.

A Note on Abbreviations and Short Titles

A number of authors and works (Donne's *Divine Poems*, for example, or Hooker's *Of the Laws of Ecclesiastical Polity*) are cited so regularly that footnoted references would clutter the pages and serve no useful purpose. The Bibliography indicates the editions to which I refer (often parenthetically) and from which I quote. I also use abbreviated titles for several standard works to which repeated reference (again, often parenthetically) is made; these are as follows:

ABCP: *The Annotated Book of Common Prayer; being an Historical, Ritual, and Theological Commentary on the Devotional System of the Church of England*, ed. Rev. John Henry Blunt. London: Gilbert and Rivington, 1866.

Bauer: *Encyclopedia of Biblical Theology: The Complete "Sacramentum Verbi,"* ed. Johannes B. Bauer. New York: The Crossroad Publishing Company, 1981. (A translation from *Bibeltheologisches Wörterbuch*, Graz, Vienna, and Cologne: Verlag Styria, 1959.)

OCEL: *The Oxford Companion to English Literature*, ed. Margaret Drabble. 5th ed. Oxford: Oxford University Press, 1985.

ODCC: *The Oxford Dictionary of the Christian Church*, ed. F. L. Cross. London: Oxford University Press, 1958.

PBD: *The Prayer Book Dictionary*, ed. George Harford and Morley Stevenson. New York: Longmans, Green, and Company, 1912.

Transfigured Rites

in Seventeenth-Century English Poetry

Let the worde of Christ dwel in you plenteously with all wise-
dome. Teach and exhort your owne selues in psalmes and hymnes,
& spiritual songs, singing with grace in your hearts to the Lorde.

ST. PAUL, EPISTLE FOR EPIPHANY 5

• • •

        you a Saint shall be
In chiefe, in this Poetick Liturgie.

HERRICK, "TO HIS KINSWOMAN"

• • •

This is LOVES sweet & heavenly sport,
To make my Days so long, & short;
That so they may a Shadow be
    Of his Eternitie,
Which, though beyond all Time it swell,
Yet is an Instant its best parallel.

JOSEPH BEAUMONT, "A CONCLUSORIE HYMNE"

Introduction

Liturgical poetry has to be among the oldest of identifiable genres for the simple reason that the Book of Psalms, whatever and whenever its ultimate beginnings, evidently was preserved for later times in the form of poetic texts appointed for liturgical use in Second Temple services dating from the sixth century B.C. Since the psalms are attributed to individuals—notably "David," of course, but also "Asaph, the chief musician"—their distinctive mode has long been (and continues to be even today) the simultaneous utterance of a private self and of a public congregation, the "I" of the individual psalmist and the composite or multiple "I" of those who join together in revoicing the words. Indeed, the customary line between singular and plural is here so blurred that the psalmist's first person singular can be interpreted nationalistically (an inversion, as it were, of the royal "we"): "R. Smend and others have maintained that the 'I' of the Psalms commonly refers not to an individual but to Israel as a nation" ("Psalms, Book of," *ODCC*, 1121A). Whatever the grammar itself may be, psalms have regularly seemed eminently appropriate not only for intensely personal circumstances or needs but also for the wider purposes of collective worship.

One might naively suppose that Christian churches automatically would confer at least equal value on New Testament hymnody, but that has not always been true. Quite the contrary, in fact, and one of the acrimonious divisions of opinion in sixteenth-century England concerned whether the hymns recorded in the Gospels should even be sung in church at all. The position taken by those opposed to the practice was that New Testament songs were entirely too individualistic to serve communal needs. Richard Hooker, defending Anglican practice in the 1590s, was forced into addressing this issue precisely because his nonconformist opponents were complaining,

> They [Anglicans] sing Benedictus, Nunc Dimittis, and Magnificat, we knowe not to what purpose, except some of them were ready to die, or except they would celebrate the memory of the Virgine. . . . These thanksgivings were made by occasion of certain particular benefits, and are no more to be used for ordinary prayers than the *Ave Maria*.[1]

---

1. Quoted in Richard Hooker, *Of the Laws of Ecclesiastical Polity*, 5.40.1 (2:154–55n).

The "Ave Maria," as it happens, was a relative newcomer to this list; in full form it "did not come into general use until the 16th cent." when "it received official recognition from its inclusion by Pope Pius V in the new Roman Breviary (1568)" ("Hail Mary," *ODCC*, 603A). In marked contrast, the "Benedictus" or "Song of Thanksgiving" (Luke 1.68–79), "Nunc dimittis" or "Song of Simeon" (Luke 2.29–32), and "Magnificat" or "Song of Praise" (Luke 1.46–55) had been used in Christian liturgy for centuries. It is undeniable, however, that they were first sung by Zacharias, Simeon, and Mary in circumstances that were not possibly repeatable in any literal way by anyone else either before or since.

This truth, as Hooker saw it, was not, however, a serious liability; indeed, in some respects for him and for others it was a potent argument for frequently resinging the songs. Lancelot Andrewes, to cite an eminent example, urges that three songs in particular be remembered for personal use: "Let us therefore sing to the Father (with *Zacharie*) *Benedictus:* and to the *Sonne* (with the *blessed Virgin*) *Magnificat:* and (with all the *Angells*) *Gloria in Excelsis*" (*XCVI Sermons*, 15). Hooker takes a comparable view, but since he is arguing rather than exhorting, one part of his strategy (*Laws* 1:155) is to focus attention on an inconsistency in the liturgical views of those on the other side.

> Seeing therefore they pretend no quarrel at other psalms, which are in like manner appointed also to be daily read, why do these so much offend and displease their taste? They are the first gratulations wherewith our Lord and Saviour was joyfully received into the world . . . the most luculent testimonies that Christian religion hath; yea the only sacred hymns they are that Christianity hath peculiar unto itself, the other [Psalms] being songs of praise and thanksgiving, but songs wherewith as we serve God, so the Jew likewise.

A weighty argument, in Hooker's view, is that the Bible itself sanctions ceremonial repetition of statements that, in their original forms, were essentially personal. Psalms, once again, is the biblical book specifically in question, but Hooker has no doubt about the rightness of extending the principle involved. "Moreover Hezekiah the king . . . commanded yᵉ Leuites to sing praise vnto the Lord, with the words of Dauid, and of Asaph the Seer" (2 Chronicles 29.30). And Hezekiah did so, Hooker says (*Laws* 2:156), because he

> was persuaded as we are that the praises of God in the mouths of his saints are not so restrained to their own particular, but that others may both con-

---

Hooker's fifth book in effect is an exposition of Anglican liturgy, but the polemical purpose dictated an organization faithful to argumentation rather than ritual. For a rearrangement and an elaborated version, see John S. Marshall, *Hooker's Theology of Common Prayer: The Fifth Book of the Polity Paraphrased and Expanded into a Commentary on The Prayer Book* (Sewanee, Tenn., University of the South, 1956).

veniently and fruitfully use them: first, because the mystical communion
. . . is such as maketh every one to be interested in those precious blessings
which any one of them receiveth at God's hands: secondly, because when
any thing is spoken to extol the goodness of God whose mercy endureth for
ever, albeit the very particular occasion whereupon it riseth do come no
more, yet . . . a small resemblance between the benefits which we and
others have received, may serve to make the same words of praise and
thanksgiving fit though not equally in all circumstances fit for both . . .
[and] last of all because even when there is not as much as the show of any
resemblance, nevertheless by often using their words in such manner, our
minds are daily more and more inured with their affections.

These several arguments presumably are designed to appeal to the
various positions that Anglicanism enabled its diverse and divergent ad-
herents to embrace. The point about emulating God's saints, even those
found in the Bible, might not be worth much to those vehemently op-
posed to the "Ave Maria" but certainly would be attractive to those who
felt otherwise. Generalizing on the theme of divine blessings, however
particular the specific instances, was and perhaps still is a recurrent hom-
iletic practice both inside and outside Anglicanism. And, of course, the
idea of fostering personal piety is scarcely one to which Hooker's most
vigorous opponents could possibly take exception.

An important point, at least for my purposes, is that Hooker's rationale
serves as a paradigm not only for the reasons why some biblical songs
were a part of some rituals but also for the motivations apparently behind
the creation of materials that were explicitly intended primarily or even
exclusively for the congregation of the self. For if it was liturgically useful
to adapt individual utterance to the worship of a group, then it also
was spiritually helpful to reverse the process: verse appropriated by the
Church continued to be claimed by individuals for personal use, and
public ceremonies themselves were converted into private accommoda-
tions that served—to requote Hooker—"to make the same words of praise
and thanksgiving fit though not equally in all circumstances fit for both."

The flexible circumstances to which Hooker refers quite accurately
imply that affiliations between liturgy and verse necessarily can be of
more than one kind. At this point, therefore, some preliminary indica-
tions are in order as to how the various aspects of the subject are to be
examined here. The simplest relationship, surely, is the one that exists
between the source of a literary work and the work itself, but with liturgy
and verse the parallels are not always completely straightforward even at
this most fundamental of levels. The first chapter illustrates these intro-
ductory facts by including parodies of prayers as well as adaptions of
them. Rites and their formal patterns can be adapted to uses either close
to or notably distant from the ones envisaged by the authors of the Book
of Common Prayer, and the second chapter accordingly examines the

initiatory rite of baptism as modified and transformed by several authors—especially Herbert, Vaughan, and Traherne—who frequently were concerned with the symbolic child of God. The Bible is a major source for liturgy and poetry alike, but in reading poems it often can be worthwhile to distinguish between the Bible itself and liturgical organizations of biblical materials. Chapter 3 addresses this point in connection with a fairly large number of major and minor writers who employ more or less comparable poetic strategies that produce, however surprisingly, remarkably different results.

Ritual necessarily takes a sacramental view of the world and of human existence. Chapter 4 explores this fact, especially as it pertains to time and eternity and to the timings of human experience. Metaphoric language is extraordinarily important here, but so also is figurative thought, and a major reason why this is the longest chapter is that the patterns of thought appear in such diverse forms. Chapter 5 describes poems for Christmas and brings together almost all of the various kinds of material in previous chapters; December 25, especially for Donne, Herbert, Vaughan, and Milton, was a microcosmic liturgical day of macrocosmic significance. Good Friday, a day of similar import, is taken up in chapter 6 for discussion of sermon literature and of poems by Donne and Crashaw. Easter necessarily is left out because there simply are no poems of genuine substance for that day, but adaptations of the rite for secular as well as sacred purposes are frequently found in Herrick, the author considered in chapter 7. Herrick and Milton died in 1674; a postscript briefly surveys developments from that year up until the death in 1974 of David Jones, an author quite as deeply committed to liturgical work as those writers who preceded him some three centuries earlier.

A large number, possibly most, of these diverse poets and various poems can be approached in terms of a guiding principle enunciated centuries ago but reiterated annually in church on the fifth Sunday of Epiphany season: "Teach and exhort your owne selues in psalmes and hymnes, & spiritual songs, singing with grace in your hearts" (Colossians 3.16). As St. Paul himself perhaps implies, and as seventeenth-century poets make both abundantly and gloriously clear, the psalms and hymns of the church are often most wonderful when transfigured by personal devotion and heard within the temple of the heart.

1 Prayers and Litanies

DONNE'S "A LITANY" AND HERBERT'S "PRAYER"

English poets of the late sixteenth and early seventeenth centuries regularly wrote verse that might accurately be called a "reappropriation" and/or "re-creation" of liturgical materials. Evidently, however, no technical vocabulary was needed for the poetry, and a possible reason why is the elaborately precise language already available in discussions of ritual itself. Donne wrote to Sir Henry Goodyer that his poem "A Litany" was an accommodation of the "divine and publique"; it was not meant "for publike service in . . . Churches" but "for lesser Chappels, which are my friends." He further observed, "Neither the Roman Church need call it defective, because it abhors not the particular mention of the blessed Triumphers in heaven; nor the Reformed can discreetly accuse it, of attributing more then a rectified devotion ought to doe."[1]

Apparently it did not occur to Donne to refer to any of the several components into which a litany and therefore his own poem, technically speaking, may be divided. Presumably, however, he knew about the various parts—after all, he includes variations on them—and took for granted that we would know them too. Since that may not actually be the case, three terms in particular are worth explaining now to save space later. The "Invocations" specifically name the "Triumphers in heaven," including (despite the objections in some quarters to the "Ave Maria") the Virgin Mary. "Deprecations" beseech deliverance from a large number of specifically mentioned evils, the manifold requests being punctuated with "Good Lord deliver us." And the "Obsecrations" list various means of divine deliverance, in each case using a formulaic repetition of "by": "By the mystery of thy holy Incarnation," for example, or "by thy Cross and Passion," and "by thy precious Death and Burial."

In so far as Donne was capable of writing poetry that seems unexciting, "A Litany" probably qualifies for most readers today, and it would not have been improved, either then or now, by weighing it down with Latinate terminology. Donne quite sensibly left out that kind of thing,

---

1. John Donne, *Letters to Severall Persons of Honour (1651)*, 33–34. Helen Gardner (*The Divine Poems*, 81), in annotating the poem, quotes part of this same letter.

5

but to apprehend some of the wit actually present in the poem, one probably needs, if not the vocabulary, at least the concepts behind it. At one point, Donne deprecates wit itself by praying, "That wit, borne apt, high good to doe, / . . . be not nothing too" (239–41). And when he writes, "Heare this prayer Lord, O Lord deliver us / From trusting in those prayers, though powr'd out thus" (125–26), he humbly deprecates his own deprecations. Donne must have expected Goodyer and other readers to see this fact, even though neither "deprecate" nor "deprecation" appears anywhere in the poem.

Reappropriation is another word not used, but "re-create" appears early on in the request, "re-create mee" (4), and both processes are in fact ongoing throughout the work. A telling indication, one particularly relevant for the point being made here, is the handling of personal pronouns. "Re-create *mee*" and "O Lord deliver *us*" both parallel and contrast to one another, and a loose pattern can be seen in that singulars outnumber plurals in early stanzas but disappear later on. Quick illustrations (with added italics) can be had by balancing the first stanza against the last. At the outset,

> Father of Heaven, and him, by whom
> It, and *us* for it, and all else, for *us*
> Thou madest, and govern'st ever, come
> And re-create *mee*, now growne ruinous:
> *My* heart is by dejection, clay,
> And by *selfe*-murder, red.
> From this red earth, O Father, purge away
> All vicious tinctures, that new fashioned
> *I* may rise up from death, before *I*'am dead.

And at the end,

> Sonne of God heare *us*, and since thou
> By taking *our* blood, owest it *us* againe,
> Gaine to thy selfe, or *us* allow;
> And let not both *us* and thy selfe be slaine;
> O lambe of God, which took'st *our* sinne
> Which could not stick to thee,
> O let it not returne to *us* againe,
> But Patient and Physition being free,
> As sinne is nothing, let it no where be.

These stanzas further illustrate the poem's tendency to be quite as knotty in thought as we expect a Donne poem to be, but they simply have not the ring, at least not today, of Donne's celebrated remark, in the seventeenth meditation of the *Devotions*, "No Man is an *Iland* [in some circumstances, possibly a *me*-land], intire of it selfe" (*Devotions*, 87). Comparable points nonetheless are being made in each case. First of all, the singular and plural pronouns, as in singing the psalms, to some extent are interchangeable. Second, the personal prayer of the speaker is presented in ceremonially public terms on behalf of all those who engage in similarly personal prayer by the very act of reading the verse. If the poem were read aloud to others, then the line between private and public might become even less distinct.

The resemblance between litany ("lite," supplication) and liturgy (people-work—from "leos" + "urgos") is largely fortuitous but not without significance. The principal theoretical aims of worship, whether private or public, are the work of prayer and praise. *"Deigne at my hands this crown of prayer and praise,"* as Donne phrases it, in both the first and the last line of *La Corona*. This work ought to be looked at in some detail and therefore is one to return to, but I mention it here as a means to move from Donne's "Litany" to Herbert's "Prayer," a poem so very personal in style that it borders on and perhaps even crosses over the line into idiosyncracy. That is one reason why it also is an excellent preliminary example of the kind of poetry I am attempting to approach.

There are, in fact, two poems called "Prayer" included in *The Temple*. The second one begins with an exclamation, "Of what an easie quick accesse, / My blessed Lord, art thou!"—an access that, in the poem's opening lines, is indifferently available to one or to many, to "our requests" (3) or to "my suit" (5). In this case, however, "my" evidently presupposes "our" since Herbert, with a reversal of Donne's procedure in "A Litany," begins in the plural but concentrates thereafter on the singular: "If I but lift mine eyes, my suit is made" (5);

> I value prayer so,
> That were I to leave all but one,
> Wealth, fame, endowments, vertues, all should go;
> I and deare prayer would together dwell.
> (20–23)

"Prayer" (II), possibly because of its later placement, seems so much more accessible than the earlier "Prayer" (I) that some readers might prefer to reverse Herbert's ordering. Herbert does provide interpretive help of his own, however, in that "Prayer" (I) is part of a subsequence of poems. "Sinne" has led to "Affliction," which has been remedied first by "Faith" and next by "The H. Communion." Prayer is a customary response in thanksgiving for the Eucharist, and the first poem with that title thus is given next. In "Faith," Herbert assures us, "A peasant may beleeve as much / As a great Clerk, and reach the highest stature" (29–30); "grace fills up uneven nature" (32). It is possible to think, even so, that Herbert's "definition" of prayer actually is rather "clerkish" or at least that the subject closely resembles such things as sin, affliction, faith, and Holy Communion in that it is considerably less simple than the simplicity of the title apparently suggests.

PRAYER

Prayer the Churches banquet, Angels age,
      Gods breath in man returning to his birth,
      The soul in paraphrase, heart in pilgrimage,
The Christian plummet sounding heav'n and earth;
Engine against th' Almightie, sinners towre,
      Reversed thunder, Christ-side-piercing spear,
      The six-daies world transposing in an houre,
A kinde of tune, which all things heare and fear;
Softnesse, and peace, and joy, and love, and blisse,
      Exalted Manna, gladnesse of the best,
      Heaven in ordinarie, man well drest,
The milkie way, the bird of Paradise,
      Church-bels beyond the starres heard, the souls bloud,
      The land of spices; something understood.

If all "shaped" verse requires that typographically visual form reflect the subject (as it does in "The Altar" and "Easter-Wings"), then this poem does not qualify. And yet typography may be the most obvious signal that, despite the seeming freedom of language and thought, Herbert has not totally departed from predetermined formality. The poem has fourteen lines, after all, and thus must be, by definition, a quatorzain. For purposes of contrast as well as comparison, one could think of Herrick's opening poem in *Hesperides*, "The Argument of his Book," with its fourteen lines and seven couplets. In Herbert, the typographical "shape" further indicates that this poem, unlike Herrick's verse, is, in fact, not merely a quatorzain but is, more precisely, a sonnet. The point is self-evident as soon as one notices it, even though the rhyme scheme cannot be labeled "Shakespearean," "Petrarchan," "Spenserian," or anything else—except, perhaps, "Herbertian." The two initial quatrains have alternating rhymes in the "English" style, and there is a concluding couplet as well. Lines 9–12, however, abandon that pattern for a quatrain that is enclosed, but imperfectly so, by "blisse-best-drest-Paradise." The rhymes certainly are in the "Italian" style, but this is a *third* quatrain in the "English" manner rather than part of an Italianate sestet. Elasticity of rhyme scheme within theoretically strict generic limits is matched by other verbal maneuvers of varying kinds. Most lines can be readily scanned, but the thirteenth ("Church-bels beyond the starres heard, the souls bloud"), despite the ten syllables, stretches itself out abnormally as it looks far above and deeply within. It leads immediately to a concluding line that is regular in its metrics but bifurcated in its thought between the physically exotic ("the land of spices") and a mental abstraction ("something understood").

If my count is accurate, there are twenty-seven successive appositives: phrases, clauses, and (in line 9) single words. No professional number symbolist is required to entertain the supposition that nine, the mysterious and divine number, projects itself here in triple or triune form. That Herbert was capable of this particular kind of wit is evidenced with great clarity by the manifold triplicities of "Trinitie Sunday," especially the third three-line stanza with its three direct objects, three prepositional phrases, and triply alliterated *r*.

> Lord, who hast form'd me out of mud,
>> And hast redeem'd me through thy bloud,
>> And sanctifi'd me to do good;
>
> Purge all my sinnes done heretofore:
>> For I confesse my heavie score,
>> And I will strive to sinne no more.
>
> Enrich my heart, mouth, hands in me,
>> With faith, with hope, with charitie;
>> That I may *r*unne, *r*ise, *r*est with thee.

In "Prayer," however, Herbert either complicates or, from one point of view, simplifies the syntax of his triadic arrangements. Connectives are uniformly omitted except in line 9, which goes to a quadruple extreme: "and . . . and . . . and . . . and." Dependent verbs and participles, both present and past, are given, but no independent verb can be found. The suppression of "is" suggests that while prayer can be a "something understood," it nonetheless defies standard definitional methods. It is *not* equatable with any one of the many items listed, whether concrete or abstract, exotic or commonplace, and it is not divine, although it appears to be more than human. In "A Litany" Donne prays, "Heare thy selfe now, for thou in us dost pray" (207). In Herbert, recognizably similar thinking appears: God's breath, for example, as it is vocalized by human speech, or "Heaven in ordinarie, man well drest" (11). Herbert's language, unlike Donne's, is largely asyntactic, however, and much of the content of the poem turns out to be so metaphoric and compact that it is neither readily nor accurately paraphrasable, even though, like prayer itself, it certainly can be understood.

Against the references to "Engine" and "Reversed thunder, Christ-side-piercing spear," one might place Herbert's poem "Artillerie," especially its assertions, "I have also starres and shooters too" (17) and "Then we are shooters both, and thou dost deigne / To enter combate with us" (25–26). And against both poems, or at least these parts of them, one might set Donne's comment (*Sermons* 3:152) on "weak prayer":

> The words of man . . . are a Canon against God himselfe, and batter down all his severe and heavy purposes for Judgements. Yet, this comes not, God

knows, out of the weight or force of our words, but out of the easinesse of God. God puts himselfe in the way of a shot, he meets a weak prayer, and is graciously pleased to be wounded by that: God sets up a light, that we direct the shot upon him, he enlightens us with a knowledge, how, and when, and what to pray for; yea, God charges, and discharges the Canon himself upon himselfe.[2]

Not all of Herbert's dense phrasing needs an elaborate gloss, in some cases precisely because the places to interpolate "is," the absent verb, are quite obvious. Or so one supposes before seeing what the results actually can be. The closing lines of a "regularized" version printed in 1697 are

> Prayer exalted Manna is,
>   And gladness of the best.
> Heaven in Ordinary 'tis,
>   Prayer is Man well drest.
>
> The Church-Bell's heard beyond the Stars,
>   It is the Souls Heart-blood,
> A kind of Land of Spices 'tis,
>   And something understood.[3]

"The six-daies world transposing in an houre" is a line that itself is transposable to mean, "Prayer in one hour abridges and changes the musical key of the harmonious universe which required six full days for its creation." If, however, this paraphrase is faithful to the original, then emending the punctuation (as Hutchinson proposes) to "six-daies-world transposing" may be desirable or even necessary.

"Churches banquet" and "Church-bels," the phrases at nearly the beginning and nearly the end, indicate that the poem as a whole, however eccentric some of it may look, is not to be regarded as hopelessly inappropriate for or alien to a public context, and the "hymn" quoted in the preceding paragraph hands over to a congregation the property that Herbert apparently stakes out as his own. Personal pronouns, one notices, whether singular or plural, are another customary linguistic feature, which in this poem Herbert scrupulously omits; "I" and "we" either are irrelevant or are equally but silently implied.

Donne's "A Litany" and Herbert's "Prayer" are two sides of one coin in that the first openly adopts in wholesale fashion a public mode of address

---

2. For comparable statements and imagery, see John Donne, *The Sermons of John Donne*, ed. George R. Potter and Evelyn M. Simpson, 2:220; 4:311; 5:223, 364 (quoted by Patrides, annotating "Prayer" [I]); 6:329; and 7:58, 306. Donne sometimes (for example *Sermons* 4:311) cites Tertullian as his authority for this kind of imagery.

3. *Select Hymns Taken Out Of Mr. Herbert's Temple* (London, 1697; Los Angeles: Augustan Reprint Society, No. 98, with an introduction by William E. Stephenson, 1962), 11.

whereas the second, far less overtly, nudges personal expressivity in the direction of churchwide, though not "churchy," application. Like the statement quoted earlier from Hooker, these poems can serve as paradigms, though more limited than Hooker in this respect, for two kinds of verse often found in the canons of their authors and in those of other writers of the time. Herbert's indirection will be the more interesting of these two strategies for most people today because it relies on verbal effects that are independent of liturgical ceremony. "A Litany," while not out of Donne's top drawer, impresses itself upon me with very considerable force, but one of the reasons why is an occasion when, with propriety thrown to the winds, I followed hard on the heels of an Episcopal priest afflicted by laryngitis and not up to singing the lines in The Great Litany that I was singing for him: with crucifer and candle-bearing acolytes ahead, full-robed and full-voiced choir behind, and an answering congregation down on its knees. In 1608, the date tentatively assigned to this poem, Donne no doubt could count on many readers being able to engage in a mental re-creating of some sort or other on their own. It also may be worth remembering that 1608 is several years prior to Donne's ordination, but Herbert's "Prayer" is the work of an experienced priest, watchful over minutiae in the ceremony but also intensely aware of the invisibly internal import of eye- and ear-catching showiness that can sometimes be jettisoned, especially if one is not dependent on the traffic signals of sensory experience for devotional and spiritual response. This particular difference between lay person and priest may be more theoretical than actual, of course, and in any case, I doubt that it could be adequate to explain each of the differences among the poems next to be cited.

VERSE LITANIES

Nashe and Crashaw

Donne's title can be "*A Litany*" (in Helen Gardner's edition) or "*The Litany*" (in C. A. Patrides's) because the poem is *a* personal adaptation of *the* public prayer. There is the further fact that "litany" is itself a generic term. The "Deprecatio Gelasii" or Intercession of Pope Gelasius (papal years, 492–496) is "the earliest extant Latin litany," according to the *ODCC* ("Deprecatio Gelasii," 390A), which adds that even "by the time of Alcuin [c. 735–804] it was probably already being superseded by the more popular Litany of the Saints." The "more popular" litany, still in use among some Romans, could hardly leave out prayers to God but receives its name from the fact that large numbers of saints also are individually named. In an introduction to The Great Litany (the only major one in the Prayer Book), *The Annotated Book of Common Prayer* points out that the Litany of the Saints, in some of its versions, has had formidably long invocations, the breathtaking examples being one in use at "the venerable abbey of St. Germain des Près," with ninety-four saints; "an old Tours form" that "has a list of saints occupying more than four columns"; and "a Litany of the ninth century . . . accomodated to the use of Paris" that "has one hundred and two such invocations" (*ABCP*, 47A). Also quoted is a directive in use at medieval York to the effect that as many saints were to be invoked as the length of the processional required ("secundum exigentiam itineris"), a hair-raising proposition unless one supposes that some names may be omitted instead of still more having to be added.

The Litany of the Saints, in one or another of its forms, is the presumable source for those stanzas of "A Litany" in which, to requote the letter to Goodyer, Donne "abhors not the particular mention of the blessed Triumphers in heaven." As the poem itself indirectly indicates, however, the long lists were drastically pared down by the Reformers, and the process of subtraction can finally leave nothing more than that from which the process of addition began. "The earliest form of the LITANY," to quote the *Prayer Book Dictionary* ("Lesser Litany," 435A), "was the repetition of *Kyrie eleison* [Lord have mercy on us] three, six, or even up to 300 times."

This is the one quoted by Thomas Nashe in "Adieu, farewell earths blisse," the "Song" from *Summers Last Will and Testament*, which often is referred to by quoting the line that reads, "Brightnesse falls from the ayre" (or possibly, though one hopes not, "from the hair").[4] The poem, in this respect rather like long versions of the Litany of the Saints, looks as if it could have been expanded or even contracted to fit any required length, and the liturgically important point is or seems to be merely that each stanza ends with "Lord, have mercy on us." The refrain, however, while invariably the same, becomes increasingly more powerful because of the changing context that Nashe, not the liturgy, supplies. The effect is not unlike that sometimes found in ballads, but because of the "Church-bels" (to requote Herbert's phrase) ringing in the background, the impact is especially intense.

> Come, come, the bells do crye,
> I am sick, I must dye,
> Lord, haue mercy on vs.

---

4. Thomas Nashe, *The Works of Thomas Nashe*, ed. Ronald B. McKerrow, 3:282–84. This song is largely independent of its surroundings (and, indeed, has been anthologized as if a separate poem). A second litany (3:292), comprised of two seven-line stanzas, is sung soon after the first; line 7 (repeated as line 14) is, "From winter, plague, & pestilence, good Lord, deliver us."

These lines from the fourth stanza suggest the audible bells of some local parish, but the singer evidently is too mortally ill to travel to church, however short the distance may be. "Earths blisse," "This world," and "lifes lustfull joys" are bid "Adieu" as the song begins: "Death proues them all but toyes, / None from his darts can flye." Wealth and health last long enough to "fade," but the plague, though "full swift" in its progress, is more enduring in its consequences. Past distances, both geographical and temporal, have been immense and have encompassed evanescent glory as far back as ancient Greece and Troy: "Wormes feed on *Hector* braue."

> Beauty is but a flowre,
> Which wrinckles will deuoure,
> Brightnesse falls from the ayre,
> Queenes haue died yong and faire,
> Dust hath closed *Helens* eye.
> I am sick, I must dye.
>   Lord, haue mercy on vs.

Even in ancient climes it seems to have been true that "man is but a flowre," as the burial office has it, for "in the middest of life, we are in death." On the far side of the church and its bells is, of course, its cemetery, and on the far side of that is "Hels executioner" who "Hath no eares for to heare." There is no getting round a trip to the grave, no matter how frequently one prays, "Lord, haue mercy on vs." One might, however, be able to evade the executioner—if, that is, God responds favorably to the prayer. Five iterations of the lesser litany, in one sense invariable and in another quite varied, are followed by a radical change in thought that, in retrospect, seems well-nigh inevitable. A partial analogue is Shakespeare's *Richard II*; in the play named for him, the king makes a final exit with the command, "Mount, mount my soul! thy seat is up on high, / Whilst my gross flesh sinks downward, here to die" (5.5.110–11). Nashe's singer, regardless of rank, has comparable aspirations as he concludes.

> Heauen is our heritage,
> Earth but a players stage,
> Mount wee vnto the skye.
> I am sick, I must dye:
>   Lord, haue mercy on vs!

Additional stanzas conceivably could have been added in the middle to swell out "this long Disease, my Life," as Pope later puts it ("Epistle to Arbuthnot," 137). Nashe's beginning and end, however, are nearly as fixed as those of human existence itself, and there is no far side of heaven. That much is clear enough, but one might ask to whom the "us," six times repeated, refers and especially who the "we" of "we mount" may be. Body as well as soul? An otherwise absent congregation filled up by Everyman? The transposable "six-daies-world," transmuted into new heavens and earth? Nashe, like Herbert, by leaving some things out, actually manages to put even more things in.

The Lesser Litany, the Great Litany, and the Litany of the Saints were (and, in some usages, still are) the ones with greatest currency, but others did (and, with the same restriction, still do) serve more specialized needs. The Litany of the Sacred Heart of Jesus, for example, proclaims its distinctive focus in the title and appears to have been a stimulus for Crashaw in writing "The Flaming Heart." The Sacred *Heart* takes its name from that part of a litany technically known as the "supplications," each of which, in this instance, begins formulaically with "Heart of Jesus" and next adds various descriptive epithets before concluding, "Have mercy on us." Hence, for example, "Heart of Jesus, glowing furnace of charity," "Heart of Jesus, pierced with a lance," and "Heart of Jesus, delight of all saints."[5]

The material is very close to some of Crashaw's, but the poem is addressed to St. Teresa (or Theresa) of Avila (1515–1582), the Carmelite nun and mystic, and comparable material already was associated with her. Her autobiography (quoted in George Williams's headnote) tells of visionary visitations by a seraph who plunged a fiery dart into her heart, an incident depicted in stylized portrayals of the saint, including the famous statue by Bernini in Rome and the plate that prefaces some editions of Teresa's work. Teresa identified her visitor as one "of those most Superiour Angells, who seem to be all in a fire; and he well might be of them, whome we call *Seraphins*." Donne, in "A Litany," partly reverses this situation and its sexuality by referring to the Virgin Mary as a "she-Cherubin / Which unlock'd Paradise" (38–39). The word *cherub* has never been satisfactorily explained, and various forms of the singular and plural at one time were in competition.[6] Seraphim, however, etymologically are "the burning ones" or, as St. Teresa has it, are "all in a fire." Milton reflects the derivation in his poem "Upon the Circumcision" when, in the first line, he links the seraphim to "flaming Powers" ("Powers," as Hughes's annotation points out, were traditionally ranked sixth among the angelic orders) and then implores that they "burn" in their "sighs" (8).

With this kind of thing ready to hand, Crashaw needed no litany for

5. Quoted from Joseph A. Nelson, *The Roman Breviary in English*; see supplementary pages 18**–21** of the volume for Winter and/or the volume for Spring.

6. See the examples given by Stella Brook, *The Language of the Book of Common Prayer* (New York: Oxford University Press, 1965), 116–17. Brook noticed that "cherubin" is to be found (probably as a singular) in the Te Deum. "Cherubims," an illogical double plural, appears in Psalter Psalm 99.1.

his initial argument that, because of the saint's flaming heart, we really ought to call the seraph a saint and "the SAINT the SERAPHIM" (11). The contrast is comparable to strategies noticed earlier, especially if "-im," the plural suffix added to the singular "seraph," is taken seriously. The sharp juxtaposition reminds me of the mixture of singulars and plurals in liturgical grammar, but in any case, it is in his conclusion that Crashaw adopts the formulaic language of a litany's "obsecrations." The word that establishes the form is "by" or, in Latin, "per"—that is, "through." Donne, for example, has "through thy gallant humblenesse" ("A Litany," 176), and the Anglican Great Litany (to requote a phrase earlier mentioned) has "By thy holy Incarnation." Williams, presumably overlooking the existence of other litanies, was misled by the Anglican formula and in consequence was surprised: "Surely it is remarkable that Crashaw should at the end of his life have returned to English forms and Anglican ways to sustain this most Roman and Counter Reformation ecstasy" (headnote, 61). Milton, in the Circumcision poem, introduced hyperbolic and seraphic flames to balance equally hyperbolic liquids, but he did not include highly exaggerated verbal formulas. Crashaw's poem, and this is a major reason for citing the Litany of the Sacred Heart, is both hyperbolic and formulaic.

> By all thy dowr of LIGHTS & FIRES;
> By all the eagle in thee, all the doue;
> By all thy lives & deaths of loue;
> By thy larg draughts of intellectuall day,
> And by thy thirsts of loue more large then they;
> By all thy brim-fill'd Bowles of feirce desire
> By thy last Morning's draught of liquid fire;
> By . . .
> By . . .
> . . . .
> By all of HIM we haue in THEE;
> Leave nothing of my SELF in me.
>
> (94–100)

And then the final couplet:

> Let me so read thy life, that I
> Vnto all life of mine may dy.

St. Teresa sensed that the seraph not only "thrust . . . through my verie Hart" but that "when he drew" the dart "back, me thought, it carried away, as much, as it had touched within me; and left all that, which remained, wholy inflamed with a great loue of Almightye God" (Williams, 62). As he ends the poem, Crashaw evidently is proposing to continue the reading of the saint's life (her "legend" in the old sense of a saint's biography), thereby attempting to make her experience his own. A vehement objection to the veneration of saints was that it seemed, to those opposed to the practice, to place distracting, unnecessary, and indeed quite useless intermediaries between the individual and God. Those on the other side, among them Crashaw, supposed that a self-destructive union with "all of HIM we haue in THEE" would be a lofty humility, a positive negation.

The thinking is transparently and deliberately illogical, but Crashaw also implies a chain of reasoning of the kind that textbooks on logic refer to as a "sorites" (literally, a "heaping"), in which the predicate of one statement becomes the subject of the next. Crashaw is too intent upon verbalizing the formulaic "by" to verbalize the successive parts of the chain, and a spelled-out version in any case was superfluous because the form is sufficiently clear. The sorites, at rather less than full length, is this: If we may invoke the saints to pray for us, as litanies do, then the "obsecrations" applied to events in the life of Christ—as in "by thy Agony" and/or "Heart of Jesus, pierced with a lance"—also may apply to imperfect echoes of those events in the lives of his saints. And if we can rightly make that first application, then we may further reapply the legends of the saints to the more severely imperfect echoes in ourselves. And if we actually succeed in doing that, then downward progression in this case can be a means of reversing our Fall in Adam and Eve and of ascending higher than the seraphim. Herbert wrote a poem for St. Mary Magdalene but usually preferred to shorten the chain: "If I imp my wings on thine, / Affliction shall advance the flight in me" ("Easter-Wings," 19–20), where "thine" refers to neither a winged seraph nor a saint but to Christ himself. Crashaw preferred to stretch it out and in doing so approximated fuller litanic splendor.

PARODIC INVERSIONS

Ignoto and Sidney

Two parodic litanies can round off this introductory material by showing with great clarity that liturgical splendor, like the secular variety, can be subverted into satiric fireworks. "The Litany of the Duke of Buckingham," a rough-and-tumble satire, was included in *Poems on Affairs of State*, first published in 1680. The anonymous author ("Ignoto" in the subheading for this section) refers in the title to the lord who also was the model for Zimri in Dryden's *Absalom and Achitophel* (published the same year), but Dryden's rapier is replaced by a blunt weapon. The poem consists of twenty triplets, each based on the form of the litany's "deprecations." The punctuating phrase in the Anglican version is "Good Lord, deliver us" and in the Latin, "Libera nos, Domine." In Buckingham's litany the Latin is partly quoted but a tacit and sardonic "Lord" (or, possibly, "Duke") must be mentally substituted for "Domine." The first triplet is enough to illustrate the strategy, no doubt effective enough for the author's own purposes. For my purposes, however, a major point is that a litany, whether English or Latin, was presumed to be so widely familiar that satiric force, also presumably, would be instantly felt.

> From a sensual, proud, atheistical life,
> From arming our lackey with pistol and knife,
> From murd'ring the husband and whoring the wife,
> 　　　*Libera nos.*[7]

A century earlier is the thirtieth poem of Sidney's *Certain Sonnets.* An amorous counterpart to Nashe's "Adieu," it commands,

> Ring out your belles, let mourning shewes be spread,
> 　For love is dead:
> 　　All Love is dead, infected
> 　　With plague of deepe disdaine.
> 　　　　　　　　(1–4)

The fact appears to be certain, the cause of the would-be lover's mortal wound is that his "Worth" is "rejected" as "nought," his "Faith fair scorne doth gaine" (5–6), and the resulting prayer is,

> 　From so ungratefull fancie,
> 　From such a femall franzie,
> 　From them that use men thus,
> 　Good Lord deliver us.
> 　　　　(7–10)

"Weepe neighbours, weepe." Love's "winding sheete is shame." There- fore, "From so ungratefull fancie, / From such a femall franzie, . . . / Let Dirge be sung, and Trentals rightly read."

> For Love is dead:
> 　Sir wrong his tombe ordaineth,
> 　My mistresse' Marble hart,
> 　Which Epitaph containeth,
> 　'Her eyes were once his dart.'
> 　　From so ungratefull fancie,
> 　. . . . .

7. *Poems on Affairs of State*, vol. 2, ed. Elias F. Mengel (New Haven: Yale University Press, 1965), 192. Other satiric litanies are scattered through the *State Poems*, and see also two satiric versions in *Rump: Or an Exact Collection of the Choycest Poems and Songs Relating to the Late Times . . . 1639 to Anno 1661*, "Part II," (London, 1662; repr. 1874), 177–88. The refrains are, "From a Rump insatiate as the Sea, Libera nos Domine"; and "From Fools and Knaves, in Parliament-free / Libera nos Domine."

This is wonderful parody, of course, but the final lines backfire on the parodist. Rage turns inward, and frenzy collapses upon its own foundations, for it is merely self-torment or the rage itself that has caused the death of love to seem momentarily real. The litany to end litanies proclaims that love yet lives, normally good news indeed, but here prefaced, ironically, with "Alas."

> Alas, I lie: rage hath this errour bred,
>> Love is not dead.
>>> Love is not dead, but sleepeth
>>> In her unmatched mind:
>>> Where she his counsell keepeth,
>>> Till due desert she find.
>>>> Therefore from so vile fancie,
>>>> To call such wit a franzie,
>>>> Who love can temper thus,
>>>> Good Lord deliver us.

2 The Child of God

An advantage of starting with litanies is that their schematic formulas leave little room for mistake or coincidence when encountering versions in verse. Of the poems cited in chapter 1, only Crashaw's "The Flaming Heart" is a doubtful case, and the important question there, from this admittedly partial and particular point of view, is not whether the language of a litany is present but whether "The Sacred Heart" is, quite precisely, the form to cite. Elaboration of highly patterned verbal formulas cannot always be discerned, however, even in liturgical materials, and poets, after all, have sometimes been restive under constraints not imposed by themselves.

There is the further fact that ritual inevitably adopts and poetry sometimes takes a fundamentally sacramental view of reality, both broadly and specifically considered. The Anglican Catechism, deliberately simplified because it was designed for very basic instruction, declares that a sacrament is "an outward and visible signe of an inward and spirituall grace."[1] "Baptisme" and "the Supper of the Lord," the Catechism adds, are the two that are "generally necessary to salvation."[2] Not to be overlooked, however, are the five "lesser sacraments," to use Anglican terminology, which pertain restrictedly to individuals at certain critically important times: Confirmation, Penance, Orders (that is, the Ordering or Ordination of priests), Marriage, and Extreme Unction for those assumed to be near death.

The standard number of sacraments, most strictly speaking, is therefore two or, less strictly, seven. To these, however, an indefinite number of others can be added, a fact explicitly established in the officially appointed Elizabethan homily on Common Prayer and Sacraments. "Nei-

---

1. The quoted material on sacraments was not added to the Catechism until 1604.

2. For this usage of "generally," one might mention—and add italics to—2 Samuel 17.11, "that *all* Israel be *generally* gathered vnto thee," and Jeremiah 48.38, "There shall be lamentation *generally* vpon *all* the house tops of Moab." Richard Hooker, *Of the Laws of Ecclesiastical Polity*, 5.60.5–6 (2:246–49), rejects the belief that baptism is unconditionally necessary for salvation; in his view, there is an unconditional necessity for the Church to *offer* baptism, but a presumed intent to be baptized is sufficient should circumstances make impossible the actual receiving of it.

ther [Orders] nor any other sacrament else, be such sacraments as bap-
tism and the communion are."

> But in a general acception, the name of a sacrament may be attributed to
> any thing, whereby an holy thing is signified. In which understanding of
> the word, the ancient writers have given this name, not only to the other
> five, commonly of late years taken and used for supplying the number of
> the seven sacraments; but also to divers and sundry other ceremonies, as to
> oil, washing of feet, and such like; . . . either for godly states of life . . . or
> else judged to be such ordinances as may make for the instruction, comfort,
> and edification of Christ's church.[3]

Religious poets, and for that matter a goodly number of secular ones,
often adopt this broadly sacramental view of life and of human activity,
including the sundry ceremonies of their art and, to quote Shakespeare's
phrasing, "the perfect ceremony of love's rite" (*Sonnets*, 23.6). A very
famous illustration of this fact is Donne's "The Canonization," poetry in
which secular and sacred lines of thought—even though presumably no
more than parallel and therefore never convergent—somehow manage to
intersect one another in overt reticulation.

The poem as a whole bodies forth love's saints and concludes with
prayers whereby lesser mortals may "thus invoke us" (37) to be "a pat-
terne of . . . love" (45). The verse etches a firmly articulated pattern in
which the word "love" ends the first and last lines of all five stanzas and
therefore has to be rhymed in an additional ten of the forty-five lines.
Rhyming syllables are highly repetitive and, in this case, powerfully cu-
mulative in effect, especially because an emotionally persuasive proof
emerges incrementally from the seemingly scattered but carefully con-
trolled appearances of the words "move," "prove," "*im*prove," and "*ap*-
prove." The intensity of the poem's commitment arises, moreover, from
the restoration of watered-down amorous language to a secular approx-
imation of the fuller strength of its ecclesiastical origins. Thomas Cam-
pion's "Follow thy fair Saint where'er she leadeth" is undeniably lovely to
sing and to hear, but its force is greatly diluted when reduced to that of
words without music. At least some of Donne's *Songs and Sonnets* were
and are singable, a truth evidenced by more or less contemporary settings
that have survived; it thus is possible that the poems were originally con-
ceived as "lyrics" for "songs" to be sung. Even if so, unheard music is a loss
not often or greatly lamented in all of the *Songs and Sonnets*, and cer-
tainly not in this one. Far more serious, at any rate, would be deafness to
the ceremonial language of amatory ritual. Also of great importance is
that exaggerated departures from saintly idioms—"For Godsake hold

---

3. *Certain Sermons or Homilies Appointed to be read in Churches in the Time of the late
Queen Elizabeth . . . And now . . . Reprinted . . . Anno MDCIII* (Oxford, 1840), 316–17.

your tongue" (1), for example, or "Call her one, mee another flye" (20)—
do not demean or coarsen "reverend love" (37) but rather magnify it all
the more.

No litany that I know of is to be listened for in "The Canonization," not
even the Litany of the Saints, but a basically reverent view of human
affairs, including love affairs and sexuality, is there taken, and a transla-
tion, as it were, of the vocabulary of prayer is made. In this respect, the
poems that I next cite do not seem to me to be any more radical than
Donne's, and they very possibly are less so. Nevertheless, the first two of
the subsections below are intended to be mostly on the safe side by being
largely concerned with loudly heard reverberations from the "generally
necessary" sacrament of baptism. Subsections three and four may be less
cautious in pursuing the more ecumenical idea that the child of God can
be of any age and in some cases is sanctified whether literally baptized or
not.

EXCEPT YE BECOME AS A LITTLE CHILD

Beaumont and Crashaw

Baptism is an initiatory rite that incorporates the recipient into the
Church, and the unique singularity of it, from an Anglican point of view,
necessarily precludes renewal in the form of literal repetition or reenact-
ment, not even to remedy an inevitable relapse from baptismal purity
into the worldliness of subsequent human experience.[4] This position does
not prohibit commemoration of baptism, however, but instead can strong-
ly support the desirableness of remembering an innocence formerly re-
gained but now again lost and of rededicating the self, however much
aged by sin, as one of God's children. The point is made by the rubric or
directive headnote for "The ministration of Baptisme, to be vsed in the
Church" when it observes that the rite is *public*, among other reasons,
"because in the Baptisme of infants," those "present may bee put in re-
membrance" of their own earlier "profession made to God." Among the
witnesses who thus "testifie," as the rubric phrases the matter, to "the
receiuing of them that be newly baptized, into the number of Christs
Church" were Herbert, Crashaw, Joseph Beaumont, Vaughan, and Tra-
herne. Their personal professing, moreover, while often colored by self-
referenced vocabulary, is worded so as to apply also to others who aspire
to metaphoric childhood. Since Beaumont, unlike the others mentioned,
is not a well-known name, describing some of his verse (rather than mere-
ly mentioning it) probably is in order. A second reason for giving a pre-

---

4. Hooker, *Laws* 5.62.4–7 (2:260–64), examines the sacramental reasons for this rule
and explains also the exceptions to it.

liminary account of his poems is that Beaumont's expansiveness can be helpful in reading between the lines of the denser work that Crashaw and Herbert compacted from approximately the same basic materials.

Beaumont shared many enthusiasms with his friend Crashaw, whom he sometimes alludes to or paraphrases, and one of their joint interests (a fact to be recurred to) was the poetry of Herbert. Brevity, however, as in most of Crashaw's *Epigrammata sacra* or sacred epigrams, was not for Beaumont a stylistic or compositional ideal. Grosart, his editor, said of *Psyche*, "It is outrageously long—the longest poem I suppose in the English language" (*Complete Poems* 1:lxxviii). And Beaumont himself confessed, in a birthday poem for his own "Natalitium . . . 1645," that he grew "tire'd with . . . PSYCHE . . . for yᵉ Song / Though wondrous hudled yet was long."

As "Natalitium" itself partly indicates, he sometimes traded one kind of prolixity for another, specifically by writing numerous poems for the anniversaries of his birthday on March 13 and of his baptism, eight days later, on March 21. He further added poems for feasts and fasts marked out in the ecclesiastical calendar—Saints' days, for example, and incidents in the life of Christ, including the birth, the circumcision (eight days later), and baptism (thirty years later). The idea being advanced by Beaumont is an "Imitation" of Christ that is based on multiple models to which varying chronologies apply: the life of Christ himself, his principles as embodied by the saints of history, and both of these as they are annually celebrated in present time by the Church. Beaumont attunes the repetitive cycle of autobiographical occasions to recurrent liturgical days and dates, and he thereby attempts to bring his interior personal life into harmony with exterior ideals, which are simultaneously both timely and timeless. He is intensely aware, however, of a childish waywardness that disrupts devotional synchronism and thus mandates continually renewed efforts to achieve it.

In theory, since any and every year would be finely suitable to recollect and redevote the self, an unlimited number of poems on these recurrent subjects could be written. In actuality, of course, there must be a stopping point of some kind regardless of theoretical freedom from restriction, and in the case of baptism, there are seven poems for Beaumont's own eighth-day christening, another one for the baptism of Christ, and a corollary poem, "The Little Ones Greatnes," which proclaims, "Heavns little Gate is onely fit / Deare Babes, for you." In this arithmetic there may be rather more meant than immediately meets the ear, but the evidence will be more persuasive, perhaps, if one backs into it from what appears to have been Beaumont's own stopping point in writing verse of this kind.

In the manuscript that survives, the last thirteen poems are dated from

June 1 through June 13, 1652. In that year, Pentecost, a movable feast dependent on the date of Easter, fell on June 6, and the unmovable date for St. Barnabas was, as always, June 11. For these days, therefore, the calendar of the Church, not Beaumont's autobiography, supplied the occasions for the poems. For the other eleven, however, Beaumont peered inward and discovered deep and lamentable self-contradiction.

"Thrift," the subject for June 1, with unseemly speed corrupts into "Avarice," the poem for the following day, and "Honor" (title for June 3) quickly shows itself to be a disguise for disreputable ambition. Indeed, behind the mask lurks Haman, not named in the poem but infamous from the Bible for "the gallowes, fiftie cubites high which [he] had made for Mordecai" (Esther 7.9), only to be hanged on it himself once his dishonorable villainy was found out. "Ambitious Sir," Beaumont warns himself, "take heed":

> who but He
> Honor's own Darling was! Yet see
> His ruines monstrous mockery,
> Who fell full fifty cubits high.

"Physik" (June 4) can be no remedy at all against "Selflove" (June 5), and the gifts of "Pentecost" (June 6), though never more "Seasonable," also were never designed to include false "Witt" (June 7) or merely physical "Entertainment" (June 8), nor have they anything to do with "Riches" (June 9), in this case a treasure *not* laid up on earth, though Beaumont wishes it were: "O had I but ten thousand pounds a year!" "The Alarm" is sounded on June 10, when the voice of "Mortalitie" rings out, and on June 11, "S. Barnabie" ("A Man like thee / In passionate infirmitie") proffers sage advice: "Pluck courage then / From hence." "The Gardin" (June 12), at least the important one, reveals itself to be Paradise as it has been lost and barred off from Beaumont's egoistic sinfulness.

> For now I'm hanted with the thought of that
> Heavn-planted Gardin, where felicitie
>   Flourishd on every Tree.
> Lost, lost it is; for at the guarded gate
> A flaming Sword forbiddeth Sin
>   (That's I,) to enter in.

Or rather, and fortunately so, the garden is Eden, not as formerly lost, but as it is to be regained; it now is relocated, however, on Calvary, the "skull" mound, where Beaumont beholds

> That Tree, made Fertile by his own dear blood;
> And by his Death with quickning virtue fraught.
>   I now dread not the thought

> Of barracado'd Eden, since as good
> A Paradise I planted see
> On open Calvarie.

According to one tradition, the nails in Christ's crucified hands incised the letters of a divine and selfless alphabet. For Beaumont's proximate source for the idea, in the unlikely event that one was required, one could look to Crashaw's epigram, "On the still surviving markes of our Saviours wounds":

> What ever story of their crueltie,
> Or Naile, or Thorne, or Spear have writ in Thee,
> Are in another sence
> Still legible;
> Sweet is the difference:
> Once I did spell
> Every red letter
> A wound of thine,
> Now, (what is better)
> Balsome for mine.

Somewhere behind Crashaw is traditional imagery that probably originated from interpreting a statement by St. Paul with what might be called symbolic literalness: "And you being dead in your sinnes . . . hath hee quickened. . . . Blotting out the handwriting of ordinances, that was against vs, which was contrary to vs, and tooke it out of the way, nayling it to his Crosse" (Colossians 2.14).[5] In "Palmestrie" (June 13), Beaumont's hands have un-nailed it by taking on a flagrant but mutually incriminatory life of their own. The specific injunction that they violate is, "When thou doest thine almes, doe not sound a trumpet before thee, . . . let not thy left hand know, what thy right hand doeth" (Matthew 6.2–3). "I'll not inquire," Beaumont says to himself, "thorough what trumpets throat / Thou spak'st the prologue to thy Gift; / Nor in what carefull pomp thou gav'st thy groat."

> Indeed no such intelligence; for I
> By Palmestrie can read it plain:
> Thy right hand to thy left did it descry,
> And now thy left tells tales again.
> What canst thou answer, who dost guilty stand
> By the cleer evidence of thine own hand?

These are the last lines of the final poem in the manuscript. Beaumont lived on until 1699, but if he added poetry for June 14 or a subsequent day of 1652 or any later year, the additional volume(s) evidently disappeared from sight.

Perhaps he had grown tired of this verse too, but it is entirely possible that the series of thirteen poems is, in fact, substantially complete. For if, in one sense, the series is not finished and, most truly considered, is not even finishable, in another sense no further additions actually were needed to establish a thematic perspective that is both evident and cohesive. These "last" poems oscillate between the palmistry to be read in the hands, actions, thoughts, and life of an unworthy sinner—"Sin (That's I,)"— and of a redeeming God, of a specifically named saint, and of the Church, Christ's body on earth. The sequential order traces out contrasts that can never be fully reconciled, no matter how many poems might be written, until the various hands clasp one another in the volume of a world of glory not yet spelled out. In the meantime, however, useful handiwork can sometimes be done, and after the return of King Charles II in 1660 and with his own fortunes restored, Beaumont set about doing it. As Master of Jesus College, he repaired the chapel at his own expense; appointed Regius Professor of Divinity in 1674, he "applied himself," as Robinson tells us (*Minor Poems*, xxviii), "with the utmost punctuality and diligence" and "took needy students into his own home."

Beaumont's several poems for baptism could not have been written at one time (nor can they be printed in sequential order) since many of them celebrate anniversaries scattered through the years. Their titles and subject, however, link them together quite as closely, though without physical proximity, as the consecutively dated "last" poems, and there may be exactly as many of them as their own unfinishable chain required. Seven, after all, was long thought to be a summary totality for the finite week of this world's time, the meaningful addition being the eighth day of resurrection and eternity and/or the ninth of divine perfection itself. Herbert's "Sunday" acts out some of this symbolism in its seven-line stanzas and verbalizes one part of it in the ninth of them, the open-ended close.

> Thou art a day of mirth:
> And where the week-dayes trail on ground,
> Thy flight is higher, as thy birth.
> O let me take thee at the bound,
> Leaping with thee from sev'n to sev'n,
> Till that we both, being toss'd from earth,
> Flie hand in hand to heav'n!

Beaumont verbalizes another part of the symbolism in "Anniversarium Baptismi . . . 1649": "Eight Days I breath'd, but did not live." "The *Baptismal Flood* . . . doth . . . roll . . . to Eternities high Shore." Beaumont's full articulation, however, is so characteristically expansive that the copi-

ous fullness of nine poems was felt to be required. I hasten to add, how-
ever, that not all of them are necessary here. Beaumont is a very useful
poet for my purposes, both now and later, and he may be an undervalued
one, but the opening and "closing" poems will be enough to illustrate the
concepts that give form to this particular series.

The first, "The Waters of H. Baptisme," traces out various "streams" of
thought that are reflective images of one another. It begins with "The
Worlds Great *Lord*" standing on the "brim of *Jordans* flood," about to
enter a literally watery stream along with that "greater stream of Men"
who answered the call of John the Baptist. The purity of the Lord, with
or without baptism, was such that an inversion presents itself: when he
stepped into the waters, "Thus were They washed . . . not He." The Holy
Ghost, although eternally acquainted with "Pure intellectuall Streames"
on high, descended in the likeness of a dove that for the first time "espyde
/ A worthy Perch" in symbolic streams below.

> Heer He his first acquaintance took;
> Then flew to ever Spring & Brook,
> Fixing on all Baptismall Streames
> His best esteem.

Water itself, in effect, had to be baptized before subsequent baptisms by
means of it could occur, and only after it has been cleansed can there be a
remedial effect on human sin, whether present or future or past. In the
final stanzas, the streams flow together and become a torrent.

> Nor new Stains, nor y^t ancient spot
> Which all ye World of Men doth blot
> Doe stick so deep & close, but they
> Wash them away.
> And wash out also that great Score
> The Deluge ought ye World before[.]
> Those Waters drown'd all Sinfull Men,
> These onely Sin.

To those not familiar with the rite, the idea of cleansing water being
cleansed and the parallel between deluged people and inundated sin may
seem fanciful conceits and perhaps rather oddly upside down. To others,
the initially surprising thing is more likely to be the fact that most of the
analogical content of the poem depends from no more than one prayer:

> Almightie and euerlasting God, which of thy great mercy diddest saue Noe
> and his family in the Arke from perishing by water . . . & by the baptisme
> of thy welbeloued sonne . . . didst sanctifie the flood Jordan & all other
> waters to the mysticall washing away of sinne: We beseech thee . . . that
> . . . these children . . . may be receiued into the Arke of Christs Church.

"Every ancient Baptismal Office," as the notes of the Annotated Prayer Book inform us, "contains this reference to the effect of our Lord's Baptism in sanctifying the element of water, and yet it is remarkable that no such doctrine is to be found in Holy Scripture" (*ABCP*, 218n). In contrast, Noah and the Ark must still be one of the more famous of biblical narratives, but as the notes also observe, the point here is "the Baptism of the world by the deluge to the cleansing away of its iniquity, and the regenerating it for a new life." From this perspective, one might wonder not why Beaumont refurbishes "conceits," which in fact are too venerable to be conceited, but rather why he adapts only one part of the baptismal office. It is impossible to know how much foresight Beaumont himself exercised, but with hindsight one can see the probable significance of the fact that the prayer partially quoted above is the *first* prayer. Its function, especially in the references to prepurification of water, is "dedicatio baptismi" (a phrase quoted from the *ABCP*), a dedicating or, as it were, a baptizing of baptism itself. The initial poem of Beaumont's discontinuous series serves in similar fashion to prepare for those that follow. It might be said, in fact, that this one, by relying so heavily on only the first prayer, silently announces its own incompleteness even as it arrives at its own pointed conclusion, "Those Waters drown'd all Sinfull Men, / These onely Sin." The "general," that is to say, the inclusive necessity of these antithetical causes and effects also is important, especially because of significant restrictions that are prominent in the "next" (though not contiguous) poem.

In "The Little Ones Greatnes," a dramatic monologue spoken by Christ, the only watery image is in reference to those so pridefully self-swollen that they are much too bulky for the Book of Life. "My Royall Seat / Is high & great . . . Without Hydropick Names of Pride." Crashaw, in his Latin epigram "Hydropicus sanatus," on the miraculous healing of "a certaine man . . . which had the dropsie" (Luke 14.2), supposed that one insatiable thirst was replaced by another: after the cure, "Cui *vitae* ex ipso *fonte* sititur aqua" or, as George Williams translates, "He thirsts for water from the very source of life." Beaumont, however, evidently locates his sometime self among those still diseased and thus, with a change of metaphor, to be numbered among the "bunched Camells" of those unable "at a Needles Eye" to pass. The "fond Kings" dismissed by Jesus are entirely too ponderous in their self-importance, but so also is the puffed-up vanity of that "Hydroptique immoderate desire of humane learning and languages" that Donne identified as his own besetting weakness (*Letters*, 51). In quantifications of this kind, the little ones are great precisely because of their smallness.

> Come then, meek Brethren, hither come
> These armes you see

> At present, bee
> The Gate by which you must goe home.

There may be an echo here of "Blessed are the meeke" (Matthew 5.5), but if so the inheritance in this case is to be heaven, not earth. For the poem as a whole, the more significant reference is to the symbolic children of Mark 10.13–16, the text for a short homily given at baptism; as quoted by Beaumont for his subtitle or epigraph, the critically important verse is, "Suffer little Children to come unto Mee, & forbid them not, for of such is yᵉ Kingdome of God." The "briefe exhortation" of the rite supplies a double application of this statement to the present occasion. Specifically and (more or less) literally,

> Yee perceiue howe by his outward gesture and deed, he declare [*sic*] his good wil toward them: For he imbraced them in his armes, he laid his handes vpon them and blessed them. Doubt ye not therefore but earnestly beleeue, that he will likewise fauourably receiue these present infants, that he will imbrace them with the armes of his mercy, that he will . . . make them partakers of his euerlasting kingdome.

More generally and tropologically, "Friends, you heare in this Gospel . . . that hee commanded the children to be brought vnto him: how hee blamed those that would haue kept them from him, how he exhorteth . . . *all* to follow their innocencie" (italics added). The Gospel and homily are prefaced by a prayer on behalf of the witnesses and children alike: "Open the gate vnto us that knocke, that these infantes may enjoy the euerlasting benediction of thy heauenly washing."

With one poem to dedicate baptism itself and a second for children of any and every age, extrapolation to one's own baptism, especially at any length, might be thought superfluous. Hiatus inevitably intervenes, however, between the ideal and one's personal attempts to embody it as well as between the recurrent attempts themselves. The gate to Paradise is continually being misplaced, after all, while roaming through the wilderness of this world. Or, as Beaumont puts it at the end of "The Voyage," the poem immediately after "The Little Ones Greatnes,"

> Thus did I come
> All shipwrack'd home
> Unto my Selfe: & there must dwell
> Private and still,
> Unlesse I will
> Another Voyage make to Hell.

This is a potent motive, therefore, for renewing earlier vows to tend the paradise within thee happier far and thus for an additional seven poems on "Anniversarium Baptismi." As printed by Robinson, these poems begin on pages 86, 285, 334, 369, 383, 389, 396, and I cite the page numbers as a quick way of showing that Beaumont's annual productivity declined quite markedly after the second anniversary (the large gap between pages 86 and 285) and came nearly to a standstill between the fifth (on page 383) and sixth (on 389). He may have been marking time, as it were, before picking up the tempo to some extent once the "end" was in sight. Details of the sixth and seventh poems support this view of the progression and, if prepared for properly, can here serve as synecdoches of the series as a whole.

First, then, I ought to say that the allusions noticed earlier to the "gate" of heaven and/or of paradise regained might, if lifted from context, be somewhat misleading. An essential point to be remembered about baptism is that it initiates the child of God to the Church Militant of this world but not—or rather, not *yet*—to the Church Triumphant of eternity. In the language of the rite, "The old Adam in these children may be so buried, that the new . . . may be raised vp in them," and to confirm the renewal, Christ "did shed out of his most precious side both water and blood." But what next is anticipated is an immediately continuing future of indeterminate length in which one is "to fight vnder his banner . . . and to continue Christs faithfull souldier and seruant" even unto "liues end." The martial imagery was and is widely used but could be reminiscent, to cite specific examples, of language also found in Herbert's "Prayer" and, especially, in the closing lines of "Artillerie." "There is no articling with thee: / I am but finite, yet thine infinitely." Beaumont obviously agreed with this sentiment and echoed Herbert to say so; in the sixth "Anniversarium . . . 1650," he ventures, in nearly terminal position, only so far as to say,

> Bold bold enough is my ambition,
> Into thy Pay to begg admission,
> And have my Name inroll'd & blest
> Ev'n in thy meanest Hirelings list.
> Alas 'tis not for famishd Me
> To article with mighty Thee.

From that humble ambition Beaumont develops the "last" poem, the "Anniver: Baptismi" for 1651.

"Courage my Soule!" is the hortatory theme announced by the poem's first words, and one of the stanzas that develops it must be quoted in entirety to illustrate its seven-line form or shape.

> Courage! This very Day must Item Thee
> Into an holy Braverie:
> This happy Day, wherein
> Thou didst begin

To win
A place in Valour's Army, and
Under the LORD OF HOSTS didst listed stand.

The "Palmes" of victory, Beaumont assures himself, "thou canst not loose."
At this stage, however, they also have not been won. Born in 1616, Beau-
mont was thirty-five in 1651; in this seventh sequel—which consists of
five stanzas, each of seven lines—he has arrived at no more than the mid-
point of a theoretical three score and ten. The ultimate goal, therefore, is
as much in the future as the place where Beaumont "didst begin" is in the
past. "This very Day," "This happy Day," itemizes both past and present,
but March 21 of 1651 (or of any other calendar year) is not a date on
which to finish but one from which to press on. Beyond seven, however, it
is not possible in this life to go, however old or young one happens to be.
From this point of view, therefore, an eighth poem endstopped with final
closure could never have been written so long as Beaumont remained
alive to write it. Or, to rephrase the matter, in terms of symbolic numbers,
only seven poems could be composed.

The doctrinal point enacted by Beaumont on an interior stage is the
one made also by the title of Crashaw's Latin epigram, "Baptismus non
tollit futura peccata," baptism takes not away future sins. Only the Lamb
of God that takest away the sins of the world can do that. The theology is
orthodox, but the title with which Crashaw enunciates it is exceedingly
dry, perhaps especially so in view of the subject. In most of the poem
itself, however, Crashaw abandons standard materials to construct an
allegorization of the myth of Achilles. Thetis represents the Church; dip-
ping her son into the Styx parallels baptism; the heel left so dangerously
vulnerable is equated with that openness to the sting of mortal sin that all
retain even after being healed from prior and innate wounds. "A curious
conceit indeed," as Williams comments in his note, but perhaps not much
more bizarre than the conceits in the English epigrams may *seem* to be
unless one has already noticed the ecclesiastical background or inverted
chronology by reading Beaumont first. Crashaw's pyrotechnics probably
were no less showy in his time than in ours, but some of his wit formerly
depended on a minimalization over and beyond epigrammatic brevity
since what Crashaw himself often takes away is one's sense of the human-
ized fleshly embodiments of traditional principles. The symbolic images
that remain behind often dazzle the eye, but at one time the effect must
have been rather like looking through an X-ray screen. Knowing that the
flesh has to be there, one marvels at the diagnostic clarity that *not* seeing
it permits.

A particularly striking example of this technique is Crashaw's epigram
for John the Baptist. Considerable information about John is available

from the Bible, not to mention post-biblical legends, and much of it was read aloud in church on June 24, John's day in the calendar of saints. The date for celebration, however, has been said to arise most specifically from John's being six months older than Christ and from John's own statement about their relationship: "He must increase, but I must decrease" (John 3.30). Midsummer thus becomes the fit time for his day because it marks John's zenith and point of decline even as the birth of Christ, six months later, heralds the newly risen Sun. *The Prayer Book Dictionary* cites St. Augustine, who shows that John 3 (specifically, the verse just quoted) "agrees with the astronomical fact that days decrease after June 24 and increase after December 25" ("Festival," 33, *PBD*, 346A). With a switch from astronomy to speech, John's was "the voyce of one crying in the wildernesse, Prepare ye the way of the Lord" (Matthew 3.3). In Crashaw's epigram, "In Baptistam Vocem," John the person is decreased to a disembodied voice, but what the voice utters could not possibly have been increased.

> Tantum habuit Baptista loqui, tot flumina rerum,
>   Ut bene Vox fuerit, praetereaque nihil.
> Ecce autem *Verbum* est unum tantùm ille loquutus:
>   Uno sed *Verbo* cuncta loquutus erat.

> So much the Baptist had to speak, so many streams of thought
>   that indeed he will have been a Voice, nothing else.
>   But lo at last he said one *Word*:
>   but with one *Word* he had said everything.
>   (Williams's translation)

There ought to be some way to recapture in translation the vertical alignment of Vox, Verbum, and Verbo within horizontal progression of thought; perhaps one also ought to be able to retain the duplication of "tantum" and "loquutus" even as one indicates that the import of the words alters somewhat because of intervening words about the Word. I finally quit trying and thankfully quoted Williams instead, but the possibility has to exist since Crashaw himself was able to recast many of the Latin epigrams, though not apparently this one, into English. An English epigram that is pertinent here is the double couplet, "On the water of our Lords Baptisme" (in the Latin version, "In aquam baptismi Dominici"), and this may be an instance where being able to read between the lines comes in handy. At any rate, that the water washes but also is itself washed by now needs no explaining, nor does the idea that blessing is conferred on as well as by means of that which is blessed. It may be added, however, that water usually can no more remain unalterably pure than can those whom it baptizes. It takes not away future sins, as Crashaw himself points out, and sometimes falls ever lower, like the river Jordan, down to a briny

Dead Sea. Providentially, however, or so Crashaw suggests in the second couplet, the salty tears of repentance for subsequent sin can be a future aid against an unfortunate fall from grace.

> Each blest drop, on each blest limme [limb],
> Is washt it selfe, in washing him:
> Tis a Gemme while it stayes here,
> While it falls hence 'tis a Teare.

Herbert, in lines from "H. Baptisme" (I), seems rather less compressed in comparison and more straightforward: "O blessed streams! either ye do prevent / And stop our sinnes . . . Or else give tears to drown them."

HERBERT'S BACKTRACKING FROM SIN

The lines just quoted from Herbert, when replaced in the context of "H. Baptisme" (I), are in no sense enigmatic but also are not without an indirection of their own, among other reasons because the "blessed streams," despite Herbert's title, are discovered neither in the baptismal font of a church nor in Jordan, the biblical river. They are instead "that water . . . / Which is above the heav'ns" (4–5), the "spring" (5) or source of which turns out to be located on earth "in my deare Redeemers pierced side" (6). And in order to perceive those waters, Herbert's eyes must overlook an obstacle or look backward and away from it.

> H. Baptisme (I)
> As he that sees a dark and shadie grove,
>   Stayes not, but looks beyond it on the skie;
>   So when I view my sinnes, mine eyes remove
> More backward still, and to that water flie,
> Which is above the heav'ns, whose spring and rent [or "vent"]
>   Is in my deare Redeemers pierced side.
>   O blessed streams! either ye do prevent
> And stop our sinnes from growing thick and wide,
> Or else give tears to drown them, as they grow.[6]

The ominous gloom of "dark and shadie" is not difficult, as it were, to see. Dante stumbled on the Inferno's entrance in a "selva oscura," Redcross Knight and Una find their way (or lose it, rather) to the Den of Error through thickly wooded territory, and Milton's Comus offers his baneful

---

6. "Rent" (the reading in line 5 given by 1633) is followed by Patrides; Hutchinson preferred "vent" (from the Tanner manuscript and 1635). "Rent" may have the advantage of suggesting the rending of the veil of the temple on Good Friday and the refusal on that same day to rend Christ's seamless robe.

cup to unwary travelers "Within the navel of this hideous Wood, / Immur'd in cypress shades" ("A Masque," 520–21). Herbert does specify "grove," however, and it is worth noting that in biblical usage the word almost always implies idolatry. A concordance turns up the fact that out of forty-one instances, in only one is "eshel" (a tamarisk) the word being translated (Genesis 21.33, "And *Abraham* planted a groue [margin: "*Or, Tree*"] in Beer-sheba"). In all others, the Hebrew is "asherah," "shrine." "The children of Israel . . . serued Baalim and the groues" (Judges 3.7); "the children of Israel did secretly those things that were not right, against the Lord their God. . . . They set them up images and groues in every high hill" (2 Kings 17.9–10). I select these particular examples, quite obviously, because in them it is *children*, though some of them must have been elderly, who have gone quite astray to become, temporarily, imps of Satan. In *Paradise Lost*, the hellish origins of devilish "shrines" (1.188) are glanced at early on in the catalogue of fallen angels, and Moloch in later times is said to have

> made his Grove
> The pleasant Valley of *Hinnom*, *Tophet* thence
> And black *Gehenna* call'd, the Type of Hell.
> (1.403–5)

The prudence of one who "Stayes not, but looks beyond it to the skie" is surely self-evident. One might want to notice, even so, an exemplary figure standing somewhere behind or possibly in front of Herbert's speaker: "At that day shall a man looke to his Maker, and his eyes shall haue respect to the Holy One of Israel. And he shall not looke to the Altars, the worke of his hands, neither shall respect that which his fingers haue made, either the groues or the images" (Isaiah 17.7–8). Herbert's phrasing is that of parable (Matthew 25.14, for example, "For *the kingdome of heauen is* as a man trauailing into a farre countrey"). The apparently external grove is assimilated, however, in semiallegorical fashion to inward sin, as if the indwelling Christ has been monstrously replaced by Baal and Moloch. Or perhaps by Osiris, a false god who ought to have been banished from the human heart as he was, in Milton's account of events "On the Morning of Christ's Nativity," from his "*Memphian* Grove" (214).

If these are the conditions that currently prevail, then looking beyond and back is not merely prudent but urgent. And since desperate situations call for desperate remedies, it is by no means too extreme to rivet one's eyes on the Crucifixion even in a poem that has "H. Baptisme" as its title; at the rite itself, after all, one is reminded that a child's renewal was enabled when Christ "did shed out of his most precious side both water and blood." Also to the present point, of course, would be thinking back to Noah's flood, that earlier "Baptism" (to requote the *ABCP*) "of the world by the deluge to the cleansing away of its iniquity, and the regenerating it for a new life." Herbert's speaker probably does that too when he refers to "that water . . . / Which is above the heav'ns." The allusion, evidently, is to Genesis 1.7, "God . . . diuided the waters, which were vnder the firmament, from the waters, which were aboue the firmament," and according to the traditional guess, those waters were being stored up, well in advance, to deluge a world of sin not yet in existence.[7] Busily backtracking from the "grove," as well as looking beyond it, Herbert has been attempting to retreat to a point in symbolic time prior to accumulated sin, whether personal or worldwide. His prayer, "Prevent / And stop our sinnes from growing thick and wide," clearly envisages the prevention of further growth of what at present is comparatively thin and narrow. Redundancy, however, is not characteristic of Herbert, and "prevent" therefore must also retain its etymological meaning of "come before": wrong growing and doing thus are being anticipated even before they can begin, inevitably, to occur, and a remedy for them was prepared, again well in advance, for later use. The kind of thinking implicit in "prevent" becomes, moreover, a major idea in the remaining lines of the poem. (I requote the ninth line parenthetically lest form and rhyme be obscured.)

> (Or else give tears to drown them, as they grow.)
> In you Redemption measures all my time,
> And spreads the plaister equall to the crime.
> You taught the Book of Life my name, that so
> What ever future sinnes should me miscall,
> Your first acquaintance might discredit all.
>
> (9–14)

Unless Herbert has lapsed into heterodoxy, these lines cannot mean that baptism cancels out future sin. Redemption, again etymologically, can certainly "buy" them "back," however, and thus foster confidence that Herbert's name, received and recorded when baptized, will *not* be "blotted out and ras'd," as were the names of Satan's followers, "from the Books of Life" (*Paradise Lost*, 1.362–63). If, moreover, one could only get back to putting first things first, in metaphoric chronology and in terms of hierarchical value, then "acquaintance" in the etymological sense ("ad," an intensifying prefix, + "cognoscere") of "to know quite well" could be a continuing process for the discrediting of sin and the triumphant credibility of grace.

"H. Baptisme" (I) ends by envisaging an immediate as well as an ulti-

---

7. For the tradition, see Arnold Williams, *The Common Expositor: An Account of the Commentaries on Genesis 1527–1633* (Chapel Hill: University of North Carolina Press, 1948), 55.

mate future, neither of which has at this point arrived. "Should" and "might," moreover, leave open the possibility that the arrival may not be accompanied by good news. "H. Baptisme" (II), the following poem, thus continues to examine the chronology of time's measurement, among other ways by means of typography. The lines repeatedly backspace themselves and then readvance until the childhood of the past is renewed as a present-future condition.

H. Baptisme (II)
Since, Lord, to thee
A narrow way and little gate
Is all the passage, on my infancie
Thou didst lay hold, and antedate
My faith in mee.

O let me still
Write thee great God, and me a childe:
Let me be soft and supple to thy will,
Small to my self, to others milde,
Behither ill.

Although by stealth
My flesh get on, yet let her sister
My soul bid nothing, but preserve her wealth:
The growth of flesh is but a blister;
Childhood is health.

"Narrow," "little," and "small" are all in antithetical contrast to "great God" on the one hand and, on the other, to the wrong growing alluded to in the first poem as it becomes a blisterous growth here in the second. A major reason, moreover, why Herbert immediately needs this second poem is that it develops—or perhaps is motivated by—an idea implicit within "Let me be soft and supple to thy will," the prayer (and line) that, quite literally, is at the poem's center. The alternative to suppleness, far from being a discrediting of sin, is to be "hard," as in "hardness of heart," a phrase with theological import of a truly terrifying kind. The significant variant is "fatness of heart," an inverted parallel whereby flinty impenetrability is associated with gross fleshiness lacking all worthwhile substance. Isaiah 6.9–10 is the crucial Old Testament text because it is quoted six times in the New, including Matthew 13.15, "For this peoples heart is waxed grosse." In the original Greek, "It is *fattened*," as Matthew Henry explains (*Commentary* 5:182A), "so the word is; which denotes sensuality and senselessness." To be even more precise, the Greek word is "pachuno," and one of its antonyms is "krataioo" or "wax *strong*," as in Luke 1.80: "And the child [John the Baptist] grew, and waxed strong in spirit." "Too stony hard, and yet too fleshly" is how Donne describes his "dry soule" in *La Corona* ("Resurrection," 1, 3). And the danger to the soul, when stony and/or fat, is enormous. The article in Bauer's *Biblical Theology* initially remarks that the condition "can be defined as 'persistent refusal when faced with the divine call.'" It is, moreover, "the result of a wrong decision which is at the same time sinful in itself and brings other sins in its wake. If this chain of sin is not broken in time through conversion to God . . . it will become a vicious circle from which there is no escape" ("Hardness of Heart," Bauer, 344A, 348A).

Herbert proposes to antedate that particular circle prior to its starting point by continuing to orient himself in rectilinear fashion along a narrow way toward a vertical gate. From a realistic point of view, however, Herbert's prayer is like some of those offered at baptism in that totally favorable response to the request simply is not possible. "All" and "ever" are usually ideals, not human realities: "Graunt that *all* carnall affections may dye . . . and that *all* things belonging to the spirit, may liue and grow."

> Regard, we beseech thee, the supplications of thy congregation, and grant that *all* thy seruants which shall be baptized in this water, may receiue the fulnesse of thy grace, and *euer remaine* in the number of thy faithfull and elect children. (italics added)

Due care, therefore, certainly is to be taken by godparents to ensure that the growing child "learne the Creede, the Lords Prayer, and the ten Commaundements in the English tongue, and all other things which a Christian . . . ought to know and beleeue to his soules health." Indeed, from this point of view, ongoing childhood *is* health, as Herbert says. And, as Herbert exclaims in the next poem but one, "Lord, with what care hast thou begirt us round!" (1). "Parents first season us" (2), "Pulpits and Sundayes" (5), "Bibles laid open, millions of surprises" (8),

> Blessings beforehand, tyes of gratefulnesse,
>   The sound of glorie ringing in our eares:
>   Without, our shame; within, our consciences;
>   Angels and grace, eternall hopes and fears.
>   (9–12)

But the title of this poem is "Sinne" (I), and the grim farce played out at the end is, "Yet all these fences and their whole aray / One cunning bosome-sinne blows quite away" (13–14).

Sin's huffing and puffing can blow down the fence, if not yet the house, because of "Nature," the subject of the poem placed in between "H. Baptisme" (II) and "Sinne" (I). Here, the heart is "rugged" (13), "Is saplesse grown, / And a much fitter stone / To hide my dust, then thee to hold" (16–18). Hardness of heart now seems nearly irremediable because its "fatness," its sensuality and senselessness, is poisonously swollen and venomously reproductive but puffed up nonetheless with mere emptiness.

> If thou shalt let this venome lurk,
> And in suggestions fume and work,
> My soul will turn to bubbles straight,
> And thence by kinde
> Vanish into a winde,
> Making thy workmanship deceit.
> ("Nature," 8–13)

"Kinde" and "winde," thanks to long standard poetic license, rhyme well enough, but one wonders about "straight" and "deceit"; licentiousness, not license, perhaps is needed instead. The venom may be locating Herbert, prospectively but not yet actually, among that "generation of vipers" (Matthew 3.7) who are warned by John the Baptist to expect a baptism, not with water, but "with the holy Ghost, and with fire" (3.11). In any case, spiritual bubbles, originating from and vanishing by "kinde" (that is, by "nature"), are the counterpart to "The growth of flesh" that, in "H. Baptisme" (II), "is but a blister." Vesications both, they are filled up with ineffectual water or with mere wind, an empty but potentially deadly parody of the Holy Ghost. To escape from or rather to cure these viciously circular orbicularities, not even baptism is quite enough. One needs, therefore, to backspace yet again, specifically to "H. Baptisme" (I), where Herbert has already noticed that it is "Redemption" that "measures all my time, / And spreads the plaister," a *hardening* agent with reductive—*not* "fattening"—properties, "equall to the crime."

VAUGHAN'S DAZZLED EYES

Vaughan obviously read Herbert with boundless enthusiasm and (not always the same thing) with meticulous attention to verbal detail. The evidence is everywhere to be found in *Silex Scintillans*, most generally, of course, in the Preface, with its reverence for "the blessed man, Mr. *George Herbert*, whose holy *life* and *verse* gained many pious *Converts*, (of whom I am the least)" (*Works*, 391). Much more specifically, Herbert's poems for baptism were among those that Vaughan not only took to heart but sometimes reworked into his own verse, a fact that is evident, in greater or lesser degree, from at least three rather different kinds of echo effects. Two sequential groups in the *Silex* are the examples of compelling interest because they include "The Retreate" from the first part, 1650, and "The Night" from the second part, 1655. Also worth looking at are "Repentance" and an incident in *The Life of Holy Paulinus*, the work published by Vaughan in 1654. While it might be difficult to exaggerate the debt to

Herbert, it also is true that Vaughan at times left not only Herbert behind but the specifically Anglican faith as well. His contemplations of baptisms (for in this case there is more than one variety) are quite informative on this point and are illustrative of that which bonds Vaughan to Herbert and at the same time differentiates the two.

In *The Life of Holy Paulinus,* Vaughan tells us that Paulinus finally yielded to repeated requests for a picture of himself to be "set up . . . before the sacred font in a fair Church" (*Works*, 364) and that he sent not only a portrait but also two sets of verse: "The first coppy relates to the *pictures*, and the latter to the *Font*." It is the verse given for the font that reminds one of Herbert and/or of ritual. "Here" one beholds "the great well-spring of wash'd Soules." "The Dove descends" and "So weds these waters to the upper springs." "A new birth doth proceede" as

> man dyes to sins,
> And lives to God; Sin dies, and life begins
> To be reviv'd: Old *Adam* falls away,
> And the new lives, born for eternal sway.
>   (*Works*, 365)

Reverence for Paulinus is as unquestionable as admiration of Herbert, but these lines, perhaps because of their origin, are standard in substance and rather routine in the verbalization of it, so much so in fact that one might like to trade some of Paulinus, if need be, for more of Herbert.

Vaughan certainly could have bartered in that way had he chose; he too was alive to the dangers of spiritual corpulence and at one point called up Herbert's "H. Baptisme" (II) in saying so.

> Lord, since thou didst in this vile Clay
>   That sacred Ray
> Thy spirit plant, quickning the whole
> With that one grains infused wealth,
> My forward flesh creept on, and subtly stole
> Both growth, and power; Checking the health
> And heat of thine: That little gate
> And narrow way, by which to thee
> The Passage is, He [the flesh] term'd a grate
> And Entrance to Captivitie.

Among the interesting facts here are that these lines are from "Repentance," a title probably not suggestive of baptism, that they nevertheless are the poem's very first lines, and that since they are adaptations of "H. Baptisme" (II), Vaughan necessarily delays alluding to Herbert's poem "Repentance," specifically until line 53. "Cut me not off for my most foul transgression: / I do confesse / My foolishnesse" (Herbert's "Repentance," 15–17); "Cut me not off for my transgressions, / . . . Lord, I confesse the heynous score" (Vaughan's, 53, 57). Partly filling the preceding ellipsis, moreover, is a reworking of Herbert's *first* "H. Baptisme": "whose spring and vent / Is in my deare Redeemers pierced side" (Herbert, "H. Baptisme" [I], 5–6); "Whose spring is in my Saviours heart" (Vaughan, "Repentance," 56). At this point, if not earlier, one suspects that, before writing "Repentance," Vaughan mentally reviewed not only Herbert's poem with the same title but also those poems immediately prior to it. Phrased another way, in reading the Vaughan poem, one probably ought also to reread the series in Herbert that, in successive order, consists of "H. Baptisme" (I and II), "Nature," "Sinne" (I), "Affliction" (I), and "Repentance." It would, in fact, be easy to draw several comparisons between Vaughan's one poem and Herbert's six. Since it also would be tedious, perhaps it is permissible to jump over protracted quotation of parallels to notice a few points of more general import.

First, upon arriving at the end of Vaughan's "Repentance," one discovers that Vaughan himself has gone beyond the end of Herbert's "Repentance" and on to the next poem, "Faith." Herbert had been working with the more than generous redeeming of human debts; the reality is, "I owed thousands and much more," but

> I did beleeve that I did nothing owe,
> And liv'd accordingly; my creditor
> Beleeves so too, and lets me go.
> (Herbert, "Faith," 13–16)

In ending "Repentance," Vaughan picks up most of the theme but varies both the wording and the meter. In *tetrameters,*

> His pure perfection quits all score,
> And fills the Boxes of his poor.
> (81–82)

And then in *pentameters* (the last lines),

> O let thy *Justice* then in him Confine,
> And through his merits, make thy mercy mine!
> (85–86)

Second, Vaughan often seems more diffuse than Herbert, partly because of less pointed phrasing but also because of our tendency to scissor through, as Vaughan himself did not, the threads between Herbert's interconnected poems. In this case, one really should notice that Vaughan is covering some of the same ground in 86 lines that Herbert traverses in 203. Also important is that Vaughan, having levied on Herbert's "Faith" for the ending of "Repentance," next moves on to consider "The Burial of an Infant," not the baptism of one, and then proceeds to his own poem called "Faith." So far as Vaughan's editors (or I) can tell, Herbert at this particular point temporarily ceases to be a helpful sounding board since no verbal imitations of Herbert's "Faith" appear to be present in Vaughan's. Absence of echoes, by definition, is negative evidence, of course, but when they suddenly stop ringing in one's ears in this way, it may not be entirely coincidental that two poems have the same title but otherwise are not verbally close. A possible implication is that not all of Herbert's thinking on the subject of "Faith" can be carried through by Vaughan himself.

One of the places where Herbert and Vaughan did, in fact, part company, though not for long nor for totally different paths, is visible in "The Retreate," a much anthologized poem often read without benefit of verse that Vaughan placed on either side. Since there can be no question about it standing up marvelously well alone, no serious harm will be done by making several suggestions here about context, although, to be frank in advance, they will be accompanied by some refusing of my own to carry them through.

"Happy those early dayes! when I / Shin'd in my Angell-infancy." The sudden "éclaircissement" or (if one prefers) "epiphany" is one of Vaughan's many impressive openings. That this early time is specifically "*Angell-infancy*" may or may not also cause a "frisson" in those ever alert for the possibility of suspect heterodoxy. In any case, the immediately following lines definitely are not Anglican, for they refer to the world, with reminiscence not of Herbert but of preexistence, as "this place / Appointed for my second race." Vaughan reviews his past progress—more accurately, his decline—from the new starting point in *this* world's time as having been marked by "sinfull sound" (16), "A sev'rall sinne to ev'ry sence" (18), the fading away of "Bright *shootes* of everlastingnesse" from "all this fleshly dresse" (19–20). This looks very much like "fatness" of soul, of course, but the methods of attempted reduction are not identical to Herbert's backspacing toward baptismal innocence. Vaughan, it is true, also at first proposes to retreat from present to past, to "travell back / And tread again that ancient track!" (21–22). This particular linear motion, however, proves impossible; "my soul . . . Is drunk, and staggers in the way" (27–28). The alternative, evidently, is to move forward so as also to retreat simultaneously backward and thus cause terminal and initial states, if not to coincide, then at least to be closely parallel because similarly disembodied.

> Some men a forward motion love,
> But I by backward steps would move,
> And when this dust falls to the urn
> In that state I came return.
>
> (29–32)

In these final lines, the route envisaged may run parallel to the back-tracking of Herbert, but the "retreat" to be made is far anterior to one's baptism. "Come, come, what doe I here?"—the next poem—also appears to be eminently suitable for Vaughan's sense of restless mortality but exceedingly remote from any renewal of one's baptismal vows.

> This restles breath
> That soiles thy name,
> Wil ne'r be tame
> Untill in death.
> (17–20)

"Midnight," however, follows "Come, come," and after the last line of it, Vaughan quotes the warning—already cited in abridged form because of possible relevance for Herbert—of John the Baptist to Pharisees and Saducees. As given by Vaughan (in italics, moreover, though I omit them here), the fuller version is, "I indeed baptize you with water unto repentance, but he that commeth after me, is mightier than I, whose shooes I am not worthy to beare, he shall baptize you with the holy Ghost, and with fire."

The hypothetical ideal reader presumably would have seen all along that the approach to Matthew 3.11 (and hence to the motif of baptism) began back in "The Retreate" and continued in "Come, come"; other readers, however, probably will be pulled up short and have to retrace their steps. In "Midnight" itself, major signposts along the way turn out to have been "firie-liquid light" (18) and the "Streames, and flames" (20) of the heavens; the prayer that needs to be "Kindled" (25) so that Vaughan's own "bloud" and "water" (22–23) may "burne, and streame" (26); and the anticipation of "bright quicknes, / Active brightnes" (28–29) when and/or where "thy spirit blowes!" (32, the concluding line). At one level, of course, quickness means life, as in "the quick and the dead." Metaphorically, "It is the Spirit that quickneth, the flesh profiteth nothing" (John 6.63); "And you being dead in your sinnes, and the vncircumcision of your flesh, hath he quickened" (Colossians, 2.13). As for the when and the where, "The wind bloweth where it listeth, and thou hearest the sound thereof, but canst not tell whence it commeth, & whither it goeth: so is euery one that is borne of the Spirit" (John 3.8).

The resonance of this usage is unquestionable in "Midnight," and hearing it there ought to affect what one has so recently heard in "Come, come, what doe I here?" In the first line, the repeated verb is self-deprecatory. The sense changes, however, to that of a repeated injunction: "Come, come! / Cut off the sum" (5–6); "Thy hand is nigh; / Come, come! / Strike these lips dumb" (15–16). For some ears, at least sometimes, it might be difficult *not* to hear the Bible's penultimate verse: "Surely, I come quickly. Amen. Euen so, Come Lord Iesus" (Revelation

22.20). With or without that specific verse in the immediate background, "Come, come, what do I *here*" clearly concerns literal and metaphoric death to this world and resurrection to a world that has *not* yet come. According to Vaughan's editors, a major concern in this poem is the death of Vaughan's brother William, a loss also lamented in "Thou that know'st for whom I mourne," to which editorial notes ask one to return. Both referential systems, the autobiographical past and the apocalyptic future, may be relevant for the last stanza, especially the final "Come, come," which probably is both deprecatory and yet also an injunction.

> Perhaps some think a tombe
>> No house of store,
> But a dark, and seal'd up wombe,
>> Which ne'r breeds more.
>> Come, come!
>> Such thoughts benum;
>> But I would be
>> With him I weep
>> A bed, and sleep
>> To wake in thee.

If the tomb-womb is ever to yield up more than Christ ("the first fruits of them that slept," 1 Corinthians 15.20), and if it is to prove true for Vaughan himself and/or his brother William that "them also which sleepe in Iesus, will God bring with him" (1 Thessalonians 4.14), then baptisms by water, by the Holy Ghost, and with fire by him "that commeth after me" almost certainly will be needed.

"Come, come" and "Midnight," evidently, are not casually or coincidentally placed next to one another; nor is "The Retreate," the poem that precedes them. "Dust," as Vaughan states in ending that poem, most definitely "falls to the urn" since all human flesh, protective urn or no, inevitably lapses into that whence it first came. This is but one of the returns, however, that Vaughan so clearly has in mind. Another is associated with him who is to "come" at the hour of "midnight." I admit that the notion of an unwritten epigraph is self-contradictory and farfetched, but it is not extravagant to view the title of "Midnight" as allusive and to suppose that somewhere in its near vicinity is the famous parable of wise and foolish virgins who were and were not able to light their lamps when "at midnight there was a cry made, Behold the bridegrome commeth, goe yee out to meete him" (Matthew 25.6). Biblical commentaries indicate that this text traditionally had multilayered meanings, but in one of them, as Matthew Henry puts it (*Commentary* 5:370B), "When he comes to us at death, we must go forth out of the body, out of the world, to meet him with affections and workings of soul. . . . There will be a cry from heaven, for he shall *descend with a shout, Arise, ye dead.*"

Matthew 25.6, given this standard view of it, conceivably could have been a prophetic biblical text with which to head all three of the poems I have been considering. My own view is that Vaughan refuses to give true "epigraphs" at the beginning of any of these three poems for the excellent reason that the refusal obviates an otherwise natural presupposition that the poems are deductively derived from a biblical statement or are externally oriented applications thereof. Vaughan presents instead an ongoing process of rediscovery leading to and temporarily terminated by a broadly applicable quotation the personal implications of which have been responded to and reconfirmed. If our own response is more or less instantaneous, then well and good. But if not, we are impelled back to "Come, come" and then further back to "The Retreate" by encountering, perhaps quite unexpectedly stumbling on, a postscript about baptisms on the other side of the last line of "Midnight."

These three poems, moreover, are by no means the only nor even the first instance of this kind of strategy on Vaughan's part in this work. Nine of the first ten poems in the *Silex* have biblical postscripts. The exception is "*Isaacs* Marriage," where a reference to Genesis 24.63 ("And Isaac went out to meditate" [margin: "*Or, to pray*"]) necessarily appears first, not last; without it, Vaughan's own first line, "Praying! and to be married?" would scarcely make sense. Among the other nine poems are "Regeneration" and "The Search," the first and the sixth respectively. Both are prototypical, in one case partly because of placement (the way to begin, in Vaughan's case at least, is not with a starting up but with a regenerative renewal), and in the other because of title (with its emphasis on searching and process rather than the enunciation of an already established personal and/or abstract truth). The cumulative effect of invariable use of quotations and, with one exception, the delayed placement of them is, of course, the establishment of a pattern that causes one to expect a biblical postscript. The eleventh poem, "The Showre," therefore looks rather odd precisely *because* no quotation is attached to it, and it is "Midnight," several poems down the line, that returns to the pattern one was led to anticipate and perhaps is gratified once again to find. E. C. Pettet once suggested that "The Showre" was "in sequence with" "Distraction" and "The Pursuit."[8] It seems more probable that since sequence clearly is significant, we should continue from "The Pursuite" right on through to "The Retreate" (the titles themselves, when so collocated, are enormously suggestive, of course) and then press on, perhaps a bit breathlessly, to the quotation at the end of "Midnight." To see what the gradually revealed line of development looks like, a horizontal table of contents would be

8. E. C. Pettet, *Of Paradise and Light: A Study of Vaughan's Silex Scintillans* (Cambridge: Cambridge University Press, 1960), 197n.

desirable at this point, but since that is impractical, a vertical column will have to do.

[Poems 1–10, "Regeneration" through "Mans fall, and Recovery"]

11. The Showre
12. Distraction
13. The Pursuite
14. Mount of Olives
15. The Incarnation, and Passion
16. The Call
17. < Thou know'st for whom I mourn >
18. Vanity of Spirit
19. The Retreate
20. < Come, come, what doe I here >
21. Midnight

The list is not particularly lengthy by any standards and actually is short when compared to an Elizabethan sonnet sequence, but it would be quite long enough if one were to read it not merely from start to finish but also, retrospectively from the vantage gained at "Midnight," from bottom to top.

At this point, however, the better direction for me to take is of the sidestepping kind. "Content," the poem after "Midnight," has no post-script, nor do the eight poems that follow. These nine may be still another sequence ending with "Buriall," a poem with an intrinsically suggestive title and one that once again is demarcated with a terminal biblical verse. In the chapter on poems for Christmas, I shall trace out a sequence in Vaughan's *Thalia Rediviva* that has "The Nativity" as its focus but moves forward from and then back to a poem very hard to overlook because its ti-tle is "Looking Back." But to attempt anything comparable here, whether or not with "Content" and "Buriall," would be to wander too far afield. Very much to the point, however, is a variation on epigraphic and post-scriptive procedures that Vaughan brings into play when he turns his attention to the symbolic child and adds a symbolic adult.

A suitable starting point in this case is "The Stone," the first of five successive poems that cite, though they do not quote, a biblical passage in between the title and the first line. I temporarily omit the other four titles because the point, so far as patterning is concerned, is that there also are four asterisks scattered in these five poems to direct one's attention to a biblical reference, but not to a quotation of it, below. The poems, as distinct from the titles, in this case do originate from a citation that later is supplemented, but the biblical words themselves are not printed. In times past (before, that is, a modern, annotated edition was available), the absolute minimum required was a search through the memory, if not first through the bookshelves, to locate the text. "Childe-hood" breaks this pattern by having neither headnote nor asterisked note, and "The Night," which follows, restores it by having both.[9]

"Childe-hood" and "The Night" are linked, moreover, by considerably more than proximity and by visually prominent devices or the conspicuous absence thereof. An exceptionally clear conceptual connection is the *"narrow way,"* italicized in the last line of "Childe-hood" (and encountered more plainly printed in some of the poems noticed earlier in this chapter). Since all sinful adults labor under the handicap of being much too big for a narrow way, Vaughan begins the poem with an open confession that childhood is too far beyond or, rather, behind him: "I cannot reach it" (1). Indeed, with an inversion of "éclaircissement," he cannot even see it properly: "and my striving eye / Dazles at it, as at eternity" (1-2). Otherwise, *"Quickly* [italics seemed worth adding here] would I make my path even, / And by meer playing go to Heaven" (7-8). Making matters worse is that workaday affairs misinform as well as tire out the soul, and "Since all that age doth teach, is ill, / Why should I not love childe-hood still?" (19-20). "Dear, harmless age!" (31); "An age of mysteries!" (35). Children, at least the symbolic kind, are gifted with insight, but in the literal sense, "there shall no man see me, and liue," as Yahweh told Moses (Exodus 33.20). Or, as Donne has it while riding westward on "Goodfriday, 1613," "Who sees Gods face, that is selfe life, must dye" (17). And not even then will the vision be possible unless, as Vaughan has it here, one first starts over again from rebirth and new childhood. "An age of mysteries! which he / Must live twice, that would Gods face see" (35-36). If so, then one would badly like to know, along with Nicodemus, "How can a man be borne when he is old? Can he enter yᵉ second time into his mothers wombe, and be borne?" (John 3.4). Vaughan also has been pondering these questions but in "Childe-hood" can perceive only the fringes of an answer.

> How do I study now, and scan
> Thee, more then ere I studyed man,
> And onely see through a long night
> Thy edges, and thy bordering light!
> O for thy Center and mid-day!
> For sure that is the *narrow way.*
> (35-40, the last lines)

Where "Childe-hood" leaves off, therefore, "The Night" and the story of Nicodemus begin. The headnote cites John 2.3, but perhaps the some-

9. I ought to note that "Abels blood," the poem after "The Night," again rebreaks the pattern. Conceivably, however, it also initiates a new series of eight poems, none of which has a headnote, the series being marked off by the appearance of "The Throne," which once again does.

time practice of reading backwards has momentarily confused either Vaughan or his printer since the numerals are improperly reversed and should be 3.2, a verse that begins, "The same [Nicodemus] came to Iesus by night." Vaughan introduces the name in his fifth line, "Wise *Nicodemus* saw such light," but in this particular case I can see no way of establishing precisely what response was expected from the initial chapter and verse numbers even if the ones given happened to be correct. "The Stone," to revert for a moment, makes excellent sense if one takes time to remember or look up the single verse, Joshua 24.27 ("And Ioshua said, . . . Behold, this stone shall be a witness vnto vs"), to which the headnote refers. One might like to think about the context, but Alan Rudrum's annotation in *The Complete Poems*, very reasonably in my opinion, quotes no more than the verse itself. "The dwelling-place," which immediately follows, refers to and requires finding out the two verses of John 1.38–39: "They said vnto him, . . . where dwellest thou? Hee saith vnto them, Come and see." And "The Ass," the next poem but one, headnotes an entire chapter, Matthew 21, though the first ten verses (recounting Christ's entry into Jerusalem on an ass) appear to be enough.

John 3.2, however, is part of an ongoing narrative with an embedded sermon. It was and is famous, among other reasons because it incorporates the statement, "For God so loued the world, that hee gaue his onely begotten Sonne: that whosoeuer beleeueth in him, should not perish, but haue euerlasting life" (3.16). A priest I used to know, as it happens a Scot named Mackensie who was much aware that "mac" means "son of," managed to work John 3.16 into, approximately, every other sermon. No doubt he also could have reeled off the preceding fifteen verses as well as the next five and thus saved me the trouble of flipping pages, but not unless he had the right numbers to trigger his response. In any case, it is impossible to think that we are to reread, with or without instant mental recall, *only* the opening words of a single verse, especially one that begins "in medias res," as it were, with "the same came." At the very least, the story line of John 3.1–21 is implied, and it may not stretch credibility too far to suppose that one might even turn over to the two continuations of it. In 7.50–51, with reference to the Pharisees, "Nicodemus saith vnto them, (Hee that came to Iesus by night, being one of them.) Doeth our Law iudge any man before it heare him, and know what he doeth?" And in 19.39–40, "There came also Nicodemus, which at the first came to Iesus by night, and brought a mixture of myrrhe and aloes about an hundred pound weight. Then tooke they the body of Iesus, and wound it in linen clothes, with the spices, as the maner of the Iewes is to bury."

One of the points of this narrative, especially as fleshed out in biblical commentaries, is that Nicodemus, though a late beginner, continued well and stayed the course. Matthew Poole remarks (*Commentary* 3:378A),

"We . . . heard of him standing up for Christ in the sanhedrim"; "we read no more of him till now, where he shows his love to his dead body." "Most blest believer he!" (7), Vaughan exclaims, especially in contrast to himself. Darkness thus has much the same attraction as childhood—if, that is, one transposes this world's customary meanings of life and death. In the earlier poem, Vaughan would "Quickly . . . And by meer playing go to Heaven"; now, if "loud, evil days" were "Calm and unhaunted as is thy dark Tent" (37–38), "Then I in Heaven all the long year / Would keep, and never wander here" (41–42).

> But living where the Sun
> Doth all things wake, and where all mix and tyre
> Themselves and others, I consent and run
> To ev'ry myre,
> And by this worlds ill-guiding light,
> Erre more then I can do by night.
>
> (43–48)

A second point established by the biblical narrative is that "Wise *Nicodemus*," as Vaughan puts it, was indeed wise when he "saw such light" (5), but he had not always been so, and he became much more learned about truly important matters in the course of his visit. Already "a man of the Pharisees" and "a ruler," he arrived with the knowledge "that thou art a teacher come from God" (John 3.1–2). Part of what he was taught was in answer to his question about how the old can be born: "Except a man be borne of water and of the Spirit, he cannot enter into the kingdome of God" (3.5). A strongly contrastive lesson that he carried away with him and into later life was, "This is the condemnation, that light is come into the world, and men loved darkenesse rather then light, because their deedes were euill" (3.19). Vaughan's imaging only appears to stand the wording of this unpalatable truth on its head. He has already reversed the secular relationships between infancy and maturity on the one hand and between life and death on the other. Dark deeds, moreover, when seen in the false glare of "this worlds ill-guiding light," often seem lightsome. With a continued reversal, therefore, Vaughan disdains physical light in favor of a light so divinely bright that it is invisible. In the closing lines,

> There is in God (some say)
> A deep, but dazling darkness; As men here
> Say it is late and dusky, because they
> See not all clear;
> O for that night! where I in him
> Might live invisible and dim.

"A deep, but dazling darkness" returns Vaughan to the first lines of "Childe-hood": "I cannot reach it; and my striving eye / Dazles at it, as at eternity." But the learning process in between has radically changed the two endpoints at which Vaughan hopes to arrive.

> O for thy Center and mid-day!
> For sure that is the *narrow way.*
>
> O for that night! where I in him
> Might live invisible and dim.

In each case, the mode is optative, not declarative, because even at the end the way has been partly misplaced and the recurrent diurnal motion from illuminating darkness to daytime obscurity has not ceased. In the second poem, however, time and space have become functions of one another—"O for that night! *where* I in him," not *when*—so that the strictly delimited linear route of a narrow way transmogrifies itself into an illimitable place beyond, or rather encompassing and turning inside out, all finitudes. The final transposition, therefore, is that the human self could scarcely be anything other than invisible and dim when totally surrounded by the dazzling darkness of God and by every other standard imaginable could never be supernally transfigured into more radiant glory.

TRAHERNE AND THE TEMPLE OF THE MIND

Whether Nicodemus was ever actually baptized by water is a moot point. "After these things"—the "things," that is, included in the story of Nicodemus—"came Iesus and his disciples into the land of Iudea, & there he taried with them, and baptized" (John 3.22). We are fast reapproaching John the Baptist, the baptism of Jesus, the presanctification of water itself, and so on, as if the two narratives given in this third chapter of John were in some sense mirroring one another. Matthew Henry possibly indicates as much in observing, "*After these things,* after he had had this discourse with Nicodemus, he came into the land of Judea; not so much for *greater privacy* . . . as for *greater usefulness*"; the point being that large numbers now were to be baptized. But "Jesus himself baptized not" (John 4.2), merely authorizing the disciples to do so. Moreover, according to received theology, as Poole reports it in commenting on John 3.5, "before the death of Christ baptism was not necessary, neither by virtue of Divine command, nor as a means to obtain salvation." Poole further reports and reproves much vain disputation about "the meaning of being *born of water,*" especially on the part of "Romanists, and rigid Lutherans," both of whom insist that "the element of baptism" is meant. For his own part, Poole (*Commentary* 3:290B–91A) is convinced, "By *water* . . . we are to understand the grace of the Holy Spirit in purifying the soul."

Thus John the Baptist foretold of Christ that he should *baptize with the Holy Ghost and fire*, that is, with the Spirit, that has the force and efficacy of fire to refine us from our dross and corruptions. Thus our Saviour plainly instructs Nicodemus of the absolute necessity of an inward spiritual change and renovation, thereby showing the inefficacy of all the legal washings and sprinklings, that could not purify and make white one soul.

In Poole's opinion, Nicodemus was truly baptized by the Spirit but in the literal sense did not even need to be.

What, however, of unbaptized adults long after Christ's death? Part Two of *Silex Scintillans* first appeared in 1655. Poole died in 1679, leaving his English commentary to be completed by others for posthumous publication in 1685. In the meantime, the Prayer Book was revised in 1660–1661, and among other changes, there was added "The Ministration of Baptism to such as are of riper years." Hitherto, only the baptism of infants had been provided for. Lessons had to be found, of course, and the Gospel appointed for the new rite consisted of the first eight verses of the story of Nicodemus. If one wonders why the lesson stops there instead of going on, part of the explanation is that verse 8 completes an initial exposition of rebirth. In verse 9, an as yet imperfectly instructed Nicodemus asks, "How can these things be?" The new rite temporarily holds back that question so as to answer it at some length in a new homily that then asks a question of its own: "Brethren, what shall we do?" The response is, "Repent and be baptized every one of you."

The Restoration bishops who approved this new rite were persuaded that the years immediately prior to 1660 had much to answer for. In particular, they were deeply offended by the effects of two beliefs, both increasingly widespread, that *only* those of "riper years," not infants, should be baptized and that one might need to be repeatedly reborn and thus be baptized more than once. In the revised Prayer Book, therefore, a new "second" Preface was inserted, and some of the language adopted therein is harshly uncompromising. A form for baptizing adults, we are told, "although not so necessary when the former Book was compiled, yet by the growth of Anabaptism, through the licentiousness of the late times crept in amongst us, is now become necessary."[10] In this particular context, "licentiousness" very probably means nothing worse than "laxity," but in the background, as Jeremy Taylor found out to his cost, is a fierce and convoluted contentiousness. In section 18 of *A Discourse of the Liberty of Prophesying* (subtitled "A particular consideration of the opinions of the Anabaptists"), Taylor first gave standard Anglican arguments in favor of infant baptism and next (speaking temporarily as an Anabaptist) proceeded to pulverize each and every one of them. First published

10. Quoted in connection with the "new" rite (of 1661–1662) by the *ABCP*, 236n.

in 1647 amidst ongoing controversy, the work was intended to show, as stated on the title page, "The Unreasonableness of Prescribing to Other Men's Faith, and the Iniquity of Persecuting Differing Opinions." Taylor, however, despite or possibly even because of his ecumenical motive, was then hotly attacked from the Anglican side. He decided to add a new subsection of counterarguments to refute the Anabaptist arguments, which his ventriloquistic voice had presented in overturning the Anglican position. The final result of all this uncharitable acrimony is a tangled treatise that, however intelligible then, is largely unreadable today.

It is worth knowing about, however, because it further indicates that Traherne, ordained in 1660 and resident rector of Credenhill in 1661, began his public ministry at that particular time in Anglican church history when the theory and practice of baptism, however surprisingly, were highly inflammatory subjects. Traherne presumably met the needs of his parishioners by baptizing infants and/or adults as the case required, but he was not always interested in "outward Busy Acts" ("Silence," 9),

> Building of Churches, giving to the Poor,
> In Dust and Ashes lying on the floor,
> Administring of Justice, Preaching Peace,
> Ploughing and Toyling for a forc't Increas,
> With visiting the Sick, or Governing
> The rude and Ignorant.
>
> (11–16)

The lines must not, of course, be taken at face value, a fact strongly evidenced by Traherne's endowment of five houses held in trust for the poor in Hereford. But however worthy such activities unquestionably are, they merely run parallel to "Th'External Rite" ("Solitude," 89), not the inner one. Traherne also explicitly acknowledged that "Churches are a place / That nearer stand / Than any part of all the Land / To Hev'n" (68–71), but that proximity had no personal meaning "Except they mov my Soul with Lov divine" (88). Traherne was certainly inside the Church, therefore, but quarrelsome statements about externalities can have held small interest for him except, perhaps, as conclusive proof that the Restoration that most was needed did not concern buildings, bishops, Anabaptists, or a literal baptism by water. Inside what ought to be the living temple of the human soul, the essential consideration is restoring the self to its status as a child of God.

In the *Centuries of Meditations*, however, by one set of standards "we are but Children of Darkness, at least but Ignorant and imperfect: neither able to rejoyce in God, as we ought, nor to liv in Communion with Him" (*Centuries*, 4.4). This kind of darkness, moreover, while eminently human but in no sense divine, is essentially *un*natural precisely because of that fact. First causes—"Glorious Principles," in Traherne's vocabulary— "in the Rubbish of Depraved Nature . . . are lost, tho when they are found by any one, and shewn, like Jewels they shine by their Nativ Splendor" (4.52). The spiritual imperative, therefore, is

> to Meditat the Principles of Upright Nature: and to see how things stood in Paradice before they were Muddied and Blended and Confounded · for now they are lost and buried in Ruines. Nothing appearing but fragments, that are worthless Shreds and Parcels of them. To see the Intire Piece ravisheth the Angels. (4.54)

The problem, when phrased in this way, is how to regain the ability to *see*. From a slightly altered perspective, however, the question is how to restore the very essence of what it means to *be*. If the "Piece" was and can again be truly "Intire," then distinctions between what perceives and what is perceived—between subject and object, that is—are themselves unnatural deprivations, and so also are those between *when* and *where*. In a fully reintegrated universe, to look at any one part of it would be to behold everything, and each locality would be coextensive with timeless infinity.

Traherne's thought is often said to be neo-Platonic and Hermetic but in this instance appears to be an extension from philosophic investigations into "placeless place." Aquinas (though he himself is building on definitions of "place" given in Aristotle's *Physics*, 2.4 and *De Caelo*, 1.3) was the standard base for Scholasticism. "It is evident," he says,

> that to be in a place appertains quite differently to a body, to an angel, and to God. For a body is in place in a circumscribed fashion, since it is measured by the place. An angel, however, is not there in a circumscribed fashion, since he is not measured by the place, but definitively, because he is in one place in such a manner that he is not in another. But God is neither circumscriptively nor definitively there, because He is everywhere.[11]

For Descartes, however, "The mind by which I am what I am" is so constituted that it "has need of no place, nor is it dependent on any material things." Thomas Hobbes went so far as to claim that place "is the phantasm of a thing existing without the mind simply," even as time "is the phantasm of before and after in motion." And Milton's Satan boasts, "The mind is its own place, and in itself / Can make a Heav'n of Hell, a

---

11. Thomas Aquinas, *Summa theologica*, pt. 1, Q. 52, A. 2, trans. Fathers of the Dominican Province, 22 vols. (London, 1922), 3:29. For the quotations which next follow, see René Descartes, *A Discourse on Method*, section 4, trans. John Veitch, in *The Rationalists* [selected works of Descartes, Spinoza, and Leibniz] (Garden City, NY: Mentor Books, 1965), 63; Thomas Hobbes, *De Corpore*, in *Works*, ed. William Molesworth, 16 vols. (London, 1839–1845), 1:94, 96.

Hell of Heav'n" (*Paradise Lost*, 1.254–55), thus managing to corrupt these ideas along with much else.

Traherne is within this broad tradition when he remarks, "To sit in the Throne of God is to inhabit Eternity" (4.72), especially because it is people or their souls that he envisages as cohabiting in that untimable placelessness. In 4.71, immediately prior to the statement just quoted, he has already undivorced Creator and Creation by saying, "To sit in the Throne of GOD is the most Supreme Estate that can befall a Creature." B*efall* is, of course, a word to keep a wary eye on, but for the moment, backtrack from 4.71 to 4.70, and "Now you may see what it is to be a Son of God more clearly." Retreat from 4.70 to 4.69, and "a natural intimat familiar Lov . . . is Blessed." "It representeth evry person in the Light of Eternity." Return to 4.68,

> And what shall we think of Christ Himself? Shall not all our Lov be where his is? Shall it not wholy follow and Attend Him? Yet shall it not forsake other Objects · but lov them all in Him, and Him in them, and them the more becaus of Him, and Him the more becaus of them · for by Him it is redeemed to them. So that as God is omnipresent our Lov shall be at once with all.

Filiation—"Sonship," as it were—is as central a concept to Traherne's thought as the Cross is to Herbert's, and at times Traherne's language can be fully as ecclesiastical. This fact is exceptionally clear if one starts looking back from 4.72 instead of from 4.71. "In this Throne our savior sitteth, who is the Alpha and Omega, the first and the last." "In Him the fulness of the Godhead dwelleth Bodily. If that bee too Great to be applied to Men, remember what follows, His Church is the fullness of Him that filleth all in all."

Sooner or later, however, one has to think all the way back to the Fall, traditionally the initial source of all subsequent depravation and thus a starting point that presumably needs to be replaced by a fresh start located in terms of new spatial chronology. "If you ask," as Traherne does, "what is becom of us since the Fall?" (4.53), the answer given opens up one of the directions that Traherne took in going beyond Herbert's Anglican "middle way" even farther than Vaughan.

Herbert and Vaughan, after all, never lost sight of their own internal flintiness nor of the continuing need to mollify it through repeated renewals of childhood's soft suppleness. This is true even when Vaughan images forth the sparkling flint, the "silex scintillans," which the human heart can sometimes be. Bosom sin, fatness of soul, bleariness of mind, unsparkling hardness of heart—for Vaughan and Herbert, such things were everyday realities of all human existence on this side the tomb. And even though these spiritual dilapidations certainly could be redeemed and inverted into images of their desirably antithetical opposites, relapse was an ever present danger.

For Traherne, however, the paradox of the fortunate Fall is scarcely a paradox at all except, perhaps, at a merely verbal level. Quite wonderful things have in fact become of us since the Fall, because—quoting again from 4.53—"Truly Now we hav superadded Treasures." "O the infinit and Eternal Change!" "In a Clear Light it is certain no Man can perish." In this case, moreover, it is not opposites that attract but rather loving subject and amiable (that is, "loveable") object that do so. Traherne articulates the rapprochement in terms of subject and object with the person as agent and God as that which is perceived, but implicit in the wording, including the use of passive voice, is the idea of a reversible interchangeableness between those relationships, an idea possibly predicated on the basis of God seeing us whether we see him or not. "Being more Delightfull and more Amiable, He is more Desirable, and may now be more Easily yea Strongly Beloved · for the Amiableness of the Object Enables us to lov it." We are back, in a sense, to John 3.16, "For God so loued the world, that hee gaue his onely begotten Sonne," but Traherne stresses a corollary proposition, that God in return is beloved by those whom love transforms into filiated children.

When Traherne maintained, "It is certain no Man can perish," he probably had one of his eyes on John 8.51, "If a man keepe my saying, he shall neuer see death." If so, then his other eye may have been on John 8.56 and 8.58, "Your father Abraham reioyced to see my day: and he saw it, and was glad. . . . Before Abraham was, I am." A major point here is that Abraham "rejoiced"—or, as Matthew Henry prefers to translate (*Commentary* 5:1006B), "*he leaped at it*"—and he did so in seeing that an originally precipitous Fall should become a Rise. Upleaping and/or uplifting, however, cannot possibly occur within "Children of Darkness." More accurately, rising up is precisely what is required to remedy the condition in which, as Traherne points out in a statement recently quoted, they are "neither able to rejoyce . . . nor to liv in Communion." A second point arises from the fact that the text being echoed by John 8.58 is Exodus 3.14, "And God said vnto Moses, I AM THAT I AM," but as Poole points out (*Commentary* 1:122B), the tense actually used in the Hebrew is future: "Heb. *I shall be what I shall be* . . . to signifie that all times are alike to God, and all are present to him; and therefore what is here, *I shall be*, is rendered *I am*, by Christ, John [8].58." A further translation into linear chronology can be managed without much difficulty, and Matthew Henry (to quote a little more of his *Commentary* on John) exemplifies the straight line that results: Christ "is the same in himself from eternity" and "the same to man ever since the fall." His "redemption" was present "to Adam, and Abel, and Enoch, and Noah, and Shem, and all the patriarchs that lived and died by faith in him before Abraham was born."

Traherne, however, declines to translate in this way because of his refusal to divorce the time frames or spatial locations of redeemer and redeemed. All "times," most "naturally" considered, must be as essentially alike when perceived in and by Creation as they are when viewed from the perspective of Creator. From this proposition, Traherne proceeds to open up interiorities of unlimited timelessness so that points on a linear line, whether universal or human, perhaps are usefully located for narrative purposes but are possessed, despite popular usage, of only metaphoric, not literal, reality. By inverting customary levels of meaning, Traherne is as guilty as Paul and Silas were said to be by those who claimed, "These . . . have turned the world upside downe" (Acts 17.6). The relevant poem here is "Shadows in the Water," where Traherne sees "A new *Antipodes*" (38). "By walking Men's reversed Feet / I chanc'd another World to meet . . . / Where Skies beneath us shine" (41–42, 45).

In the *Centuries*, however, it is Time and descriptively linear vocabulary that often become antipodean or topsy-turvy. Oxymoron and paradox (in the sense of "contrary to received opinion") can defy all translations, but one (inadequate) way of phrasing those at work here is to say that the interior self is naturally and truly born and even reborn in time schemes irrelevant to the merely physical and external habitation wherein, according to conventional views, it is "placed." The Pharisees responded to "Before Abraham was, I am" by looking round for stones to hurl, but the response made possible by Traherne's sense of filiation is something like this: Yes indeed, and so also, therefore, was-am-shall-be I. In "The Anticipation," Traherne remarks, God's "Name is NOW, his Nature is forever" (26). Now-ness and ever-ness evidently characterize humanity too since the following line asserts, "None Can his Creatures from their Maker Sever." "Now you may see what it is," requoting from 4.70 in order to add what comes next, "to be a Son of God": "It is ordained to hold an Eternal Correspondence with Him."

Traherne continues to replicate necessarily incomplete wordings of this thinking down to the end of *The Fourth Century* and through the first ten meditations of the *Fifth*, the supposition being that single versions and even heaped up profusion could not possibly be more than mere approximations of the true reality. Traherne also resorts to the use of numbers and quantitative patterns as well as words to attempt a partial realization of an ultimately unwritable reality. It is highly unlikely that any amount of quotation on this side of reproducing nearly everything could capture Traherne's strategies and the effects thereby produced. Perhaps, however, on grounds of pragmatic necessity, a workable substitute can be the citation of two kinds of numerical progression in the *Fifth Century*. Each of the first four "centuries" does indeed consist of one hundred meditations, but in the fifth one, the tenth section is followed by nothing more than "11," a numerical figure standing at the top of vacant space. The final meditation therefore is wordless (the implications of this suggestion will have to be put off for just a moment), and the numbering of it must have been carefully precalculated, or so it seems to me, precisely because of its numerical (rather than verbal) "content." The numerical progressions that lead up to eleven perhaps resulted from (by now) deep-rooted habits of mind rather than careful precalculation, but in either case, the patterns can be shown by quoting the first complete "sentence" (or loosely defined syntactical "unit").

Arithmetically (from 5.2 to 5.4. to 5.8): "The Infinity of God is our Enjoyment, because it is the Region and Extent of his Dominion" (5.2). "Were it not for this Infinitie, Gods Bountie would of Necessitie be limited" (5.4). "One would think that besides infinit Space there could be no more Room for any Treasure" (5.6). "Eternitie magnifies our Joys exceedingly" (5.8).

Geometrically (from 5.1 to 5.3 to 5.9): "The objects of Felicitie, and the Way of enjoying them, are two Material Themes; wherin to be instructed is infinitly desirable, becaus as Necessary, as Profitable" (5.1). "Creatures that are able to dart their Thoughts into all Spaces, can brook no Limit or Restraint, they are infinitly endebted to this illimited Extent, becaus were there no such Infinitie, there would be no Room for their Imaginations; their Desires and Affections would be coopd up, and their Souls imprisoned" (5.3).

> His Omnipresence is an ample Territory or Field of Joys, a Transparent Temple of infinit Lustre, a Strong Tower of Defence, a Castle of Repose, a Bulwark of Security, a Palace of Delights, an Immediat Help, and a present Refuge in the needfull time of Trouble, a Broad and a vast Extent of fame and Glory · a Theatre of infinit Excellency, an infinit Ocean by means wherof evry Action, Word and Thought, is immediatly diffused like a Drop of Wine in a Pail of Water, and evry where present evry where seen and Known, infinitly delighted in, as well as filling infinit Spaces. (5.9)

The openings of 5.5 and 5.7 are paired. "Infinity of Space is like a Painters Table ["canvas"], prepared for the Ground and feild of those Colors that are to be laid theron." "Eternity is a Mysterious Absence of Times and Ages: an Endless Length of Ages always present, and for ever Perfect." 5.10 begins, "Our Bridegroom and our King being evry where . . . no Danger or Enemie can arise to hurt us." It ends with a consideration of "Lov" as "a pure and simple Act . . . perfecting and compleating our Bliss and Happiness." After all this is the number 11, and after that is blankness. The doubled single digit represents uncountable counting, the vacancy has reference to unlimitable space, and the implication is that all of space-time infinitely stretches itself out from—or perhaps is included comprehensively within—the remainder of the unfilled and unfillable page. From Traherne's point of view, after all, writing necessarily is activity, not pure Act; it limits perfection and can never be complete, however felicitous its suggestiveness may be.

I cannot feel guilty about being more fascinated by the *Centuries* than by Traherne's verse. Ridler's introduction points out that Traherne did not repeat stanza patterns, a fact that probably points toward dissatisfaction with the strictly delimited and thus intrinsically imperfect. There is, however, no use denying the side effect that Ridler also takes note of: "Few of his poems reach a complete formal perfection" because refusing to repeat patterns "meant that he never became entirely at ease with any." There is the further fact, however, that the prose is extremely helpful in placing (or "timing") the infancy to which the poems do so repeatedly refer.

A true but partly deceptive statement about the verse is that it sometimes sounds like Herbert's, perhaps most specifically when Traherne "ante-dates" his chronology. In Herbert's "H. Baptisme" (II), "Thou didst . . . ante-date / My faith." In the first poem ("For Man to Act") from the *Christian Ethicks*, "Belief doth, if not conquer Fate, / Surmount, and pass what it doth Antedate" (27–28). In "The Evidence," God's "*Works*" affirm what Traherne would "Wish" prior to the wishing itself: "my Wish they antedate" (14). (Traherne immediately straightens out this particular time scheme by remarking, "Before I was conceiv'd, they were / Allotted for my great Inheritance" [15–16], but by that point anachronism has already occurred.) The stupendous example occurs "When Eternity Stoopd down to Nought" ("The Designe," 1). "When," the line's first word, functions narratively, as it often does in ordinary use, but in this case simply cannot be related to customary chronology. Subsequently (as it were), Eternity—so "That . . . It other Toys might Antedate" (13–14)—did "take such Care about the Truth, / Its Daughter, that even in her Youth, / Her face might Shine upon us" (10–12).

Less striking is the idea, but perhaps not the language, that "a Sight of Innocence" is "An Antepast of Heaven sure!" ("Innocence," 55, 57). And the last line of the same poem, "I must becom a Child again" (60), may not seem striking at all after reading Herbert and Vaughan, especially if one also notices "My Heart did Hard remain / Long time" ("The Approach," 19–20) and "our stony Hearts make no Reply!" ("Bells," 22). "The vigor of mine Infant Sence" ("The Improvement," 67), "Mine Infant-Ey" ("Sight," 1), "My Infancie . . . Opes its Eys" ("The Designe," 57), and the title "An Infant-Ey" are among the repeatedly proliferated spiritual exercises whereby to penetrate to orderly "Beauty" behind "Ten thousand Heaps of vain confused Treasure" ("The Vision," 13). The diffuse methodology is dictated by the seeming diffuseness of the subject-object under consideration and is not totally abridged even when "I" and "Ey" become rhymed homonyms. "I / Forgot the rest, and was all Sight, or Ey" ("The Preparative," 35–36). This all-ness is less total, however, or at least less permanent than it at first appears to be, for Traherne goes on to say, "My Soul retire, / Get free, and so thou shalt even all Admire" (69–70, the concluding lines). And "Flight" itself, though surely one way of getting free, turns out to be "but the Preparative" ("The Vision," 1).

All of this is familiar in an odd or disconcerting way, and so also is the idea of being "drownd in Glorious Rays of purer Light, / Succeeded with a Black, yet Glorious Night" ("Nature," 59–60). In this same poem, however, Traherne speaks of "A Secret self I had enclosd within" (19) and senses a "Dilating of it self" (34). Herbert, one recalls, in "H. Baptisme" (II) wanted to "Write thee great God, and me a childe" (7), and Vaughan proposed, admittedly with reversals of usage, to "live invisible and dim" when surrounded by divine darkness ("The Night," 54). Traherne proposes instead to be so conclusively reborn of the spirit that total filiation is achieved. The "rigid Lutherans," chided by Poole for insisting always on a literal baptizing by water, sometimes insisted also on the ubiquity of the Son of God, that is to say, "that Christ in His human nature is everywhere present" ("Ubiquitarianism," *ODCC*, 1385B). Donne, it is true, scoffed at "that dream of the Ubiquetaries, That the body of Christ must necessarily be in all places at once" (*Sermons* 9:201), but he was arguing a theological point and adopting the official Anglican position, not thinking of spiritual filiation, when he did so.[12]

Traherne, as an equally official Anglican priest, surely did dispense baptismal water when and as needed, but as a poet he also dispensed with it, particularly when emulating "*David*," who

> a Temple in his Mind conceiv'd;
> And that Intention was so well receiv'd
> By God, that all the Sacred Palaces
> That ever were did less His Glory pleas.
> ("The Inference" [II], 1–4)

Traherne also took ubiquitarianism at least one step farther than most Lutherans probably would be willing to go. For if the Son of God truly is everywhere, then all of God's true children may be likewise. "All my Mind was wholy Evry where / What ere it saw, twas ever wholy there" ("My Spirit," 57–58); "tis all Ey, all Act, all Sight" (29). Or, as Traherne has it in the concluding lines of "Insatiableness,"

---

12. Hooker, *Laws* 5.53.4 (2:211), also discounts "ubiquity . . . which human nature admitteth not." In 5.55–56 (2:218–34), he explains the Anglican position.

> Till I what was before all Time descry,
> The World's Beginning seems but Vanity.
> My Soul doth there long Thoughts extend;
> No End
> Doth find, or Being comprehend:
> Yet somwhat sees that is
> The obscure shady face
> Of endless Space,
> All Room within; where I
> Expect to meet Eternal Bliss.

In Traherne's opinion, "No End" could possibly be in sight despite the visual prominence of the phrase in its medially placed and self-terminated line. Quite the contrary, in fact, for the internal rediscovery made by the filiated Child of God is that the self once was and again can become both timelessly and infinitely great.

3 Prayers and Pericopes

NAMES OF GOD'S SERVANTS

Donne, Jonson, Milton

Four names must on no account be omitted from the rite of baptism: "I baptize thee [first name] in the name of the Father, and of the Son, and of the Holy Ghost." In the rite, inherited surnames are ignored as irrelevant, and in poems for baptism even the personal "Christian" name appears to be of small consequence since individuality—the "*one*-ness" of the self—is devalued in favor of communion with all others who (in Donne's words) "are of the houshold of the faithfull . . . matriculated, engraffed, enrolled in the Church, by that initiatory Sacrament of Baptisme" (*Sermons* 9:319). What one is called matters rather less than what one is being converted into. No suggestion is made, of course, that personality is in any sense obliterated by unification to or within a larger and faceless identity. On the contrary, all of God's children are knowable and known in their unique particularity throughout their careers in the Church Militant of this world; God is further requested to remember "thy servant [name]" in time of affliction and after death; in heaven, St. Paul is positive, "I shall know even as also I am knowne" (1 Corinthians 13.12). "Then long Eternity shall greet our bliss / With an *individual* kiss" (Milton, "On Time," 11–12).

Individuality is in fact stressed by the first-name basis—in this case, more accurately the baptismal name—on which divine acquaintance is predicated. It is invariably thy servant "George," for example, and *not* "George Herbert," who is to be remembered and recognized. The temptation may sometimes be strong to expand "H. Baptisme" ingeniously into "Herbert's Baptisme" as well as "Holy," especially because of the line, "You taught the Book of Life my name" (12), but it is far from certain that Herbert himself would have done so. Donne, it is true, in the "Hymn to God the Father," repeatedly punned on his own last name: "When thou hast done, thou hast not done." The strategy is remarkable, however, among other reasons because of what the word "Donne" turns out to mean.

A major confessional point in this poem is a continuing discovery,

"Thou hast not done, for I have more." And what Donne has more of is a personal existence so intricately involved with sinful corruption of self and of others that its alien alterity requires superabundant forgiveness if ultimate reconciliation with God is to be possible. Since the inherited consequences of the Fall, unlike surnames, cannot possibly be ignored, original sin comes first, "that sinne where I begunne, / Which is my sin, though it were done before" (1–2). Actual sins, "those sinnes through which I runne" (3), continually add to innate guiltiness because they are run through, "though still I doe deplore" (4), but somehow are never left totally behind. There seem always to be more of them just down the road on that broad highway that leads to the lake of perdition. Making terribly bad matters even worse, Donne has done injury to others as well as himself, is guilty of "that sinne by which I wonne / Others to sinne" (7–8). There is also, and in this case quite understandably so, "a sinne of feare," of distrust or incipient despair, "that when I have spunne / My last thred, I shall perish on the shore" (13–14).

Two full stanzas and the opening two lines of the third establish an entity signified by "Donne" who (or which) can be equated with manifold sins that have been, are being, and shall continue to be *done*. This entity is profligately wasteful and self-destructive, expending itself to the point of having been entirely spun, and nothingness now threatens to obliterate all traces of selfhood so that "Donne-ness" not only is not worth having but at this rate cannot long continue to exist. This grim proposition is evident from "perish on the shore," but the far worse horrors that accompany the erasure of one's name from the Book of Life are yet to come: "And death and hell were cast into the lake of fire: this is the second death. And whosoeuer was not found written in the booke of life, was cast into the lake of fire" (Revelation 20.14–15). Donne asks, "Wilt thou forgive that sinne which I did shunne / A yeare, or two: but wallowed in, a score?" (9–10). Depending on the chronology of events, the answer may well be no.

The Epistle to Hebrews is emphatic on this matter. "For it is impossible for those who were once inlightned. . . . If they shall fall away, to renue them againe vnto repentance: seeing they crucifie to themselues the Sonne of God afresh" (6.4, 6). Against this peril is the protective weight of a grievously needed "anker of the soul" (6.19). One of its two flukes is the oath sworn by Yahweh to Abraham to "blesse thee," an oath that, "because he could sweare by no greater, he sware by himselfe" (6.13, paraphrasing Genesis 22.16–17). The other is the keeping of that oath in the person of "the forerunner" (another runner through sins but only those of others, not his own), "*even* Iesus, made an high Priest for euer" (6.20). Donne's prayer, "Sweare by thy selfe" (15), an immutable and eternal self, is precisely the requisite request when one's own self has been and still is one's own undoing. "Sweare by thy selfe, that at my death thy Sunne / Shall shine as it shines now, and heretofore" (15–16).

Donne-ishness needs to disappear now lest it disappear later in second death; alternatively phrased, "my self" needs to be replaced by "thy self" so that the disservice of an iniquitous Donne may be finished, be done and over with, and so that God's servant John can be remembered. If, moreover, divine forgiveness should keep pace with personal sin, then the entity named Donne will not need or want or even possess itself. "And, having done that, *Thou* hast done." "*I* have no more."[1]

Since the whole poem turns on the negative deconstruction that sinful selves engage in, a positive assertion at the end would be misplaced. If that were not the case, however, and to some extent, even though it is, the last line might itself be convertible so as to imply, "I have regained so much by losing my self that there is no more to be feared or requested or required." Two of the annotations in Gardner's edition are worth quoting in this connection. On "I have no more": "*1633* reads 'I feare'; *Ash* reads 'I aske' (*S* 962, 'I'le aske'); *E* 20 reads 'I need.'" On the poem's title (for which variants also exist, including "To Christ"):

> The best title would be no title at all. The poem has no sense of distinction of Persons; it ends with an appeal to the Godhead. "Sweare by thy selfe" is the cry of the man who, as Walton reports, "would often say in a kind of sacred extasie—Blessed be God that he is God only, and divinely like himself."

Five names, not four, are indispensable at a wedding, and ecclesiastical usage permits, possibly fosters, the view that those of the bride and bridegroom are specifically and equally godly. "I [name] take thee [name]" is the conjunctive formula repeated by both parties, and the spaces to be filled are for first names, not last. There is, of course, no use blinking the fact that the bride's last name was about to be changed, but it may be difficult, even so, to see that much can be gained by minimizing the additional fact that surnames theoretically are much more significant outside the doors through which the couple exit than inside the household of God. And on still the third hand, it certainly has been true of actual practice on both sides of the doors that even the "Christian" name of the wife has frequently vanished behind "Mrs."

In this respect as in certain others, rank has had a built-in advantage: "Princess [name]," for example, or "[name], Duchess of [titular name]." Or, to approach two poems in particular, "Lady Jane, Marchioness of Winchester." When Jane, the daughter of Thomas, Viscount Savage, died

1. The word "more," repeated in much the same way as "done," sometimes has been interpreted as a pun on the name of Donne's wife, Anne More. A pun on "Anne," if one could be found, might be suitable, but since "Donne" in this poem is pejorative, "More" would have to be similarly so or in sharp contrast; neither possibility looks plausible to me.

on April 15, 1631, her name had long since become, because of her marriage, Jane *Paulet* and/or "the Marchioness of Winchester." Jonson lamented the death in a hundred-line poem (*Underwood*, 83), which dilates the totality to which the numerous virtues of her person added up. The "dotes" (gifts, endowments) of her character and life "were such / . . . no notion can express how much" (25–26), but Jonson makes a brave effort to afford the "admiration and applause" (62) due to her on earth and thus to balance, imperfectly, the fact that "angels" now "sing her glories" (63). Jonson's hundred lines imply at least another hundred that cannot be written out; "her mortality / Became her birthday to eternity" (67–68), and she now "Speaks heaven's language" (71).

Jonson by no means skips over the biographical details that Jane was wife to John Paulet, Marquis of Winchester, and mother of Charles Paulet, later to be the sixth Marquis and the Duke of Bolton, nor does he omit the circumstances that she died in childbirth and that the second child did not itself survive. It is her personal integrity and exemplary function, however, as distinct from her familial and social status, which enliven others despite the double death of mother and child: "What she did here by great example well / To enlive posterity, her fame may tell" (33–34). I have deliberately delayed giving Jonson's title for this poem, "An Elegy on the Lady Jane Paulet, Marchioness of Winchester." Jonson could not refer to the deceased by her maiden name, but in this case the poem's title and the names there mentioned quite accurately indicate Jonson's emphasis. In first position is the "Christian" name of the person herself; her married name comes next; and her position, third. The first two of these, moreover, were supplied, not by necessity, but by free choice, and the proof for that fact is Milton's poem for the same occasion.

Milton's title is "An Epitaph on the Marchioness of Winchester," and it too is informative about the poem that it heads. Without editorial assistance, one would scarcely know anything about the deceased except for the roles, evidently quite well played, of lamented wife and mother. Very unlike Jonson, Milton and other students at Cambridge were writing dutiful poems for an august and remote personage, possibly glimpsed at a distance if her husband, the university's nonresident chancellor, brought her along on one of his ceremonial visits. "Here be tears of perfect moan" (55), Milton writes, with complete but also exceedingly distant propriety,

> And some Flowers and some Bays
> For thy Hearse to strew the ways,
> Sent thee from the banks of *Came*.
> (57–59)

The poetic "flowers" are "Devoted to thy virtuous name" (60), and yet the personal name is nowhere mentioned. Milton can have had little or no direct acquaintance to draw upon, however, so that one can scarcely fault him for falling back on whatever served as newspaper society pages and funeral notices at that time.

> This rich Marble doth inter
> The honor'd Wife of *Winchester,*
> A Viscount's daughter, an Earl's heir.
> . . . .
> Her high birth, and her graces sweet,
> Quickly found a lover meet.
> . . . .
> The hapless Babe before his birth
> Had burial, yet not laid in earth,
> And the languisht Mother's Womb
> Was not long a living Tomb.
> 　　　　　　　　　(1–3, 15–16, 31–34)

Milton had to find material somewhere, after all, with which to start and then to fill up the middle of his poem. He further needed to discover a suitable conclusion based on something other than personal knowledge about Lady Jane, which he himself did not possess.

At this stage, therefore, we appear to be back at the solemnization of matrimony, both generally speaking for a concentration on wifeliness rather than individuality, and more specifically for a prayer that disappeared when the Prayer Book was revised in 1660–1661. Prior to that time, one supplication was that the bride "be louing and amiable to her husband, as Rachel" (translating the pre-Reformation Latin, "amabilis . . . ut Rachel"), "wise as Rebecca, faithful and obedient as Sara, and . . . a follower of holy and godly matrons." Of these possible exemplars, it was Rachel whom the Marchioness had followed, even unto the tomb and on to its other side. For Rachel also died in childbirth, and the offspring, while named Ben-oni ("son of sorrow") by the dying Rachel herself, was renamed Ben-jamin ("son of the right hand") by Jacob so as to translate a bane into a blessing (Genesis 35.18). Milton turns the prayer, the situation, and its narrative reversals into an early version of the Fortunate Fall. Here on earth are tears of perfect moan,

> Whilst thou, bright Saint, high sitt'st in glory,
> Next her much like to thee in story,
> That fair *Syrian* Shepherdess,
> Who . . . .
> The highly favor'd *Joseph* bore
> . . . .
> And at her next birth, much like thee,
> Through pangs fled to felicity,
> Far within the bosom bright

Of blazing Majesty and Light;
There with thee, new welcome Saint,
Like fortunes may her soul acquaint,
With thee there clad in radiant sheen,
No Marchioness, but now a Queen.
(61–65, 67–74)

Milton draws his parallel as closely as he can, and since he had to rely on honorifics, not names, he not only omits "Jane Paulet" but also substitutes "Syrian Shepherdess" for "Rachel." To mention Jacob, the biblical husband, and either Ben-oni or Ben-jamin would be to introduce pointless and unparallel specificity, but it is not entirely cynical to say that an implicit comparison of the young Charles Paulet to "highly favored *Joseph*," the elder biblical brother, might be a politic as well as a graceful gesture for a dutiful student to make.

BANQUETING WITH GOD AND WITH SATAN

Herbert and Milton

My explanation for the presence of Rachel in Milton's poem makes reasonably good sense, I hope, but at very best one is considering no more than probabilities. Hanford's suggestion, made long ago but still current because incorporated in Merritt Hughes's headnote, was that Milton had Dante in mind, specifically the third rank of the Celestial Rose, where Rachel is placed with Beatrice. No one doubts that Milton was aware of Dante, but a rock-solid certainty is that he had read the Bible, and that is the place, after all, where Rachel most fundamentally is to be found, not the *Paradiso* or the marriage rite. At issue here is an indisputable fact, which thus far I have attempted to evade, that ritual makes repeatedly and enormously heavy use of biblical words that necessarily possess a totally independent existence of their own. Therefore, two questions, both of the nagging variety, have to do with surrounding context and with presence or absence of interpretive aid from that context. The same words can and do appear both in scripture and in the liturgy, but in each case within larger surrounding verbal structures, not a void. The larger structures, moreover, are distinguishably different since biblical passages in the liturgy are preceded and followed either by passages from other parts of the Bible, sometimes widely separated in scripture itself, or by nonbiblical passages peculiar to the rite.

Phrased more technically, the distinction here is between the Bible and a liturgical pericope, etymologically a "section" and defined by the *ODCC* ("Pericope," 1045B) as "a passage from the Scriptures, esp. one appointed to be read in the Church services." From this point of view, the best known of all liturgical pericopes surely must be the Lord's Prayer, appointed for use at various points of various services, but it is doubtful that knowing that fact can regularly be of much help in interpreting literary allusions to the prayer. Not quite so much to the forefront, since few words could be, but perhaps not lagging too far behind is the angelic song that heralded the birth of Christ, "Glory to God in the highest, and on earth peace, good will towards men" (Luke 2.14). With so small a difference as may seem trivial, these are the words placed after "Finis," the End, which in turn is appended to Herbert's "Love" (III), the final poem of "The Church."

FINIS.
Glory be to *God* on high
And on earth peace
Good will towards men.

Memories of children improbably disguised as cherubs for Christmas pageantry and of choirs standing on tiptoe to belt out "in the HIGH est" in Handel's *Messiah* cannot always be blotted out and in this case, despite anachronisms, perhaps should not be. Herbert's reference, even so, is not only and, indeed, probably not so much to Luke as it is also to the Gloria, the hymn at the end of Communion.[2] To some extent, however, this may indeed be a case of both/and rather than of either/or. The Gloria begins, as Herbert does, with "Glory be to God on high" and, when sung, a slight but nonetheless perceptible pause must be made after "peace." The hymn, however, also gives "*in* earth," as does the Geneva translation of Luke, but the Authorized Version, like Herbert, has "on."

In any case, a major point here arises from the positioning of the words. Luke, after all, has barely begun, but Herbert and the Communion service are almost finished. One has to add, of course, that "Love" (III), the preceding poem, is Eucharistic. According to C. A. Patrides, it "celebrates not the sacrament in the visible Church but the final communion in Heaven," a statement that is true but also incomplete. Another thing to be added, therefore, is that much of the situational conflict presented in the poem develops from a problem (sometimes highly and most unsuitably visible in church) that is referred to, technically, as "noncommunicating attendance."

The entry under that term in the *Prayer Book Dictionary* (483B–84B) explains that the question behind the terminology is "whether those who do not propose to communicate at a particular celebration of H[oly] C[ommunion] ought to be allowed to remain throughout the service."

2. The Gloria was positioned at the end of the service in 1552 and thereafter; in the first Prayer Book of 1549, it was sung toward the beginning of Communion (as it is once again in rites that parishes in the United States began using in 1976).

Except for those who have communicated at an earlier service, the answer, generally speaking, is or should be no. "Those who do not feel able to communicate should, as Chrysostom argues, regard themselves as under penitence, and should, in consequence, modestly depart." Suitable opportunity for departure therefore must be provided; otherwise, "the heretic, the unbeliever, and the self-excommunicate are practically invited to remain." It is in that last category of self-excommunicates that Herbert, in "Love" (III), provisionally places himself, but instead of being asked to leave, he is pressed to stay.

> Love bade me welcome: yet my soul drew back,
>   Guiltie of dust and sinne.
> But quick-ey'd Love, observing me grow slack
>   From my first entrance in,
> Drew nearer to me, sweetly questioning,
>   If I lack'd any thing.
>
> A guest, I answer'd, worthy to be here:
>   Love said, You shall be he.
> I the unkinde, ungratefull? Ah, my deare,
>   I cannot look on thee.
> Love took my hand, and smiling did reply,
>   Who made the eyes but I?
>
> Truth Lord, but I have marr'd them: let my shame
>   Go where it doth deserve.
> And know you not, sayes Love, who bore the blame?
>   (1–15)

The Prayer Book's version of this scene takes the form of exhortations to be delivered, according to the directive rubric, "at certaine times, when the Curate shall see the people negligent to come to the holy Communion." I have never heard these exhortations in church, and they were omitted from the rites for Eucharist that the Episcopal Church of the United States approved in 1976. Herbert, however, may have found it incumbent upon himself actually to speak the words. In the preceding prayer "for the whole state of Christs *Church militant* here in earth," grace is beseeched for "all Bishops, Pastours, and Curates, that they may both by their *life and doctrine* set foorth thy true and liuely word, & rightly and duely administer thy holy Sacraments" (italics added). In "The Windows," Herbert asked, "Lord, how can man preach thy eternall word?" (1), and one of the answers was, "Doctrine and life" (11). As for "The Church Militant," that is, of course, the longish poem after "Love" (III), "Finis," and "Glory be."

"At *this* time," however, the exhortation to the negligent is being heard in Herbert's mind and needs to be heard in ours. (Despite apparent length, it is quoted here with very heavy abridgement and with added italics.)

We bee come together at this time (dearely beloued brethren) to feede at the Lords Supper, vnto the which *in Gods behalfe* I bid you all that be here present, and beseech you *for the Lord Jesus Christs sake*, that yee will not refuse to come thereto, being so *louingly* called and *bidden of God him-selfe*. Yee know how grieuous and *vnkinde* a thing it is, when a man hath prepared a rich feast, decked his table with al kind of prouision, so that there *lacketh nothing* but the *ghests* to sit downe, and yet they which bee called (without any cause) most *vnthankefully* refuse to come. . . . [You] say, I am a grieuous sinner, and therefore am afraide to come: wherefore then doe you not repent and amend? . . . When you should returne to God, will you excuse your selfe, and say that you bee not readie? . . . And as the sonne of God did vouchsafe to yeelde vp his soule by death vpon the crosse for your health: Euen so it is your duetie to receiue the Communion to-gether in the remembrance of his death, . . . And where as you offend God so sore in refusing this holy banquet, I admonish, exhort, and beseech you, that vnto this *vnkindnesse* ye will not adde any more: Which thing ye shall doe, if yee stand by as *gazers* and *lookers* on them that doe communicate, and be not partakers of the same your selues.

Juxtaposition of the two texts exposes correspondences between them with respect to situation and imagery, including Herbert's ashamed con-viction that one who cannot partake had best depart and not look. Quick-eyed and smiling Love, however, has here replaced both its own earthly curate and the irrascible host seeing his rich feast go to waste, a change that profoundly affects the tone. Since the exhortation was heavily re-vised in 1661, the *ABCP* (178n) adds a historical note: "As this Exhorta-tion originally stood, it contained a strong passage [partly quoted above] about the ill effects of habitually remaining to 'gaze' without receiving the Communion, which shows that the habit was an extremely common one at that time." The *ABCP* also remarks (179n), "The admixture of grave warning and tender encouragement in this Service is indeed truly wonderful." Herbert, from this point of view, in effect both splits and exaggerates the admixture. He finds himself unworthy, unkind, guilty, marred, and—with a pun on grace—ungrateful, and he discovers Love to be extraordinarily gracious and encouraging. Love is "observing," but Herbert maintains, "I cannot look" and asks that his "shame / Go where it doth deserve." The argument from merit is speedily met, however, by quick-eyed Love, who already has borne the blame, so that Herbert next proposes to "serve" the meal but apparently not to be a guest who par-takes of it. That also will never do, however, for what this speaker lacks most of all is the quickening and regenerative force of Love's banquet.

In M. M. Mahood's opinion, this "last and culminating poem . . . turns upon an unspoken pun on the word *host*."3 "Consecrated bread,"

3. M. M. Mahood, "Something Understood: The Nature of Herbert's Wit," in *Meta-*

the Eucharistic meaning of that word, certainly is well worth hearing, but the way to bridge over the distances between *ob*serve, *de*serve, and "serve"—as well as go beyond them—is by invoking the assistance of a different prefix that is invisibly present in the poem's closing lines. "There lacketh nothing but the ghests to sit downe," as the exhortation has it.

> You must sit down, sayes Love, and taste my meat:
>
> [The bodie of our Lord Jesus Christ . . .
> The blood of our Lord Jesus Christ . . .
> *pre*serue thy bodie and soule into euerlasting life.]
>
> So I did sit and eat.
>
> • • •

"Only deign to sit and eat . . . sit down and eat." The words might almost be manuscript variants for Herbert's poem but in actual fact occur in the second book of *Paradise Regained* as part of an elaborate Eucharistic parody. By the time Milton published the poem, he may have thought that curates of the established church were likely to be hirelings in the devil's pay, whether they knew it or not, but here, at any rate, it is Satan himself who takes on the role of one who prepares a rich feast, decking his table with all kind of provision, and it is Jesus, of course, who rightly declines to partake.

The exhortation to the negligent makes reference to a holy "banquet," a word that in modern times has tilted its meaning toward the heavy side. It formerly shared one of the meanings of "buffet" or sideboard and some-times referred to a light repast of a relatively insubstantial kind. Hence, for example, Donne's warning, "Except thou feed (not banquet) on / The super-naturall food, Religion, / Thy better Growth growes withered, and scant" ("An Anatomie of the World," 187–89).[4] In the banquet scene of *Paradise Regained*, Satan evidently has it in mind to establish his own variety of the Anglican "middle way" by combining the best, that is to say the worst, from both sides of these linguistic and culinary worlds. He conjures up

> A Table richly spread, in regal mode,
> With dishes pil'd, and meats of noblest sort
> And savor, Beasts of chase, or Fowl of game,
> In pastry built, or from the spit, or boil'd,
> Grisamber steam'd; all Fish from Sea or Shore,
> Freshet, or purling Brook, of shell or fin.
>
> (2.340–45)

---

physical Poetry, ed. Malcolm Bradbury and David Palmer (Bloomington: Indiana University Press, 1970; repr. 1971), 127.

4. John Donne, *The Anniversaries*, ed. Frank Manley, 73; cf. Manley's annotation: "*Banquet* is used in its common seventeenth-century meaning of a dessert of nuts, fruit, and wine."

It is difficult to pinpoint exactly where Satan begins to overreach himself in this scene, but in line 345 he clearly oversteps a strictly drawn line. What Satan has earlier claimed is true enough: "nor mention I / Meats by the Law unclean" (328–29). What he later claims, "These are not Fruits forbidden" (369), also is no lie. In offering shellfish, however, Satan— with seemingly casual but also insidious nonchalance—includes prohibited fare. "Whatsoeuer hath no finnes nor scales in the waters, that shall bee an abomination vnto you" (Leviticus 11.12). The availability "at a stately sideboard" of "wine / That fragrant smell diffus'd" (350–51) might or might not rouse suspicion had it been mentioned five lines earlier than unclean seafood, but since it is placed five lines later, another echo perhaps is to be heard: "Doe not drinke wine nor strong drinke . . . when ye goe into the Tabernacle of the Congregation" (Leviticus 10.9).

The Levitical laws pertained only to the old dispensation, of course. "Stripling youths" (352) and "Nymphs" (355), however, do not strongly remind me of the chalice bearers I am accustomed to seeing at Eucharist, but then "*Arabian* odors" (364) and "charming pipes" (362) also are not quite like the thurible's incense or the organ at my local parish church. All of this lushness is placed in "a pleasant Grove" (288), and that is an idolatrous place of false images, as previously noticed in connection with Herbert's "H. Baptisme" (I), quite certainly one to be backed away from and looked beyond. In these circumstances, there is wonderfully monstrous perversity in "only deign to sit and eat" (336), "What doubts the Son of God to sit and eat" (368), "sit down and eat" (377). But the finest equivocation of all those uttered in this superlatively high-church "Splendor" (366), with its "gentle Ministers" (375), is the claim made for "these viands pure" (370), that

> Thir taste no knowledge works, at least of evil,
> But life *preserves*, destroys life's enemy,
> Hunger, with sweet restorative delight.
> (371–73, italics added)

This "preserving" may be to everlasting death but certainly not actually to life, and Jesus continues to take the stance of the "negligent," despite all "exhortations." Lest, however, we carry the parody where this poem's Jesus does not, also to be noticed is his assertion that he could

> Command a Table in this Wilderness,
> And call swift flights of Angels ministrant
> Array'd in Glory on my cup to attend.
> (384–86)

It is the giver, the mode of giving, and the implications that are corrupt, not necessarily Communion tables and cups themselves. St. Paul long ago made the point, "Yee cannot drinke the cup of the Lord, and the cup of deuils: yee cannot be partakers of the Lords Table, and of the table of deuils" (1 Corinthians 10.21).

PARAPHRASED PERICOPES

Wither, Herbert, Henry More, Milton, Sidney

St. Paul's statement certainly could have been appointed for liturgical use but, so far as I know, in fact never was, and there are no allusions to it in the exhortations to the negligent where it might have been, perhaps rather harshly, appropriate. Also true is that the banquet scene is not placed last in *Paradise Regained*, nor does it include a Gloria; indeed, since no communion, devilish or otherwise, has in fact occurred, no hymn at all need be sung. These necessary omissions are partly made up later as angels set forth "A table of Celestial Food" (4.588), and Jesus, "from Heavenly Feast refresht" (637), "Home to his Mother's house private return'd" (639). Yet even here, although the angels sing "Heavenly Anthems" (594), the words supplied by Milton (597–635, "True Image of the Father") are not a paraphrase of "Glory be to God on high." The only reminiscences (if, doubtfully, any at all) appear in, "Hail Son of the most High . . . on thy glorious work / Now enter" (633–35). We have arrived at the closing lines of the poem, but the Gloria simply cannot supply an appropriate ending; in the poem, after all, what has been prepared and opened is an entry way into glorious work, not an exit from the experiencing of it.

Milton thus takes over what he can use and lets the rest go, a scarcely surprising strategy since few poems, whether by Milton or not, are designed to be close paraphrases of something else. Some of George Wither's rhymes, however, are exceptions to this rule, including those in the collection titled *Halelviah* or, to quote more of the title page, "praisefull and Poenitentiall *Hymnes, Spirituall Songs*, and *Morall-Odes . . .* advancing the glory of GOD." The first hymn, according to Wither's own headnote, is "A generall Invitation to praise GOD." The verse itself begins by paraphrasing the Venite—the "Invitatory," as it sometimes is called—of Morning Prayer. The Prayer Book's "O Come, let us sing vnto the Lord" is versified into "Come, oh come in pious *Laies*, / Sound we *God-Almighti's* praise." From a purely biblical point of view, what Wither is versifying is Psalm 95; that psalm and the Venite are identical except for the minor verbal differences between the translation in the Prayer Book on the one hand and in the Authorized Version on the other. It is the positioning, not the paraphrasable content, that unmistakably indicates the presence of a pericope.

Since, however, the Psalter and the Authorized Version do not exactly agree in their wordings, this is the place to notice that allusions that appear to be to Psalms—the biblical book, that is—sometimes in fact are not. Herbert's "The Quip" presents a striking illustration. The *OED* defines "quip" as a "sharp, sarcastic remark" and/or "verbal equivocation," and the situational context is put on view in the poem's first stanza.

> The merrie world did on a day
> With his train-bands and mates agree
> To meet together, where I lay,
> And all in sport to geere at me.

Among the mates are Beauty, Money, Glory, and a compound personification called "quick Wit and Conversation," each of them being allowed a full stanza in which to jeer, none of them receiving a single word in reply.

> They . . . laide snares for mee: and they that went about to doe me euill, talked of wickednes, and imagined deceite all the day long. As for me, I was like a deafe man, and heard not: and as one that is dumbe, which doeth not open his mouth. I became euen as a man that heareth not: and in whose mouth are no reproofes.

The quotation is from the Prayer Book's Psalter, but the Authorized Version of Psalm 38.12–14 would do equally well up to this point. Accounting for this self-willed silence to the world, the Authorized Version of the psalm next adds: "Thou wilt heare, O Lord my God." The explanation as given in the Psalter, however, differs greatly: "Thou shalt answere for me, O Lord my God." It is the latter, not the former, which Herbert paraphrases four times (and in Hutchinson's text, in italics): "But thou shalt answer, Lord, for me."

Seeing this fact does not clarify Herbert's poem except in the sense that it removes an obstacle or puzzle that reading the Authorized Version unnecessarily obtrudes. The point, moreover, is not that Herbert is willfully obscure or obtruding obstacles himself. He understandably alludes to the version of the psalm that he knew best from continual recitation of it in church. If he scrupulously followed the directions of the Prayer Book, he heard it aloud on the eighth day of every calendar month unless a special day of feast or fast, with its own specially appointed psalms, took precedence over the schedule whereby the 150 psalms would all be used each month. Had Herbert been equally scrupulous and a secret Roman Catholic, he would have read all of them in Latin every week.

This also is another place to take into account the sometime importance of surrounding context. Easter is an example of a special day on which proper psalms replace those called for by the monthly calendar, and among those specially appointed for the day is Psalm 57, which includes the command, "Awake lute and harpe." Lest I seem to claim too much, let me freely admit that this psalm surely is not a model for Thomas Wyatt's famous lyric, "My lute awake!" John Hall, professing to be scandalized by Wyatt's amorous verse, fired back with a religious parody, "MY lute awake and prayse the lord," but Easter and Psalm 57 are no more needed in reading Hall than they are for Wyatt.[5] The point here is that Herbert considers "Easter" in a poem with that title, and "Awake, my lute" is the command given in the poem's seventh line; with that kind of context, it probably ought to be difficult *not* to hear the psalm. Herbert's words might also, of course, evoke Wyatt, or even Hall, but that is merely a possibility, not a near certainty.

A similar situation occurs when Wither at one point chooses to paraphrase St. Paul. Since Wither can't possibly have needed any help from the Book of Common Prayer in finding his way to 1 Corinthians 15, it is context that once again indicates that liturgical usage is, in fact, significant. For St. Paul, it is quite specifically Judgement Day when "the trumpet shall sound" (1 Corinthians 15.52), and there "shall bee brought to passe the saying that is written [quoting Hosea 13.14], Death is swallowed up in victory. O death, where is thy sting? O graue [margin: "*Or, hell*"], where is thy victory?" (verses 54–55). The next thing to observe is that this passage is part of a pericope for Evensong on the Tuesday after Easter. Wither jumps the gun by a couple of days, but it can be no accident that his hymn for Easter concludes with a paraphrase:

> emboldned now we grow,
> Triumphantly, to say or sing
> Oh *Hell*! where is thy *Conquest* now?
> And, where oh Death! is now thy *sting*?

Pericopes for Eucharist normally include a passage from one of the New Testament epistles and one from the Gospels. On the Monday of Holy Week, however, the epistle is the dialogue that opens Isaiah 63.

> Who is this that commeth from Edom, with died garments from Bozrah? this that is glorious in his apparell, trauelling in the greatnesse of his strength? I that speake in righteousnesse, mighty to saue.
> Wherefore *art* thou red in thine apparell, and thy garments like him that treadeth in the wine fat?
> I have troden the winepresse alone, and of the people *there was* none with mee.

According to traditional interpretation, the questioner is Isaiah, and the respondent is the Messiah who is to come when time shall be. Lancelot

---

5. See Thomas Wyatt, *The Complete Poems*, ed. R. A. Rebholz, 144 (poem cix); and John Hall, *The Court of Vertue*, ed. Russell A. Fraser, 169–72. Hall's preceding poem is a parody of Wyatt's "Blame not my lute."

Andrewes, taking the passage as his sermon text for Easter 1623, gives an elaborate exposition, especially of the winepress as a symbol of the Cross and the Passion on Good Friday. This sermon thus demands that the congregation contemplate Easter, the climax of Holy Week, by reconsidering a pericope with which the week began.

Henry More does roughly the same kind of thing in "An Hymn Upon the RESURRECTION of Christ" in that the verse looks back to Good Friday in addition to celebrating Easter.

> Who's this we see from Edom come,
> With bloudy Robes from *Bosrah* Town
> He whom false *Jews* to death did doom,
> And Heav'n's fierce Anger had cast down.
>
> His righteous Soul alone was fain
> The Wine-press of God's wrath to tread,
> And all his Garments to distain,
> And sprinkled Cloaths to die bloud-red.

The trouble with this kind of thing, of course, is that it *is* paraphrase, not poetry. Sometimes, however, one is lucky enough to be given both. In Herbert's "The Agonie," Christ's "skinne" and "garments bloudie be. / Sinne is that presse and vice, which forceth pain" (10–11). This particular press is a winepress as well as a vice that results from human vice; wine and blood become interchanged, however, as at the Eucharist. "Love is that liquour sweet and most divine, / Which my God feels as bloud; but I, as wine" (17–18). The poems next to appear are "The Sinner," "Good Friday," "Redemption," "Sepulchre," and "Easter," at which point Herbert is ready for Psalm 57 and "Awake, my lute."

And sometimes one is given something that definitely is poetry and probably is paraphrase, but the language has been so thoroughly assimilated into the verbal fabric of the poem itself that its force is infused by the poet much more powerfully and fully than by the "source" one detects behind it. A self-evident truth is that much of the language of *Paradise Lost* can be called "English" only if one firmly inserts the adjective "Miltonic." A specific case in point is that Morning Prayer, as celebrated by Adam and Eve in book 5, is fully Miltonic and not confusable with anything else. Nevertheless, as Bishop Newton pointed out long ago, their hymn of praise is

> an imitation, or rather a sort of paraphrase, of the 148th Psalm, and (of what is a paraphrase upon that) the Canticle placed after *Te Deum* in the Liturgy, "*O all ye works of the Lord, bless ye the Lord*, &c." which is the song of the three children in the Apocrypha.[6]

6. *Paradise Lost*, ed. Thomas Newton, 2 vols. (London, 1749), 1:322.

From one point of view, Newton is talking about three separate or separable things in addition to Milton's poem: the psalm itself; the apocryphal part of chapter 3 of the Book of Daniel (apocryphal because no Hebrew for this part of the chapter exists, only the Greek translation); and, finally, the Benedicite, the hymn used at Morning Prayer as an alternative to the Te Deum. The Benedicite and the song in Daniel 3 are the same in paraphrasable content for many practical purposes; indeed, so far as general structure goes, there is not much to choose from in talking about any of the three texts that Newton mentions. The account of the Benedicite in *The Prayer Book Dictionary* (95B–96A) thus applies, except for verse numbers, indifferently to the other two as well: "The invitation to praise which is its simple theme is worked out in great detail; first the heavenly powers are invoked (*vv.* 1–5), then the heavenly bodies and atmospheric phenomena (*vv.* 6–17), then the earth and sea (*vv.* 18–22), then living creatures (*vv.* 23–25), and finally man (*vv.* 26–32)."

Differences can be seen within this structural framework, however, and one of them is that the canticle and Milton's lines contain more specific examples than does the psalm of those created things that offer up praise. In the canticle, but not in the psalm, an unvarying refrain—"Blesse yee the Lord: praise him, and magnifie him for euer"—is repeated after each verse. Milton also includes a refrain, but it varies from "sound his praise" to "resound his praise," "still new praise," "advance his praise," "tune his praise," and finally, "taught his praise." The opening words of Milton's hymn, "These are thy glorious works," are measurably closer to those of the canticle, "O all ye workes," than to those of the psalm, "O praise the Lord of heauen," but the psalm arrives at works quite quickly itself. The Benedicite, but not the psalm, calls for praise from "ice and snow," "frost and cold"; Adam and Eve, of course, as yet know nothing of such matters. Their hymn is freer in its progress than its precedents are; it seems more spontaneous, less formulaic or predetermined, and quite fittingly so.

> For neither various style
> Nor holy rapture wanted they to praise
> Thir Maker, in fit strains pronounct or sung
> Unmeditated, such prompt eloquence
> Flow'd from thir lips, in Prose or numerous Verse.
> (5.146–50)

The hymn in *Paradise Lost* also is "More tuneable than needed Lute or Harp" (152), instruments later available for more than one purpose but not yet strung in Eden. The last four lines (205–8) refer back to Eve's ominous dream of the night before ("if the night / Have gather'd aught of evil or conceal'd, / Disperse it"); no equivalent exists, for obvious reasons, in the background materials.

In light of these various facts, it seems fair to me to say that Milton did not begin with the Book of Psalms nor with the apocryphal part of Daniel 3 as sung by Shadrach, Mishack, and Abed-nego in the fiery furnace. Instead he re-created a canticle for Morning Prayer into a hymn for the "Orisons, each Morning duly paid" (145) by Adam and Eve. It also is clear that he did not write merely a paraphrase of the canticle but a hymn that is itself finely "tuneable" for the larger poem in which it is placed and for the singers of it.

Changing the singers from Adam and Eve to anyone else at any other time would further require changing at least some of the song's material. One therefore would be astounded not to find at least some differences when Morning Prayer and Evensong are celebrated in Arcadia, however close that classical setting at times may be to prelapsarian Eden. Sidney is the poet in this case, the singers are Strephon and Klaius, and the foundation for the song is Isaiah 40, assigned in the Anglican calendar to December 13 but read in Roman churches on Christmas day. From an Anglican point of view, the season is Advent ("ad-venio," come to), the four-week process of the "coming" of Christ to be climaxed by his arrival on December 25; from the Roman perspective, he is already here by the time Isaiah 40 is read. Either the prophecy of verse 4 will shortly be fulfilled or it has been on the very day appointed for its reading, but in either case, "euery valley shalbe exalted, and euery mountaine and hill shalbe made low."

The occasion for "Yee Gote-heard Gods" is not a coming, however, but a departure, specifically of Urania, "thought a Shepeherdes Daughter, but in deed of farr greater byrthe." Inverted celebration thus is called for, and since the lament is cast into a double sestina, six terminal words must be rotated in strict sequence, not once but twice, in the six lines of each of the twelve stanzas. In stanza one, the six words appear in this order: "mountaines" and "vallies," "forrests" and "musique," "morning" and "evening." "Forrests" and "musique," the inside pair, represent the relatively personal and private elements of where these speakers are located and of the musical activity in which they are engaged. The others, antithetically correlated, prove to be ceremonially public words that vary in their relationships and meaning even as their positionings change from stanza to stanza.

As the poem opens, the mountains are perceived to be "grassie," the valleys "pleasant," but as Strephon and Klaius search for a means adequate to the expression of their grief, these Edenic features of the Arcadian landscape gradually become externalizations of internal conditions. One of the staggering things about this poem is that the technicalities of its extraordinarily artificial form become massively powerful vehicles in portraying psychological intensities. The mountains begin to look "savage" (8) and "monstrous" (16) while the "wofull" (10) vales seem "foule affliction's vallies" (17). By the fourth stanza, "molehilles seeme high mountaines"; by the fifth, are hyperbolically "highest mountains"; and by the sixth, Klaius says,

> Long since I hate the night, more hate the morning:
> Long since my thoughts chase me like beasts in forrests,
> And make me wish my selfe layd under mountains.

Molehills inevitably suggest much ado about nothing, but any comedy discoverable here is of the deadly serious and grimly ludicrous kind. It is not unlike that in *Paradise Lost*, when God the Son first comes upon the battle scene of the war in heaven, having "into terror chang'd / His count'nance" (6.824–25).

> They astonisht all resistance lost,
> All courage; down thir idle weapons dropp'd;
> O'er Shields and Helms, and helmed heads he rode
> Of Thrones and mighty Seraphim prostrate,
> That wish't the Mountains now might be again
> Thrown on them as a shelter from his ire.
>
> (838–43)

The allusion in both cases is to St. John's apocalyptic vision (Revelation 6.15–17) of the last Advent of Christ on Judgement Day.

> And the Kings of the earth, and the great men, and the rich men, and the chiefe Captaines, and the mighty men, and euery bondman, and euery free man, hid themselues in the dennes, and in the rockes of the mountaines,
> And saide to the mountaines and rocks, Fall on us, and hide us from the face of him that sitteth on the Throne, and from the wrath of the Lambe:
> For the great day of his wrath is come, and who shalbe able to stand?

This vision of the Last Coming also is foreseen in the Anglican Collect for the first Sunday of Advent, "Giue vs grace . . . that in the last day when hee shall come againe in his glorious Maiestie, to iudge both the quicke and the dead, we may rise to the life immortall."

St. John and the Church are looking so very far ahead at this point that they have arrived at the end of all of time. Meanwhile, however, the first Advent of Christmas must recur, and mountains must be made low. Opening the second half of the poem, Strephon beholds, or thinks he does, precisely that distortion:

> Me seemes I see the high and stately mountaines,
> Transforme themselves to lowe dejected vallies.

And this transformation opens the way for other metamorphoses, scarcely less remarkable, as forests seem "ill-changed" (39), "Nightingales doo learne of Owles their musique" (40), and "Me seemes I feele the comfort of the morning / Turnde to the mortall serene of an evening" (41–42). This projection of grief upon an external world reflexively alters the subjective apprehension of it, and the external scene next seems to degrade still further the internal landscape of those who have changed it. Strephon would destroy that world if he could ("I wish to fire the trees of all these forrests," 49), his motive being bitter hostility ("I doo detest night, evening, day, and morning," 54). Klaius would isolate himself from it ("Shamed I hate my selfe in sight of mountaines, / And stoppe mine eares, lest I growe mad with Musicke," 59–60). In both cases, however, the setting and its features, including the sounds, are by now so fully internalized that no withdrawal or escape is possible. "Curse to my selfe my prayer is" (55); "My state more base, then are the basest vallies" (57).

The increasingly devastating truth is that Urania, "Heaven," has left, not come, apparently never again to return. "For she, with whom compar'd, the Alpes are vallies, . . . Is gone, is gone" (67, 71). The liturgy of Strephon and Klaius, like other rites, quite properly offers up prayer and praise but is itself transformed, even as they and their world and the terminal words for their sestina have been changed, from a canticle of celebration into a Morning Prayer and Evensong of despair. The three-line conclusion of a sestina is obligated to gather up all six of the terminal words that have been ending previous lines; three of the six words therefore must be transposed back to an earlier position. In this case (73–75, with italics added),

> These *mountaines* witnesse shall, so shall these *vallies*,
> These *forrests* eke, made wretched by our *musique*,
> Our *morning* hymne this is, and song at *evening*.

TRUE CIRCUMCISION OF THE SPIRIT

Beaumont, Crashaw, Harvey, Herrick, Quarles, Wither, Milton

When Urania absents herself, even an Arcadian landscape is blighted, becoming a place of "spoyld forrests" (72), "Turning to desarts our best pastur'de mountaines" (73). When it is God who arrives, each circumstantial detail is charged with grandeur, even the circumcision of a child. In the secular calendar, a new year is ushered in by Janus, the bifronted god who faces both past and future, but in church the eighth day after Christmas is both January 1 and Circumcision day. It too initiates a new chronology but of a kind that challenges the validity of how a pagan world measures time. Among those who marked down the date were the poets and versifiers named immediately above, and an important reason why this verse could be written is that, while bloody circumcision of foreskin by no means is discounted on January 1, metaphoric values are especially paramount. Implicit within the Circumcision of the infant Christ is the Passion on Good Friday, and a prime lesson taught on this day in church concerns the imperative need for true circumcision of the spirit whether the flesh be circumcised or not. Milton's poem for the day will never replace the Nativity poem or "Lycidas" but is impressive in its own—admittedly more limited—way. Crashaw's, as usual, is quite flashy, and Joseph Beaumont's is more effective than the work of an obscure writer is supposed to be. The others are useful, as shadowed backgrounds often are in highlighting something else, but they are mostly prosaic and can be cited briefly.

At this point, I also need to include the fact, hitherto skipped over because as yet not needed, that commentaries on scripture have sometimes been organized in terms of liturgical use. They necessarily disregard where and how the material appears in the Bible itself and comment instead on why the particular passages are proper to the day. In some cases they also unfold the meanings of prayers and canticles; the aim is to contemplate the import of biblical events in the fullness of their annual liturgical celebration.[7]

A strictly ordered account of the verse for January 1, therefore, would probably require quoting the Communion pericopes in the Prayer Book's translation and other lessons from the Authorized Version, next citing the liturgical commentaries on the pericopes, and then comparing this background material to the poems and the poems to one another. That method is, in fact, worth adopting, at least more or less, for a later chapter on poems for Christmas, but considerable liberty is taken with it here.

Luke 2.21, part of the Communion Gospel, could scarcely have been left out since it records, uniquely, "And when the eight day was come, that the child should bee circumcised, his name was called Jesus." I count 84 other examples of "circumcise," "circumcision," and related forms scattered through the Bible, a number of them clustered in other lessons appointed for the day: Genesis 17 (the imposition of circumcision by Yahweh on Abraham and his seed), Romans 2 and 4 (St. Paul's initial interpretation and adaptation), and Colossians 2 (Paul's further translation of a carnal rite into symbolism). Joshua 5, however, also turns out to have multiple appearances of the word *circumcision* but nonetheless was passed

---

7. *The Golden Legend* is the famous medieval compilation of traditional materials for dates in the church calendar, including January 1. A modern counterpart is Toal's four-volume translation of patristic materials for major feasts and fasts. Among the successors to Hooker's work were those by Boys, Sparrow, and—a century later and thus less directly—Wogan, all of them explaining what is done in church and why; these works were intended to serve as guides for perplexed Anglicans, especially those feeling pressure from Roman Catholics on one side and from Protestants on the other. The editions used here are cited in my bibliography.

over in favor of Deuteronomy 10, a chapter in which the word occurs only once—as a significant metaphor, however, in a statement soon to be quoted. An inference here is that the lessons represent considerably more than a mere anthology of random passages that happen to mention circumcision. Liturgical commentaries, at any rate, take the position that the pericopes were chosen carefully so as to serve as the foundation on which several cornerstones of theology rest.

An informing concept is the unquestioned necessity of the narrowly defined and very specific fulfillment of that part of the Old Testament covenant between Abraham and Yahweh, which required that every male child be circumcised. Also assumed, however, are the implicit totality of the first shedding of blood by Christ and the consequent easement for others from the letter of the old law. Anthony Sparrow maintains, "As by his Birth we received the adoption of sons; so by his Circumcision, the redemption of the Law: and without this, his Birth had not availed us at all" (*Rationale*, 129). In the first of three poems for the event (N–97), Herrick remarks that without this further act, "The Birth is fruitlesse."[8] "Our Church," Wither writes in a prose headnote for verse on the subject, "solemnizeth this . . . [so] that taking notice how soone he began to shed his blood for us, and to smart for our Sins, we might be the more thankfull for the same: and be provoked to repentance, by considering how easier a Sacrament [baptism] he hath left for our initiation into his *Church*." The idea of an unmerited gift of grace quickly presents itself at this point. Herrick's three titles for three separate poems are "The New-yeeres Gift, or Circumcisions Song" (N–97), "Another New-yeeres Gift" (N–98), and "To his Saviour. The New yeers gift" (N–125). The third one proposes an exchange: in thanks for the Circumcision, Herrick will "returne a bleeding Heart." Christopher Harvey asks, "What shall I give"; discovering that he has only himself to offer, he prays that the self be made worthy: "Circumcise my heart." Wither's prosaic summary in verse, from which the first lines have been lopped off, is helpful here precisely because it explains itself.

> 2. LORD! let thy smart make us repent.
> And, *Circumcised-Hearts* desire.
> Yea, by that milder *Sacrament*,
> Which follow'd This, thy Grace inspire:
>   For, He that either is *Baptiz*'d,
> Or *Circumcized* in Flesh alone,
> Is but as one Vncircumciz'd;
> Or, as an Vnbaptized one.

8. When referring to poems for the Circumcision, I seldom specify exact titles since all of them refer either to "New Year" or (far more frequently) to "Circumcision" ("The," "On the," "Upon the," "Of the," "For the").

> 3. The *Year*, we now anew begin;
> And *outward-Gifts* received be.
> Renew us, also, LORD, *within*,
> And make us *New years-Gifts* to Thee.

An exchange of gifts is, moreover, only one aspect of the doubleness important to this day. John Boys, speaking as the dean of Canterbury Cathedral, wants us to know why the naming of Jesus and the first shedding of his blood should coincide. "To show that Christ our Mediatour betweene God and man, was both a man in being *circumcised*, and God in being *Iesus*, that is, a Sauiour" (*Festivall*, 132). Beaumont adds bifronted Janus to the idea and writes,

> FAIND *Janus* now forget thy Name,
> And both thy faces hide for shame,
> The Nobler Face of Heavn & Earth
> Are joynd in this Great Infants Birth,
> Who in His double Nature now is come
> To ope ye year at *Bethlehem*, not at *Rome*.

Alternatively, Boys continues, "Christ happily was called *Iesus*, and *circumcised* at the same time, to signifie that there is no remission of sinne without shedding of blood" (*Festivall*, 132). Beaumont was acquainted with that idea too.

> Shine out blest Year; 'twas not to cause
> A Blush, that Blood drop'd on Thy Face,
> Those Circumcision Drops will dresse
> Thee in bright Purple Blessednesse.
> The Paschall *Lamb* doth sprinkle his most pure
> Blood on Times Doore to keep it safe & sure.

Crashaw, very possibly a model for Beaumont in the lines just quoted, tosses off glittering antitheses.

> Rise, thou best & brightest morning!
>   Rosy with a double Red;
> With thine own blush thy cheeks adorning
>   And the dear drops this day were shed.

Francis Quarles extends the motif for a double title, "Of our Saviours Circumcision, or New-yeares day," explaining that these "Did make a double Birth-day to appeare, / One of our happinesse, one of the yeare." Boys, however, indicates that the concept of two in this case is not entirely adequate, for circumcision actually is

Three fold,
{
Carnall, vnder the Law.
Spirituall, vnder grace.
Celestiall, in the kingdome of glorie.
}

(*Festivall*, 133)

Carnal circumcision is the physical act but applies to no more than the letter of the law, a point made by St. Paul in Romans 2, the second lesson for Morning Prayer. What Boys refers to as spiritual circumcision is the one demanded by Deuteronomy 10, "Circumcise therefore the foreskin of your heart." Colossians 2 amplifies the image to "putting off the body of the sinnes of the flesh" so as to be "quickened together with" Christ. For Boys (and, presumably, for the poets already cited), this is "a circumcision of the heart . . . in the spirit . . . when as the regenerate by the sword of the spirit . . . doe not onely circumcise the foreskinne: but all the powers of the soule, and all the parts of the body" (*Festivall*, 133–34). Over and beyond carnal and spiritual circumcision is the celestial kind, the one to occur "in the world to come," possibly implied by the lessons but certainly not identified by them, "when all superfluity shall be cut off vtterly, when as wee shall appeare before Gods throne without any spot in our soule, or corruption in our body" (*Festivall*, 134). For Boys, the ultimate significance of an eighth-day circumcision is, "Seuen daies signifie the time of this present world, and the eighth day the resurrection, when all corruption of the flesh shall be cut off" (*Festivall*, 136).

Christopher Harvey, his heart as yet not circumcised, is ill prepared to anticipate an ultimate future. He asks, however,

> Must smart so soon
> Seize on my Saviour's tender flesh, scarce grown
> Unto an eighth-daie's age?

He further inquires about this day's purpose: "Is it to antidate Thy death" or "to begin Thy passion / Almost together with thine incarnation?" Whatever the specific answer, it is clear that the Circumcision "seals Thy covenant" and thus becomes a symbol for the entire pattern of sacrifice and service that the day initiates. Herrick's "To his Saviour. The New yeers gift" (N-125), a poem mentioned earlier, consists—perhaps not coincidentally—of eight lines; the final word is an italicized "*all.*"

The Circumcision was a much weightier occasion than at first might be supposed, but I doubt that any amount of background would fully prepare one for Milton's poem on the subject except in the sense of enabling a perception, otherwise quite literally imperceptible, of how vast an improvement it is over other verse written for the day. This statement remains true, even though there are verbal similarities to some of the phrases in other treatments, including the sealing of covenant by an early wounding that smarts. (I quote from Hughes but alter the indentation of 27–28 to conform to that of 13–14 and add—for reasons shortly to be explained—the odd-looking scheme for the rhymes.)

	Ye flaming Powers, and winged Warriors bright,	f
	That erst with Music and triumphant song	g
	First heard by happy watchful Shepherds' ear,	e
	So sweetly sung your Joy the Clouds along	g
5	Through the soft silence of the list'ning night,	f
	Now mourn; and, if sad share with us to bear	e
	Your fiery essence can distill no tear,	c
	Burn in your sighs, and borrow	d
	Seas wept from our deep sorrow:	d
10	He, who with all Heav'n's heraldry whilere	c
	Enter'd the world, now bleeds to give us ease;	a
	Alas, how soon our sin	b
	Sore doth begin,	b
	His Infancy to seize!	a
15	O more exceeding love or law more just?	ee
	Just law indeed, but more exceeding love!	ff
	For we by rightful doom remediless	cc
	Were lost in death, till he that dwelt above	ff
	High-thron'd in secret bliss, for us frail dust	ee
20	Emptied his glory, ev'n to nakedness;	cc
	And that great Cov'nant which we still transgress	cc
	Entirely satisfi'd,	dd
	And the full wrath beside	dd
	Of vengeful Justice bore for our excess,	cc
25	And seals obedience first with wounding smart	aa
	This day; but Oh! ere long	bb
	Huge pangs and strong	bb
	Will pierce more near his heart.	aa

An extraordinary feature of this poem, particularly evident when it is approached from the direction of Herrick and Crashaw, not to mention Wither and company, is its tone. Grandiose language and syntax replace sentiment on the one hand and epigrammatic jewel work on the other, and the poem is nearly as "high-thron'd" (19) as its subject is said to have been. One could hardly fail to notice this fact, but a possible result is that the rhyme scheme, though unquestionably fundamental to any rhymed poem, might not be noticed at all. The two go hand in hand, however, for both are versions, in many ways inverted, of the "heroic." The exclamation of line 14 leads to the rhetorical question of line 15, a shift in mode (though by no means jarring, and another exclamation follows immediately) that is paralleled by changes in line length and of rhyming syllables. Two halves, both of sonnet length, are thus exposed, and each consists of two quatrains and a sestet in upside-down order. The procedure is certainly unorthodox but not so radical as to be unrecognizable. Further irregularities, though less unusual, also are audible. Rhyme linkage (dependent on "-ess") occurs between "sestet" and initial "quatrain" in the second half, the side effect being a partial isolation of the last four lines. Lines 26–27 end with "-ong," however, and thus reflect back to lines 2 and 4, especially because of "along" (4) and "long" (26). Pentameters, the norm for sonnets, are interrupted in both halves by trimeters and dimeters that occupy correspondingly positioned lines.

The right-side-up analogy to this verse form is the "heroic sonnet" as found in poems that Milton addressed to Fairfax, Cromwell, and Vane. Each begins with a name ("Fairfax, whose name in arms," "Cromwell, our chief of men," "Vane, young in years") the lofty meaning and value of which are to be spelled out in the succeeding lines. The sonnet to Lawes ("Harry, whose tuneful and well measur'd Song") may be an informal variant of the technique appropriate for Milton's collaborator in the masque usually referred to as "Comus." In these poems the name progressively expands in significance until one realizes, somewhere in the middle of the poem, that "Cromwell," for example, has both actual and symbolic existence; in these cases it is the name, as it were, rather than the style that makes the man or is, at any rate, the shorthand form of that which he represents.

"Upon the Circumcision" works in similar fashion. Sooner or later—in my view, not later than the fourteenth line—one ought to be hearing a rhyme scheme that articulates sestet and quatrain(s). Only a pause, moreover, can be made after line 14; or if, erroneously, a terminal stop is heard because of the exclamation point, then the next line quickly corrects the mistake. In any case, those familiar with standard materials for the day would certainly be expecting to hear more than has been said by the end of the fourteenth line. Much has been indicated about appropriate angelic and human reactions to the single declarative statement: "He . . . now bleeds" (10–11). Much no doubt has been implied by that statement and by the externals with which it is surrounded, including the suspended, nearly epic syntax and a diction that would be excessively ponderous and hyperbolic if one did not know that the event is in fact a momentous one. Little of the internal meaning, however, has yet been presented except in the addition of purpose or motive to explain "now bleeds": "to give us ease." It would be very strange to omit completely the "great Cov'nant" that is being "entirely satisfi'd" (21–22) and/or to leave out that Christ "seals obedience first" (25) on this day as a prelude to the Passion yet to come.

This last point is intimated, as it happens, considerably earlier than the closing lines, for it first suggests itself in "Emptied his glory" (20), an allusion to Philippians 2.7–8. Christ

> made himselfe of no reputation [translating "heauton ekenosin," literally "emptied himself"], and tooke upon him the forme of a seruant, and was

made in the likenesse of men. And being found in fashion as a man, he humbled himselfe, and became obedient vnto death, euen the death of the Crosse.

The text is the foundation for the doctrinal theory of kenosis, "a self-emptying of the Lord's deity . . . in the sense that, while remaining unimpaired, it accepted union with a physically limited humanity" ("Kenotic theories," *ODCC*, 763–64). The passage, for self-evident reasons, also was a pericope for Communion on the Sunday immediately prior to the intensely human events of Holy Week. "Emptied his glory, ev'n to nakedness" applies quite as fully to the Cross as to the cradle, possibly more so.

Doubleness, a frequent motif in other poems for the day, appears here in the contrast between "Just law indeed, but more exceeding love" (15). Foreskin, however, while inextricably pertinent to the former, is itself only external flesh, something to be cut off and discarded. The heart of the matter, and I do not apologize for this phrasing, is indeed the heart. And that is the location being gradually approached from the outset of the poem, though not totally arrived at even in the last lines: "Huge pangs and strong / Will pierce more near his heart." January 1 starts something not yet finished, and the Passion of Good Friday is itself an event that recurs annually until Last Advent appears at the end of all future history. Milton spells his way down to (not away from) "heart," the symbolic word, and his subject is not a General Cromwell nor a Lord Fairfax but the King of Glory, the great exemplar of those who unfurl the banners of the Cross. Jesus himself took on the form of a servant whose name means "saviour," but he is—as Milton puts it in "The Passion" (13–14)—the "Most perfect *Hero*, tried in heaviest plight / Of labors huge and hard." These heroics, however, turn a secular world's heroism inside out even as Circumcision day spins bifronted Janus around and turns him upside down. Milton thus inverts heroic sonnet form so as to match his theme and in order to signal the process of conceptualization whereby the sharp knife of merely carnal circumcision is converted into the piercing spear of the Passion as well as a keen-edged sword for the soul.

These poems probably would not exist, and they certainly could not have their present shape, were it not for the prior existence of liturgy and its pericopes. Liturgical prayer was a less needed prerequisite for this verse, but an informing concept within all of it, including Milton's elevated loftiness, is the one set forth by the Anglican Collect for this day:

> Almightie God, which madest thy blessed sonne to bee
> circumcised, and obedient to the law . . . grant vs the true
> circumcision of the Spirit.

4 Now Is the Day of Salvation

METAPHORS AND FIGURES

Verse for the Circumcision normally is written as if it concerned an event taking place, not centuries ago, but on January 1 of whatever year it currently happens to be: "Faind Janus now forget thy name"; "Rise thou best & brightest morning." One might expect to find something that could be paraphrased with "Feigned Janus did forget his name back in the past when that most unusual morning rose," but the seventeenth-century verbs actually do not distort one kind of literal truth since the day being celebrated, January 1, really is recurrently present. The day's significance nonetheless is defined by (and hence cannot be divorced from) a first shedding of blood that occurred long ago and at no other time whatsoever. And yet the historical event also is persistently displayed as if still in process: "Must smart so soon / Seize on my Saviour's tender flesh"? "He . . . now bleeds to give us ease." Despite chronological disparity, immediacy is predicated both of an annual event and of a historical incident that cannot possibly be repeated. "Now-ness," it seems, either is movable (rather than precisely sited) or is expandable far beyond the limits of that chronological moment to which it apparently refers.

The verbs in liturgical verse and prose are, in fact, quite regularly conjugated in this flexible present-tense fashion, and there are at least four good reasons why. First is a devotional point, that the current moment of each and every feast or fast can be critical, if for no other reason, because it may be—for some, inevitably *shall* be—the last one ever to be experienced. "Therefore take the *time* of the *text*," as Lancelot Andrewes urged his congregation on Ash Wednesday 1611: "And that *time*, is at this *time, now*," for "It may be the last *spring*, the last *Swallow*-time, the last *wednesday*, of this name or nature, we shall ever live" (*XCVI Sermons*, 202). And again on Ash Wednesday 1619: "*Now*, is the onely sure part of our *time*. That which is *past*, is *come* and *gone*. That which is *to come*, may peradventure *never come*. Till to morrow, till this Evening, till an houre hence, we have no assurance. *Now therefore*" (*XCVI Sermons*, 213).

Since January 2 might easily be one day too late for anything other than one's own funeral, timely celebration of that which is itself a cele-

bration of something else is not necessarily too inward or excessively rari-
fied. A second point, even so, is that there are times when the ongoing
significance of an event simply must override the fact of its own unique
singularity. Strictly speaking, Milton *ought* to have written, "The infant
Jesus then bled so as to give easement from the Law in time past and also
to give that same easement both now and in times yet to come." Milton,
no doubt, could have managed less awkward phrasing, but not even an
elegant filling out of the verb tenses could serve any useful purpose; the
stress is on the tremendous impact of the Circumcision, regardless of when
its force, chronologically and on a specifically individual basis, is felt.

A third reason is that if easement were not uninterruptedly at work,
then January 1 would be only another day (perhaps like Washington's
birthday, to cite a random example) marked off on the calendar in honor
of some famous personage. The corollary result for baptism would be
disastrous, for the rite, now cut off from the source of its effectiveness,
would be *merely* ceremonial and not a sacrament of God's grace. And a
fourth reason is that the Circumcision itself cannot be severed from other
happenings that are anterior or subsequent to the moment of its own
occurrence. Had circumcision not been imposed on Abraham, the infant
Jesus would not have had that law to fulfill; if later baptisms were not
sacramental, a major purpose of that fulfillment would not have existed.

Retrospectively, then, it can be seen that the baptism of Joseph Beau-
mont (on March 21, 1616) and the Circumcision of Jesus (theoretically, on
January 1 in the year 0 A.D.) are in multiple reflexive action with one
another. Beaumont's eighth-day ceremony presupposes the prior exis-
tence but also the continuing remedial presence of an eighth-day rite
centuries earlier in time. Reversing the order of the two preceding chap-
ters would mirror the historical chronology but also complicate matters,
not simplify them, since the Circumcision makes presuppositions of its
own. The ancient covenant between Abraham and Yahweh was self-pos-
sessed of inherent value, and yet important parts of the agreement and of
what it meant came into actual existence only much later; the Circumci-
sion, by fulfilling the contract of Hebraic law, thus validates and in turn is
validated by its own past history. It also anticipates the Passion to occur
some years later in a different month, and it does so, among other rea-
sons, in order to "baptize" January 1 and every other date (including
March 21, 1616) on which baptisms take place. Until these later effects
become visible, however, the significance of the causes behind them can-
not be adequately known. One therefore must bear witness to the Cir-
cumcision of Jesus in order to comprehend the earlier covenant, and to
see how and why the Circumcision worked in the past, one needs to see
baptism still working in the present. John Boys, moreover, would further
insist that the full reality cannot be known until present time is validated

by the future tense of eternity, "when," to requote, "all corruption of the flesh shall be cut off."

"Circumcision," in Donne's wording, therefore "carried a *figure* of *Baptisme, & Baptisme* carries a *figure* of that *purity*, which we shall have in *perfection* in the *new Jerusalem*" (*Devotions*, 100). These distinctions have little to do with foreskin or water as such and turn instead on a completed past action, on process coextensive with time but largely independent of datable chronology, and on untimable finality. The last of these is verbalized, perhaps inescapably, by means of a metaphor ("the new Jerusalem") but nonetheless is fully possessed of an absolutely complete metaphysical reality. The other two are phenomena that can be described in nonmetaphoric language but even so are figurative; baptismal "cleansing," which from a modern perspective probably looks to be "metaphoric," is considerably closer to nonfigurative reality—to total and final purification, that is—than any merely physical excision, including the Circumcision of the Christ child, could possibly be.

Figure-carrying events, therefore, can be dated in so far as they are history, but the figures that are being carried by those events are continuously present at all times on this side of eternity. A running chronology at the top of the pages in Matthew Henry's *Commentary* confidently dates the covenant between Yahweh and Abraham as having been made in 1898 B.C., the Creation having occurred back in 4004. Henry, however, also takes care to observe that "the covenant of grace is everlasting. It is from everlasting in the counsels of it, and to everlasting in the consequences of it; and the external administration of it is transmitted with the seal of it to the seed of believers, and the internal administration of it by the Spirit to Christ's seed in every age" (*Commentary* 1:112).

Henry's remarks, helpful though they are, might be usefully supplemented with some dictionary definitions, and a handy work to consult is Thomas Wilson's *A Christian Dictionary*, first published in 1611 and augmented for the third edition in 1623 (759 quarto pages, with supplements for Revelation, Canticles, and Hebrews). Turning to C, one finds these four entries in consecutive but slightly irregular alphabetical order: "To Circumcise," "Men of Circumcised eares, lips, and hearts," "Circumcision," and "Circumcision made without hands." The first definition given for "To Circumcise" is, "To cut off, or to pare away the fore-skinne of the flesh, to witnesse thereby an entrance into the Couenant of mercy with God, for forgiuenesse of sinne, and newnesse of life, Genes. 17, 10, 11. This is to Circumcise Sacramentally." The last entry, under "Circumcision made without hands," is, "It is a Sacrament of the olde Testament, signifying and sealing vp to the people of yᵉ Iews their entrance into Couenant with God, for the remission of their sinnes, and mortification of their lusts by faith in Christ to come, Rom. 4, 11."

Even in these definitions, the developed senses have become so dominant that primary meanings have nearly become secondary in importance. This kind of relative significance is especially clear from the two middle entries. "Circumcision" (as distinct, evidently, from "To Circumcise") means "the whole legall ceremonious worship of God, by a Synecdoche of the part for the whole," and also has reference to "those which bee truely godly persons, spiritually circumcised in their heart." "Men of Circumcised eares, lips, and hearts" are "such as haue the inward spirituall effect and grace of Circumcision, together with the signe: as on the other side, vncircumcised lips, eares, and heart, be affirmed of such as haue the outward signe onely, without the signified grace, Acts 7, 51." And add the entry under "Vncircumcised": "circumcised outwardly; yet because their harts were not renewed, they were inwardly vncircumcised." Circumcision, if restricted to the physical and hence no more than an outward sign, thus turns out to mean *un*circumcision, a reversal of meaning that looks odd at first though in fact making excellent sense. The figure that ought to be carried is more important than the carrier itself; indeed, so very much so that, when the figure is lacking, the carrier inverts its meaning. The thrust, however "unliteral" and/or "metaphoric" from a modern perspective, concerns purpose and effect rather than physical act. From Wilson's point of view, therefore, a crucial point about "Circumcision" is that it "assured to the Iewes (as Baptisme doth to vs) their engrafting into Christ."

"Now" and "present tense" are not entry headings in Wilson's dictionary, but his definitions of various kinds of "Day" serve well enough to establish that timings themselves are irregular, not strict. As a term, "Last dayes, or latter dayes and times," most simply considered, merely refers to "a long while after, or heereafter in time to come." But the phrase also means,

> The whole time wherein the Gospell is preached, to wit, betweene the first and second comming of Christ, called by *Paul*, Fulnesse of time. . . . The reason why the times betweene Christs first and second comming are called last dayes, is because in these dayes all figures, types, prophesies, were to bee fulfilled.

"Day of saluation" is defined as that "time of the Gospell, wherein the glad tydings of Saluation are [*not* "were"] offered. 2 Cor. 6, 2. *This is the Day of Saluation*." "Day of the Lord, or of Christ" means, "The time of his comming in the flesh, to live amongst us" and/or "the time of his second comming to Iudgement in Glory and Maiesty." "Day of Visitation" is "the time wherein God of his great Mercy shall conuert a Sinner." "This Day" refers to "every Day, or the day present which now is." And, perhaps most tellingly, "To Day" is "the whole season of our calling to

God, euen all the time of this life, wherein God offereth vs grace, and calleth vs to him." One should notice, however, that the "today" of present grace may be quite brief, and in no case is it long; Wilson's very first definition of "Dayes" is, "The short time of mans life." Some of the "days" defined by Wilson happen unchronologically or repeatedly or even simultaneously, but from his point of view they are quite genuinely "literal" rather than metaphoric; they actually do occur, and despite their apparent irregularity they by no means are haphazard.

Thinking of this kind does not, of course, imply that the importance of metaphors has somehow been diminished. Far from it, in fact, since earlier writers supposed the ultimate source of ambivalent language to be God's own ambivalent doubleness. Donne, for example, places his remarks on figurative circumcision and baptism within an extensive discussion, which is itself highly metaphorical, of God's use of metaphors. One of his major points, moreover, is that Christ quite often is more "metaphorical" than "real." The words just quoted are the ones Donne himself used, but even in 1624 a statement of that kind evidently would have invited serious misapprehension if not well prepared for in advance. Prior to making it, therefore, Donne firmly insists that God is "a *direct God . . . a literall God, a God* that wouldest bee understood *literally,* and according to the *plaine sense* of all that thou saiest" (*Devotions,* 99). On the other hand—but "let no *prophane mis-interpreter* abuse it"—

> Thou art also . . . a *figurative,* a *metaphoricall God* too: A *God* in whose words there is such a height of *figures,* such *voyages,* such *peregrinations* to fetch remote and precious *metaphors,* such *extentions,* such *spreadings . . .* and such *things* in thy *words,* as all *prophane Authors,* seeme of the seed of the *Serpent,* that *creepes;* thou art the *dove,* that flies.

Remarks of this kind about figurative *language* presumably would have occasioned no surprise, nor would the comments that follow about figurative *events.* This is the context for the statement, already quoted, about circumcision and baptism.

> Neither art thou thus a *figurative,* a *Metaphoricall God,* in thy *word* only, but in thy *workes* too. The *stile* of thy *works,* the *phrase* of thine *Actions,* is *Metaphoricall.* The *institution* of thy whole *worship* in the *old Law,* was a continuall *Allegory; types & figures* overspread all; and *figures* flowed into *figures,* and powred themselves out into *farther figures; Circumcision* carried a *figure* of *Baptisme, & Baptisme* carries . . . (*Devotions,* 100)

Elsewhere, the narrative base for "allegory" is or, at any rate, may be "fictional" but clearly is not so here; "types" and "figures" also remain rooted in an authentic reality of their own even as they typify and prefigure or postfigure something else.

Not until after this rather elaborate preparation (and I have greatly shortened it) is Donne ready for symbolic metaphors. "How often, how much more often doth thy *Sonne* call himselfe a *way*, and a *light*, and a *gate*, and a *Vine*, and *bread*, than the *Sonne of God*, or of *Man?* How much oftner doth he exhibit a *Metaphoricall Christ*, than a *reall*, a *literall?*" (*Devotions*, 100). Whether Donne could or could not have got away with asking that rhetorical question at the outset may be itself a question not worth asking; in either case, he decided to lead up to it. When he does ask it, there can be no suggestion whatsoever that Christ was not historically real or that the Gospels are fictional narratives that function as an extended "metaphor" or "allegory." An important idea instead is that the language and also the life of Christ often are metaphoric—and thus more than merely "literal"—in that they "carry figures" forward to the ultimately unfigured and totally absolute reality that is signified by and discoverable within the new Jerusalem. A second idea being emphasized is that reality, whether figured or not, must sometimes be expressed metaphorically.

Donne adds that it is the divine model that "hath occasioned thine ancient *servants*, whose delight it was to write after thy *Copie*, to proceede the same way in their *expositions* of the *Scriptures*, and in their composing both of *publike liturgies*, and of *private prayers* to thee" (*Devotions*, 100). It further occasioned the pouring forth of figures upon figures throughout many of these devotions, among them the metaphoric "voyage" into manifold significations of "waters," which Donne immediately launches into here, including "a *Remedy* against the deepest *water*, by *water*; against the *inundation* of sinne, by *Baptisme*."

One has to be aware of figures of speech so prominent in "publike liturgies" (to borrow phrasing from the *Devotions*) and conspicuous also in "private prayers" as well as private verse. One also needs to be wary since apparently similar language often refers to figure-carrying events and timings that are not metaphoric, at least not as that word commonly is used today. This difference is frequently important in the verse taken up in the sections that follow, but there appears to be no terminology that is both apt and widely accepted, and some of my subheadings, therefore, are deliberately artificial.[1]

1. It seemed desirable to cite seventeenth-century authors in the preceding paragraphs, but this kind of thinking was, of course, a part of their heritage. A very basic text (certainly for Andrewes and Donne, probably for Wilson, and possibly for Matthew Henry) would have been Part 1, Question 1, Article 10 of Thomas Aquinas's *Summa theologica*, "Utrum Sacra Scriptura sub una littera habent plures sensus" (whether the Holy Scriptures contain multiple senses beneath a literal one). The distinctions there drawn are fundamental to the *Summa* itself and concern the significations of biblical words (both literal and metaphoric) as they relate to the figurative significations of biblical events. See Aquinas, *Summa theologica* 1:10–12.

DOUBLE DAYS OF SALVATION

Hammond, Beaumont, Donne

Some verse, if approached with wayward assumptions about figures and metaphors, probably will seem largely pointless or, if not that, then either artificially precious or oddly specious. Glaring examples are three poems that rely for their very existence on "analogies," which may seem to be—but in actual fact are not—senselessly strained or wrenched about by ingenious efforts to be clever. Deleting metaphors that were never there in the first place may make this poetry seem merely different, not better, but that, after all, is a separate problem.

The poem by William Hammond (1614–?) is "Upon the Nativity of Our Saviour and Sacrament then Received," and one reason for citing it first is the doubleness of the title. In this respect it is reminiscent of some of the poems for Circumcision (Quarles's "Of our Saviours Circumcision, or New-yeares day," for example), and the resemblance is not entirely fortuitous. Since this is a Nativity poem, the timing of it necessarily is tied to December 25, and implicit in the date are two solar motions that Hammond refuses to take for granted. Even though one of these motions is nearly invisible, he sets out from the proposition that the Janus-like features of January 1 also are discoverable, eight days earlier, on Christmas day. "See," he begins,

> See from his watery tropic how the Sun
> Approacheth by a double motion!
> The same flight, tending to the western seas,
> Wheels northward by insensible degrees;
> So this blest day bears to our intellect,
> As its bright fire, a duplicate respect.
>
> (1–6)

Because of the duplicate respect, Hammond next transplants bifronted Janus from Rome to Bethlehem and thence to seventeenth-century England. The god continues to be two-faced, of course, but not for purposes of duplicity; indeed, the ability to look two ways becomes an asset, even a necessity:

> None but a two-fac'd Janus can be guest,
> And fit himself unto this double feast,
> That must before jointly the manger see,
> And view behind the execrable tree;
> Here the blest Virgin's living milk, and there
> The fatal streams of the Son's blood appear.
>
> (7–12)

In church settings as they exist *outside* the poem, the manger is often enough a focus of attention for part of Christmas day, but when the Eucharistic elements are consecrated, the Cross and the Passion necessarily become central. Eight days ahead (from the perspective of Christmas) but also much earlier (looking back from the Passion) is Circumcision day, when the infant born in the manger antedates the Crucifixion. *Inside* the poem, double vision is needed in order to behold an oxymoron, but the double feast would itself wear a false front if merely the visible or most obvious half of it were to be looked at instead of both halves being viewed simultaneously.

From a purely metaphoric perspective, the bread and wine of Communion on December 25 seem to have been mentally transferred to the invisible body and blood that in turn have conjured up an image of the "execrable tree" of the Cross. And the Passion evidently has next assumed control so completely that the Eucharistic elements, although the presumed starting point for the association of ideas, disappear even before they can be mentioned. Hammond thus appears to be engaged in some deletion of his own, but if so, then the point of the absence almost certainly is to indicate presence, specifically "the Real Presence of Christ."

Capitalization and quotation marks are needed because the phrase refers to an article of faith that supposedly is cherished by every Roman, Lutheran, and Anglican who participates in Communion. The Sunday scorecard handed out at my church regularly states that visitors, whether Anglicans or not, are invited to communicate if they have been baptized, are in good standing elsewhere, and "acknowledge the Real Presence of Christ" in the Sacrament. I have very little idea what other parishioners make of the statement, but the language is technical:

> In (esp. Anglican) Eucharistic theology an expression used to cover several doctrines [including Roman "transubstantiation" and Lutheran "consubstantiation"] emphasizing the actual Presence of the Body and Blood of Christ in the Sacrament, as contrasted with others that maintain that the Body and Blood are present only figuratively or symbolically. An early instance of its use is in H. Latimer, who . . . held that "this same presence may be called most fitly a real presence, that is, a presence not feigned, but a true and faithful presence." ("Real Presence, The," *ODCC*, 1141B).

Metaphoric and/or symbolic presence, in short, is expressly being denied as not merely inadequate to the truth but fundamentally false. It is in some other sense, unfeigned and faithful, that the elements "really" are the body and blood, even though the exact nature of this reality evidently is uncommonly difficult to define.[2]

2. Joseph Hall, in 1631, claimed universal agreement on the basic point. "That Christ Jesus our Lord is truly present, and received in the blessed sacrament of his body and blood, is so clear and universally agreed upon, that he can be no Christian that doubts it." Hall

A major foundation for Hammond's poem, at any rate, is the basically *un*metaphoric assertion of essential identity between "sacrament received" and "presence of Christ." Some of the events happening on Christmas day thus concern a birth long past; others, a sacrifice still happening in the present. The "time," however, is the same, and, as Hammond has it, "The difference only this, the Deity / Born to our flesh, into his spirit we."

The poems by Donne and by Sir John Beaumont the Elder (1583–1627) have closely similar titles, "Upon the Annunciation and Passion falling upon one day 1608" and "Vpon the two great Feasts of the Annunciation and Resurrection falling on the same day, March 25, 1627." Donne's poems were not published until 1633 and hence not until after Beaumont's death, but since they circulated in manuscript, Donne's poem for 1608 could have prompted Beaumont's for 1627. Any conclusion based on the very similar wording of the two titles would, however, be hasty. It is extremely difficult to verbalize this kind of subject without using this kind of language, a point illustrated by the fact that even the *PBD* ("Occurrence and Concurrence," 489B) resorts to comparable phrasing: "When two holy-days fall on the same day they are said to 'occur.'"

"Occurrence" does not usefully apply to Hammond's title since verse of more or less the same kind presumably could be written for large numbers of other days in the year ("Upon the Ascension and Sacrament then received," to invent an example, or "Upon S. Barnabas day and . . ."). Hammond himself evidently saw a contemplative advantage (as distinct from an opportunity for shifty semantics) in viewing the birth and sacrifice of his redeemer at the same time, but very little, if anything at all, can be gained by speaking of the Sacrament "falling on the *same* day" when, after all, it could be received on *any* day.

With Beaumont and Donne, however, there may be scarcely any alternative to phrasing of this sort. In both cases, the subject proposed is not, in fact, the Annunciation itself, nor is it either the Passion or the Resurrection. The titles indicate instead that the poems concern the simultaneity of two events that, despite chronological separation, "occur" together. The doctrine of the Real Presence also may be implicit in Beaumont's poem since Eucharist has to have been celebrated on Easter in 1627, but in any case, in 1608 and again in 1627 the temporal co-incidence of two days was a reality. For Donne and Beaumont this whole idea was a "donné," a

---

immediately adds, however, "But in what manner he is both present and received is a point that hath exercised many wits" (*A Plain and Familiar Explication of Christ's Presence in the Sacrament*, in *The Works . . . of Joseph Hall*, ed. Philip Wynter, 8:768). Jeremy Taylor opens *The Real Presence . . . Proved Against . . . Transubstantiation* (*The Whole Works of the Right Rev. Jeremy Taylor*, ed. Reginald Heber, 6:1–168) by reviewing "The State of the Question." Heber (Taylor's editor and Bishop of Calcutta) maintained, "The word 'real,' as Taylor has introduced it, is unmeaning or worse" (*Works* 1:cxcvii).

"given" that they could and did take for granted, but it may not be amiss here to explain why occurrences can and do occur.

Since at least two time schemes almost always are operative inside church, collisions between them are inevitable. First, the calendar year is deeply charged with spiritual meaning by church usage, but it does employ a large number of "normal" calendar dates. In addition to the Circumcision and Christmas, one might mention the Saints' days encountered earlier in connection with Beaumont and Crashaw: June 11 for St. Barnabas and June 24 for St. John the Baptist. Or there is the Annunciation, nine months to the day before Christmas, and it is worth noticing that March 25, to which the Annunciation was fixed, probably determined the date of Christmas, not the other way around.[3]

A second methodology, however, has always controlled the timing of other feasts and fasts. Easter, far and away the most important example, is the first Sunday following the first full moon to appear on or after the vernal equinox. The practical consequence is that the date for Easter can be as early as March 22 or as late as April 25. Also sliding forward and back, to keep proper pace, are the dates determined by Easter—Good Friday (three days earlier), Ash Wednesday (forty weekdays earlier—Sundays are not counted), Ascension Thursday (forty weekdays later), and so on. The underlying cause for this variableness is that the Christian year, in this respect, is an adaptation of the Hebrew lunar year. Passover is tied to the appearance of the vernal full moon, specifically to the fourteenth day of the month Nisan; since Easter was to be the new Passover, it had to be timed to occur in similar fashion.[4]

From an astronomical point of view, discrepancies between lunar and solar calendars cause inconsistent measurements, and the lunar calendar must be adjusted periodically lest the discrepancies become too great. At the end of a leap year, to cite one notable example, the Hebrew calendar adds Veadar (sometimes called Adar Sheni [in translation, "second Adar"] because it follows Adar), an extra month of twenty-nine days. From a liturgical perspective, the collisions caused by shifting relationships often result in double days. From either perspective, it could be argued that an "occurrence" is a "real incidence or co-incidence" (as distinct from a

3. Hippolytus (c. 220), working backward from his own time, calculated that the Crucifixion took place on Friday, March 25, 29 A.D. Assuming that the death occurred on the thirty-second anniversary of the Incarnation, he fixed the Annunciation to March 25 and thus placed Christmas nine months later. The *Ecclesiastical History* of Eusebius (c. 260–c. 340) is the source for this information, but I have taken it from the *PBD* (339B, "Festival, 5—Calculation").

4. In early times, in some places of Asia Minor, Easter was celebrated "on Nisan 14, whatever the day of the week, and not (as elsewhere) on the following Sunday"; those who insisted on doing so "survived as a sect down to the 5th cent." (*ODCC*, 1131B, "Quartodecimanism").

merely factitious coincidence); it is time that is being measured by two systems in two different ways, and the double days being celebrated are, after all, indisputably and actually there.

Both Beaumont and Donne, at any rate, unfold the co-incidences referred to in their titles by pairing the various disparities that are thereby conjoined, and Beaumont's opening, not unlike Hammond's, rejoices that the "happy day"

> sweetly do'st combine
> Two hemispheres in th' Equinoctiall line:
> The one debasing God to earthly paine,
> The other raising man to endlesse raigne.
> Christ's humble steps declining to the wombe,
> Touch heau'nly scales erected on His tombe.

These particular contrasts work well enough, but the collocation of "wombe" with "tombe" turns out to be entirely too beguiling and leads to an inappropriate turn of thought. Easter is abandoned, in fact, and the poem regresses to Holy Saturday, the day before, when Christ is still subject to the bonds of death. At this point, therefore, it is Crashaw who supplies an instructive comparison. The relevant sacred epigram is "Vpon our Saviours Tombe wherein never man was laid."

> How Life and Death in Thee
> Agree?
> Thou had'st a virgin Wombe
> And Tombe.
> A *Joseph* did betroth
> Them both.

Crashaw was able to balance Joseph, the husband of Mary, against Joseph of Arimathea because of a "coincidence" in the modern sense: two individuals, apparently by mere happenstance, once shared the same name. Beaumont, in similar fashion, compares Gabriel, the "angelus" (the "messenger," that is) of the Annunciation, to those "angels" who had the dissimilar mission of guarding the tomb. Worse yet, the Incarnation becomes a fanciful marriage, and "night" is said to be "conqu'ring" at the very moment when, by the standards of faith, it is being most conclusively conquered. The resulting hodgepodge is this:

> We first with Gabriel must this Prince conuay
> Into His chamber on the marriage day,
> Then with the other Angels cloth'd in white,
> We will adore Him in this conqu'ring night:
> The Sonne of God assuming humane breath,
> Becomes a subiect to His vassall Death.

Beaumont's poem—and there is considerably more of it—could be written off, of course, as no great loss, but tossing out Donne's similar poem at the same time would be an entirely different affair. Since even Homer is said to have nodded on occasion, it is reasonable to think that Donne sometimes slept, but in this case, his language does verbalize the inward concept that informs the poem. And since it now is the Passion, not the Resurrection, that occurs with the Annunciation, the simultaneity is of the conception and death of Christ, his temporal beginning and end. Donne at first cannot make up his mind whether to "feast" because "Christ came" or to "fast" because he "went away." Feast-fast, at first glance, may not seem far removed from womb-tomb, but this disparity actually does mirror the liturgical occasion and the customary observance of feasts and fasts. This particular occurrence further requires that Mary be "seen / At almost fiftie, and at scarce fifteene." "At once" (at one and the same time, that is) "a Sonne is promis'd her, and gone"; "Gabriell gives Christ to her" and Christ on the Cross gives "her to John." And since Christ himself is "at once, not yet alive, and dead," his "first and last concurre" to form a "circle."

Picking up a circular image used also in the "Hymne . . . in my sicknesse," Donne acknowledges that this day "makes one / (As in plaine Maps, the furthest West is East) Of the' Angels *Ave,* 'and *Consummatum est.*" "Hail" (Ave) salutes the rise of a Son-Sun whereas "It is finished" (Consummatum est) signals the setting. Since beginnings and endings necessarily encompass "all betweene," this day presents "Th'Abridgement of Christs story." Indeed, liturgical time has compacted the story so densely that Donne concludes by proposing a subsequent daily distribution of the heaped up treasures that the Church so lavishly "affords" on this double day.

> So though the least of his paines, deeds, or words,
> Would busie a life, she all this day affords;
> This treasure then, in grosse, my Soule uplay,
> And in my life retaile it every day.

DISTRIBUTED TIME

Donne's *La Corona* and Carey's "Crucifixus pro Nobis"

Since the Annunciation and the Passion had already "occurred" in 1597, Donne himself could have written two poems in two different years for the same double day, and exactly the same subject could have been addressed back in 1524 or once again in 1692.[5] Either of the two inci-

---

5. To find the calendar years mentioned, I worked with the tables given in the *OCEL*, 1126–47 ("The Calendar").

dents, moreover, certainly could be the subject for a separate poem in any year whatsoever, whether the days for them coincided or not. The date of *La Corona* is usually said to be earlier than 1610 and possibly 1607. "Annunciation," the second sonnet of that sequence, and "Crucyfying," the fifth, therefore could be regarded as indicating what actually happened when—in 1607 or 1609 (or in 1608, for that matter)—Donne chose to examine the two events as they usually appear rather than as they very occasionally do. Some support for this view might be had from the "treasure" alluded to in the closing lines of "Upon the Annunciation" and from the "treasury" mentioned in the third line of *La Corona*. Looking at the two component parts of a co-incidence as two events could, of course, quite easily lead to looking at several more.

In these terms, "Th'Abridgement of Christs story," as made in the double day and in the poem for it, is unfolded in *La Corona* through six incidents spaced out in time and distributed over six sonnets, all of them being prefaced by an introductory seventh poem. *"Salvation to all that will is nigh"* is the announcement heard first. The next three are "Annunciation," "Nativitie," and "Temple" (where the twelve-year-old Jesus instructed the rabbis); "Crucyfying" and "Resurrection" resume the story, and "Ascention" carries on to the end. Linear progression within narrative sequence is visible in the events to which these titles refer, but if one is thinking in terms of the biblical narrative itself, then enormous amounts of wonderfully rich material necessarily have been dropped out. This version, therefore, is indeed rather less of an "Abridgement of Christs story" than the one made earlier, but it by no means is full. On the other hand, the Ascension is up to the heaven whence deity made its descent to become incarnate in the first place. The point of origin and place of return thus "concurre" (as the first and last were said to do in "Upon the Annunciation and Passion"), but the circumference of the new circle, by encompassing eternity as well as time, is so very huge that it could scarcely be larger. The story line as a whole, therefore, turns out to be nonlinear and, far from being abridged, it proves to be much fuller by implication than even "unabridged" could suggest.

Fullness also turns out to be characteristic not only of the linear circularity as a whole but also of each one of the constituent parts. Phrased another way, the successive sonnets dilate the narrative events far beyond the limits of the time and space in which the events themselves presumably are to be located. The Annunciation announces a conception, but "thou" (Mary)

> Wast in his minde, who is thy Sonne, and Brother,
> Whom thou conceiv'st, conceiv'd; yea thou art now
> Thy Makers maker, and thy Fathers mother.

The Nativity happens in a manger, but "Seest thou, my Soule . . . how he / Which fils all place, yet none holds him, doth lye?" "The Word but lately could not speake, and loe"—in the "Temple"—"It sodenly speakes wonders." Crucifixion becomes an oxymoron by "Measuring selfe-lifes infinity to'a span"; the Resurrection specifically signals Easter but also enables one to "*Salute the last, and everlasting day*"; and in "Ascension," Christ is a "Bright torch, which shin'st, that I the way may see."

In effect, therefore, the composite oneness of "Upon the Annunciation and Passion" has been divided in half, and the life as a whole has further been split into six parts. And yet each of the separated segments of chronological time expands toward infinite timelessness. They also contract into the movable present tense of the moment when they are being considered. More than thirty years elapse in the course of Christ's story from conception to ascension, all of it past history, but the various incidents of sonnets 2–7 are all happening "now." The word as such is not insisted upon and appears only twice. "Thou art now / Thy Makers maker" (Sonnet 2).

> the worst are most, they will and can,
> Alas, and do, unto the immaculate,
> Whose creature Fate is, now prescribe a Fate,
> Measuring selfe-lifes infinity to'a span.
> (Sonnet 5)

The idea of now-ness is, however, continually and currently present. "Kisse him, and with him into Egypt goe." "*Joseph* turne backe; see where your child doth sit."

> Loe, where condemned hee
> Beares his owne crosse, with paine, yet by and by
> When it beares him, he must beare more and die.

One of Donne's letters—dated "July 1607" by Donne himself—mentions the "inclosed *Holy Hymns and Sonnets*" (Gardner, *Divine Poems*, 55). The reference may be to *La Corona* and, if so, then the date of the letter also dates the verse. I mention that kind of timing, however, primarily because it highlights so clearly the very different sort that is happening in the verse. *La Corona*, unlike the letter, is deeply involved with a distant past that continually recurs in present-tense time so as to enable the work of personal salvation. Wilson's definitions of "This day" and "To day" and Andrewes's insistence on "now" are closely parallel to Donne's conceptualizations, and underlying the usage of all three authors are several biblical texts that I have been reserving until now. "And you that were sometimes alienated, and enemies in your minde by wicked workes, yet now [translating "nuni," at this moment] hath he reconciled" (Colossians 1.21). "What fruit had ye then in those things, whereof ye are now

ashamed? for the end of those things is death. But now ["nuni"] being
made free from sinne, and become seruants to God, yee haue your fruit
vnto holinesse, and the end euerlasting life" (Romans 6.21–22). "Now
["nuni"] therefore performe the doing of it" (2 Corinthians 8.11). I also
must add 2 Corinthians 6.2 because the verse is of great importance:
"Behold, now is the day of salvation." The Greek word is "nun" (now)
rather than "nuni," but this was a key text, and Wilson (in an entry ear-
lier quoted from the *Christian Dictionary*) added an emphasis of his own
by translating, "This is the Day of Saluation."

"This" day can be any day, of course, but some people are most in-
tensely aware of its presence when experiencing church time in their own
lives. March 25 and December 25, from this perspective, mark new be-
ginnings in different ways and yet can be equally and fully expressive of
the workings of God. This also is true of the first Sunday after Epiphany,
when the visit of young Jesus to the Temple is annually celebrated. Good
Friday, Easter Day, and Ascension Thursday speak for themselves in this
regard, and these events to some extent mirror earlier ones. Or rather,
and more accurately, it is the other way round. As Donne later said,
Christ "found a *Golgotha*, (where he was crucified) even in Bethlem,
where he was born . . . the Manger as uneasie at first, as his Crosse at
last" (*Sermons* 7:279).

> All that Christ said, or did, or suffered, concurred to our salvation, as well
> his mothers swathing him in little clouts, as *Iosephs* shrowding him in a
> funerall sheete; as well his cold lying in the Manger, as his cold dying upon
> the Crosse; as well the *puer natus*, as the *consummatum est*; as well his
> birth, as his death is said to have been *the fulnesse of time*. (*Sermons* 6:333)

Six instances of time's fullness are especially particularized in *La Corona*.
Others conceivably could have been added, but about each and every one
of them it is to be said that this day, this very day, now is and is now the
present day of the Lord.

There are large numbers of such days in any given year, but it would be
laborious, if not impossible, to determine exactly how many. If one is
using a solar calendar, the figure to start with, of course, would be 365 or,
in leap years, 366. Fifty-two Sundays plus days in between make for 364.
Lunar calendars are still in use, but I trust I am not alone in being unable
to calculate when and how intercalary days are inserted, as they must be,
in seven years out of every nineteen. In church time, double days for
occurrences increase the totals but by variable amounts depending on
how many collisions result from the changing relationships between lu-
nar and solar time. "We count three hundred," Herbert says in "Easter"
(11–12, the concluding lines), "but we misse: / There is but one, and that
one ever."

Also missable is the exact number of lines in *La Corona*. Helen Gardner and C. A. Patrides give each sonnet its own line numbers; John Shawcross uses cumulative numbers through the sequence as a whole. All three give subtitles for sonnets 2–7, though Gardner adds that she doubts their authenticity. No one, however, tries to print the poem in circular form or to assign two consecutive numbers to a single line, and that is the totally impractical typography needed here. Each sonnet ends with a line that is exactly repeated to start the next, a practice that extends to and includes the seventh poem since its last line repeats (and/or is repeated by) the line with which the sequence begins. With shared lines printed twice and counted both times, the total runs to 98; otherwise it is 91. The reason for mentioning these transparently absurd figures is that the actual number of lines in the work cannot, in fact, be known. And the reason why is that the sequence has no lines that are independently final. Line 14, to cite the first relevant example, ends the first poem but also is either a new line 1 for the next sonnet (Gardner and Patrides) or is line 15 of the ongoing sequence (Shawcross); the "twenty-eighth" line (ending the second sonnet) also serves either as a third line 1 or, in the cumulative system, as line 29; and so on through the rest of the poems. In order to arrive at the "end" of the seventh sonnet (the ninety-eighth and/or ninety-first line and/or seventh appearance of number 14), one necessarily returns to and rereads precisely the same words that began the first poem. In theory, therefore, there also can be no choice about going on through the rest so as to re-reach the last line and thus rereach once again the first. One has to keep circling round and round and is never allowed even to stop reading, much less take time off to worry about the arithmetic.

This may look like thought too relentlessly pursued to be worth thinking about, but one of Sidney's poems conclusively proves that coronas, despite their circularity, actually can be stopped. "I Joye in griefe, and doo detest all joyes," from *The Fourth Eclogues*, runs to ten stanzas, each of ten lines, before making a full return. Line 1 and 101 thus are the same: "I joye in griefe, and doo detest all joyes." But as soon as this return to the first line of stanza 1 *is* made, a halt immediately is called. Lines 102–4 are firmly end-stopped, and so is the poem that they conclude:

> But now an ende, (ô *Klaius*) now an ende,
> For even the hearbes our hatefull musique [de]stroyes,
> And from our burning breath the trees do bende.

Circularity aside, if for any reason at all one did choose to return from Donne's seventh sonnet back to the first, then at least some of the initial poem almost surely would be a jolt the second time through. I have been delaying as many references as possible to that first poem (and omitting line numbers for the others) because its first-ness turns out to be illusory.

There is no other place to print it, true enough, but *La Corona*, including the title, is about as self-consciously circular as any poem can be, given the inevitable constraints imposed by successive lines of verse and by the necessities of typography. Only the shapes of Herbert's "The Altar" and "Easter-wings," for example, could visibly reflect content more clearly. Because of the endless circularity in which last becomes first, the sestet of the first poem simply has to be looked at more than once and thought through at least twice. (In quoting it, I have tinkered with the typography, but it is the space opened up, not the specific spacing, that is the point.)

The ends crowne our workes,	but thou crown'st our ends,
For, at our end	begins our endlesse rest,
This first last end,	now zealously possest,
With a strong sober thirst,	my soule attends.
'Tis time	that heart and voice be lifted high,
Salvation to all that will	*is nigh.*

Change the preceding period to a comma, and one has the line that opens sonnet 2, the second line being,

That All,   which alwayes is All   every where[.]

All in all ways is all, always is so, and for that matter is "every where" as well. I spread out the line to fill available space, but its nearly monosyllabic shortness actually reverses the technique and achieves the same effect by means of contraction. The preceding lines bifurcate themselves regardless of how they are printed and thereby exaggerate antitheses that interact: a first last end, an end that begins endless rest, ends that crown (Gardner: "completes worthily" and "blesses or rewards") but which also are crowned. The wording is strongly ambivalent, and so is the syntax that immediately follows. In Gardner's opinion, "'Possest' qualifies the soul, which is 'wholly occupied' by its thirst." This may well be true, but "possest" probably will be attached to "first last end," the preceding phrase in the same line, before it can be reattached to the next line. In the couplet, "'Tis time" and "*is nigh,*" in emphatic initial and terminal position, are present tenses that are differently present.

These details interrupt linear progress quite forcefully by calling into question the location of first and last or beginning and ending; they raise doubts about when something is "possest" and even about when "is" actually *is*. They represent, in fact, another contraction, in this case of the strategies in the liturgy for Advent. Gardner saw a major part of this point quite clearly and proposed that a suitable subtitle for this sonnet would be "Advent." She further suggested that leading ideas and phrasing were derived from the lessons for Advent in the Roman Breviary. Some allowance has to be made for the Breviary's Latin, but the parallels are indeed both numerous and close, including the Breviary versions of Revelation 1.8, 11 (in English, "I am Alpha and Omega, the beginning and the ending . . . the first and the last") and of Isaiah 28.5 ("erit Dominus exercituum corona gloriae . . . residuo populi sui," the Lord of Hosts shall be a crown of glory for the remnant of his people). What needs to be added, or probably so, is that Advent consists of the four Sundays prior to Christmas but nonetheless is unbounded by time. The season of the "Coming" of the Lord "began" when the Word in all eternity first decided to come, and it "ends" after Judgement Day, the Last Coming, when eternity begins again. The season includes the day of the Lord when the Word becomes flesh on Christmas but also extends through all other days, regardless of calendar date, when the Word is internalized in human hearts. "Coming," in fact, is not so much an event as an ever-present process, a "now" that confers meaning on the recurrently circular measurements of time. Most truly regarded, it is not quantifiable and therefore is not measurable. Numbers, one might say, simply don't count.

There is one number in *La Corona*, however, the presence of which cannot possibly be denied. Whatever the total number of lines may be, there certainly are seven sonnets. Among Donne's own glosses are these:

> The Sadduces put a case to Christ of a woman maried successively to *seven* men; let seven signifie infinite.
>
> *Seven* is ever used to express infinite.
>
> *Seven* is the holy Ghosts Cyphar of infinite.
>
> Seven, in this *Arithmetike*, is *infinite.*
>
> These two parts of our devotion, Prayer and Praise, . . . doe not onely consist together, but constitute one another. . . . As that Prayer [the Lord's] consists of seven petitions, and seven is infinite, so by being at first begun with glory and acknowledgement of his raigning in heaven, and then shut up in the same manner, with acclamations of power and glory, it is made a circle of praise, and a circle is infinite too, The Prayer, and the Praise is equally infinite.[6]

Given these remarks, especially those on infinitely circular prayer and praise, the first-last line of *La Corona* should be (re)quoted too: *"Deigne at my hands this crown of prayer and praise."*

Narrative, whether biographical or autobiographical, necessarily rests upon chronological sequence. Many biblical narratives, including the

6. Quoted from *The Sermons of John Donne*, ed. George R. Potter and Evelyn M. Simpson, 6:89; *Essays in Divinity*, ed. Evelyn M. Simpson, 59; *Sermons* 5:270–71; 7:411; 8:77. For comparable statements, see *Sermons* 4:96; 7:52, 247, 396; 9:406. This numerology was, of course, traditional.

Gospels (but excluding the parables, for example), are conventionally thought to represent, not legendary occurrences, but a true history constituted from authentic events. At a personal level, all sorts of things really were happening to John Donne in, shall we say, 1607–1610, and we know very well what some of them were. We also know, or so it seems to me, that he was imaginatively engaged in reliving New Testament history in an internal space that permits spiritual autobiography to become, not merely a kind of metaphoric relocation, but also a continuation of the biblical story into a personal and genuinely real present-tense time that extends into an indefinite future. The living out of life often has to be cut up and distributed in terms of before and after, of then and now and not yet, but Donne evidently conceived of this distribution as a series of continually recurrent moments that can and should manifest the now-ness, the is-ness, of the fullness of time. *La Corona* is characterized by elaborate artifice or, from the hostile point of view, by inordinate artificiality because it is an externalization of this interior concept. Since consecutiveness is inherent in the idea itself of sequence, including sonnet sequence, perhaps the most that can be done is to turn linearity against itself as early on and as frequently thereafter as is practicable. And indeed, if there is to be any hope of transforming sequence into an image of a real presence that ought to be within sequentiality and yet transcendent to it, then great artfulness, surely, will be required.

• • •

John Boys, commenting on Ascension day, indicates that a retrospective summation is called for by the very nature of the day itself. "Christ's assension," he remarks (*Festivall* 2:138), "is the consummation of all that which he did, and taught, whilest hee dwelt among vs."

> He laboured six daies, and then he rested on the seuenth. His *natiuity* was the first; his *circumcision* was the second; his *presentation in the Temple* the third; his *baptisme* the fourth; his *passion* the fifth; his *resurrection* the sixth; and then followed his *ascension*, in which hee was *receiued into heauen, and now sitteth at the right hand of God*, as hauing finished the whole worke for which hee came into the world.

Boys knew full well that very shortly he himself would be making a fresh start, as it were, by rounding off his comments on Ascension and turning his attention to Pentecost, when the Holy Ghost descended to continue and sustain "the whole worke for which" Christ "came into the world." Indeed, within the same paragraph Boys anticipates that day, referring to the "sending of the holy Ghost in the forme of fiery tongues."

Donne, in contrast, had no further days in *La Corona* with which to work, but perhaps he thought that his verbal strategies already indicate that the abiding presence of the Spirit is a condition without which his

104   Transfigured Rites in Seventeenth-Century English Poetry

seven sonnets either could not have been written at all or would have been drained of all meaning except for the strictly historical kind. For a Whitsunday sermon, possibly preached in 1630 (George R. Potter and Evelyn M. Simpson, Donne's editors, are uncertain), Donne chose John 14.20 as his text, "At that day shall ye know, that I am in my Father, and you in me, and I in you" (*Sermons* 9:232). When Jesus spoke these words to his disciples, the phrase "at that day" had primary reference to a future New Testament time that by 1630 was long since past. Thanks, however, to figurative continuity, "that" historical day becomes synonymous with "this" present day on which the sermon is preached. "So I say of this day, This day, if you be all . . . in perfect charity," the Holy Ghost "shall fill you all" (ibid., 241).

In this same passage, Donne supplements exhortation with rebuke by taking to task the person "that celebrates any Holy-day" on only "one day": "that never thinks of the Incarnation of Christ, but upon Christmas-day, nor upon his Passion, and Resurrection, but upon Easter, and Good-friday." The immediate point concerns weekday time; there is no use dressing up the soul "with your best habits to day," merely to "returne againe to your ordinary apparell to morrow." More generally, any holy day should be not only this day but also every day hereafter. "He that loves the exercise of prayer so earnestly, as that in prayer he feeles this vehemence of the Holy Ghost, that man dwels in an everlasting Whitsunday: for so he does, he hath it alwayes, that ever had it aright." I know of nothing in the Prayer Book that would enable overt celebrations of multiple simultaneities, but Donne's line of thought is that "this" day, whichever one it is, can "occur" simultaneously with any other "day," or even with all of them, no matter what the calendar says. From this point of view Pentecost may be implicit throughout *La Corona* despite the fact that it nowhere is mentioned.

In any case, Patrick Carey's "*Crucifixus pro Nobis*" quite certainly turns upon the idea of one day being not only itself but also another.[7] "What bruises do I see! / What hideous stripes are those!" This scene is much like the one in the "Crucyfying" sonnet of *La Corona*, it is happening in its own present-tense time, and it meets the expectations aroused by "Crucifixus" in Carey's title. The lines quoted are not, however, from the opening of the poem but from the third of the four stanzas. Stanza 1 is subtitled "Christ in the Cradle," and stanza 2, "Christ in the Garden." We see these events before viewing "Christ in his Passion," but all of them are happening "now." "Look, how he shakes for cold!" "Look, how he glows for heat!" Present tense is by no means the only thing these stanzas have in common.

---

7. Carey's poem was first printed in 1819 by Walter Scott (in that year, not yet "Sir Walter") and again, with additional poems, in 1906 by George Saintsbury in *Minor Poets of the Caroline Period* (the edition used here); the date given in the manuscript is 1651.

They also share an identical rhyme scheme that, while not particularly complex, is rather like that of a sonnet and sufficiently elaborate to reveal strong parallelism, especially since line 5 in every case is carefully left unrhymed. The third stanza illustrates the patterns of all four:

a	What bruises do I see!
b	What hideous stripes are those!
a	Could any cruel be
b	Enough, to give such blows?
x	Look, how they bind his arms
c	And vex his soul with scorns,
d	Upon his hair
d	They make him wear
c	A crown of piercing thorns.
e	Through hands and feet
e	Sharp nails they beat:
f	And now the cross they rear:
g	Many look on;
g	But only John
f	Stands by to sigh, Mary to shed a tear.

Another part of Carey's formal patterning is the similarity within difference of closing lines. The cradle on December 25 is bitterly cold; "All th' heat he has / Joseph, alas! / Gives in a groan; or Mary in a tear." The garden, in baleful contrast, is flaming with heat; "For all this flame, / To cool the same / He only breathes a sigh, and weeps a tear." Medially placed in the second stanza, Christ's "Agony" echoes the language of the earlier Christmas and is itself echoed by the later Good Friday, and all three occur in a movable "now" that stretches both forward and back.

By 1651, however, "now" has long since become "then," or so, at least, it momentarily seems. In the fourth stanza, Carey wants to know, "Why *did* [italics added] he shake for cold? / Why did he glow for heat?"

> Those bruises, stripes, bonds, taunts,
> Those thorns, which thou didst see,
> Those nails, that cross,
> His own life's loss,
> Why, O why suffered he?

The answer, "'Twas for thy sake," is no surprise, but the implication of *thy* sake is that what was past must again become present. The sacrifice continues, and it ought to elicit the same reaction "now" as it did in the "now" of long ago. Carey's last lines, therefore, return from past to present:

> If then his love
> Do thy soul move,
> Sigh out a groan, weep down a melting tear.

Appended to the poem is the phrase "Ex dolore gaudium": from sorrow, joy. Easter, even though it has not yet arrived, also always is. Except, of course, for those (to adapt Donne's phrasing) who don their "best habits to day" but "returne againe" to "ordinary apparell to morrow."

FORESHORTENED HOURS OF SIN AND GRACE

Carey's format is one that I have not stumbled across elsewhere, but one of the principles behind it is embodied in poems that work with daily hours of prayer and with the calendar year of the saints. Abstractly stated, a very basic consideration in each case is what might be called expansive abbreviation. Every single day of prayer and/or each of the hours specifically appointed for worship can be far more intensely time-consuming than hotly pursued but quotidian worldly affairs, and the days of the saints tightly compress the legend of a lifetime down to those spiritually profitable moments that border on eternity. "To be short," as Vaughan begins some recapitulatory advice in *The Mount of Olives*, "live a *Christian*, and die a *Saint*. Let not the *plurality* of *dayes*, with the numerous *distinctions* and *mincings* of thy *time* into *moneths, weeks, houres* and *minutes* deceive thee, nor be a means to make thee misspend the *smallest portion* of it" (*Works*, 188).

Putting this theory into practice has not always been easy even in monastic circumstances, but St. Benedict set down guidelines for doing so in his *Rule for Monasteries*. The seventh chapter, on the twelve degrees of humility, should not be overlooked in this connection, but it is chapters 8–20 that are specifically relevant here. Even though ample precedent, some of it biblical, clearly existed, it is to these regulations that the organization of the monastic day into set hours for prayer is to be traced and from which later church practice derived. In pre–Reformation England, as elsewhere, prayer was to be offered seven times a day, and references to these various "hours" occasionally appear in much later literature. A possibly surprising instance is that Milton's Adam and Eve pray at "that sweet hour of Prime" (*Paradise Lost*, 5.170) prior to beginning their tasks for the day. Vaughan also uses this term in a poem shortly to be quoted, and a further example, to be delayed a little longer, is Donne's "nocturn" for St. Lucy's day.

The seven hours largely disappeared, however, after England broke with Rome, and the Prayer Book has services only for Mattins or Morning Prayer and Evensong or Evening Prayer. In a poem I looked at earlier, these are the hours with which Sidney's two shepherds propose to begin and end each day: "Our morning hymne this, and song at evening." In "Ye Gote-heard Gods," a possible implication is that the intervening time is to be filled with similar devotions, and in *The Mount of Olives*, Vaughan is more explicit on the matter. "Admonitions for Morning Prayer" are followed by "Preparations for a Journey" (preferably to church, in which case "How to carry thy self in the Church" will be helpful, but the distance involved may be as short as stepping out of one's house). "A Prayer . . . When thou art come home; or in the way if thou beest alone" leads to "Admonitions for Evening Prayer," including "When thou art going into bed." During business hours of the day, numerous occasions for prayerful "Ejaculations" will surely arise. Indeed, by some standards, many of those specifically mentioned might easily represent full-time activity: "When[ever] the Clock strikes," "When thou intendest any businesse," "Upon any disorderly thoughts," "Upon thought of thy sins," not to mention "When thou art provoked to anger," "Upon any losses," and especially, perhaps, "When thou art weary of the cares and vanities of this world."

Herbert's comment on the sometime sorry state of worldly days is a three-poem minisequence. The first title is "Mattens"; the third, "Evensong"; what fills up the middle, of course, is "Sinne." It does so, however, with emptiness. Sin is (de)privation, a negation of anything positive; as Herbert says, "It wants"—lacks, that is—"the good of *vertue*, and of *being*" (5). In this respect as in others, "Sinne is flat opposite to th' Almighty" (4), and its emptiness is a corrupt inversion of the process previously encountered in Milton's poem for the Circumcision: the "kenosis" or "emptying" of his glory by Christ. One part of Christ's fullness, as Donne points out, "was a strange fulnesse, for it was a fulnesse of emptinesse; It was all Humiliation . . . all evacuation of himselfe" (*Sermons* 4:289). In Herbert, the favorable result is that divine kenosis can more than balance sinful emptiness, a visual sign being that "Sinne," though it hollows out the center of the three-poem sequence, by that very fact can be surrounded by liturgical "hours" filled up with prayer to which God responds. "I Cannot ope mine eyes, / But thou art ready there to catch / My morning-soul and sacrifice" ("Mattens," 1–3).

> Yet still thou goest on,
> And now with darknesse closest wearie eyes,
> Saying to man, *It doth suffice*:
> *Henceforth repose; your work is done.*
> ("Evensong," 17–20).

"Not one poore minute scapes thy breast," "And in this love, more then in bed, I rest" (30 and 32, the concluding lines).

Rotations through sin are synonymous, in effect, with every twenty-four-hour period from birth to death. Any Evensong, moreover, may be the last one of all, a truth recognized at the service by singing the Nunc

Dimittis or Song of Simeon, "Lord, now lettest thou thy seruant depart in peace: according to thy word. For mine eyes haue seene: thy saluation" (from Luke 2.29–30; the colons indicate break points for antiphonal utterance and response). Herbert's acknowledgment of these truths is made by means of ambivalent signification. "Henceforth repose; your work is done" is a line that specifically refers to nothing more than the end of a single day, but there is no need for Herbert to add that there may or may not be a tomorrow in which to do more. Especially is this true when night is imaged in spatial terms as a coffinlike "ebony box":

> *Henceforth repose; your work is done.*
> Thus in thy ebony box
> Thou dost inclose us, till the day
> Put our amendment in our way,
> And give new wheels to our disorder'd clocks.
>
> (20–24)

Dawn, almost by definition, is a time for fresh beginnings, but the gift of totally new wheels is not likely on this side of the new Jerusalem. The idea is varied in a second "Euen-song," excluded from *The Temple* but found in the Williams manuscript. "The Day is spent," Herbert begins. "I and the Sunn haue runn our races, / I went the slower, yet more paces, / ffor I decay, not hee." A daily decaying into darkness cannot be helped, but God's light is invisibly bright, and thus there can be hope that "my darknes may touch thine. . . . Since Light thy Darknes is." And sooner or later—quite possibly, of course, "this night thy soule shalbe required of thee" (Luke 12.20)—one's hope must be not to greet the dawn but to "wake with thee for ever."[8]

Counterparts to Herbert's poems include George Gascoigne's "Good-Morrow" and "Good-Night," George Wither's "A Morning Hymn" and "An Evening Hymn," Joseph Beaumont's poems with exactly the same titles, and "Hymn for the Morning" and "Anthem for the Evening" by Thomas Flatman (1617–1688), whose claim to fame in the *Oxford Companion to English Literature* is this: he "was much esteemed as a painter of miniatures and also wrote poetry. *Poems and Songs* (1674) contains 'A Thought of Death', 'Death, a Song', and 'The Dying Christian to his Soul', the last of which was imitated by Pope."[9]

8. The symbolism adopted by Herbert and others appears to be both obvious and inherent in the "hours" themselves, but it sometimes was elaborately explained. Jodocus Clichtoveus (Josse Chlictove, d. 1543), for example, observes that at Compline one comes "at last to the vespers and end and last point of life" (translated from *Elucidatiorum ecclesiasticum . . . quatuor libros* [Basil, 1519], sig. 45ᵛ); "dawn is described [in a hymn by Prudentius], and by means of metaphor it is applied to the coming of grace to our souls, after the darkness of sin" (sig. 11ᵛ).

9. *OCEL*, 352. For Pope, see "Minor Poems" in *The Poems of Alexander Pope*, ed. John

These poems are like many of those for the Circumcision in that they are worth knowing about if only to safeguard against the supposition that such work in some sense is outré when in fact it was relatively common. A suitable substitute, however, for many unmemorable lines can be one of Sir Thomas Browne's rare excursions into verse, especially since Browne obviates the need for commentary by appending his own.

> Howere I rest, great God, let me
> Awake again at last with thee.
> And thus assur'd, behold I lie
> Securely, or to awake or die.
> These are my drowsie dayes, in vain
> I now do now wake to sleep again:
> O come that hour, when I shall never
> Sleep again, but wake for ever.

"This," Browne says, "is the Dormative I take to bedward; I need no other *Laudanum* than this to make me sleepe; after which I close mine eyes in security, content to take my leave of the Sun, and sleep unto the resurrection."[10]

Also worth notice are Vaughan's "The Morning Watch" and "The Evening Watch" because the poem for evening departs from the form that this kind of verse customarily takes. Instead of a prayer, Vaughan writes a dialogue between body and soul. The body evidently is aware of only a literal night and a literal dawn, but it somehow implies far more than it realizes and hears from the soul much more than it can comprehend.

> Farewell! I goe to sleep; but when   *Body.*
> The day-star springs, I'le wake agen.
> Goe, sleep in peace.   *Soul.*

This opening conversation just possibly might be preparatory for any good night's rest. The Soul, however, continues with anticipations of a future repose and state wherein the Body is to lie "Unnumber'd in . . . dust," and the Body, failing to understand, uneasily wants to know, "How many hours do'st think 'till day?" The Soul's response ends this poem, this hour, this day, and this time.

Butt et al., 6:90–93. Flatman is mentioned by Pope's editors whereas Pope himself cited Hadrian and Sappho as his models. Possible connections arise from the fact that Flatman knew the work of Vaughan, who in turn had paraphrased Hadrian. Except for Hadrian ("the saddest *poetrie*, that I ever met with," Vaughan says [*The Works of Henry Vaughan*, ed. L. C. Martin, 173]), this verse is not distinctive, and the Sappho is merely a fragment. It therefore is impossible to prove, but Pope may have imitated Flatman, who imitated Vaughan, who paraphrased Hadrian, who imitated Sappho. My reason for taking note of this convoluted affair is indicated by the first sentence of the next paragraph above.

10. *Religio Medici*, 2.12, in *The Works of Sir Thomas Browne*, ed. Charles Sayle, 1:107–8.

> Ah! go; th'art weak, and sleepie. Heav'n
> Is a plain watch, and without figures winds
> All ages up; who drew this Circle even
>   He fils it; Dayes, and hours are *Blinds*.
> Yet, this take with thee; The last gasp of time
> Is thy first breath, and mans *eternall Prime*.[11]

Throughout these poems, the process visibly present is a narrowing of twenty-four-hour periods down to a single "hour" that then reexpands. Joseph Beaumont exaggerates this strategy in "A Preparatory Hymne to the Week of Meditacions upon, & Devout Exercise in the Historie of Christ" and in "A Conclusorie Hymne to the same Week." To start this week off properly, Beaumont vows, "From Morn to Evening I / The History / Of LOVE through all my houres will spread." "With LOVE I'l Rise, & Goe to bed." This week evidently was set aside after Midsummer day had come and gone; its "Days now shrinck & shorter grow." Or rather, when measured by solar movement, they do. When filled with "LOVES deer History," they "so long appear, / That in each Week, I live a Year." And yet, as the thought turns itself upside down, Love "Pours out it self so wide / That every Day" hastens "To bed too soon, though 'twere an Age to Night." Since not nearly so much time can be expended as Love deserves,

> My Days look but like Minutes now,
> My Houres like wretched Nothings show:
> Whilst yet me thinks I but Begin
>   The Evening rusheth in.

Beaumont thus oscillates between "Preparatory" and "Conclusorie," morning and evening, shrinking days stretched out into years and expanded hours diminishing into nothingness. Extremes separate out and become increasingly more extreme as if a gaping distance were opening up between Love's abundant fullness and Beaumont's limited capacity to be filled. The fullness of time is entirely too full, as it were, to be encompassed by means of time, but the oxymoron that is the problem leads, with a final turn of thought, to the oxymoron that is the solution.

> This is LOVES sweet & heavnly sport,
> To make my Days so long, & short;
> That so they may a Shaddow be
>   Of his Eternitie,
> Which, though beyond all Time it swell,
> Yet is an Instant its best Parallel.

11. Alan Rudrum notes in *The Complete Poems:* "*blinds* pretenses, which obscure from us God's real purposes; cf. *OED* blind *sb* 6"; "*eternal prime* a paradox and possibly also a pun: 'prime' refers to the period of greatest vigour, before strength begins to decay; it may also refer to the first canonical hour of the day."

> And straitned in this Vastnes may
> I ever be! Let every Day
> Less than a Minute seem; yet such
> As no Age can outreach:
> Whilst my Devotions sweetly rove
> In this deer Riddle of divinest LOVE.

"Content," I should add, is the poem that follows. Its headnote cites Philippians 4.11, but verses 12–13 also are part of Beaumont's starting point: "I haue learned in whatsoeuer state I am therewith to be content. I know both how . . . to bee full, and to bee hungry, both to abound, and to suffer neede. I can doe all things through Christ, which strengtheneth me."

THE CALENDAR OF ETERNITY

The saints frequently have been regarded as those whom Christ strengthened most, but the Anglican position often has been ambivalent or, indeed, ambiguous about the extent to which they are to be venerated. The twenty-second of the Thirty-Nine Articles roundly condemns "Invocation of Saints" as "Romish"; it is but "a fond thing, vainly invented." The Anglican calendar, however, has always set aside numerous days for the birthdays of the saints into heaven and, for St. John the Baptist, has reserved a second day for his birth on earth. As Donne remarks on John's day in 1622, "For, though we finde the dayes of the Martyrs still called, *Natalitia Martyrum*, their *birth-dayes*, yet that is always intended of the dayes of their *death*; onely in *John Baptist* it is intended literally, of his naturall birth; for, his spirituall birth, his *Martyrdome*, is remembred by another name, *Decollatio Joannis, John Baptists beheading*" (*Sermons* 4:146).

In an undated sermon, possibly from 1624–1625 (the guess made by Potter and Simpson, *Sermons* 9:1), Donne invites his congregation to "Consider the Church of God collectively, and the Saints of God distributively" (9:331). Earlier in this same sermon, however, one is warned not to consider them too much. "Certainely it were . . . a strange circularity, in a man that dwelt at Windsor, to fetch all his water at London Bridge."

> They that come so low downe the streame . . . they will go lower, and lower, to Gravesend too; They that come to Saints, they will come to the Images, and Reliques of Saints too; They come to a brackish water, betweene salt and fresh, and they come at last, to be swallowed up in that sea which hath no limit, no bottome, that is, to direct all their devotions to such Saints. . . . So that this may be Idolatry, in the strictest acceptation of the word, Idol. (*Sermons* 9:321–22)

On the one hand, Herbert both titles and addresses a poem "To all Angels and Saints." They are "glorious spirits": "ev'ry one is king, and hath his crown." On the other, however, he says that he must "forbear . . . to crave your speciall aid." If, moreover, the choice were his alone to make, then Herbert "would addresse" his "vows . . . most gladly" to the Virgin Mary. "But now alas I dare not," for Christ the King "Bids no such thing." Browne may or may not have had the Anglican saints in mind when he remarked, "There are many (questionless) canonised on earth, that shall never be saints in Heaven" (*Religio Medici*, 1.26). The seventy-three saints in the calendar of Browne's time may seem more than enough today, but they represented only a small selection from pre-Reformation days; and except for four saints quite closely associated with England, all of them died before 1000 A.D.

(Since Browne and Herbert had mixed feelings about honoring even biblical saints, it may be worth wondering parenthetically about their reaction to later developments. In 1660, the Martyrdom of King Charles I was attached to January 30 and remained there until January 17, 1859, when a royal proclamation abolished the day. An American calendar from 1963 sets aside February 27 for Herbert and March 31 for Donne as well as August 14 for Jeremy Taylor, September 26 for Lancelot Andrewes, November 3 for Richard Hooker, and—possibly the astonishing example—January 10 for Archbishop William Laud, executed on Tower Hill by Order of Parliament on January 10, 1645.[12] The Collect for Donne is:

> ALMIGHTY God, who in this wondrous world dost manifest thy power and beauty: Open the eyes of all men to see, as did thy servant John Donne, that whatsoever has any being is a mirror wherein we may behold thee, the root and fountain of all being; through Jesus Christ, thy Son our Lord. *Amen.*

The one for Laud:

> ACCEPT, O Lord, our thanksgiving this day for thy servant William Laud; and grant unto us constancy and zeal in thy service, that we may obtain with him and thy servants everywhere a good confession and the crown of everlasting life; through . . .

I can end this parenthesis by noticing that these prayers are modern, among other ways, in that God's servants are referred to by last name as well as first.)

Some days are listed in the calendar—St. Lucy's, for example, December 13—without, however, having pericopes or collects appointed for them. Even when lessons are supplied, Anglican materials always are

---

12. *The Calendar and the Collects, Epistles, and Gospels for the Lesser Feasts and Fasts* (New York: The Church Hymnal Corporation for the Episcopal Church, 1963).

skimpy compared to those in a Roman Breviary, which regularly includes the legend of the saint and much else besides. If Donne had wanted to refresh his memory about what might be appropriate for a nocturn on December 13, a Breviary would have been useful, but the Prayer Book would have been no help at all.

Perhaps for these various reasons, poems for Saints' days were not numerous in English, and special circumstances of one kind or another often apply to those that were written. An example is "To St. Peter and St. Paul" by Henry Constable (1562–1613), remembered in the *OCEL* as the author of *Diana*, one of the seemingly innumerable sequences of amorous sonnets in the 1590s. This particular holy sonnet appeals to me because the bifurcated subject is neatly worked out in tripartite form: a quatrain for each saint and then a sestet for both. Constable also partially captures the pose of naiveté adopted so successfully at times by Herbert: "O three tymes happy twoe," he exclaims, opening the sestet. By the time this poem was written, Constable had converted—in his view, reconverted back—from the Anglican to the Roman church. His subject probably reflects this fact since the Roman calendar reserves June 29 for a joint celebration of Peter and Paul, but the Anglican does not. In any case, the closing lines achieve unity from twos and threes and even manage to balance the Rome founded by Romulus and Remus against the eternal city; this particular oneness is, however, highly tendentious from an Anglican point of view because it centers, quite specifically, on the Pope.

> O three tymes happy twoe: O golden payre
> who with your bloode, dyd lay the Churches grounde
> within the fatall towne which twynnes dyd founde.
> And setled there the Hebrew fishers chayre,
> where fyrst the Latyn sheepehyrd rais'd his throne,
> and synce the world, & Church were rul'd by one.

A saint frequently celebrated on the continent was St. Mary Magdalene, probably the favorite saint of the Counter-Reformation, and she was popular in England too. In this case, even Herbert relaxed his scruples, and among other examples in English are poems by Southwell, Constable (four holy sonnets), Vaughan, and—notoriously—Crashaw ("The Weeper"), who turned to Saints' days for several other poems as well. Poems for the Magdalene are, in fact, entirely too numerous to be looked at without obscuring the point needed here that Saints' days, like the hours for prayer, cut across the planes of chronological time. To see how and why, Joseph Beaumont once again is the useful author to cite.

Beaumont is reputed to have made a digest in prose of the lives of the saints and martyrs, one for each day. He was not quite so industrious in verse, but there are twenty-six poems on these subjects, and the series as a whole reflects a couple of significant facts. First, I have been pretending that the church calendar begins on—or rather, *only* on—January 1. In the tables prefatory to the Prayer Book, January does indeed appear first, and the day was regularly referred to as New Year's, as in verse for the Circumcision. The first Saint's day, however, is *not* January 8, for St. Lucian, Priest and Martyr (d. 290 A.D.). It is instead November 30 for St. Andrew. Several points are at issue here, including the fact that Andrew was the first disciple called by Jesus and the further fact that the first Sunday of Advent, the preparation for Christmas, is "defined" as that Sunday that falls on or closest to St. Andrew's day. (The wording of the definition is to confer explicit honor on the saint—otherwise, "November 30" would suffice; the reason for the definition itself, as distinct from the wording, is to ensure that there will be four Sundays of Advent, no more and no less, before Christmas day.) Since St. Andrew comes first, the last Saints' day is the one that is celebrated five days earlier: November 25, the day for St. Katharine, Virgin and Martyr. But unless one wants to count St. Cecilia on November 22 because of the odes (notably, of course, Dryden's and Pope's) and the musical celebrations for her, then the last *major* day is All Saints on November 1. Confirming these points is the organization adopted by John Boys. He begins his *Exposition* of the year of the saints with St. Andrew; *The Third* [and final] *Part* (separately published in 1615) announces on its title page that the days included will be those "from S. Iohn Baptists Nativitie to the last Holy-day in the *whole yeere*"; and that last holy day does indeed turn out to be All Saints.

In the first of the poems in Beaumont's series, it is St. Andrew whom we discover marching steadfastly through Thrace and Scythia, his last and most eloquent sermon being preached from a cross of martyrdom ("Long was His Sermon, for his last it was"). Beaumont borrows the story line from the Breviary or, possibly, *The Golden Legend*, and he makes similar borrowings in successive poems while doing some steadfast marching of his own through this kind of year down to All Saints. If Beaumont's *Psyche* is one's measuring stick, then the length of any one or indeed of all these poems is scarcely worth mentioning. "St. John Baptist" does run to 600 lines, however, as if, with a whole year to work with, Beaumont felt no need to be excessively brief. When All Saints rolls round, however, time is fast running out, and—here is the other point I wanted to stress— this kind of year is revealed to have been as inadequately long as was the week spent in "Meditacions upon, & Devout Exercise in the Historie of Christ." At this late stage, "The year . . . Grows scant and narrow." "More saints" exist than "could with Feasts be furnished." Saints, moreover, "Are not Times flitting brittle Breed, / But borne to be / Eternallie." Necessarily, therefore, the "years poor Round" can never extend itself to "Their great Dimensions bound." All Saints, however, solves this problem by its distillation of immensity down to short but intensely concentrated time that is compactly full. "All yᵉ year" is "Now grown lesse fair & wide / Then these few Hours, the vast Epitomie / Of what excelld yᵉ years Capacitie."

> As when We see
> In one rich Mixtures Unitie
> Each Tribe & kinde
> Of Sweets combinde,
> And by Art taught to dwell
> In one small chrystall cell,
> Such is yᵉ quintessentiall Confluence We
> Finde in this single generall Feast to be.

All Saints thus reveals itself to be an

> Illustrious Day,
> In which yᵉ whole year doth display
> It selfe, & more.

When the broad limits of time prove to be not nearly broad enough, then the best way to be aware of the fullness of time evidently is to focus on smallness: an instantaneous moment that parallels eternity, a quintessential confluence in one small crystal cell, a single general day that somehow is more than the year of which it is a part. Beaumont expresses oxymoron without resorting to negative language, but he is dealing, as he himself points out, with a year that is imperfect and inadequate for the saints who more than fill it. When that which *is* perfect needs to be described, then negation is not merely helpful but frequently indispensable. Milton's angels, to mention one notable example, fill out an entire line (*Paradise Lost*, 3.373) by referring to the deity as

> Im[-]mutable   Im[-]mortal,   In[-]finite.

Donne, to mention one more, secularizes the usage in "Negative Love" (Patrides: "In a few MSS entitled *The Nothing;* in others, given both titles"):

> If that be simply perfectest
> Which can by no way be exprest
> But *Negatives*, my love is so.
> To All, which all love, I say no.

DONNE AND ST. LUCY

"Negative Love" is far outside the calendar of saints and somewhere inside the *Songs and Sonnets*, but it is difficult to pinpoint the poem's exact location because the proper order of these poems, if indeed there is one, by no means is certain. They were first collected together under the now usual title in the second edition of the *Poems* in 1635, but the one given pride of place in 1635 ("The Flea") had been the thirty-fourth of the fifty-three songs scattered about in separated groups in the first edition of 1633. A. J. Smith, in dealing with these discrepancies, attempted to be "neutral," as he put it, by substituting an alphabetical order, a decision mentioned here because the fortuitous result, in this case a serendipity, is that "*Ne*gative Love" alphabetically precedes "A *No*curnall upon S. *Lucies* day, being the shortest day," a poem also much concerned with negation. No justification exists, so far as I know, for placing the "Nocturnall" and "The Canonization" in close physical proximity, but these two also go well together. The idea of sainthood alluded to in the titles, unparalleled by any of the other *Songs and Sonnets*, is one reason. A second has to do with length and form. They are the only two of these poems that run to forty-five lines, and both consist of five stanzas, each of nine lines, with identical rhyme schemes.

Despite the distraction of a digression, some comparisons are in order to show that the similarities just noted are, in fact, unusual. Other *Songs and Sonnets* do have nine-line stanzas but not five of them: "The Flea" (3 stanzas), "Goe and catch a falling star" (3), "The Indifferent" (3), "Valediction to his booke" (7), "Twickenham Garden" (3), "A Valediction of weeping" (3), "The Will" (6), and "Negative Love" (2). In "The Indifferent" and "Valediction to his booke," rhyme schemes are the same as in "The Canonization" and "A Nocturnall," but total length obviously is not. A second nine-line rhyme scheme is shared by "The Flea," "The Will," and "Negative Love"; "Goe and catch" gives a third variation; and "Twickenham Garden," a fourth. If one is concerned with total number of lines but not stanzaic form, then the only poems longer than forty-five lines are "The Will" (54 lines), "A Valediction of my name" (60), "Valediction to his booke" (63), and "The Extasie" (76). Those nearly as long: "Sweetest love, I do not goe" (40), "Loves exchange" (42), "The Blossome" (40), "Farewell to love" (40). Those with fewer than twenty lines: "The Computation" (10), "The Expiration" (12), "A Jeat Ring sent" (12), "Witchcraft by a picture" (14), "The Apparition" (17), "Womans constancy" (17), and "Breake of day" (18). Those between twenty and forty lines: the remaining thirty-six of the fifty-three given in 1633 and 1635.

Still a third reason for comparing "The Nocturnall" and "The Canonization" is that the law of contraries applies here in much the same way that it does to Milton's "L'Allegro" and "Il Penseroso" or to Crashaw's "For Hope" and Cowley's "Against Hope," poems originally published together. "The Canonization" isolates the lovers from the trivial superficialities of an external universe so as to magnify and elevate the world that they create for themselves to inhabit and share. In the Douai translation, Psalm 67.36 proclaims, "God is wonderful in his saints" (translating

"Mirabilis Deus in sanctis suis"); the equivalent verse in the Prayer Book Psalter is 68.35, "O God, wonderfull art thou in thy holy places." And both versions of the verse parallel these sanctified lovers in their wondrous world.

In "The Canonization," however, the total number of love's true saints appears to be no more than two, and if so, then mutuality is of utmost importance; in effect, they sanctify one another. The five stanzas of the "Nocturnall" are not a desanctification, but they do establish dissolution of mutuality into agonizing separation, and the poem proceeds through increasingly greater stages of negation as it makes a precipitous retreat from that which is to that which is not.

From a more or less technical point of view, astonishing virtuosity is on display in the articulation of this retreat. By the eighth line, the world is "Dead and enterr'd"; by the ninth, its pieces "seeme to laugh, / Compar'd with mee, who am their Epitaph." On Beaumont's All Saints day, "Art" combines "Sweets"; "quintessentiall Confluence" is visible. But in Donne's second stanza, love's

> art did expresse
> A quintessence even from nothingnesse,
> From dull privations, and leane emptinesse:
> He ruin'd mee, and I am re-begot
> Of absence, darknesse, death; things which are not.

In the third, "I, by loves limbecke, am the grave / Of all, that's nothing." This stanza also makes reference to some earlier past time, when "oft did we grow / To be two Chaosses . . . and often absences / Withdrew our soules." Since primeval chaos preceded the existence of everything created from it, "two Chaosses" may suggest a twofold uncreation. In any case, Donne next mentions "the first nothing," perhaps the one prior to second or third nothings; as "the Elixer" of it, he clearly cannot be merely "an ordinary nothing." The simplest and totally devastating statement begins stanza five: "But I am None." The ancient philosophical adage was "nihil ex nihilis" ("Nothing will come of nothing," as Lear translates, terrifyingly, for Cordelia [1.1.90]). But in the "Nocturnall" nothing—all kinds of it, each more negative than the last—can come and does come from nothing. Not only has all something-ness been taken away; nothingness itself has been emptied out.

The shorthand way to refer to this process is, once again, "kenosis" or "emptying," and this time around, some details of what the term abbreviates are worth noticing. The "Nocturnall" presents what might be called serious parody of the religious concept and in this respect, as in others, resembles "The Canonization," but with this difference: the vocabulary associated with sainthood had long since been appropriated for amorous purposes whereas that for "kenosis" had not. In both cases, however, Donne turns divinity inside out or upside down to stake out a profoundly serious position. His remark about the strangeness of Christ's fullness, previously quoted in connection with Herbert, is much to this point, especially if the ellipsis that I earlier made to avoid a distraction is now filled in.

That fullness, to requote, "was a fulnesse of emptinesse; It was all Humiliation, all exinanition [the word previously sidestepped], all evacuation of himselfe" (*Sermons* 4:289). Exinanition cannot have been in the active vocabulary of everyone in the congregation, and Donne therefore surrounds it with more familiar words with similar meaning. Philippians 2.7 is the biblical base, another fact previously mentioned, but unlike most of Donne's biblical references, the verse is not identified in the original Folio volume by a marginal note, perhaps because a simple citation would have been pointless. In the Great Bible (supplying the Epistle for Palm Sunday) and in the Authorized Version, Christ is said to have "made himself of no reputation," but for Donne's purposes, "reputation" might have been a distracting word because taking time out to retranslate it would probably be required.[13]

Terminology aside, the idea is that Christ possessed fullness of deity prior to the Incarnation and that thereafter he united fully divine and completely human natures in one incarnated person. In doing so, as Philippians 2.7–8 points out, he "tooke vpon him the forme of a seruant . . . he humbled himselfe, and became obedient vnto death," and for that to occur, his divine glory had to be laid aside and his deity had to be "vailed" or—again the terms vary—"shadowed" or "clouded." To this position there are two further corollaries. First, since the name of God is "I am that I am" (Exodus 3.14), it follows that when Christ emptied out his deity, he identified himself with "I am not." Cornelius à Lapide, when commenting on Philippians 2.7, places this idea in the context of creator and creature. (In translation, but with critically important parts of the Latin parenthetically included:)

> Even as the name of the creator is I am who I am ("Ego sum qui sum") or pure essence and an ocean of being itself; so the name of the creature is I am

---

13. Donne could have quoted the Bible of Junius-Tremellius-Beza ("ipse se inanivit" ["inanio," make void]) or the Vulgate ("semetipsum exinanivit"—hence the Douai's "emptied himself") or the Greek ("heauton ekenosen"—hence the term "kenosis"), but a paraphrase probably would still have been needed. In Edward Leigh's "Observations upon All the Greek Words of the New Testament" (part 2 of *Critica sacra*), the entry under "kenoo" refers to Tertullian, "*exhausit, Made himself nothing*," and to "learned *Beza*": "*Ex omni ad nihil seipsum redegit*" (roughly, he reduced himself from totality to nothingness). In the English translation (from Italian) of Diodati's *Pious and Learned Annotations*, the pertinent note on Ephesians asserts that Christ "annihilated himself."

not ("Non sum"), for all being which it has, it has from God . . . so much so, in fact, that were God to withdraw his hand, immediately the creature would lapse into nothingness, whence it came, and disappear ("evanescit"); even as, when the sun has set or its rays are withdrawn, light everywhere fades from the air.[14]

The point recurs in Donne's Christmas sermon for 1627. "The name of the Creator is, *I am*, but of every creature [it is,] rather, I am not, I am nothing."

> As Man had an eternall not beeing before the Creation; so he would have another eternall not-being after his dissolution by death, in soule, as well as in body, if God did not preserve that beeing. . . . And. . . . As man had one eternall not beeing before, and would have another after, so for that beeing which he seemes to have here now, it is a continuall declination into a not being. . . . Every change and mutation bends to a not being, because in every change, it comes to a not being that which it was before; onely the name of God is *I am*. (*Sermons* 8:144–45)

A second corollary is that, since the basis of being merely human is not being, identification with Christ in his emptiness is the way to transform one's own nothingness into something-ness: as he emptied himself to become human, so ought we to empty our selves to become divine. Donne takes the self-humiliation of Moses before Yahweh to be a prefigurative example of the idea and adds, "This exinanition of our selves is acceptable in the sight of God" (*Sermons* 8:143). Pearson intimates the thought when he notices that it is as impossible to empty "any thing that hath no fulnesse, as to fill any thing which hath no emptiness." Quite explicit are two statements quoted in the *OED* (under "exinanition"). Henry Bull (in 1577): "God's power taketh no place in vs vntill we be vtterly . . . exinanited"; Henry More (in 1686): "The scope . . . is a perfect exinanition of ourselves, that we may be filled with the sense of God."

The saints trace out this pattern in that they martyr themselves (in the developed sense of "martyr") in order to be "witnesses" (the etymological meaning) for God. In their legends, however, this idea invariably is phrased from a favorable point of view. They are said to give up something not worth having in order to achieve something that is. Much of the language of Beaumont's poem for "May-Day" (the title) about "SS. Philip & James" (the subtitle) is highly negative, but the point being made is affirmative.

14. Cornelius à Lapide, *Commentaria in . . . Pauli Epistolas*, 571B. Cf. John Pearson (1612–1686), expounding Article 2 of the Creed: "Beside, he was not in the form of a servant, but by the emptying himself, and all exinanition necessarily presupposeth a precedent plenitude; it being as impossible to empty any thing that hath no fulness, as to fill any thing which hath no emptiness" (*An Exposition of the Creed*, 174–75).

> For Saints, while they are living here
> But all yᵉ while a dying are:
>   That gasp wᶜʰ we
>   Fooles think to be
>   Their dying breath
>   Breath's out their Death;
> It breathes it out, & sets them free.

Crashaw approaches Donne's line of thought more closely in the concluding lines of "The Flaming Heart," his poem for St. Teresa, but self-destruction, in this particular context, unmistakably represents self-discovery.

> By all of HIM we haue in THEE;
> Leaue nothing of my SELF in me.
> Let me so read thy life, that I
> Unto all life of mine may dy.

In all these instances, personal exinanition is a means of unification with Christ, with true Being and true Fullness. In effect, therefore, Beaumont and Crashaw are clarifying what it can mean, as Vaughan put it, in a passage previously quoted, to "live a *Christian*, and die a *Saint*." In the "Nocturnall," however, Donne's status has formerly been founded on the presence of a love that now is absent. Instead of achieving an amorously holy place and mutual self-fulfillment therein, the very basis on which the continuation of his existence has been predicated no longer exists. From the point of view of theology, the analogy is to the lapsing into *I am not* that would inevitably occur were the sustaining power of *I am* to be withdrawn. Or, in the language of Donne's sermon, "It is a continuall declination into a not being." Lapide's comparison was to the situation obtaining when the sun sets or its rays are occluded and light fades from the air. The setting for the "Nocturnall" includes among its initial details a similar enervation. "The Sunne is spent, and now his flasks / Send forth light squibs, no constant rayes." For other lovers, this "lesser Sunne / At this time to the Goat is runne / To fetch new lust." But Donne's greater Sun has not merely stopped in its tracks; it and the zodiac have vanished.

Consider for a moment—whether Donne himself did or did not—what the consequence would be of deconstructing the universe that the lovers of "The Canonization" created out of themselves for one another. "You whom reverend love / Made one anothers hermitage" (37–38)—but if either lover were permanently absent, that mutual hermitage would become a wasteland. "Your eyes . . . did all to you epitomize" (41, 43)—and there could be no epitome of anything because only a broken half of it would be left. "Beg from above / A patterne of . . . love" (44–45). The pattern, however, since now rent asunder, could not possibly be invoked by anyone at all, not even by either of those who earlier participated in the creation of it.

In the "Nocturnall," this hypothetical situation, or one very like it, has become the reality. Even worse, the possibility of restoration or re-creation is explicitly ruled out. "I am None; nor will my Sunne renew." A search for anything positive would thus be absurd; achieving something, anything at all, would only serve to increase the already unbridgeable distance between the self and the no longer present beloved. And since union with that which formerly was but now is not could never be realized merely by becoming something else, one needs instead to engage in minimalization or reduction away from is-ness in the direction of not-ness. May Day celebrations, even of a religious kind, as in Beaumont's poem and in the church calendar for SS. Philip and James, obviously would be grotesque. Midsummer day and time at its broadest limits, whether devoted to John the Baptist or not, also are nothing to the point. Only "St. Lucy's day, being the shortest day" could possibly be appropriate, and even on this briefest day, major reversals of customary usage must be made.[15]

The name of St. Lucy means light, but when light has evanesced, the liturgical hour for celebration needs to be one of unlighted darkness. On the day of celebration, every saint is annually present to be reborn into life everlasting, but in this case absence, not presence, needs to be intensified, and what must be affirmed with increasingly powerful emphasis is denial and loss. As the poem is concluding,

> Since shee enjoyes her long nights festivall,
> Let mee prepare towards her, and let mee call
> This houre her Vigill, and her Eve.

Vigil is a night service, of course, often most strongly associated with the vigil on Holy Saturday for the dawn of the Resurrection and the festival of Easter day. To "prepare" is to engage in the "preparation," the opening prayers of Eucharist. The "hour," as in the phrase "canonical hour," in this case specifically is that part of the night office referred to as a nocturn. These words normally are optimistic in their import, but not so here.

They also are not quite final, and the only process actually included in this poem is of the kind required to accommodate the limitations of hu-

---

15. Donne's editors regularly verify Donne's claim that Lucy's is the "shortest day" by referring (as Patrides puts it) to "the old calendar in use in Donne's time." According to the *PBD* ("Calendar," 120A): "Two errors, operating in reverse directions but not compensating each other, accumulated . . . [so that] The Vernal Equinox in 1582 fell on Mar. 11, ten days too early." As a result, the shortest day also was occurring too soon. To correct matters, "In the Roman C., October 5, 1582, was called Oct. 15. In the English C., Sept. 3, 1752, was called Sept. 14." (In 1752, as a side effect, it thus was impossible to celebrate St. Eunurchus on Sept. 7 or the Nativity of the Blessed Virgin Mary on Sept. 8.)

man perception. Raphael's comment to Adam about how the world came to be applies also to how this one ceased to exist. "Immediate are the Acts of God, more swift / Than time or motion, but to human ears / Without process of speech cannot be told" (*Paradise Lost*, 7.176–78). The immediacy of collapse in the "Nocturnall" is revealed by the fact that the first line,

'Tis the yeares midnight, and it is the dayes,

is quite closely paralleled by the words that actually do end the poem.

since this
Both the yeares, and the dayes deep midnight is.

More than forty lines separate these statements, but the duplicated present tense indicates that no time at all has elapsed in which anything whatsoever could possibly have occurred. Except—and it is a very important exception—an unfolding of what the first line implicitly but also imperceptibly contained within itself. Present in the last line but not in the first is a short word of vast significance. The word is "deep," and what it signals is a moment in time so close to being no time at all that the profundity of its depth could not have been sounded without the layered linearity of speech. Alteration of syntax adds a further depth of its own. The delay of the verb and the postponed completion of syntactic sense result in a rhyme that affirms "this / is." And the this-ness now insisted upon by emphatic terminal position and by rhyme is the not-ness of *Non est, ergo non sumus, et ergo à fortiore non sum.* "This" definitely and emphatically *is*, and not only that, but that which it so forcefully is, is that she is not, we therefore are not, and I all the more and quite certainly am not.

The condition verbalized by the poem is the stasis of "not," but the verbalization itself moves in two antithetical directions and does so simultaneously. The timing of the poem prepares for this fact in that St. Lucy's day closes out the annual seasonal cycle of the sun but appears a mere two weeks after St. Andrew's day and, thus, is placed very early on in the increasingly abundant calendar of the saints. In terms of decrease, the poem moves toward ever lowering depths of anguish as temporary nadir turns out to be a zenith in comparison to the lower nadir opening up beneath it. An inexact parallel is the discovery made by Milton's Satan (*Paradise Lost*, 4.76–78);

in the lowest deep a lower deep
Still threat'ning to devour me opens wide,
To which the Hell I suffer seems a Heav'n.

Much closer is the one made by Adam (ibid., 10.842–45). Cut off from God, alienated from Eve, and his world reduced to a shambles, Adam "to himself lamented loud":

into what Abyss of fears
And horrors hast thou driv'n me; out of which
I find no way, from deep to deeper plung'd.

One definition of hell has been "that place where God is not," and the worst torment of all has been said to be a blind inability to experience the beatific vision. The Donne of the "Nocturnall" is much like what Milton's Adam presumably would have been had the presence of Eve and God not been restored. He is in that place where his beloved is not, and all that he can see is midnight darkness.

The second and antithetical movement of the poem, as distinct from what it verbalizes, is toward formal perfection and a sense of finality, a movement that is completed by the not quite circular return of the last line to the first. This movement both undercuts and reinforces the one that appears to be in contradiction to it. It does so because the perfection achieved is of the kind defined in lines already quoted from "Negative Love": "If that be simply perfectest / Which can by no way be exprest / But *Negatives*, my love is so." Perfection also implies immutability, and in this case the stasis apparently arrived at in the end is in fact the unchangeable nullity already present when the poem began. The abyss—etymologically, "not-bottomed"—that seems to open up in this poem is rather like Milton's deity in being not finite, not mutable, and in a sense not even mortal. "But I am by her death, (which word wrongs her) / Of the first nothing, the Elixir grown" (28–29). Non-death, non-life, non-being—I am tempted to say "non-nothing"—these nonentities decline into or add down (not up) to a perfect quintessence of perfect nothingness. In the poem's last line, the antithetical extremes of negation and perfection coincide. A search for formal perfection implies a search for unity, and so it is here. Donne and the beloved are indeed united or reunited, and they are so because they share not that which is but that which is not. Kenosis, the fullness of emptiness, is the basis of this non-sainthood, but it has been transvalued (though not *de*valued) from the divine, where miracles of creation out of nothingness are possible, to human uncreation, where the most potent of all tremendously powerful affirmations is *Non sum*, the instantaneous totality of self-annihilation translatable by "I am none."

In 1633, the "Nocturnall" was the second poem in the first separate handful of *Songs*. The group was repositioned in 1635 when all the *Songs* were gathered in one place, but the internal ordering of the group itself was not changed. In both editions, therefore, the following seven poems appear together as a consecutive series. (I give mnemonic quotations to supplement titles.)

The Message
(Yet send me back my heart and eyes,

That I may know, and see thy lyes)
A Nocturnall . . .
Witchcraft by a picture
    (My picture vanish'd, vanish feares,
    That I can be endamag'd by that art)
The Baite
    (That fish, that is not catch'd thereby,
    Alas, is wiser farre than I)
The Apparition
    (When by thy scorne, O murdresse, I am dead,
    And that thou thinkst thee free)
The Broken heart
    (Yet nothing can to nothing fall,
        Nor any place be empty quite,
    Therefore I thinke my breast hath all
        Those peeces still, though they be not unite;
    And now as broken glasses show
    A hundred lesser faces, so
        My ragges of heart can like, wish, and adore,
        But after one such love, can love no more.)
A Valediction: forbidding Mourning
        (Thy firmnes makes my circle just,
        And makes me end, where I begunne.)

This order may, of course, be no more significant than one produced by "neutral" alphabetizing. Connections of some kind might be made among any seven randomly selected poems by Donne simply because all of them, after all, *are* by Donne. It is tempting, nonetheless, to perceive a progression from a message having to do with unfaithfulness to a deep sense of devastating alterity and thence to such matters as witchcraft, an alluring bait, the ghostly apparition, and almost finally to a broken heart that, despite the shattering of it into shards, does not fall totally into nothingness nor admit of complete vacuity. Love affairs have been known to end with an estrangement that at first seems romantically catastrophic and tragic but realistically turns out to be a good riddance. A farewell without tears, in theory, might be an eminently suitable, if cynical, termination for a love affair of that kind. This particular valediction, however, reaffirms presence despite absence and by means of the celebrated compass arrives at transcendent togetherness. The poem really does say, or at least it certainly appears to, that this *is* rather than this is *not*. If this group of seven poems actually is sequential, then the last lines of the "Valediction" do rather more than make Donne end where, in that particular poem, he began. They revert back to the situation that presumably existed prior to sending "The Message." If that is a genuine possibility, then reading any one of these seven poems—including "A Nocturnall"—

requires rereading them all in light of one another, and in that case, the shortest day—indeed, the longest day—might scarcely be sufficient.

PARADISE REGAINED

Empty Time and God's Due Seasons

Biathanatos, Donne's defense of suicide—or "self-homicide," as he calls it—is a paradox in the formal sense: an argument against ("para") received opinion or standard doctrine ("doxe"). As in other works of the kind, statements cannot automatically be taken at face value because any one of them could be a parodic subversion of customary views. So far as I can tell, however, Donne is straightforward enough when he considers Christ's remark: "I lay down my life for my sheepe." The question asked is, "Why Christ saies this in the present time"—before the crucifixion and actual death, that is; the answer is, "I rather thinke, (because exposing to danger, is not properly call'd a dying,) that Christ said this now, because his Passion was begun; for all his conversations here were degrees of ex-inanition" (*Biathanatos*, 188). In Donne's view, the kenosis of Christ was an empty*ing*, a continuing process leading up to Good Friday and finished by the "actuall emission of his soule, which is death, and which was his own act" (190).

From a slightly altered perspective, the emptying was intermittent, partly because of ongoing process but also because either of Christ's two natures, the fully human or the totally divine, might predominate over the other at any given moment. When Christ performed miracles, to mention obvious examples, he must have been filled with his own deity in order to perform them, and an early instance (to revert back briefly to *La Corona*) was that even at the age of twelve, when visiting the Temple, "He in his ages morning thus began / *By miracles exceeding power of man*" ("Temple," 13–14). If, however, it had been deity itself that encountered Satan in the wilderness, then the magnitude of Christ's victory would have been enormously reduced or, if not that, then vastly different in import. The standard view, therefore, was that Christ experienced genuine hunger and that it was as a human person, not as a god, that he successfully withstood temptation. Also present is the idea that Adam and Eve both could and should have done the same; in regaining paradise, Christ demonstrates, among other things, that it need never have been lost.

These assumptions are often a focus of attention and the basis for elaborate discussion in expositions of the first Sunday of Lent, when the temptation annually recurs in church time. Patristic sermons for the day do not greatly differ from their later and specifically Anglican counterparts in this particular respect, and if one is willing to overlook almost everything except subject matter, then *Paradise Regained* is comparable to the ninth book of Beaumont's *Psyche*, subtitled "The Temptation." Milton, however, decided to develop these ideas in conjunction with concepts of secular (even demonic) chronology on the one hand and of divine timing on the other, and this combination, as one can tell from its absence in Beaumont's treatment of the event, was *not* more or less obligatory.

This particular choice is consistent with but does not in itself result from or reflect the heterodoxy of Milton's personal views during the period when, presumably, the poem was written. *Paradise Regained*, it is true, clearly pursues several lines of thought considerably further than conventional thinking would care to go, but the basic distinction between chronological time and "appropriate time" or "due season" was entirely traditional. A fact noticed earlier was that Satan proposes to celebrate a fake Communion, and a character who parodies the Eucharist perhaps might be expected to parody liturgical time as well. Satan, at any rate, is feverishly worried about the expiration of his own kind of time and does attempt to force the pace of God's due seasons. One of the results is an adaptation of liturgical patterns that extends them quite possibly to, but not in fact beyond, their breaking point. Despite the intervening years, *Paradise Regained* and "Upon the Circumcision" do not voice mutually exclusive views, and the degree of Milton's heterodoxy and the precise nature of it, while potentially complex matters of intrinsic interest, do not seem to me to be highly problematic here.

Definitely peripheral—and quite fortunately so—is an issue far more formidable than those posed by Milton's customary insistence that he be allowed to think for himself. Two questions raised by modern biblical scholars are whether "biblical time" differs from "western" (especially Greek philosophical) time and, if so, then whether the difference is reflected by consistent patterns of usage in Old Testament Hebrew and New Testament Greek. Oscar Cullmann's widely influential answer to both questions was yes indeed, but James Barr pointed to apparently *in*consistent usage in the languages and, therefore, urged a cautious approach to the thought being expressed.[16] These questions about "time" and the vocabulary for it are well worth asking when reading Milton's poem, but twentieth-century discussion is anachronistic in more senses than one. Cullmann and Barr, after all, attempt to determine what the original Hebrew and Greek truly signify, but the thing needed here, quite luckily, is much less than that: merely how the words formerly were interpreted, regardless of what they actually mean.

---

16. Oscar Cullmann, *Christ and Time*, trans. Floyd V. Filson (Philadelphia: Westminster Press, 1950); James Barr, *Biblical Words for Time*, 2d rev. ed., Studies in Biblical Theology, 1st Series, 33 (London: S.C.M. Press, 1962).

Redefining the problem in this way has obvious advantages but does not simplify matters as much as one would like, among other reasons because of technicalities in seventeenth-century discussion. I do not want to belabor this point unnecessarily, but the fact of the matter is that the Jesus of Milton's poem is capable of using technical vocabulary himself. And one of the things to be noticed is that this Satan frequently has almost no idea what this Jesus is talking about. Lancelot Andrewes and Edward Leigh are extremely helpful at this point in supplying information that, despite barriers to easy access, allows one to avoid traps into which Satan unwittingly falls.[17]

The text announced by Andrewes for his Christmas sermon in 1609 is taken from Galatians 4.4–5; as given by Andrewes, it begins, "When the fulnesse of time was come, GOD sent his Sonne." In this context, the process whereby time is filled may be self-evidently important; less obvious, perhaps, is that time needs no emptying because in itself it already is so. "Of it selfe, *time . . .* hath nothing in it *. . . Empty dayes, Psal.* LXXVIII. *v.* 33. *Voyd moneths*, without any thing to fill them, *Iob* VII. *v.* 3." In very strong contrast, "That which *filleth time*, is some memorable thing of *Gods* powring into it, or (as it is in the Text) of *His sending*, to *fill* it withall." Partial filling resulted from "many memorable *missions*" (etymologically, "sendings") in the course of Old Testament history. "He *filled* up certaine times of the yeare under *Moses*, and the *Prophets*: all which, may well be termed, *The implements* [Latin, "impleo," pour in or fill] *of time*."

> But, for all them, the *measure* was not yet *full: filled* perhaps to a certaine *degree*, but not *full* to the *brimme: full* it was not (seeing it might be still *fuller*) till *God sent* That, then which, a more *full* could not be *sent*.
>
> And, That *He* sent, when *He* sent *His Sonne*, a *fuller* then whom, *He* could not *send*, nor *Time* could not *receive*. Therefore, with the *sending Him*, when that was, *Time* was at the top, that was the . . . *plenitudo temporis*, indeed.

Time is to be understood as "measure," therefore, and up to this point Andrewes is content to follow at a distance the philosophic definition found, among other places, in Plato and Aristotle. Specifically, time is the

---

17. I cite Andrewes and Leigh because they, like Milton, were accustomed to working with Hebrew and Greek Bibles. Donne's exposition (*Sermons*, 6:331–48) is too *untechnical* (and/or too metaphoric) for my purposes here. I cannot even try to deal directly with the biblical passages because, as a concordance quickly reveals, there simply are too many of them: in Hebrew, about 270 instances of "eth" (usually translated as "time," with "season" a distant second choice); fifteen of "zeman," a substitute for "eth" to which Andrewes refers in a passage soon to be quoted above; in Greek, about fifty-five instances of "chronos" ("time" or, less frequently, "season"); and about eighty of "kairos" (usually "season" but also "time").

measure of motion—or, as Milton has it in the second of his two poems for the death of Hobson, the Cambridge coach driver, "Time numbers motion, yet (without a crime / 'Gainst old truth) motion number'd out his time" (7–8). To understand only that much, however, is to apprehend not nearly enough since measure itself is empty, void, or vain. Andrewes thus leaves classical philosophy behind in order—temporarily, as it were—to define time in terms of *what* is happening rather than "when"; that which is filling supplies the meaning, not that which is being filled. The entry under "Hour" in Bauer's *Encyclopedia* has been very heavily influenced—but not openly so—by Cullmann's views and thus should be read with caution; nonetheless its initial distinctions (379B–380A) are helpful in seeing an important part of Andrewes's point.

> In the bible *hour* does not simply refer to a unit of time into which the day . . . or the night is divided. . . . Corresponding to the Hebrew ["eth"] it also commonly stands for the period of time during which an action takes place (eg [*sic*] the phrase 'in that hour'). The Semitic experience of time is less of the spatial-temporal order than dynamic, determined by the experience of the event which fills or takes up time. . . . Hence there are special 'hours' in which, following on the divine decision, some specific event will take place which will have significance for the salvation of the world.

In 1609 Andrewes wanted to move on to "what" was sent and to *why* that what-ness filled time to the brim, and he therefore deferred consideration of "when." "And let this be enough, for this point; more there is not in the *text*. But if any shall further aske, why . . . iust then, and neither sooner nor later," then the answer is, "Then was the time, for that was *Tempus praefinitum à Patre*, the time appointed of the Father":

> *The Times and seasons He hath put in His owne power, it is not for us to know them* [closely paraphrasing Acts 1.7]. This is for us to know, that, with His appoyntment, we must come to a full point. So doth the *Apostle*, and so let us, and not busie our selves much with it, *time* is but the *measure* or caske, that where with it is *filled*, doth more concerne us. To that therefore let us come.

When Andrewes returned to this topic on Christmas 1623 a major consideration was God's appointment of proper or due time for divine action. The text announced is Ephesians 1.10, "That, in the dispensation of the fullnesse of the times, He might gather together into one all things, both which are in heaven, and which are in earth, even in Christ." "Fullnesse of times" is a phrase in which Andrewes continues to be deeply interested, and again he supposes that it is the filling—in this case, by "gathering together again in one"—that confers meaning on that which is being filled.[18]

---

18. In the paragraph just concluded and in those that immediately follow, I am para-

"Time" and "times," pivotal in the Authorized Version of the texts for these two sermons, disguise the fact that different words are being translated from the Greek. The nominative singular of the noun in Galatians is "chronos" but in Ephesians is "kairos." Andrewes, therefore, retranslates the phrase in Ephesians with "fulnesse of seasons" and adds an explanation. (The brackets in the following quotation are mine; I am substituting transliterations of Andrewes's Hebrew and Greek as well as adding dates.)

> We have heeretofore dealt with the *fullnesse of time* [marginal note: "At Christmasse A. D. 1609"]: and now [in 1623] are we to deale with the *fullnesse of Season. Time* and *season* are two, and have in all tongues, two different words, to shew, they differ. In *Hebrew* [zeman] & [eth]. In *Greeke*, [chronos], and [kairos]: In *Latine, Tempus* and *tempestivum.*

Divine full seasons, precisely because they are divine, cannot easily be defined, but they can be thought of by analogy to seasons of the year or of human life and may even be compared to the Christmas season being celebrated when Andrewes delivers his sermon. "Set this downe then (to beginne with:) There are *seasons;* as in our common yeare (of twelve moneths) So, in the great yeare, whereof, every *day* is *a yeare* (by *Daniel's*) nay, *a thousand yeare* (by *Saint Peter's* calculation)." Duration as usually measured, therefore, is not always applicable to season. "*Time* is taken at large, any time: *Season,* not so; but is applied to that, with which it suites, or for which it serves best." There was "A *season* of the *Law unwritten,*" "A *season* of the *Law written,*" and "Then came all the *Prophets*"; and at last "to this plunge it was come, . . . It was time for Him to come, *qui venturus erat* [who was to come]." "Now, when the *seasons . . .* at last brought forth *Him, . . .* in whom it pleased the FATHER, all fulnesse should *dwell,* then were they at the *full.*" Since the arrival of Christ, as Andrewes pointed out in 1609, results in the total filling of time, it follows that fullness of time and fullness of seasons in effect coincide.

Beyond this point in analysis, however, no one except the Father can possibly go. "But, why GOD, in the *dispensation* of the *seasons,* did so order, that at such a *yeare* of the *world,* such a *moneth* of the *yeare,* such a day of the *moneth,* this should fall out just [so]; this is more, then I dare take upon me to define." The fact is that God did ordain matters in this

---

phrasing and quoting from Launcelot Andrewes, *XCVI Sermons*, 23–32. The process of filling depends on "Gather together in one," the Authorized Version for "anakephalaiosasthai" (a word appearing only in this verse). Andrewes cites the Authorized Version but prefers to translate with "gathering together into one *againe.*" He emphasizes the prefix "ana" (together), contrasting it to "apo" (from) and also to "syn" (with), because "a *returning* to, implies a *departing from:* a *gathering together againe,* a *scattering in sunder* before," and both imply "a former being *with.*"

way, and in Andrewes's view, a tremendously important point to remember is that what is being anticipated by both times and seasons is the condition wherein

> there shall be neither *time*, nor *season* any more. No *fullnesse* then, but the *fullnesse of aeternitie*, and in it the *fullnesse* of all *joy*. To which, in the severall *seasons* of our being *gathered to our fathers*, He vouchsafe to bring us; that (as the yeare, so) the *fullnesse* of our *lives* may end in a *Christmasse*, a *merry joyfull Feast*, as that is.

Given the need for homiletic exhortation, Andrewes subordinates times and seasons to an ultimate eternity, but his comments are useful here because of the distinctions made between time in its general acceptation (whether empty or being filled) and the seasonable time for proper activity (whether human or divine). Andrewes restricts the meanings of four pairs of words from Hebrew, Greek, Latin, and English in order to place one concept on each side of a clear-cut verbal distinction. This strategy does not accurately reflect translatable meaning and English usage as found in the Authorized Version (a fact explicitly acknowledged when Andrewes substitutes his own translations). It also appears to impose firmer distinctions on the *words* (as distinct from conceptual thought) than the original languages themselves actually warrant; homiletic need, therefore, again may be at work.

Leigh, at any rate, indicates that the *verbal* categories cannot always be so strictly delimited and yet nonetheless gives strong support for supposing that one should distinguish between the concepts themselves.[19] In the relatively brief entry under "eth," he remarks that it, like "kairos," can mean time itself but also may indicate "fit" or "suitable" time. ("Ut Graecis [Kairos], ita Hebraeis hoc nomen, nunc tempus ipsum, nunc temporis opportunitatem seu occasionem significat.") Under "kairos," which heads a much longer entry, "tempus" (time, that is—*not* season) is the meaning given first. The dominant sense, however, quite clearly is taken to be "mature and seasonable time." "The Greeks," he says, "make a difference between [chronos], *Time*, and [kairos], *Season*; and in the Scripture they also are distinguished." "*Time* is more generall; *Season* implyeth that part which is fit for doing a thing. [Kairos] signifieth in a large acceptation, Seasonablenesse of circumstance, whether of time, place, or any occasion; but most properly a seasonable time: . . . *Opportunitie*, or present occasion, that present fit time, wherein any thing to be

19. In writing his definitions, Leigh shifts in and out of English, Latin, Greek and, less often, Hebrew; they seem to have been more or less simultaneously present in his thinking. The definitions are entered, of course, under the untransliterated Hebrew and Greek words being defined. Where possible, I quote the English and elide the rest; square brackets, however, indicate my transliterations.

done may be done fitly and happily . . . that fit opportunitie, and fit occasion offered of well-doing." Several biblical texts, clearly of critical importance, are referred to along the way, including 2 Corinthians 6.2: "Now is the accepted time [kairos] . . . now is the day of salvation." The most useful text presumably is Acts 1.7; also paraphrased by Andrewes, it is quoted three times by Leigh (and since the preceding verse establishes context, I give it too):

> When they therefore were come together, they asked of him, saying, Lord, wilt thou at this time [chrono] restore againe the Kingdome to Israel? And hee said vnto them, It is not for you to know the times [chronous] or the seasons [kairous], which the father hath put in his owne power.

The emergent points as explained by Andrewes and Leigh, therefore, are these: Mere time (frequently but not always a matter of "chronos" in the sense of *chrono*logy) is necessarily and inexorably repetitive—days, months, years—but in itself also is intrinsically empty of all value or meaning. Seasonable time *is* seasonable precisely because it signifies a period that is being filled, partly or totally, with meaningful events. Value is conferred, moreover, by varying kinds of filling: natural processes or annual seasons of growth and/or decay; human actions that are rightly chosen to conform to the season for doing them; liturgical seasons, including (though by no means limited to) Christmas; and, finally, those divinely ordained events that regulate the course of universal redemptive history.

One of the summary texts is Ecclesiastes 3.1: "To euery thing there is a season, and a time to euery purpose vnder heaven." Another inclusive text is 2 Corinthians 6.1–10, the Communion Epistle for Lent 1. Much of this pericope concerns those who are charged to be, quite specifically, "the ministers of God" (verse 4), but the text presumably applies by extension to everyone. The extended meaning may be evident enough from the paraphrase and interpretation of Isaiah 49.8 given in verse 2 (one of those quoted by Leigh): "For he saith, I haue heard thee in a time accepted, and in the day of saluation haue I succoured thee. Behold, now is that accepted time; Behold, now is that day of saluation." When this text is expounded, the "accepted time," as Matthew Poole explains (*Commentary* 3:617A), "is the same with what the apostle calls, *the fulness of time*, Gal. iv.4." Galatians 4.4, in turn, was the text for one of the two sermons in which Andrewes addressed these topics. And consider John Boys (*Dominical* 2:4), commenting on Lent 1: "*In a time accepted, and in the day of salvation*, that is, in the fulnesse of time, Galat.4.4. . . . *relativè ad Deum*, in respect of God, an accepted time: *relativè ad homines*, in respect of men, a day of salvation." "Worke your salvation in feare and trembling," Boys adds, "while it is called to day."

On this particular day in church, the specific means or model for the working of one's salvation is Jesus in his role as Second Adam, overcoming Satan in the wilderness, reestablishing a paradise, and exemplifying a way of life for the offspring of Adam and Eve to emulate. One more summary text, therefore, is the Anglican Collect for this recurrent day of salvation:

> O Lord, which for our sake diddest fast fourtie dayes and fourtie nights: giue vs grace to vse such abtinence, that our flesh being subdued to the spirite, we may euer obey thy godly motions in righteousnesse and true holines, to thy honour and glory, which liuest and reignest, &c.

The temptation of Christ, from a divine point of view, could only have occurred exactly when it was deemed appropriate or due for the time period that it filled. From a human perspective, it recurs annually or, indeed, even daily as a present moment, the elastic "now" of "today," during which the work of salvation takes place. Critical days thus can be either chronologically repetitive or seasonally unique and often should be both at the same time. But on Lent 1, to round matters off, it is necessary that Christ's divinity be temporarily emptied out so as to enable the filling up of times and seasons both for himself and for others.

When this process begins in *Paradise Regained*, an initially important point is that Satan, despite centuries of experience and expectation, is ill-prepared to understand either the "what" or the "when" of that which unfolds before him.

> Long the decrees of Heav'n
> Delay, for longest time to him [God] is short;
> And now too soon for us the circling hours
> This dreaded time have compast, wherein we
> Must bide the stroke of that long threat'n'd wound,
> At least if so we can, and by the head
> Broken be not intended all our power
> To be infring'd, our freedom and our being
> In this fair Empire won of Earth and Air;
> For this ill news I bring, the Woman's seed
> Destin'd to this, is late of woman born.
>
> (1.55–65)

The speech jumbles parts of the truth in, admittedly, an appropriately nightmarish way; when seen through devilish eyes, dreaded time and destined event, after all, will prove to be exactly that and will *not* seem opportune or seasonable. The lines also expose self-contradictory emphases on circling hours that seem simultaneously both long and slow in their delay and yet excessively short and far too soon in their coming. Underlying these perceived appearances is the unalterable truth that not much demonic time is left, but Satan rushes toward a corollary conclusion that turns out to be false. He clearly supposes that the time for God's overt vengeance has now arrived and that he must somehow deflect an open attack.

This particular occasion, however, is no more than one for "deeds . . . in secret done" (1.14–15), an action concluded when Jesus "unobserv'd / Home to his Mother's house private return'd" (4.638–39, the poem's last lines). Later on, Jesus will turn water to wine (though not stones into bread) and will feed the multitudes with baskets miraculously full; he will serve as a true oracle to his people, celebrate a eucharistic Last Supper, establish a kingdom, accomplish and/or become more or less everything else that Satan now places on view. None of these things will occur, however, until the proper "season comes" (4.146). Satan's ongoing argument is, among other things, an insidiously intended appeal to speed matters up so as to match his own sense of inexorable time; Jesus, on the other hand, must refuse to anticipate his own future history. For the moment, his strategy is to "endure the time" (4.174) and thus, in effect, to decline to do anything at all: he needs to abstain, not act.

These divergent positions emerge quite strikingly in a scene played out in the third book. Satan claims to be looking back to Old Testament prophecy but in fact is keeping an eye on his own kind of fit occasion or opportunity, the one sometimes known as "the main chance."

> Zeal and Duty are not slow,
> But on Occasion's forelock watchful wait.
> They themselves rather are occasion best,
> Zeal of thy Father's house, Duty to free
> Thy Country from her Heathen servitude;
> So shalt thou best fullfil [*sic*], best verify
> The Prophets old, who sung thy endless reign,
> The happier reign the sooner it begins.
> Reign then; what canst thou better do the while?
> (3.172–80)

The response derives from the comment about times and seasons recorded in Acts 1.7, the verse closely paraphrased by Andrewes and quoted three times by Leigh.

> To whom our Savior answer thus return'd.
> All things are best fulfill'd in their due time,
> And time there is for all things, Truth hath said:
> If of my reign Prophetic Writ hath told
> That it shall never end, so when begin
> The Father in his purpose hath decreed,
> He in whose hand all times and seasons roll.
> (181–87)

The allusion is unmistakable, and "roll," a word with no verbal counter-part in the biblical text, reveals with great clarity that in the mind of this Jesus, all seasons as well as times revolve. The temporal and seasonal contexts established by Milton for the wilderness temptation thus approximate those established in church, but in asserting the existence of this parallel, I must also immediately acknowledge divergence from it. The Gospel for Lent 1 is Matthew's account of the temptation, and in this version the pinnacle scene is placed second. Milton, however, follows Luke's order in placing it last. He also supplements the biblical record with additional incidents in the early life of Christ and causes the cycles of time to rotate far more repetitively in the poem than they do in church. These are large discrepancies, but their effect is to exaggerate the devotional and moral meanings of Lent 1 by augmentation in both of the possible directions, toward a greater number of timely events on the one hand and toward tighter circularity on the other. Since Milton supposed the whole Reformation had not yet gone nearly far enough, the notion that he expanded and improved upon Lent 1 does not seem inherently improbable to me. It may, however, be prudent to reapproach this particular point by making an altogether easier one about the poem's narrative technique.

A major reason why the hours circle in this poem is its form. An epic, even a brief epic, customarily "hastes into the midst of things," as the "Argument" to the first book of *Paradise Lost* puts it. A structural principle, to some extent, therefore, is inverse chronology instead of sequential time, and *Paradise Regained* begins, accordingly, "in medias res" with the baptism of Jesus. Milton's resumés of antecedent action are atypical, however, of classical epic practice. Virgil, to cite a standard example, fills in the essential background by means of one extended speech, the story told by Aeneas to Dido of what befell him and his comrades prior to their arrival at Carthage. The equivalent passage in *Paradise Regained*, in so far as one exists, is the interior monologue given in 1.197–293. The lines survey the past as Jesus remembers it but are doubled in interiority by incorporating words uttered by Mary at some earlier time and now re-stated by Jesus as heard again within his own mind. This strategy allows direct knowledge of previous history to be supplemented with indirect information already knowable by an omniscient deity but available to a human Jesus only if he is informed by someone else. The Annunciation, the Nativity, and the Purification are events entirely too remote for Mary's son to recall them, but since they are indispensable for even a partial understanding of his own life, he calls up in his own memory what Mary has earlier remembered.

Placing Mary's introspective speech inside the interior monologue of Jesus is effective strategy, but it does not make nearly as much history available as quite obviously is required. The narrator reminds us of the first temptation in Eden, God the Father reminisces to Gabriel about the recent Annunciation and the old temptation of Job, and Jesus mentions to Satan the forty days of fasting endured by Moses and Elijah. Satan, providing some history of his own, thinks back to his expulsion from heaven, recalls his dealings with Job and with Ahab, and boasts of his success as an oracle among the Gentiles. And these examples are no more than a sampling from those appearing in the first book alone.

Milton's handling of inverse chronology thus differs from Virgil's and does so in easily seen ways. Instead of one major disruption of narrative time, there are multiple dislocations that are distributed in piecemeal fashion. The overall difference in effect is very considerable since Virgil, once the background story of Aeneas is out of the way, moves more or less straightforwardly ahead.[20] Milton, however, repeatedly interrupts the line with backward glances at the past. One therefore reads many of the scenes in *Paradise Regained*, but not in the *Aeneid*, with a sense of "déjà vu," of having encountered, however briefly, the present moment earlier on.

Deepening this impression are various thematic motifs, including frequent allusions to the trial of Job as an analogue for the action of the poem as a whole. The Dove of the Holy Spirit descends three times within the opening 280 lines, once as described by the narrator, again as mentioned by Satan, a third time as remembered by Jesus. The visit to the Temple at the age of twelve, traditionally regarded as the first miracle, is here alluded to—though its miraculous import is not—by three different characters in three disconnected speeches. Jesus recalls it as an indication of precocious knowledge (1.209); Mary, as a cause for hope that her son's current absence, like the previous one, is in pursuit of "His Father's business" (2.99); and Satan (4.215–21), as an excuse to survey Greek philosophy in tempting Jesus with secular wisdom. As the second book begins, Andrew and Simon, worried by the inexplicable absence of their master, "Began to doubt, and doubted many days" (11). "Plain Fishermen" (27), when similarly troubled, pray to the "God of *Israel*, / Send thy Messiah forth, the time is come" (42–43). "But," with a quick change of heart, they resolve to "wait" and "out of their plaints new hope resume" (58). Mary also expresses "troubl'd thoughts" (65), asking "where delays he now" (95) before deciding to "wait with patience" (102). In the mean time, Jesus "Into himself descended" (111) to resolve self-doubt, and Satan, "doubting" (147), addresses his assembled cohorts. The plain fish-

---

20. Some of Virgil's characters (especially those met in the underworld) do review their own past; others (especially those met soon after arrival in Italy) give history lessons to Aeneas; some do both. Given the length of the poem, however, these interruptions are neither long enough nor sufficiently frequent to undermine the claim made here, that the narrative moves more or less straightforwardly ahead.

ermen have been assuming, "*Now, now* [italics were worth adding, I think], for sure, deliverance is at hand, / The Kingdom shall to *Israel* be restor'd" (35–36), an idea later to be tested, of course, by Satan's offer of the kingdoms of Parthia and Rome. The Father, however, has previously intimated that his Son's warfare and kingdom would be of a spiritual kind; and Jesus has already identified "the promis'd Kingdom" with the "work" of "Redemption" (1.265–66). John the Baptist, earlier still, had proclaimed "Heaven's Kingdom nigh at hand" (1.20), but three books later Jesus waits until his "season comes to sit / On *David's* Throne" (4.146–47), and Satan continues to wonder whether the kingdom is "Real or Allegoric" (4.390).

These illustrations are not even comprehensive, much less exhaustive, but perhaps they can suffice as suggestive reminders of the insistence with which the poem backtracks upon itself. An enormous amount of "what happens" in *Paradise Regained* continues, in fact, to happen repeatedly; "the circling hours" (to requote Satan's phrase) revolve, while the times and seasons "roll" with extraordinary frequency and rapidity. Since the time line itself by definition must be rectilinear, the seeming circularity probably should elicit a reaction of two complementary but dissimilar kinds: (1) On the one hand, there is the multilinked chain that inescapably and quite horribly binds not only Satan but also all of those for whom he is the Prince of the Air. The specifically *human* implications of this kind of time are ruthlessly implacable and ghastly to contemplate, for the only possible termination is the eschatological day of wrath and irremediable second death. (2) On the other hand, bending the time line back upon itself makes possible repeated references that function as measuring rods: by means of them one can gauge the progressive maturation of Jesus into a second Adam who redeems vain time by filling not only his own due seasons to the brim but also the seasons of those who are to inhabit his kingdom.

The Satan of this poem has been unfavorably compared to the Satan of *Paradise Lost*, partly because of his ineptitude. In *Paradise Lost*, however, he at least knew the identity of those to whom he chose to be the adversary, and here he does not. Toward the end, it is true, the angels sing of a reconquering hero and a refallen foe:

> him long of old
> Thou didst debel, and down from Heav'n cast
> With all his Army; now thou hast aveng'd
> Supplanted *Adam*, and by vanquishing
> Temptation, hast regain'd lost Paradise.
>
> (4.604–8)

Jesus, the human "Queller of Satan" (634) on earth, becomes identifiable as the divine Son of God who long ago quelled Satan in heaven. Now he can be saluted as "heir of both worlds" (633). This double identity, how-ever, is not heralded by the angels until nearly the end of the poem and has not previously been apparent. God's "first-begot we know," Satan says, "and sore have have felt, / When his fierce thunder drove us to the deep; / Who this is we must learn" (1.89–91). It simply does not occur to him—and how could it?—that the first begot and newly begot are equally the only begotten. And having mistaken his ground at the outset, Satan never thereafter recovers. He probes and tests and tempts with ever di-minishing returns, but not until just prior to the moment of his downfall does he grasp the hard truth that this fully human son of Mary is also the completely divine Son of God.

That truth, moreover, difficult to rational thought though it be, is merely the traditional view of the matter. In this poem, Satan's difficul-ties are compounded by the fact Jesus has emptied himself so fully and is refilling himself so gradually that recognition, even self-recognition, is well-nigh impossible at any point earlier than the climactic stand atop the pinnacle. Milton makes grand gestures toward conventional think-ing, the angelic hymn in the fourth book being a prime example. In addi-tion, he incorporates large quantities of traditional material, especially Old Testament typology and the frequently encountered idea that Christ was the true prophet, priest, and king. But Milton also bifurcates almost completely the two existences of Christ as god on the one hand and as human being on the other. He further indicates that this Jesus, internally confused when the poem begins, experiences self-doubt about his own identity and is a potentially culpable person emerging from a childhood during which he set himself ungodly aims. From a purely orthodox per-spective, this is the point at which some of the times and seasons, whether rolling or not, do become unmistakably unconventional.

As a child, Jesus says, "All my mind was set / Serious to learn and know" (1.202–3). That mentality was devoid, however, of all recollection of former and divine existence, and it occasionally reached false conclu-sions in the course of reeducating itself. At one time, to mention a forceful example, this Jesus entertained hopes of founding a worldly empire de-pendent on the prowess of armed might. "Victorious deeds" (*not* the pri-vate deeds of the poem)

> Flam'd in my heart, heroic acts; one while
> To rescue *Israel* from the *Roman* yoke,
> Then to subdue and quell o'er all the earth
> Brute violence and proud Tyrannic pow'r,
> Till truth were freed, and equity restor'd.
> (1.216–20)

Three books later, "quell" will be echoed by "Queller of Satan," but this earlier aspiration is, transparently, the stuff of which tyrannic emperors, not to mention hellish rulers, are sometimes made, and it is the ambition to which Satan appeals in offering Parthia and Rome. Satan, characteristically, acts too late, too *in*opportunely, but there have been at least two occasions when the offer might have been propitious. The first is the time when Jesus admits to profound uncertainty about himself and his role: "O what a multitude of thoughts at once / Awak'n'd in me swarm" (1.196–97). The second is when Jesus reaches a hasty conclusion as erroneous in its own way as the one so quickly embraced by Satan. "I knew," he says (but in actuality not so),

> the time
> Now full, that I no more should live obscure,
> But openly begin, as best becomes
> The Authority which I deriv'd from Heaven.
> (1.286–89)

Even the lines that immediately follow may *seem* to supply Satan with fit occasion and opportunity since Jesus enters the desert with faith in God's purposes but no knowledge at all as to their precise nature or of how they are to be fulfilled.

> And now by some strong motion I am led
> Into this Wilderness, to what intent
> I learn not yet; perhaps I need not know;
> For what concerns my knowledge God reveals.
> (1.290–93)

In actuality, however, divine revelation is not required, or at least no more of it is needed than has previously been given. Prodded externally by Satan, Jesus instructs himself as to his own personality and about his responsibilities to self and to God. He learns, for example, to avoid intemperance and distrust in God's providential care, to distinguish between secular learning and sacred wisdom, and—most significantly in view of earlier hopes—to prefer the kingdom of God before an earthly throne. Jesus learns too much, in fact, and does so both too quickly and too subtly, for any short summary to suffice. One can notice, however, that this education is cumulative and that it ends where the Father foresaw it would when he referred to Jesus as "This perfect Man, by merit call'd my Son" (1.166). The angelic testimonial to this accomplishment is the chorus that identifies Jesus as heir of both worlds.

Since the hero of *Paradise Regained* finally stands forth as an emergent deity, a son of Mary who grows up into godhead and becomes, by merit more than birthright, Son of God, Milton could not possibly have followed the order of events as given in Matthew's account. The pinnacle is there placed second, not last, but that was the only biblical scene that potentially contained within itself a climactic revelation of maturation into deity. And even there, the fulfilling or refilling could not have been manifested had Milton not adopted a minority view about what sort of place the pinnacle was. In the Greek text, the word is "pterugion," a "little wing." Translated with "pinnas" in the Junius-Tremellius-Beza Bible (in the Vulgate, "pinnam"), its meaning is *"turret* or *battlement"* (the Greek *Lexicon* of Liddell and Scott, defining the Greek); "a raised part of an embattled parapet, a merlon or sim[ilar] structure" (the *Oxford Latin Dictionary*, defining the Latin); "projectura aut prominentia" (Leigh's entry under [pterugion]). Or, as John Diodati (*Commentary*, fol. C3ʳ), more expansively explains: *"A pinacle* Ital. *the edge of the roof: viz.* the roof of the Temple being flat according to the fashion of those times and places, there was round about it a certain edge, hem, or cornice, jetting out, as well for ornament as to convey away the rain-water; and there it should seem the Devil did set the Lord."

With flat-roofed architecture of this kind, the temptation becomes an appeal to self-willed presumption. As Beaumont's Satan puts it, "If *God* thy father be, leap down from hence, / In witness of thy filial Confidence" (*Psyche*, 9.218.5–6). There is, however, an alternative but less likely possibility, as Diodati himself next adds: "It was upon the roof of the porch of the Temple, sixty cubits high, *Ezra* 6.3." (The verse referred to reads, "Let the foundation thereof bee strongly layd, the height thereof, threescore cubits.") Beaumont, despite the lines just quoted and perhaps attempting to make the best of both prospects, refers to "the Temple's highest Spire" (9.215.5). In any case, Milton's scene towers above Beaumont's in more senses than one.

> *Jerusalem,*
> The holy City, lifted high her Towers,
> And higher yet the glorious Temple rear'd
> Her pile, far off appearing like a Mount
> Of Alabaster, top't with golden Spires:
> There on the highest Pinnacle he set
> The Son of God, and added thus in scorn.
>   There stand, if thou wilt stand; to stand upright
> Will ask thee skill; I to thy Father's house
> Have brought thee, and highest plac't, highest is best,
> Now show thy Progeny; if not to stand,
> Cast thyself down; safely if Son of God.
>
>   (4.544–55)

In giddy heights such as these, "to stand . . . Will ask thee skill" becomes gross understatement, and the question is not whether a fall will occur but rather whether it will be fatal. If not, miraculous angelic intervention will be required:

> For it is written, He will give command
> Concerning thee to his Angels, in thir hands
> They shall up lift thee, lest at any time
> Thou chance to dash thy foot against a stone.
>
> (556–59)

Should the old promise of Psalm 91 be met, then at very least, some of Satan's nagging doubts will be dispelled, but if otherwise, why then so much the better. Satan's cleverness, far from inept, ordinarily would be foolproof, but it makes no allowance for a more than human stand nor for a blinding revelation of deity.

> To whom thus Jesus. Also it is written,
> Tempt not the Lord thy God; he said and stood.
> But Satan smitten with amazement fell.
>
> (560–62)

The purely human times that preceded this momentous stand also were of gravest importance. The suggestion is that something might have gone irretrievably wrong since Jesus had the free will to choose and, thus, might actually have chosen to be a worldly philosopher or a benevolent despot. But having refilled himself to become heir of both worlds, Jesus can "enter" on his "glorious work" and "begin to save mankind" (4.634–35). Other events, to be sure, of necessity must follow, including the scandal of the Cross and the glory of the Resurrection. The end of the work, however, has been assured.

> For though that seat of earthly bliss be fail'd,
> A fairer Paradise is founded now
> For *Adam* and his chosen Sons, whom thou
> A Savior art come down to reinstall,
> Where they shall dwell secure, when time shall be
> Of Tempter and Temptation without fear.
>
> (4.612–17)

In a "now," which itself is now long ago, paradise was regained as the habitation of the redeemed when time shall be. Due seasons of the past thus insure the result of future chronology, and this is one reason why times and seasons revolve throughout the poem. Another is that the cyclic chronology of human affairs must be modeled on divinely appointed seasons if the wilderness of this world is to become a new Eden. The experience of Jesus in the desert, though uncontestably unique, fulfilled its Old Testament prefigurations, including the wandering sojourn of the chosen seed for forty years and the fasts of Moses and Elijah for forty days. It continued and continues to be the pattern for subsequent reenactments by others. Indeed, those who refuse to subordinate their own timings to

God's due seasons will discover for themselves—on Judgement Day, if not earlier—the truth of what the Satan of this poem said long ago, "And now too soon for us the circling hours / This dreaded time have compassed."

When this particular time and season were full and when, therefore, this Jesus became able to begin the work of salvation, a corner in history was irrevocably turned so that a fundamentally important now-ness was permanently located in time. Prior to that moment was the whole of human history, from Adam and Eve and the happy garden that Milton erewhile sang on down through the events narrated by Mary to her son. That past history derives its meaning from Jesus because everything imperfectly was until he came. The "now" of the poem's present tense is this due season in the wilderness, one of the many that roll in the Father's hand but fully answerable to the demands of the past and to the needs of the future. The future itself included and includes the subsequent due seasons of Jesus when his hour comes and also the acceptable times of salvation for everyone else, those recurrent moments when a garden can be raised internally in the wilderness of the human heart so as to prepare toward the unfigured reality of the new Jerusalem. Precisely when empty time would be totally displaced by the fullness of eternity, Milton could not possibly know, but he did not need to. The moment to focus on is "now," the present-tense time of "today," this very day of days, for "Now," even now, "is the day of salvation."

5 Come Thou Long Expected Jesus

There can be no question about Easter being "the greatest and oldest feast of the Christian Church" ("Easter," *ODCC*, 432B) nor about the wide sway of a belief that without the Resurrection the individual Christian's "faith would be in vain and the preaching of the apostles a delusion" ("Passover," Bauer, 647A). The associated literature—theological treatises, sermons, devotional materials, and so on—is of staggering proportions, some of it monumentally so, but if the seventeenth century often has been regarded as a glorious period for English religious verse, then poems for this day have not been a major reason. "Resurrection, imperfect" is the title of Donne's effort, a poem that breaks off with "Desunt caetera," the rest is lacking. Both of the quoted phrases might almost be broadly allegoric, even though the word "imperfect" presumably means only that the poem is incomplete.

Backing up three days to Good Friday makes for a big difference, one of them being Donne's "Goodfriday, 1613," and going back to Christmas makes for an even bigger one. The liturgy for the season, while less electrifying than for Easter day, is itself spectacular and has fascinated all sorts of writers. Versifiers (George Wither, for example) and minor poets (John Collop) seem never to be in short supply, whatever the season may be, but an interesting thing about Christmas is that authors sometimes rise above themselves when enchanted by this subject. An example worth singling out is Rowland Watkyns, an Anglican priest about whom little is known apart from the publication of his *Flamma sine fumo* ["flame without smoke"] *or Poems without Fictions* (London, 1662).[1] The book's contents indicate that Watkyns took an interest in medical matters, as Collop also did, and that he was fond of proverbs, although he did not publish a counterpart to Herbert's collection of *Outlandish Proverbs*. The immediate point, of course, is that Watkyns, again like Collop and Herbert, wrote a poem, and by no means a bad one, for the Nativity. Among more prominent names with which Watkyns thus associates his own are those

1. Watkyns was the subject of a note by Joseph A. Bradney, *The Journal of the Welsh Bibliographical Society* 2, no. 4 (May 1920): 145–47. I later quote the poem from *Signet Classic Poets of the 17th Century*, ed. John Broadbent, 2 vols. (New York: New American Library, 1974), 2:273.

of Donne, Jonson, Herbert, and Vaughan. In the sections that follow, I attempt to give an invoice of this embarrassment of riches by balancing the shape of the ritual for Christmas against the configurations of works by the authors just mentioned and by several others as well. Some of these writers can and should be read in the same order in which they are encountered in literary history, but Jonson stands somewhat apart, and the poem to put last simply must be the one written by Milton for Christmas 1629. Except in terms of a merely secular chronology, a concept largely irrelevant to the symbolic timings within the season and verse written for it, Milton's "On the Morning of Christ's Nativity" both crowns and recapitulates the tradition of which it is a part.

ADVENT AND EPIPHANY

In my neighborhood, seasonal decorations—in step, perhaps, with advertisements for "pre-holiday sales"—begin to appear absolutely no later than the weekend after Thanksgiving. I doubt, however, that this practice reflects awareness that "Christmas" refers not only to December 25 but also to a fairly lengthy liturgical season that begins on the first Sunday of Advent and lasts until the day before the Sunday that used to be called "Septuagesima."[2] Those two days represent, as it were, the temporal circumference of the cycle, while the Nativity (December 25) and Epiphany (January 6) are the poles about which it revolves. A formulaic description of the underlying theology is that Christmas concerns the Advent ("Coming") and Epiphany ("Manifestation") of "Theanthropos" (theos + anthropos), the "god-human" who uniquely and fully unites two antithetical orders of being within one person. The central personage, when identified in this way, quite clearly is the living embodiment of an oxymoron, and it thus follows, almost of necessity, that the coming and manifestation of that person will transcend the usual categories of logical thought. Somewhat less abstractly, Christ manifested himself as completely human at one point, as totally divine at another, as both at a third; he first came long ago, continues to do so at all times in the Eucharist and when reborn within the heart, and shall come again in glory when time shall be.

The liturgical (re)presentation of this thinking approaches circularity in that what is "manifested" is the "coming," and what comes is "Theanthropos" in manifested form. For purposes of discussion, however, two

2. The Latinism has been dropped from the Prayer Book in use since 1977 in most churches of the United States. Septuagesima, Sexagesima, and Quinquagesima "are the three Sundays bef. Lent; the last is exactly 50 days bef. Easter, but the other two are named loosely" (*PBD*, 342A, "Festival," 15).

of these ideas may be examined separately, and there are two reasons why Advent is the one with which to begin. First, a few gestures already have been made in the general direction of that season in connection with a right-side-up version (in the introductory sonnet of Donne's *La Corona*) and an amatory inversion (the departure of Urania, in Sidney's "Ye gote-heard Gods"). Second, and more importantly, it is the concept of Advent that controls the shape or form of the Christmas cycle as a whole.

First, then, although popular usage very likely identifies Christmas day as the one on which Christ came, the Coming was and is a process coextensive with the outermost limits of universal redemptive time, and the four Sundays of Advent, even though there are only four of them, move so irregularly back and forth within this vastness that Advent itself has no readily determined beginning or end. This is a point both established and illustrated by the Communion Gospels. Matthew 21.1–13, appointed for Advent 1, begins more or less in the midst of things with the story of Christ's entry into Jerusalem so that (among other reasons) "it might be fulfilled which was spoken by the Prophet, saying, Tell yee the daughter of Sion: behold, thy King commeth vnto thee" (see Zechariah 9.9). This entrance, itself an oxymoron since triumphal and yet made by riding meekly on an ass, was greeted by the cry, "Hosanna to the sonne of Dauid: Blessed is hee that commeth in the Name of the Lorde." Luke 21.25–33, on Advent 2, next takes one to the end of the world by means of Christ's prophecy of that time when all shall "see the Sonne of man come in a cloude, with power and great glory" and thereby know that their "redemption draweth nigh." A week later, Matthew 11.2–10 presents two disciples of John the Baptist asking of Christ, prior to his entry into Jerusalem, "Art thou hee that shall come?" And on Advent 4, John 1.19–28 portrays the Baptist himself, earlier still, as crying in the wilderness, "Make straight the way of the Lord . . . he it is, which though he came after mee, was before me." For the starting point whence these comings originated, one has to add John 1.1–14, the Gospel for Christmas day: "In the beginning was the Word. . . . He came among his owne. . . . And the same word became flesh, and dwelt among vs."

A verbal pattern clearly emerges from repetitive use of come and/or coming, but equally clear are irregularities among the frames of time to which the verbs refer. The coming of Christ first is happening in the present, then is prophesied as an event of the eschatological or ultimate future, next is questioned and anticipated in anterior time, and finally has already begun to have occurred in a past so undatably remote that it is "in the beginning." The season of Advent definitely begins on that Sunday that falls on or closest to St. Andrew's day, November 30, but definitive answers may be very hard to come by if one asks when the Word first began to come or when it will do so for the last and most final of all final times.

A fairly simple way to account for the scope of this inverse chronology is to say, along with Dom Pius Parsch, that it arises from the interaction of three "planes of time," those of history, of grace, and of eschatology.[3] For a brief indication of what is meant, Wither's verse "For the Advent Sundayes" is an appropriate source to cite here.

> When CHRIST our *Lord* incarnate was,
> Our *Brother*, then he *came* to be.
> When into us he *comes* by Grace,
> To be our *Spouse*, then *cometh He.*
> And *Comes*, when he shall *come* agen
> To judge both Dead and Living-men.

The symmetry is neatly concise, but it is gained only at the expense of some distortion or, if not that, then potential misdirection. The apparent implication is that Christ's coming occurs in terms of sequential time and that Advent—or at least the "narrative" that Advent presents—has, as it were, a beginning, a middle, and an end. Sequential time, however, while unquestionably relevant, tells only part of this particular story; it may account for variation in verb tense but inadequately clarifies why the tenses appear in disorderly fashion.

John Boys perhaps takes a better course. "There is," he says,

> a three-fold comming of Christ, according to the
> three-fold difference of
>
> time $\begin{cases} \text{Past.} \\ \text{Present.} \\ \text{Future.} \end{cases}$
>
> Which *Bernard* hath vttered elegantly:
>
> venit $\begin{cases} \textit{ad homines.} \\ \textit{in homines.} \\ \textit{contra homines.} \end{cases}$

> He came among men in time past, when as the Word was made flesh and dwelt among vs: he comes into men in the present by his grace and holy Spirit. . . . He shall in the future come against men, to iudge both the quicke and the dead. (*Dominical* 1:27–28)

This exposition reads very like a prose version of Wither's verse, but Boys next goes on to yoke together the first coming and the last, and when he does so, the Nativity is replaced, however surprisingly, by Christ's

---

3. Dom Pius Parsch, *The Church's Year of Grace*, trans. William G. Heidt (Collegeville, MN: The Liturgical Press, 1964), 4. A more informative title for this book would be "The Breviary Explained."

entry into Jerusalem, the event described in the Gospel for Advent 1. To continue,

> to iudge both the quicke and the dead: but the Sonne of Man hath but two commings in the forme of man: his first comming in great meeknesse, his second in exceeding maiestie. At his first comming he rode vpon an Asse: in his second . . . he shall ride vpon the clouds. In his first comming he came to be iudged: in his second hee comes to iudge. In his first comming the people did triumph and reioyce, crying *Hosanna:* but in his second comming the people shall be at their wits end for feare.

"First" and "second" are insisted upon, and yet the "first coming" in this case was not in fact the first to occur, and the "second" will be, but is not yet, the last one of all. Christmas day itself, moreover, has temporarily disappeared, though Boys does not, of course, continue to leave it out. Not much mileage, if any at all, can be had from the present tense—"in his second hee comes"—of merely one clause, but Boys obviously is not conjugating the tenses of time in terms of customary grammar.

To see the implications of this point more or less explicitly, one needs to follow Boys back to the twenty-fifth Sunday after Trinity, the last for which pericopes are appointed and hence the final Sunday of the liturgical year. The year itself is ending, but the Collect and Communion "Epistle" (in this case, not from the Epistles at all but from Jeremiah) are not looking back but rather ahead to the year about to be renewed. The prayer begins, "Stirre vp wee beseech thee, O Lord, the wils of thy faithful people." (I have heard this day called "Stirrup Sunday," but the usage evidently is not historically old, merely old-fashioned.) The first verses (Jeremiah 23.5–6, Prayer Book translation) of the lesson are,

> Behold, the time commeth, sayth the Lord, that I will raise vp the righteous branch of Dauid, which King shall beare rule, and he shall prosper with wisedome, and shall set vp equitie and righteousnesse againe in earth. In his time shall Juda bee saued, and Israel shall dwell without feare. And this is the Name that they shall call him, The Lord our righteousnesse.

Commenting on Advent 1, Boys remarks, "Christ is *Alpha,* and *Omega,* the first and the last, the beginning and ending; wherefore the Church allotting a seuerall Scripture for euery seuerall Sunday throughout the whole yeere, beginnes and ends with the comming of Christ" (*Dominical* 1:11). Of Trinity 25, he says, "The Church ends, as she began, with hir onely Lord & Sauiour," an idea for which the image or metaphor is an "*annulus Christianus,* as it were the Christians round, or ring":

> As then on the first Sunday, the Gospell intimating that Christ is come . . . and the Epistle teaching that we must imitate our King being come . . . , are in stead of a Preface: so this Epistle and Gospell on the last Sunday (the one prophecying that the Lord of our righteousnes shall shortly come, . . .

and the other preaching that hee is already come, . . .) may serue for a conclusion or Epilogue to all the rest of the whole yeere. (*Dominical* 4:224)

The Coming and its timings could scarcely have much meaning, however, apart from that which came, comes, and is to come. "From Christmas to Epiphany," Anthony Sparrow tells us, "Holy Churches design, is, to set forth Christs *Humanity*, to make Christ manifest in the flesh, which the offices do" (*Rationale*, 136). The two offices he has in mind are those for the Sunday after Christmas and for Circumcision day, and the Gospel for the former, taken from Matthew 1, is the famous (possibly notorious) series of genealogical "begats" wherewith "the booke of the generation of Jesus Christ" (Matthew 1.1) is recorded. The elongated list does stretch itself out, but the basic point is that it "intimates in particular" (in detailed particularity, that is) "how Christ became the Sonne of man, that hee might make vs the sonnes of God" (*Dominical* 1:87).

"But," Sparrow immediately adds, "from *Epiphany* to *Septuagesima*, especially in the four next Sundays after Epiphany," the Church "endeavours to manifest his glory and *Divinity*, by recounting some of his first miracles, and manifestations of his Deity, so that each Sunday is in this respect a kind of Epiphany."[4] Behind this remark are the diverse events recounted in the Gospel lessons: first, the display of divine knowledge by the twelve-year-old Jesus to the rabbis in the temple (Luke 2.41–52); next, the transformation of water into wine for the wedding feast at Cana (John 2.1–11); third, the healing of a leper and of a centurion's servant (Matthew 8.1–13); and fourth, the calming of a tempest and the dispelling of demons (Matthew 8.23–34). Epiphany 5 also concerns a miracle but of a considerably different kind. The Gospel, Matthew 13.24–30, is the parable of the tares and wheat that, growing together for the time of this world, at length are severed, the tares to be burnt, the wheat to be gathered in the barn of God. This ingathering and casting out necessarily end Epiphany season since further manifestations, after all, are scarcely imaginable—except, that is, for the beatific vision itself, the vision of "our good God, in whose light we shall see such light, as the eye of man hath not seene, neither eare hath heard, neither heart sufficiently can conceiue" (*Dominical* 1:235—Boys's final comment on Epiphany 5 and, hence, on the entire Christmas cycle).

4. In theory, there were five Sundays of Epiphany, the number for which pericopes were appointed, but in practice the number varied because the Christmas cycle had to end on the day before Septuagesima when the preparation for Lent began, and the beginning of Lent was determined by the variable date of Easter. When Lent fell quite early, the lessons for Epiphany 5 and, if necessary, Epiphany 4 were inserted in between Trinity 24 and Trinity 25 to fill out the liturgical year just prior to the onset of Advent. (I adopt past tense because these statements are not entirely accurate for Prayer Books printed in 1662 or later.) For purposes of discussion, John Boys and Anthony Sparrow assumed that all five Sundays invariably were celebrated in their appointed sequence.

On Epiphany or Manifestation day itself, however, multiple displays of divinity occur, the reason being that "epiphany" turns out to refer to more than one incident in Christ's life. The history behind this fact is that in the Eastern Church, the word (and hence the feast) primarily signified the baptism of Christ and the divine pronouncement, "This is my son." In the fourth century, when the feast was introduced to the West, the word and day became associated most strongly with the journey of the three wise men or Magi and rather less strongly with the baptism of Christ and with the miracle performed at the wedding at Cana. In the Prayer Book, history is glossed over in favor of symbolic co-incidence. Sparrow explains:

> This Feast is called in Latin *Epiphaniae*, *Epiphanies* in the plural; because upon this day we celebrate *three* glorious apparitions or manifestations, all which happened upon the same day, though not of the same year. . . . The first manifestation was of the *Star*, (mentioned in the Gospel [Matthew 2.1–12]) the . . . guide to Christ. The Second Epiphany or Manifestation was that of the glorious *Trinity* at the baptism of Christ, mentioned in the second Lesson at Morning Prayer, S. *Luke* 3.22. The third was of Christ's Glory or *Divinity*, by the miracle of turning water into wine, mentioned in the second Lesson at Evening prayer. (*Rationale*, 135)[5]

One of these epiphanies, moreover, manifests the humanity as well as the divinity of Christ. This is the illumination of the Magi, and the story of their journey is suggestive in and of itself. They traveled to worship the "King of the Iewes," but they discovered a "yong child with Mary his mother, and fell downe and worshipped him." Within the human child they somehow saw a king, and within the king they perceived a god. Their gifts, as traditionally interpreted, were providentially chosen: gold for the king, incense for the god, myrrh for the mortal child. Yet "in offering all these . . . the *Magi* gaue not here some gifts vnto God, and other vnto man: but all vnto one Christ" (Boys, *Festivall* 1:153–54).

Since Christ was revealed to the Magi in both of his natures, Epiphany is central to the manifestation of Theanthropos, but Manifestation ought not be isolated from Coming any more than Advent should be detached from that which comes to be manifested. Also important is the idea that the Magi signify all Gentiles whereas the shepherds represent all Jews. Because of these symbolic counterparts, Epiphany is attached most specifically to "twelfth day" but also can signify "Christmas-day, when Christ was manifested in the flesh" (*Rationale*, 134). Even more generally, as Donne points out,

---

5. As Sparrow inadvertently indicates, the pericope from John 2 that narrates the miracle of turning water into wine served double duty: at Evensong on January 6 and also as the Communion Gospel on Epiphany 2.

Every action and passage that manifests Christ to us, is his birth; for, *Epiphany* is *manifestation*; And therefore, though the Church doe now call Twelf-day Epiphany, because upon that day Christ was manifested to the Gentiles, in those Wise men who came then to worship him, yet the Ancient Church called this day, (the day of Christs birth) the Epiphany, because this day Christ was manifested to the world, by being born this day. Every manifestation of Christ to the world, to the Church, to a particular soule, is an Epiphany, a Christmas-day. (*Sermons* 7:279)

And since the wheat and tares of Epiphany 5 cannot be totally divided until the last coming, "The haruest is the end of the world" that initiates the arrival of "the kingdome of glorie" (*Dominical* 1:234–35). As epiphany season ends, one thus discovers not only the end of the Christmas cycle but also its beginning, the coming of Christ when time was-is-shall be. The Collect for Advent 1 is a prayer for that day, for the Christmas cycle that begins on that day, and for the entirety of all the cycles and years yet to come before all seasons and times, filled full to the brim, flow over and into the amplitude of eternity.

Almighty God, giue vs grace that wee may cast away the workes of darkenesse, and put vpon vs the armour of light, nowe in the time of this mortall life (in the which thy Sonne Jesus Christ came to visite vs in great humilitie) that in the last day when he shall come againe in his glorious Maiestie, to iudge both the quicke and the dead, we may rise to the life immortall, through him, who liueth and reigneth with thee and the holy Ghost, now and euer. Amen.

DONNE, WATKYNS, COLLOP, SOUTHWELL, CRASHAW, AND OTHERS

Immensitie cloysterd in thy deare wombe,
Now leaves his welbelov'd imprisonment,
There he hath made himselfe to his intent
Weake enough, now into our world to come;
But Oh, for thee, for him, hath th'Inne no roome?
Yet lay him in this stall, and from the Orient,
Starres, and wisemen will travell to prevent
Th'effect of *Herods* jealous generall doome.
Seest thou, my Soule, with thy faiths eyes, how he
Which fils all place, yet none holds him, doth lye?
Was not his pity towards thee wondrous high,
That would have need to be pittied by thee?
Kisse him, and with him into Egypt goe,
With his kinde mother, who partakes thy woe.

The poem is "Nativitie," the third sonnet in Donne's *La Corona*, and if one were to refuse, for a moment, to consider anything other than the events alluded to, then a fair assessment of the poem would be that it merely turns chronological biblical narrative into verse. Gabriel announced to Mary, "Thou shalt conceiue in thy wombe . . . the sonne of the Highest" (Luke 1.31–32); "because there was no roume . . . in the Inne" (Luke 2.7), she gave birth in a manger or, as Donne has it, a "stall." "There came Wise men from the East" (Matthew 2.1) seeking the king of the Jews, a consequence of their enquiry being that king "Herod . . . slew all the children that were in Bethlehem" (2.16). Jesus escaped, however, because an angel had previously appeared "to Ioseph in a dreame, saying, Arise and take the yong childe, and his mother, and flee into Egypt" (2.13).

This narrative order is not, of course, the one that is followed in liturgical (re)presentation of the happenings. The Annunciation, since attached to March 25, cannot possibly fall inside the Christmas cycle; the day, as shown by Donne's and Beaumont's poems for co-incidences, must occur inside the Easter cycle instead. In church, Herod's "doom" and Christ's escape into Egypt are recalled prior to the visit of the Magi, not afterwards. Annual celebration occurs on Holy Innocents day, December 28, when the Communion Gospel is Matthew 2.13–18, the passage whence Donne has borrowed the slaughter and the flight. In the poem, the Magi (since associated with January 6) thus arrive too soon, as it were, and may seem to do so in more senses than one since the shepherds usually encountered on December 25 have not even been mentioned, much less paid a visit of their own.

All sorts of things are happening in *La Corona* as a whole, some of them on the highly complicated side, but one simply cannot expect a fourteen-line poem to present numerous details nor to adopt inverse chronology in presenting those for which room can be found. Paring down, however, very possibly exaggerates and certainly does not diminish the force of the present-tense timing of the specific events that do appear. The moment from which the poem starts out is, astonishingly, that very instant when Christ himself emerges from the womb. "Immensitie . . . Now leaves," having been sufficiently weakened (and localized both spatially and temporally) "now into our world to come." The "welbelov'd imprisonment," so mysteriously vast in its narrowly human straitness, contrasts favorably to the larger inn that has no room of any kind, and Mary therefore is to "lay" (but evidently has not yet laid) the child in "this stall." Epiphany lies twelve days off, but wise men "will travell" to "prevent" ("pre" + "venio," arrive before) Herod's murderous decree, the grim results of which are known, though they have not as yet come about.

As the sestet begins, a new and altered present tense allows the "Soule" to perceive how the child "doth lye" in the creche in which Mary presumably has even now placed him, and a redefined future appears as an imperative: "Kisse him, and with him into Egypt goe." This thirteenth line, moreover, tacitly anticipates Christ's future return not merely from Egypt but also from the tomb and from heaven at the end of time. The allusion is to Psalm 2, a proper psalm for Easter and one that anticipates last Advent on Judgement Day: "Be wise now therefore, O ye Kings. . . . Kisse the Sonne lest he be angry, and so ye perish from the right way: if his wrath be kindled" (Psalter Psalm 2.10, 12). And one ought to notice that parabolic time probably is implicit not only in the "day" that calibrates both the poem and its subject but also in the language of oxymoron that so frequently appears. The womb is dear but is an imprisonment and yet is well beloved; immensity becomes weak, it fills all place, is held by none, but lies confined to a manger; God's pity "towards thee" demands human pity in response. If these past-present conditions were to be lost sight of, then the present-future return would find the "Soule" left woefully behind, condemned to Egypt for all eternity.

"Nativitie," like *La Corona* itself, is a bigger poem than it looks to be, and one of the reasons is that each of the several motifs that it so tightly compacts could be expanded, more or less separately and almost at will. Donne refers to the etymological meaning of "advent" in a single infinitive, "now into our world to come." Wither's verse "For the Advent Sundays" was earlier mentioned, but one can add Jeremy Taylor's two "hymns for Advent, or the Weeks Immediately Before the Birth of our Blessed Saviour." In one of them, "Christ's Coming to Jerusalem in Triumph," the Gospel for Advent 1 is rhymed so as to raise to the surface a meaning that Donne's present tense indirectly conveys: "Ride on triumphantly," Taylor writes; "welcome to our hearts."

This also is the place to reintroduce "Upon Christ's nativity, or Christmas," the poem by Rowland Watkyns, a poet who decided to scrutinize the idea of "coming" from a rigorous theological point of view.

> From three dark places Christ came forth this day:
> First from his Father's bosom, where he lay
> Concealed till now; then from the typic law,
> Where we his manhood but by figures saw;
> And lastly from his mother's womb he came
> To us, a perfect God and perfect Man.

The coming "began" from several apparently dissimilar starting points: from the unknowable internality of a Father of lights too brilliant for mortal eyes to see; from Old Testament prefigurations ("types / And shadows," as Milton calls them [*Paradise Lost*, 12.232–33]); and from the seed within the Virgin's womb. Divine darkness signified godhead; the "typic Law," humanity; the Virgin birth, both.

Having arrived at Theanthropos in his sixth line, Watkyns immediately amplifies the oxymoron of an incarnate god.

> Now in a manger lies the eternal Word:
> The Word he is, yet can no speech afford;
> He is the bread of life, yet hungry lies;
> The living fountain, yet for drink he cries;
> He cannot help or clothe himself at need
> Who did the lilies clothe and ravens feed;
> He is the light of lights, yet now doth shroud
> His glory with our nature as a cloud.

Donne wondered at the profound pity and mercy of God in deigning to become flesh but also added an allusively made reminder of the angry god to come in future time. Watkyns addresses a comparable point from the opposite point of view: "Little he is, and wrapped in clouts, lest he / Might strike us dead if clothed with majesty." Donne's reference to a proper Psalm for Easter day probably should summon up Holy Week within the mind. Watkyns more openly makes a similar demand by linking, chiastically, Christ's birth and death.

> Christ had four beds and those not soft nor brave:
> The Virgin's womb, the manger, cross, and grave.

Or, in diagram form,

Womb and grave: two darkly enclosed sources of light; manger and cross: the one "as uneasie at first," to requote from Donne's sermon (7:279), as the other "at last." Within the womb is discoverable the tomb; within the stall, the cross; and within the beginning, the end. By no means "soft," whatever one's standards may be, but also not "brave" (that is, not "splendid") by those that customarily prevail, these beds are glorious in their effects, not in their appearance.

Implicit glory leads Watkyns to his conclusion, but if the traditional materials thus far have been surprisingly well served in view of the author's obscurity, the final couplet is a comedown. The thought ought to be elevated, but the language falls flat. "The angels sing this day, and so will I / That have more reason to be glad then they."

Among Donne's brief references is the one to "*Herods* jealous generall doome" upon the Holy Innocents. Crashaw's lengthy expansion is a free rendering of Marino's "Sospetto d'Herode," the Suspicion of Herod, and among the sacred epigrams are two treatments, each of them in Latin and also in English. Oxymoron is useful on this day too, as in "To the Infant Martyrs":

Goe smiling soules, your new built Cages breake,
In Heav'n you'l learne to sing ere here to speake,
Nor let the milky fonts that bath your thirst,
      Bee your delay;
The place that calls you hence, is at the worst
      Milke all the way.[6]

Holy Innocents is one of the three days placed immediately after December 25 to celebrate three kinds of martyrs (etymologically, "witnesses") to the coming of Christ: on December 26, Stephen Protomartyr, a martyr both by his own intent and because of the way he died; on the December 27, St. John, who intended to be a martyr but legendarily survived immersion in boiling oil; and on December 28, the Holy Innocents, martyrs by the fact of their death though not of their own choice. Conventional time schemes once again are irrelevant. Stephen, though celebrated first and known as Proto- or First-Martyr, was the second of these to perish. John, though celebrated second, outlived the others into old age. The infant Innocents were slain first but are celebrated third. Nor did any of these deaths occur on or even near the day of Christ's own birth. The Innocents were slaughtered at least several days, perhaps as much as two years, later; for Stephen and especially for John, their final witnessing was long postponed. The days, clearly, are arranged in terms of symbolic, not literal, values: however long or short the actual chronology may be, an immediate consequence of Christ's divine birth on earth is human rebirth into heaven. William Alabaster, in opening "St. John the Evangelist," does not stretch the truth, liturgically speaking at least, when he writes, "High towering eagle, rightly may thy feast, / Be held so near to Christ's solemnity." Other authors place poems for one or more of these days immediately after verse for the Nativity: Joseph Beaumont includes poems for Stephen and John; Francis Quarles, for Stephen and the Innocents; and Jeremy Taylor, for John and the Innocents. All three of these days are suggestive analogues of one another, and it therefore is possible (even though I can see no way of knowing for sure) that Donne's allusion to the Innocents celebrated on December 28 should evoke the events of December 26 and 27 as well. If so, then "Nativitie," already

6. The image of the Milky Way may have been less strained then than it seems to be now. Cf. Thomas Washbourne (1606?–1687), "The Impartial Judgment" (of Judgement Day, that is); Christ's throne is

    Not like to Herod's throne, that was dy'd red
    With blood of infants which he massacred;
    Nor sullied o'er with falsehood and with wrong,
      But like the milky way, clear all along.

The Poems of Thomas Washbourne, ed. Alexander B. Grosart (n.p.: Fuller Worthies Library, 1868), 165.

more concisely expansive than most fourteen lines can be, becomes an even larger epitome of the long day of symbolic (re)births and multiple (be)comings.

The reference to Epiphany, "from the Orient, / Starres, and wisemen will travell," also neatly summarizes several principal themes of the day, but one of them has been omitted: the obligation to offer a gift to the Child, even if the only one ready to hand should be one's own unworthy self. "Ah my dear Lord," John Collop asks in "On the Nativity," "what shall I give / To thee, who gav'st thy self for me? . . . I have no treasury to ope. / I can no spices off'rings bring." Instead, "I tribute bring / Myself thine Image to my King." "Orient," "Starres," "wisemen," and "travell," four important words in Donne's two lines, suggest the other four important themes.

"Travell," with a pun on "travail" more or less built in, may be the best known of these today, for some audiences because of familiar carols about the wisemen or possibly thanks to Menotti's opera, *Amahl and the Night Visitors;* for others because of Lancelot Andrewes's sermon and T. S. Eliot's echo in "The Journey of the Magi." "A cold *comming* they had of it," as Andrewes remarked on Christmas day in 1622, "at this time of yeare; just the worst time of the yeare, to take a journey, and specially a long journey in" (*XCVI Sermons*, 143). The journey of Crashaw's Magi has been similar.

> We, who strangely went astray,
> Lost in a bright
> Meridian night,
> A Darkenes made of too much day,
> Becken'd from farr
> By thy fair starr,
> Lo at last haue found our way.
> To THEE, thou DAY of night! thou east of west!
> Lo we at last haue found the way.
>   ("In the Glorious Epiphany," 15–23)

Crashaw's imagery makes clear the further fact that the journey involved much more than travel-travail. The wisemen started out from the East ("We three kings of Orient are," as the carol has it), and yet their destination was "Oriens": the "day spring [margin: *Or, Sunne-rising*] from on high hath visited us" (Luke 1.78). The Old Testament verse behind Luke's own is Zechariah 6.12, "Behold a man, the Orient is his name" (Douai translation). According to Crashaw's Magi, "The EAST is come / To seek her self in thy sweet Eyes" (13–14).

Searching out the true Orient—the East or Light or the Son who is also the Sun—associates itself with two other motifs traditional for Epiphany, the insight of the wisemen in discerning badges of royalty in circumstances of poverty and the conversion to Christ that enabled them to return "into their owne countrey another way" (Matthew 2.12). Robert Southwell develops the first idea in "New Prince, new pompe."

> This stable is a Princes Court,
>> The Crib his chaire of state;
> The beasts are parcell of his pompe,
>> The wooden dish his plate.
>
> . . . .
>
> With joy approach o Christ wight,
>> Do homage to thy King;
> And highly prise this humble pompe,
>> Which hee from heaven dooth bring.

The king of the Jews whom the Magi expected to worship was in fact found, but since appearance and reality did not coincide, "humble pompe" had to be reinterpreted and then recognized as the "new pompe" appropriate for this "New" kind of "Prince."

Without that recognition, a return by any way at all would have been merely regressive physical motion. With it, the Magi were able to turn themselves away from the pathways of idolatry; looking back toward Christ, they carried him forward in their hearts. A point insisted upon in biblical commentary was that false religion thus lost its old power, giving way to Truth.[7] Crashaw, in the Epiphany poem recently cited, insists on it too. "No longer shall the immodest lust / Of Adulterous GODLES dust / Fly in the face of heau'n" (101–3). "Cheap AEgyptian Deityes" (88)— including "fatt OSYRIS" and "his fair sister cow" (96–97)—are revealed to be "All-Idolizing wormes" (113), objects of "blind idolatry" (170), now both unmasked and eclipsed by "The supernaturall DAWN of Thy pure day" (174). Christ's own departure from Bethlehem into Egypt, the incident with which Donne's "Nativitie" concludes, also relates to this theme since it was said to have resulted in the displacement of those cheap Egyptian deities to whom Crashaw refers. Boys was moved by this idea to exclaim, "O the deepnesse of the riches of Gods mercy! Babylon and Egypt whilome were *malorum officinae*, the very shops of all villainie: but now behold the Wisemen come from the one, and Christ here fleeth into the other" (*Festivall* 1:122).

CHRISTMAS IN *THE TEMPLE*

There may be no way of knowing exactly how much of the Christmas cycle is condensed into Donne's "Nativitie"—perhaps as much (or, for

7. See the materials gathered for Epiphany by M. F. Toal, ed., *The Sunday Sermons of the Great Fathers*, 1 ["From the First Sunday of Advent to Quinquagesima"]: 228–69, esp. 244–45 (translating the *Catena aurea* of Aquinas), 258 (Chrysostom), and 259 (Leo).

that matter, as little) as prior experiencing of the cycle itself allows one to see. In any case, an unarguable fact is that the poem does not restrict itself to Christmas day itself. Also beyond dispute is that contextual values are normal in verse for this subject. Watkyns expands toward the undeterminable Beginning and the unknowable End. The poems of Southwell and Collop, though I introduced them to illustrate themes of Epiphany, were written for the Nativity. Gentiles both, Southwell and Collop included the significance of their symbolic predecessors in their understanding of what the Nativity means. Watkyns adds the continuing importance of Advent in its multiple senses, and others—including Donne himself—call to mind the ongoing witnessing of Christ by the martyrs and saints.

Crashaw's epigrams aside, these several poems are longer than "Nativitie" but are less comprehensive, and that fact is worth noticing too. Other poets tend to focus attention on some one incident even when they drive toward meanings very like those suggested by Donne. Or they prepare a series of poems, each complementary to its companions, on one or more of the major events. Since Joseph Beaumont and George Wither may have worn out their welcome, a fresher name to recur to is William Alabaster, who wrote fifteen sonnets for the Incarnation alone, the first being "A Preface to the Incarnation."

Or there is one of Herbert's sequences, especially appropriate here since I doubt that anyone could recognize all of its four parts for what they actually are without knowing about Advent in general and about Advent 4 in particular. The initial poem is "Deniall," and no helpful biblical narrative is given wherewith to explain the title. Instead, Herbert sets forth a speaker whose patience has long since been exhausted by a seemingly interminable waiting for God. The need has been so urgent for so long that this speaker, close to despair, has concluded that continuing delay is incomprehensible unless God has declined to hearken to prayer and intends not to come. This lamentable state is not illustrated by a picture, but the stanzas are emblematic because of their jaggedness and the unrhymed fifth line.

DENIALL.

When my devotions could not pierce
   Thy silent eares;
Then was my heart broken, as was my verse:
  My breast was full of fears
5   And disorder:

My bent thoughts, like a brittle bow,
   Did flie asunder:
Each took his way; some would to pleasures go,
   Some to the warres and thunder
10   Of alarms.

As good go any where, they say,
As to benumme
Both knees and heart, in crying night and day,
Come, come, my God, O come,
15 But no hearing.

O that thou shouldst give dust a tongue
To crie to thee,
And then not heare it crying! all day long
My heart was in my knee,
20 But no hearing.

Therefore my soul lay out of sight,
Untun'd, unstrung:
My feeble spirit, unable to look right,
Like a nipt blossome, hung
25 Discontented.

Desperate though this situation is, it is no worse than the plight of those in church on the last Sunday of Advent. They too have been waiting, in calendar time for merely four weeks, but in spiritual time much longer, and prayers have been both fervent and profuse for the coming of God. "O Come, O Come, Immanuel" has long been a standard hymn whereby to voice the plea, especially on Advent 1. And when it is Advent 4 rather than Christ that arrives so disappointingly, then the period of waiting seems entirely too protracted. "Through our sinnes and wickenesse," as the Collect for this day says, "we be sore let and hindered," nor can there be any relief unless God "come among vs, and . . . speedily deliuer vs."

> The sense of urgency fills the collect, in which we pray that God will come in his might to our succour. Our need is great, since through the *sins* we commit, and the underlying *wickedness* of which they are the expression, *we are sore let and hindered in running* the way of God's commandments; and our prayer is that the help we need may come speedily. The collect is as it were a last appeal to God, an appeal which on Christmas morning we shall know to be answered.[8]

In "Deniall," sinful thoughts have taken to pleasures and alarms; fully aware of these lapses into waywardness, Herbert finds his soul untuned, his verse disordered, nor can he discover a remedy within himself. Like the Church, he presumably knows that the crying to God will in fact be answered, but when one's heart is in one's knee, apparently to no purpose, then the numbing possibility of no hearing—

But no hearing (15)
And then not heare it crying (18)
But no hearing (20)

8. Harold Riley, *The Eucharistic Year* (London: S.P.C.K., 1951), 28.

—is agonizing. *"Come, come, my God, O come"* (14) is not, however, Herbert's own last appeal. A final plea has been reserved for the stanza not yet quoted. In making it—and thereby ending this poem but not this sequence—Herbert orders his rhyme for the first time and thereby indicates that the long deferred promise of Advent will be fulfilled on Christmas day.

> O cheer and tune my heartlesse breast,
>> Deferre no time;
> That so thy favours granting my request,
>> They and my minde may chime,
>> And mend my rhyme.

Mending the rhyme audibly accompanies mending the time, but even in this fifth stanza the lines themselves remain craggedly broken. "Christmas," the following poem, manages to smooth out the rough edges by means of sonnet form, but December 25 poses some irregularities of its own. Herbert, it seems, has made a tiring journey in pursuit of the erroneous pleasures mentioned in "Deniall"; his travel and travail, in fact, have taken a decidedly wrong turn. The Magi, however, sought for one kind of king and unexpectedly found another, and Herbert's quest, though improperly oriented at first, is similarly rewarded.

> CHRISTMAS.
> All after pleasures as I rid one day,
>> My horse and I, both tir'd, bodie and minde,
>> With full crie of affections, quite astray,
> I took up in the next inne I could finde.
> There when I came, whom found I but my deare,
>> My dearest Lord, expecting till the grief
>> Of pleasures brought me to him, readie there
> To be all passengers most sweet relief?

This seemingly personal narrative is so charged with symbolism that it may be as allusively comprehensive in its own way as Donne's "Nativitie" is. The old allegory of horse and rider, or body and soul, reinforces or is reinforced by the beastliness of a "full cry" like the one uttered by "hounds in the chase" (*OED*, "cry," sb. 11). The irony that the one who "came" should be Herbert rather than Christ is more than balanced by the greater irony that the Lord has been "expecting" (awaiting, that is) the arrival of this world-weary traveler. All pleasures but one bring merely grief, but not quite hidden is a point from which, potentially, a change of direction may be made. All we—the whole Church, in fact—like sheep have gone astray (Isaiah 53.6, Old Testament lesson for Epiphany 2), and even though this traveler exaggeratedly has gone "quite astray," another way to turn or return is in the process of opening before him.

One detail, the finding of God in the next wayside inn, merely seems momentarily to be present. As the sestet reveals, this lodging place, like the biblical one, evidently is much too crowded with other guests for there to be any room for God.

> O Thou, whose glorious, yet contracted light,
>> Wrapt in nights mantle, stole into a manger;
>> Since my dark soul and brutish is thy right,
> To Man of all beasts be not thou a stranger:
>> Furnish & deck my soul, that thou mayst have
>> A better lodging then a rack or grave.

Christ is now quartered in a manger and later will be a racked on a cross before repose within a grave, but if the force of his own long waiting for Herbert's slow coming is to be felt, then an internal dwelling must be prepared.

The third poem begins with the shepherds of December 25, but since most of the dramatic action of this series is internally staged, the pastoral landscape quickly changes to the locale requested by Herbert at the end of "Christmas": the newly decked out soul as now furnished with a flock of transformed thoughts and words and deeds. The Word made flesh demands an answering song, and with a motif partly transplanted back from Epiphany, the true Sun and Son are to beam forth both externally and internally.

> The shepherds sing; and shall I silent be?
>> My God, no hymne for thee?
> My soul's a shepherd too; a flock it feeds
>> Of thoughts, and words, and deeds.
> The pasture is thy word: the streams, thy grace
>> Enriching all the place.
> Shepherd and flock shall sing, and all my powers
>> Out-sing the day-light houres.
> Then we will chide the sunne for letting night
>> Take up his place and right:
> We sing one common Lord; wherefore he should
>> Himself the candle hold.

["And there shall be no night there, and they neede no candle, neither light of the Sunne, for the Lord God giueth them light," Revelation 22.5.]

> I will go searching, till I finde a sunne
>> Shall stay, till we have done;
> A willing shiner, that shall shine as gladly,
>> As frost-nipt sunnes look sadly.

["And the citie had no neede of the Sunne, neither of the Moone to shine in it: for the glory of God did lighten it, and the Lambe is the light thereof," Revelation 21.23.]

> Then we will sing, and shine all our own day,
>   And one another pay:
> His beams shall cheer my breast, and both so twine,
> Till ev'n his beams sing, and my musick shine.

In "Deniall," God's ears seemed closed and unhearing but in fact were not; since God answered and thus not only hears but also is heard, Herbert in turn must not be silent. The soul, untuned and unstrung in its disconsolateness in the first poem and worn out at the end of one day's travail in "Christmas," now will outsing daylight itself in praise of him who came "Wrapt in nights mantle." Earlier, that soul also hung discontented like a nipped blossom, but it is this world's sun that proves to be "frost-nipt" by the winter birth of "Oriens," the day-spring that from on high hath visited us. And the expectation that Christmas so thoroughly satisfied must nonetheless continue to fall short of total fulfillment until the journey is terminated by the last and final coming together of the soul and the Lamb in the new Jerusalem. There the true Sun shall sing, Herbert's song shall shine, and music will have untuned the sky.

Herbert could have finished this brief sequence with "The shepherds sing" and indeed, from one point of view, could not possibly go further since the "willing shiner" shines brightest at the end of time, not earlier. Herbert chose, however, to cap the series with "Ungratefulnesse," a poem that closes out one line of thought even as it starts up another. The last stanza explains the title:

> But man is close, reserv'd, and dark to thee:
>   When thou demandest but a heart,
>   He cavils instantly.
>   In his poore cabinet of bone
>   Sinnes have their box apart,
> Defrauding thee, who gavest two for one,

These closing lines also prepare for the following poem, "Sighs and Grones," a title that names two of the consequences and/or exemplifications of human cavils against divine law.

Most of "Ungratefulnesse," however, is a theologically minded commentary, if not quite a sermon, on the experience acted out in the preceding poems, and the language serves to extend as well as clarify the significance of what has gone before. To be specific, the first stanza turns back to the "rack or grave" mentioned in "Christmas" so as to expose the redemptive effect of the Cross, and it adopts the Epiphany theme of idolatry being replaced by true faith.

> Lord, with what bountie and rare clemencie
>   Hast thou redeem'd us from the grave!

> If thou hadst let us runne,
> Gladly had man ador'd the sunne,
> And thought his god most brave;
> Where now we shall be better gods then he.

God's bounty, by an association of ideas by this time hardly surprising, suggests the bounty of the wisemen, who "opened their treasures." God's gifts, of course, are much more rare.

> Thou hast but two rare cabinets full of treasure,
> The *Trinitie*, and *Incarnation*:
> Thou hast unlockt them both,
> And made them jewels to betroth
> The work of thy creation
> Unto thy self in everlasting pleasure.

There probably is an echo here of "All pleasures," the ones sought in the first line of "Christmas." More prominent is the wedding ring of the Lamb and the soul, the union between Creator and creature, the betrothal to eternity of the timely work of six days. Adorning this ring are precious stones (possibly immortal diamonds, though Herbert does not specify), and the light reflected from one of them is entirely too brilliant or perhaps too dark for merely mortal eyes to perceive.

> The statelier cabinet is the *Trinitie*,
> Whose sparkling light accesse denies:
> Therefore thou dost not show
> This fully to us, till death blow
> The dust into our eyes:
> For by that powder thou wilt make us see.

The other jewel, since cut in the shape of Theanthropos, might also be impenetrably dark were it not for the fact that one of its facets is the Incarnation, an embodiment or carnalization experienced by every human soul. Herbert thus can round off the preceding poems, even though this one is not quite finished, by concentrating on the elemental simplicity of Christ's birth on Christmas day. Especially is this true because he has already manifested in multiple ways the subtleties of the event and of the season in which it occurs. There is, however, a complication that in Herbert's view simply must not be left out. Jewel *cabinets* (as well as the jewels themselves) have been stressed in preceding stanzas. These now become *boxes*, and while the change seems small and perhaps rather homely, the implication is that the cabinet of the Incarnation redeems the coffin box of mortal flesh.

> But all thy sweets are packt up in the other;
> Thy mercies thither flock and flow:

That as the first affrights,
This may allure us with delights;
Because this box we know;
For we have all of us just such another.

I also should not forget, since in the forward-looking last stanza Herbert himself does not, that "Sinnes have their box apart, / Defrauding thee, who gavest two for one."

"LOOKING BACK" IN *SILEX SCINTILLANS* AND *THALIA REDIVIVA*

Setting aside the symbolic density of "Christmas," one can observe that Herbert's sequence often must be more diffuse than Donne's "Nativitie" if only because some of the same materials are being distributed over four poems, not one. Those attracted to the subject may well find the fuller treatment the more satisfying of the two, however, because Herbert fleshes out the skeleton without misplacing any of the bones. Multiple time schemes, the language of oxymoron, structural diversity, and imagistic richness—all of these enliven Herbert's series, and it thus has the further advantage of translating narrative into highly dramatic monologue and biblical history into intensely personal experience.

It was, after all, the Magi who journeyed, the shepherds to whom angels sang, and it is the Church that customarily offers a Collect and provides a pulpit. Herbert, however, imaginatively plays all the roles himself, bringing past time into the present and making old situations seem autobiographically fresh and new. Each script—the plea, the quest and discovery, the song, and the homily—could be enacted independently, a fact clearly demonstrated in verse by other writers, but equally clear is that these versions lend substance to one another. Herbert's surprise and relief in "Christmas," though fully understandable in their own terms, assume added dimension when they follow the bitter disappointment of "Deniall." The emotional hyperbole of "The shepherds sing," while not much greater (if at all) than that of other poems for Christmas, becomes particularly vivid when set off by the theological commentary of "Ungratefulnesse." The first and fourth poems not only benefit from but probably *require* sequential reading. "Deniall" and "Ungratefulnesse," after all, are not titles that automatically conjure up Christmas, nor are they likely to be recognized without the two poems in between.

Sequence is important for other Christmas poems but not often so critically. Wither and Taylor label their Advent verse in large, easily read letters; the former mentions three major comings while the latter versifies a pericope for Advent 1. Herbert, however, starts out from the Collect for Advent 4 and does so without announcing the fact in advance. Alabaster's fifteen sonnets on the Incarnation loudly proclaim their subject; Herbert's discourse is "Ungratefulnesse." In the 1648 edition of *Steps to the Temple,* Crashaw's "In the Holy Nativity" is followed by "New Year's Day" and next by "In the Glorious Epiphanie." Since the second poem is one for Circumcision day, the three can be read sequentially, and an advantage of doing so, perhaps not otherwise gained, is noticing that the symbolism of "Oriens," one of Christ's names, links all three of them. In 1646, however, the Nativity and Circumcision poems were separated by other verse, and the Epiphany poem (presumably—or at least possibly—not yet written) was not given at all.[9]

For Vaughan, however, sequence—or, to be scrupulous in the wording, sequential proximity—was even more important than for Herbert. I earlier brought up this idea, without making comparisons to other writers, in connection with poems leading toward or away from baptism. I need to return to it here because of poems placed on both sides of verse for the Nativity, specifically two small clusters in *Silex Scintillans* and a fairly numerous assemblage in *Thalia Rediviva.* In each of these groups, discrete contemplations of unrelated subjects appear to be following one another in no discernible order until one poem in particular calls a momentary halt by demanding a consideration of how Vaughan got there and/or of where he may be heading next.

"The Shephards" is a poem in the *Silex* that makes this demand. Since these are indeed the visitors to the manger on Christmas day, there is nothing mysterious about their identity or mission except for how they could have been so fortunate as to find the way. "How," Vaughan asks,

> How happend it that in the dead of night
> You only saw true light,
> While *Palestine* was fast a sleep, and lay
> Without one thought of Day.
> (5–8)

One of the answers is that the shepherds, not unlike the Magi who arrive twelve days later, were guided by stars, and the evidence is "The Constellation," the preceding poem.

That these stars have no overt connection to a birth in Bethlehem is a point that must be temporarily conceded. The providentially designed purpose of their "Fair, order'd lights" (1) is to demonstrate inherently

---

9. George Williams, in his headnote for the Epiphany poem, was quite confident that it "should be considered as one of a trio" (*The Complete Poetry of Richard Crashaw,* 39; and see 76 for a similar remark heading the Nativity poem). His format, however, precluded printing them together in liturgical order, and despite the meticulous work by Williams and Martin on Crashaw's text(s), the relationships among the various versions and printings of Crashaw's poems, including these three, are less certain than one would like.

"exact obedience" (5) to the First Mover and hence to serve as exemplary beacons to "*Obedience, Order, Light*" (29).

> So guide us through this Darknes, that we may
> Be more and more in love with day.
> Settle, and fix our hearts, that we may move
> In order, peace, and love,
> And taught obedience by thy whole Creation,
> Become an humble, holy nation.
>
> (53–58)

Alan Rudrum's annotations establish that a probable background for this prayer is the civil and religious strife so virulently rampant in the 1640s and the 1650s. What Vaughan sees is a situation round about him in which, alas, "guides prove wandring stars" (46); he is persuaded that it is "*these* mists" (italics added) and the "black days" of his own time for which erroneous false lights especially "were reserved" (47). "The Constellation," however, long has been and still is visible to anyone at all who chooses to look aright, and from this perspective, obscurity results from perversely miasmic vision rather than absence of light. An historical proof, from Vaughan's point of view, is that Jewish shepherds found their way, though not provided with a life-giving Gospel and with the dead of night all about them, to the fairest and most obedient Light ever to have been seen, a Light grievously needed by self-blinded Gentiles in the 1640s and 1650s and, surely, in other decades as well. In these poems, Vaughan has been evaluating his own present time, among other ways, by rereading two of God's great books, the created universe on the one hand and the Bible on the other, and by discovering an essentially similar corrective message in both. I probably should add that he also has been rediscovering the appalling human capacity to pay scant heed to Truth, regardless of its source and whatever the consequences of error may be; persuasive testimony to this last fact is "Misery," the poem that follows "The Shephards."

Also positioned with considerable care is "Christs Nativity," a title that heads forty-eight lines, which are divisible into two parts or, possibly, two separate poems. Rudrum assigns cumulative line numbers (1–48); L. C. Martin, however, divides 1–30 from part "II" (with new numbers 1–18) and separately enters "How kind is heav'n to man!" (Rudrum's line 31) in his index of first lines.[10] Part I directly concerns the biblical event, but part II, to quote Martin's note, arises from the "Act of Parliament, 23

---

10. Alan Rudrum comments in *The Complete Poems*, 564: "There seems no way of being conclusive [about this matter]; the arrangement in 1650 leaves the matter open." In the hope of some much needed clarity, I refer to part "I" (= Rudrum's lines 1–30) and to what Martin (*The Works of Henry Vaughan*, 443) has already labeled part "II" (= Rudrum's lines 31–48).

December 1644, abolishing observance of Christmas and Good Friday."
(It is worth adding that the Prayer Book was abolished in 1645.) On the
one hand, therefore, ancient history is being relived:

> Awake, glad heart! get up, and Sing,
> It is the Birth-day of thy King,
>   Awake! awake!
>   (Part I, 1–3)

On the other hand, the consequences of recent events are still unfolding:

>   Are we all stone, and Earth?
>   Neither his bloudy passions mind,
>   Nor one day blesse his birth?
>   Alas, my God! Thy birth now here
>   Must not be numbred in the year.
>   (Part II, 14–18)

Balefully conjoining the intervening years is ill health as discoverable
in the past as well as in the present. In the first part, Vaughan draws upon
a pericope read on Epiphany 3 about the miraculous cure of a leper.

>   Let no more
>   This Leper haunt, and soyl thy doore,
>   Cure him, Ease him
>   O release him!
>   (25–28)

But the immediately preceding lines make abundantly clear that the malady
is spiritual, not physical, and that this particular leper's name is "Vaughan."

> I would I had in my best part
> Fit Roomes for thee! or that my heart
>   Were so clean as
>   Thy manger was!
> But I am all filth, and obscene,
> Yet, if thou wilt, thou canst make clean.
>
> Sweet *Jesu*! will then; Let no more
> This Leper . . .

Vaughan's personal life, like the world he sees round about him, has
fallen on evil days. A principal difference, and it is, of course, of para-
mount importance, is that his own spirit is willing, even though the flesh
be not merely weak but corrupt. "Man . . . *should* rise / To offer up the
sacrifice" (Part I, 11–12; italics added). The reply to, "And shall we then
no voices lift?" (Part II, 5) certainly ought to be yes. But external laws of
an inimical Parliament and, for that matter, internal tyrannies of sin—
both are bonds impossible to burst asunder unless the prayer of the first

part is answered: "And let once more by mystick birth / The Lord of life be borne in Earth" (29–30).

This double poem, as I think it now may fairly be called, examines past and present history at the levels of both personal and national experience. Either portion of it conceivably could be anthologized separately, but the whole is greater than a simple sum of its parts. The remedy for a pervasive problem in both sections is the mystic birth positioned in lines 29–30, but at the end of "How kind is heav'n to man," in despite of the kindness, the Nativity itself is not numbered in the year. Vaughan evidently was not sanguine about the immediacy of easement and relief; between him and last Advent at the end of time there stretches out an undetermined—in 1650, an undeterminable—future, and that future appears to be bleak.

"Christs Nativity" thus has much to say about conditions in dire need of inner and outer change but includes nothing directly to the question of their cause. For that point, quite obviously, one must go not forward but back, and in this case that means returning to the poem called "Corruption." Two others are to be met with in between, and a table-of-contents listing therefore takes this form:

Corruption
H. Scriptures
Unprofitablenes
Christs Nativity [I and II]

Since, however, it is the fourth item on this list that looks back to the first, reading the poems themselves, as distinct from glancing at a table of contents, pretty well has to be bidirectional. As it happens, several surprises are in store from either direction, among them the initial discrepancy between the title of "Unprofitablenes" and its opening line: "How rich, O Lord, how fresh thy visits are!" The incongruity evidently arises from the fact that personal experience has long been cyclic: "bleak leaves hopeles hung" (2), but "since thou didst in one sweet glance survey / Their sad decays, I flourish" (7–8). This renewal looks distinctly promising, but the Psalter sounds a warning note: "I my selfe haue seene the vngodly . . . flourishing [Authorized Version: "spreading himself"] like a greene Bay tree. And I went by, and loe he was gone: I sought him, but his place could no where be found" (Prayer Book Psalm 37.36–37). "But, ah, my God!" Vaughan exclaims; "what fruit hast thou of this?" (13).

> What one poor leaf did ever I yet fall
>   To wait upon thy wreath?
> Thus thou all day a thankless weed doest dress,
>   And when th'hast done, a stench, or fog is all
> The odour I bequeath.
>   (14–18, the concluding lines)

"Unprofitablenes" balances Vaughan's personal account against the more general ledger that is reckoned up in "How kind is heav'n to man," the second part of "Christs Nativity." Richly fresh visits, it seems, have been no more profitably bestowed on Vaughan than kindness on a people who refuse to include the birth of their savior in the official calendar year. "H. Scriptures" opens up similar parallels. "Welcome dear book," it begins. "Thou art the great *Elixer*" (6), "The Key" (7), "The *Word* in Characters, God in the *Voice*" (8). These are indeed glad tidings, but the best news of all, from the purely personal perspective of one who must "plead in groans" (10), is the sacrificial tragedy behind the words italicized (by Vaughan and/or his printer) in the last line: *"Sweet Saviour thou didst dye!"* In Vaughan's ordering, at least in this particular group of poems, the Passion precedes the Nativity and confers even greater value on it; one of the consequences is that the two events appear with chronological inversion in the question asked in the second part of "Christs Nativity": "Neither his bloudy passions mind, / Nor one day blesse his birth?"

"Corruption" takes one back not only to the far distant cause behind subsequent events, both good and bad, but even to the sinless condition that preceded corruption itself. It also will take one forward to the ultimate future but not immediately. "Sure, It was so," Vaughan asserts in opening the poem, as if with another sudden "epiphany," he had never before noticed the sharp contrast between what "was so" and what is. "Man in those early days . . . shin'd a little" (1, 3), "saw Heaven o'r his head, and knew from whence / He came" (5–6), "sigh'd for *Eden*, and would often say / *Ah! what bright days were those?*" (19–20). But now, "Almighty *Love!* where are thou now?" (29). Man "raves" (31), "Sin triumphs still, and man is sunk below / The Center" (35–36). The change evidently began when the preexistent soul first "came (condemned,) hither" (6), but a further alteration, devastating in its consequences, dates from first sin: "He drew the Curse upon the world, and Crackt / The whole frame with his fall" (15–16). Corruption has been flourishing like the bay tree from that day to this, ever more so in fact as darker times have succeeded times already darkened, despite fresh visits, holy Scriptures, a Passion followed by a Nativity, and God's lavish kindnesses.

If, however, the present time of 1650 was grim and the future both bleak and not determinable, the final outcome, in Vaughan's opinion, was by no means unpredictable.

> All's in deep sleep, and night; Thick darknes lyes
> And hatcheth o'r thy people;
> But hark! what trumpets that? what Angel cries
> *Arise! Thrust in thy sickle.*
>
>   ("Corruption," the closing lines)

> And I looked, and behold, a white cloud, and vpon the cloud one sate
> like vnto the Sonne of man, hauing on his head a golden crowne, and in his
> hand a sharpe sickle. And another Angel came out of the Temple crying
> with a loud voyce to him that sate on the cloud: Thrust in thy sickle and
> reape, for the time is come for thee to reape, for the haruest of the earth is
> ripe. (Revelation 14.14–15)

Because the human soul "came (condemned,) hither," Christ began to
come even earlier; he continued and continues his coming through the
Incarnation and by means of "mystick birth"; and he shall come again
to gather "the vine of the earth, and cast it into the great wine-presse
of the wrath of God" (Revelation 14.19). For St. John, that day, that
day of wrath is surely coming, and whatever else might be darkly ob-
scure, Vaughan evidently agreed that at least that much is harrowingly
clear.

But what of the infants, those who in their own "early days" have
already been reaped? Vaughan's praise of their innocence and the sharp
sickle of Revelation 14 directs attention to Holy Innocents day, December
28, and to the pericope, also taken from Revelation 14, appointed in
place of the Epistle: "And they sung as it were a new song before the seate
. . . and no man could learne the song, but the hundreth and xliiii thou-
sand, which were redeemed from the earth" (14.3). Boys, commenting on
this day, supposes the new song to be little different from "*Adams* old
song before his fall, to praise God for his creation in holinesse and righ-
teousnesse" (*Festivall* 1:114). The newness as such, Boys continues, con-
sists in "our redemption and regeneration, whereby Gods image lost by
sinne is restored in vs againe." Newness, one might say, is old innocence
re-created from corruption.

Vaughan's "Corruption" thus doubles back upon itself in the conclud-
ing lines and does so all the more after one becomes aware of "Christs
Nativity," one leaf of the book away. "Thick darkes . . . hatcheth" in
dark parody of the Holy Ghost brooding o'er the vast abyss to make it
pregnant, but the Nativity, accompanied by multiple Advents, announces
the arrival of new Light and of the new-old Song. New heavens and
earth, moreover, inevitably will rise from the chaos of this world when
time shall be whether Parliament and Vaughan are prepared for them or
not. At the present moment, however, when Christmas cannot be cele-
brated at all because of outside law nor be fully realized because of inside
sin, then the medial position of "Unprofitablenes" becomes ponderable:
with "Corruption" and "H. Scriptures" before and the two-part "Christs
Nativity" after, it looks to be, both visually and thematically, heart-
breakingly placed in between.

By 1678, when *Thalia Rediviva* (Thalia, the muse of comedy, revived)
was published, the political and official ecclesiastical center had shifted,

but titles and internal allusions (as Martin and Rudrum point out) indicate that much of the volume's content dates from many years before.[11] The book divides into three parts—one for occasional verse, a second for verse translations from various sources, a third for verse under the subtitle "Pious thoughts and Ejaculations"—plus an appendage ("Daphnis. An Elegiac *Eclogue*"). I doubt that "Thalia" is anything more than a nominal convenience (the title does have fine syllabic resonance), but perhaps Vaughan had divine comedy in mind as the broadly inclusive backdrop for the many spiritual ironies presented in the third of his sections.

About halfway through the pious thoughts is "The Nativity. Written in the year 1656." The title implies a twofold interest, the original happening of so many years ago but also the remembrance of it so many years later, and Vaughan follows up this insinuation by starting the poem with a series of questions and answers that relate to both present and past. "Peace? and to all the world?"

> sure, one
> And he the prince of peace, hath none.
> He travels to be born, and then
> Is born to travel more agen.
> Poor *Galile*! thou can'st not be
> The place for his Nativity.
> His restless mother's call'd away,
> And not deliver'd, till she pay.
>
> (1-8)

Since I have called attention to present tense so repeatedly, Vaughan's verbs by now may look sufficiently pious to be above suspicion. "Till she pay," however, might be viewed—especially by puritans—as low cunning on Vaughan's part. It opens the way for a second question and answer, "A *Tax*? 'tis so still! we can see / The Church thrive in her misery." And this variation is topical: "Vaughan probably refers to the Decimation Tax imposed on Royalists in 1655. The tax was extended at the end of 1656 so as to fall on lower incomes" (Martin's annotation).

The poem's title exposes the chronological disparity between the event and its timely celebration—or rather, since the ceremonies and the Prayer Book containing them had been abolished, the untimely lack thereof. And the poem itself immediately asserts simultaneity in order to underline spiritual disparity between what should be and what is. In 1656,

---

11. A secular example is "The King Disguised. *Written about the same time that Mr.* John Cleveland *wrote his.*" "Presumably written soon after 27 April 1646, when Charles left Oxford dressed as a gentleman's servant" (Martin's note, *Works*, 757); "Cleveland's *The King's Disguise* [was] first printed in 1647" (Rudrum's note, 648).

Christmas is primarily doleful, not cheerful, but (Vaughan adds), "Great *Type* of passions! come what will, / Thy grief exceeds all *copies* still" (15–16). Slightly earlier, Christ's own royalty lay concealed: "A *stable* was thy *Court*" (21); a "poor *Manger* was thy *Throne*" (24). Even now, in 1656, "thy Star runs *page*, and brings / Thy tributary *Eastern* Kings" (33–34). If a western Commonwealth were to follow suit, all might still be well. "Lord! grant some *Light* to us, that we / May with them find the way to thee" (35–36). As it is, however, a re-creation of some kind will be required, for in 1656, primordial chaos has come again.

> Behold what mists eclipse the day:
> How dark it is! shed down one *Ray*
> To guide us out of this sad night,
> And say once more, *Let there be Light*.

As "The Nativity" ends, one is looking ahead to what may be an exceedingly distant future redress for present ills, but one also and unquestionably is looking back at the anciently remote origins of everything. Taken alone, this poem, despite its subject, seems no more optimistic than "Christs Nativity" proved to be. Context, however, especially the somber tones of "Corruption," darkens one's view of the poem in *Silex Scintillans*, or at any rate ought to, and the context of *Thalia Rediviva* ought to operate in contrary fashion when reading the poem for 1656. This point, as I see it, is worth making in its own right, and a second advantage in tracing out the pattern of "Pious thoughts and Ejaculations" is that it indicates why as well as how Vaughan threads poems together. With this proposition out in the open, the following list of titles in ongoing consecutive order probably gives away part of my argument in advance, but if this series is to be kept in mind, then being able to glance ahead from Vaughan's exceedingly odd starting point will be necessary.

> Looking back
> The Shower
> Discipline
> The Ecclipse
> Affliction
> Retirement
> The Revival
> The Day-spring
> The Recovery
> The Nativity. Written in the year 1656

Looking forward from "Looking back," those acquainted with Vaughan's other work will perceive a wealth of suggestive detail, partly from the titles themselves. There is, moreover, a process at work the existence of which may not be suspected any earlier than "The Day-spring" or "The

Recovery," and perhaps "The Nativity" itself is needed to make apparent that a subject these ten poems share is the (re)birth and recovering of the dayspring who from on high hath visited us. It is clear, at any rate, that having reached "The Nativity," it is we who need to be looking back at the preceding poems.

Backing up, therefore, to "The Recovery," one notices an Epiphany motif in the initial address to the sun, "Fair *Vessell* of our daily light," and Vaughan's announcement, "I have a *Sun* now of my own" (12). Diurnal light, by no means the "willing shiner" of Herbert's "The Shepherds sing," is instead, by invidious comparison, a "weak *Shiner*" (16). Only "blind *Persians*" (or possibly not yet converted Magi) would "bow" (16) toward that lesser light; the truer "*Sun*,"

> which tramples on thy head,
> From his own bright, eternal *Eye* doth shed
> One living *Ray*.
> (17–19)

The phrasing is too verbally close to the slightly later prayer, "Shed down one *Ray*" ("Nativity," 38), to be accidental, and the momentarily curious thing is that the subsequent prayer has been answered before Vaughan ever uttered it. One might conclude, tentatively but with impeccable orthodoxy, that God's prevenient grace anticipated Vaughan's need and that if the Ray had not already been shed, then the later request for it could not have been made. What "The Recovery" recovers, therefore, is evident, even though no verbal echoes of the title are to be heard in the poem: the Son, displaced by the sun, particularly in blind religions, is newly rediscovered and repossessed. The unfavorable side of this situation is that somewhere and somehow in the small vacant space between "The Recovery" and "The Nativity," the Son-Sun has again been temporarily lost.

The process of recovery did not begin, moreover, in the poem with that title. "The Day-spring," one poem earlier, backs one up to literal and symbolic dawns. God's "loving *Dove*," it is true, often can "soare about us, while we sleep" (33),

> but always without fail
> Before the slow Sun can unveile,
> In new *Compassions* breaks like light,
> And *Morning-looks*, which scatter night.
> (35–38)

A symbolic reason why this can be so is the presence of "Oriens," the dayspring himself. The Douai translation of Zechariah 6.12, "Behold a man, the Orient is his name," was quoted earlier (in connection with

Crashaw) as the Old Testament text behind the New Testament variant in Luke 1.78. The Vulgate and/or Septuagint version of Zechariah would have done just as well, but I skipped over the Authorized Version (and the Hebrew) because Orient is *not* the name given there: instead, "Behold, the man whose name is the Branch." Biblical commentators were able to reconcile these differences, but the point needed here is that Vaughan's title alludes to one version, and the poem's first lines to the other.

> Early, while yet the *dark* was gay,
> And *gilt* with stars, more trim than day:
> Heav'ns *Lily*, and the Earth's chast *Rose*:
> The green, immortal BRANCH arose;
> And in a solitary place
> Bow'd to his father his bless'd face.

Vaughan adds a marginal reference to Mark 1.25: "And in the morning, rising vp a great while before day, he went out, and departed into a solitary place, and there prayed."

Return to "The Revival," and in that poem's last line one sees "The *Lilies* of his love"; the flowers prepare for "Heavn's *Lily*" as very shortly revealed in the lines just quoted. Retreat a bit more, and in the opening lines of "The Revival" there is an urgent imperative to human flowers who are as yet unsanctified.

> Unfold! unfold! take in his light,
> Who makes thy Cares more short than night.
> The Joys, which with his *Day-star* rise,
> He deals to all, but drowsy Eyes.

Return with Vaughan to "Retirement," and one discovers a solitary place suitable for prayer and also a pastoral landscape wherein "*rural shades* are the sweet fense / Of piety and innocense" (21–22). "If *Eden* be on Earth at all, / 'Tis that, which we the *Country* call" (27–28, the last lines).

This pastoral locale is not far removed from the traditional Christmas scene, and that the comparison is not factitious is evidenced by the Advent cry heard in "Affliction," the preceding poem: "O come, and welcom! Come" (1); "O come" (13). The title reminds me of Herbert's "Deniall," possibly because "The Ecclipse" has already explained Vaughan's ardent cry by setting forth a situation in which Son and Sun have so disappeared from sight that Vaughan feels impelled to ask, "Whither, O whither did'st thou fly / When I did grieve thine holy Eye?" (1–2). The grievance itself explicitly and previously occurred in "Discipline," where "Acts of grace and a long peace / Breed but rebellion and displease" (7–8). "Fair prince of life, lights living well" is the first line of "Discipline," an ironic one as it turns out, and for the living well itself, one needs to back

up to the opening line of "The Shower": "Waters above! eternal Springs!"
Even this fountainhead, however, is not quite the starting point.

"Looking back," generally speaking, would be a strange title with
which to begin anything, but except for the prefatory "To his Books," this
is nonetheless the first of the "Pious thoughts and Ejaculations," and as
eventually becomes apparent—though rather later than sooner—there is
exceptional propriety in the fact that a series of poems so repeatedly and
consistently regressive should commence in this way. There is spiritual
propriety to be discerned as well. In terms of personal experience, the
title is explained by Vaughan's penchant for introspective memories of his
own past innocence, and the looking back is to "The *days* and *nights* of
my first, happy age" (3). In terms of transcendental experience, intro-
spection of the self in its original condition—as created, that is, in the
image of God—can lead one to look even farther back to perceive behind
the image the divine Creator who fashioned it. The idea is in no way
idiosyncratic or peculiar, but the imperfection of postlapsarian human
vision emerges here in imagery that is both strikingly paradoxical and
very much in keeping with the series of poems that follows. Alluding to
Yahweh's pronouncement in Exodus 33.3, "Thou shalt see my backe parts:
but my face shall not be seene," Vaughan ends "Looking back" with an
exclamation. "How brave" (how splendid, that is) "a prospect" ("pro"
[forward or ahead] + "specto" [see]),

> How brave a prospect is a bright *Back-side*!
> Where flow'rs and palms refresh the Eye:
> And days well spent like the glad *East* abide,
> Whose morning-glories cannot dye![12]

Since a farther retreat is scarcely imaginable, it is from this starting point
that Vaughan prospectively views the light of "Oriens": created and re-
created in and by Christ, manifested in The Day-spring, eclipsed through
lack of human discipline, rediscovered in affliction and retirement, re-
peatedly obscured, and also revived (whether celebrated or not) on the
annual recurrence of Christmas day.

These ten poems, then, from "Looking back" through "The Nativity,"
are not only consecutive but unconventionally sequential. Given "The

12. Rudrum points out (*Complete Poems*, 679) that the first of these four lines "found its
way into D. B. Wyndham-Lewis's *The Stuffed Owl*, an anthology of sublimely bad verse";
he further remarks, "Vaughan was incautious in using the word ["backside"]; it has biblical
sanction, but *OED* illustration of its sense of 'posterior or rump' goes back to about 1500."
The point, however, is that Vaughan follows the Bible and Prayer Book, both of which also
violate modern canons of taste; the Hebrew word translated by "backe parts" in the Autho-
rized Version of Exodus 33.3 is "achor," elsewhere translated as "hinder part(s)," as in the
Psalter's version of Psalm 78.67, "Hee smote his enemies in the hinder parts: and put them to
a perpetual shame."

Nativity," one can retrace associated ideas and themes and symbols. What the procedure, itself an unequivocal "looking back," enables one to perceive is the necessarily reiterated and continuing coming of God to a fallen humanity that persistently alienates itself from the very source of its being. On Christmas day, however, God *has* come, and the subject modulates, again necessarily, to how people may replicate the shepherds and the Magi in coming back to God.

> Thou cam'st from heav'n to earth, that we
> Might go from Earth to Heav'n with thee.
> And though thou found'st no welcom here,
> Thou didst provide us *mansions* there.
>
> ("The Nativity," 17–20)

Eight poems follow "The Nativity" to close out the "Pious thoughts and Ejaculations," and in them Vaughan ponders what things might (and might not) be profitably considered by pilgrims en route to "mansions there." Titles and subjects again are discrete entities, but with Christmas as an enlightening (as well as a fresh) point of renewed departure, the cumulative effect is soon felt.

The return includes observing the principles of "The true Christmas" despite parliamentary prohibitions against celebrating the day, and it depends on a sacramental partaking of what "The Request" refers to as "those rare *Repasts*." Three Latin poems next appear: "Jordanis" or Jordan, the scene of Christ's baptism and the symbolic source of all purifying waters; "Servilii Fatum, *sive* Vindicta divina," "The Fate of Servilius or Divine Punishment," a contemplation of the rewards for good and evil lives; and "De Salmone" or "Concerning a Salmon," a mindless fish that takes a deceitful lure. The salmon, more or less allegorically, is mankind, the bait is the guile of evil, and the sullying stream or whirlpool ("gurges") where the fish is beguiled is this world. An immediately subsequent poem examines "The World" in search of "the sure *rode*" to the "last and lov'd *Abode*." "The Bee," in the poem that follows, furnishes a clue with "her unwearied Industry"; Vaughan proposes to take the hint and hence to "fly home, and *hive* with" God. The eighth poem, "To Christian Religion," bids farewell to the Church Militant of this world in anticipation of "the next *Nativity* / Of Truth and brightness." This one, whenever it rolls round, will be the last Advent of all, the one to occur when "*The Spirit and the Bride say, Come.*"

An abiding concern within the series as a whole is the continually variable relationships between two comings, God's to his people and his people's to him. Some of these relationships are predicated on the comings manifested in the Christmas cycle; others, on manifestations of divine providence in natural phenomena that function as guides and signposts for human efforts to look back and return to the ultimate source of all existence. The "rapprochement" of the natural, the human, and the divine is exceptionally clear in "The Day-spring," and since that is true, requoting lines 1–6 in order to add 7–20 will not be, I hope, an excessive redundancy.

> Early, while yet the *dark* was gay,
> And *gilt* with stars, more trim than day:
> Heav'ns *Lily*, and the Earth's chast *Rose*:
> The green, immortal BRANCH arose;
> And in a solitary place
> Bow'd to his father his bless'd face.
>   If this calm season pleas'd my *Prince*,
> Whose *fullness* no need could evince,
> Why should not I poor, silly sheep
> His *hours*, as well as *practice* keep?
> Not that his hand is tyed to these,
> From whom *time* holds his transient *Lease*:
> But *mornings*, new Creations are,
> When men all night sav'd by his Care,
> Are still reviv'd; and well he may
> Expect them grateful with the day.
> So for that first drawght of his hand,
> Which finish'd heav'n and sea and land,
> The *Sons* of God their thanks did bring,   Job *c.* 38.
> And all the *Morning-stars* did sing.   *v.* 7.

"This calm season" is, first of all, the early morning when Christ went forth to pray, thereby providing Vaughan a pattern for the time of prayer as well as the activity, "hours" and "practice" both. Also suggestively present is the morn of Christmas day when the Day-spring came forth from darkness. I admit to being influenced here by the fact that Vaughan's marginal reference (reproduced above from Martin's text) alludes to the same passage in Job—when God "layd the foundations of the earth . . . the morning starres sange together, and all the sons of God shouted for joy"—that Milton found appropriate in composing "On the Morning of Christ's Nativity."

> Such music (as 'tis said)
> Before was never made,
>   But when of old the sons of morning sung,
> While the Creator Great
> His constellations set,
>   And the well-balanc't world on hinges hung.
>   (117–22)

But in addition to Milton and Job, "When the time was full come, God sent his sonne made of a woman" (Galatians 4.4, Epistle for the Sunday after Christmas), and then was born "the Prince of Peace" (Isaiah 9.6, Old Testament lesson for Christmas day). This calm season also is or may be any and every dawn. Up until that final moment when time's lease expires, new mornings will succeed one another to illuminate the way to the Pastor of poor, silly sheep who so frequently (as in Isaiah of old and more recently in Herbert's "Christmas") have gone so far astray. Over and beyond but not separate from everything else, Christmas day and each morning thereafter, including those on which Christ and Vaughan went forth, are prefigurative re-creations: they hearken back to the original foundation of the world and, if rightly regarded, anticipate new heavens and earth that restore first heavens and earth. By progressing forward to the end, the mornings of time glance back and ultimately return themselves to the invisible beginning when the Word in all eternity began to come.

Forward motion, in short, is retrogressive in its effect, and that is the informing rationale behind this entire series of poems. Foreshadowed by "Looking back" and exemplified thereafter, the point emerges with greatest clarity when, in "To Christian Religion," Vaughan looks forward to another return. O *"Morning-star"* (5), "O blessed *shiner*, tell me whither / Thou wilt be gone, when night comes hither?" (7–8). The answer, however, is foreknown, among other reasons because Herbert had ended *The Temple* with "The Church Militant," a poem in which he followed the westward progress of the Church—and also of Sin—until the west became once again the east and The Church Triumphant stood forth in glory. "A *Seer*," Vaughan writes, elevating Herbert from poet to prophet,

> A *Seer* that observ'd thee in
> Thy Course, and watch'd the growth of Sin,
> Hath giv'n his Judgment and foretold,
> That *West-ward* hence thy *Course* will hold:
> And when the day with us is done,
> There fix, and shine a glorious Sun.
>
> (9–14)

If, however, the glorious Sun even now is on its way to displace darkness "there," then what it is leaving behind "here" is diminishing light and ever more pervasive gloom. Another and final return needs, therefore, to be looked for.

> O hated *shades* and *darkness*! when
> You have got here the Sway agen,
> And like unwholsome *fogs* withstood
> The light, and blasted all that's good:
> Who shall the happy *shepherds* be
> To watch the next *Nativity*

> Of Truth and brightness, and make way
> For the returning, rising day?
> O! what year will bring back our bliss,
> *Or who shall live, when God doth this?*
> (15–24)

Vaughan's rhetorical question implies its own answer, even though no calendar year or date can be specified. When the looking back is so comprehensive that what once was shall have been again, when the future becomes quite completely the past, then paradise lost shall have been regained, and no one will live for all shall be changed. Vaughan appends to this poem a quotation from Revelation 22, that is to say from the last chapter (though this is not quite the last verse) of the Bible's last book. The postscript is an oxymoron in that it looks hopefully forward but nonetheless is about as final as anything could possibly be:

> *Revel.* Chap. last, vers. 17.
> *The Spirit and the Bride say, Come.*

JONSON'S HYMN

Christmas was an optic glass through which Vaughan viewed time from Creation to Judgement Day. It magnified diverse objects from salmon at one extreme to the Day-spring at another but also reduced to manageable proportions the scope of the whole. Each event in this long history, whether personal, natural, or biblical, tends to be a partial synecdoche in which, providentially, the part stands for much of the whole, and Advent in its various senses at varying times becomes, as it were, the synecdoche of the synecdoches. The Christmas cycle was a lens for other poets as well, and if most of them saw rather less through it than Vaughan did, they frequently saw quite enough. Journeys to "Oriens," worthy and unworthy gifts, creation and re-creation of micro- and macrocosmic worlds, manifestation of Truth and displacement of idolatry, time and its epochs shifting themselves down into transposable moments that expand toward eternity—these are wide-eyed visions, but they are what Christmas can allow one to behold, and many Christmas poems take advantage of the opportunity thus afforded.

And yet—this point must be emphasized, not merely acknowledged—the themes and motifs just catalogued have always been optional, not obligatory. The fact is intrinsically obvious, no doubt, but one might think of the many extraordinarily lovely carols, including medieval ones, which conclusively establish it. Or one might consider a poem by Ben Jonson.

A HYMN
ON THE NATIVITY OF MY SAVIOUR

I sing the birth was born tonight,
The author both of life and light;
   The angels so did sound it,
And like, the ravished shepherds said,
Who saw the light and were afraid,
   Yet searched, and true they found it.

The Son of God, the Eternal King,
That did us all salvation bring,
   And freed the soul from danger;
He whom the whole world could not take,
The Word, which heaven and earth did make,
   Was now laid in a manger.

The Father's wisdom willed it so,
The Son's obedience knew no No,
   Both wills were in one stature;
And as that wisdom had decreed,
The Word was now made flesh indeed,
   And took on him our nature.

What comfort by him do we win,
Who made himself the price of sin,
   To make us heirs of glory!
To see the babe, all innocence,
A martyr born in our defence,
   Can man forget this story?

In pre–Reformation England, three masses were customary on Christmas day. Gospels for the first two were supplied by the simple expedient of dividing Luke's historical narrative into two parts, 2.1–14 and 15–20; John 1.1–14, the theological account of the Word made flesh, provided the third.[13] In his first three stanzas, Jonson preserves this order but inverts the ratio between the parts: one for history and two for significance. He next adds a fourth stanza that, if the poem were a sermon, would be an "application": the moral correlation between the pericope(s) and one's personal life. Jonson asks rhetorical questions instead of preaching, but "heirs of glory" and "babe . . . innocence . . . martyr" function in much the same fashion as homiletic exhortations.

Within this stanzaic structure Jonson develops progressively more inclusive human involvement with the divine event and its import for later times. He begins personally, "I sing," but since Christ assumed "our nature" and thus brought salvation to "us all," by the end of the poem, the

13. Riley, *Eucharistic Year*, 31.

broadly impersonal question is, "Can man forget this story?" The two modes partially parallel the personal immediacy of a human child and the impersonal remoteness of the unincarnated Word, but smooth progressions from singular to plural pronouns (I . . . us) and then to a collective noun (Mankind) downplay the oxymoron that underlies and informs the thought.

Understatement, in fact, characterizes the entire poem. Since the one "born in our defence" was Theanthropos, Jonson does not totally dispense with oxymoron, but overt examples are few and, in comparison to those found elsewhere, are decidedly subdued. "The Word, which heaven and earth did make, / Was now laid in a Manger." "The Word was now made flesh indeed." The continuing relevance of history is assumed to be true, but Jonson does not transpose the planes of time to make this point. He "applies" the past to the present in, "What comfort by him do we win"; the line reminds me—and has some of the same force—of the injunction at Eucharist, "Heare what comfortable [not "soothing" but *strengthening:* "cum" + "fortis"] words our Sauiour Christ saith vnto all that truely turne to him." The present moment in which Jonson sings nonetheless continues to be firmly distinct from the past time of the Nativity itself. Jonson recognizes, as other poets did, that Christmas day does not stand in splendid isolation, but he introduces no multiple advents nor any epiphany travels. Instead, he darts an eye back to causation ("The Word, which heaven, and earth did make") and briefly glances ahead to purposive effect ("To make us heirs of glory"). In short, Jonson omits as much oxymoron as possible and attenuates that which remains. Making small use of methods so favored by others, Jonson as usual elects to write his own kind of poem. His hymn, even so, would be finely appropriate and perhaps all the more forcefully felt if sung and heard in church at midnight on Christmas.

"ON THE MORNING OF CHRIST'S NATIVITY. COMPOSED 1629"

While some of the pericopes for December 25 have been scattered about in preceding pages, the reason for bringing them together at this point is that, when taken collectively, they intensify one's perception of the extraordinary splendor of Milton's poem for Christmas. A systematic list could start with the Old Testament and thus with the six proper psalms (19, 45, 85, 89, 110, and 132) and much of Isaiah 7 and 9; Luke 2 and John 1 supply the Gospels; and the Epistles are taken from Hebrews 1 and Titus 3. With invaluable assistance from the expositions of Boys and Sparrow (to whom blanket acknowledgment is thankfully made, in lieu of strung-out footnotes), one sees rather quickly that these pericopes must have been chosen with meticulous care.[14]

Psalm 19.5, customarily interpreted as Messianic, speaks of "the Sunne" that "commeth foorth as a bridegrome out of his chamber." The image of the sun elicits associations with "the light shineth in ye darknes. . . . That light was the true light" (John 1.5 and 9); with "the people that walked in darknesse haue seene a great light" (Isaiah 9.2); and with "the bright-nesse of his glory" (Hebrews 1.3). The "Bridegrome" of Psalm 19 antici-pates the epithalamic language of Psalm 45, "So shall the King haue plea-sure in thy beautie" (vs. 12); "thou shalt haue children: whome thou mayest make princes in all lands" (17). Psalm 45.7–8 further asserts, "Thy seate (O God) endureth for euer: the scepter of thy kingdome is a right Scepter. Thou [the Bridegroom] hast loued righteousnes, and hated iniq-uitie: wherefore God, (euen thy God) hath anointed thee with the oyle of gladnesse aboue thy fellowes." Hebrews 1.8–9, quoting the Psalm, identi-fies the Bridegroom as Christ and the right scepter as Righteousness: "But vnto the sonne, he saith, Thy seat O God, shall bee for euer and euer, the scepter of thy kingdome is a right scepter: Thou hast loued righteous-nesse, & hated iniquitie. Wherefore God (even thy God) hath anointed thee."

The motif of Righteousness in turn suggests Psalm 85.10, the meeting place of the age-old four daughters of God: "Mercie and trueth are met together: righteousnes & peace haue kissed each other." "The Prince of Peace" is, of course, one of Messiah's epithets in Isaiah 9.6, and the proph-ecy in that verse, "Vnto vs a childe is borne, vnto vs a Sonne is giuen," was intimated two chapters earlier, "Behold, a Virgine shall conceiue and beare a sonne" (7.14). When "the same word became flesh, and dwelt among vs" (John 1.14), prophetic utterance was fulfilled, and God began to be speak more directly through the Son. "God in times past, diuersely and many wayes spake vnto the Fathers by Prophets: but in these last daies he hath spoken to vs by his owne sonne, whom he hath made heire of al things, by whom also he made the world" (Hebrews 1.1–2). The idea of "heire" recurs in Titus 3.7, "Being justified by his grace, wee should bee made heires according to the hope of eternal life," and the creative force of the Son is broadened by John 1.3, "All things were made by it [the Word], and without it was nothing made y^t was made."

Cursory description and fragmentary quotation do scant justice to the pericopes but perhaps can suffice to indicate how often they are evoked in Milton's lines. The Word by whom everything was made is "the Creator

14. Since some of the passages next to be quoted are familiar in many quarters because of continued use on Christmas, a reminder may be in order that I do not quote the Commu-nion pericopes and the psalms from the Authorized Version but rather from the 1604 Prayer Book and Psalter (and hence as translated in the Great Bible).

Great" (120) who "cast the dark foundations deep" (123), and the prophets through whom the Word spake in sundry times and diverse manner—among them, Isaiah and the psalmist—are those "holy sages" who "once did sing" (5). The Prince of Peace works us "a perpetual peace" (7), sends down "the meek-ey'd Peace" (46) in the course of a "peaceful . . . night" (61), and thereby enables a fleeting glimpse of three other radiant daughters of God, "Truth" and "Justice" and "Mercy set between" (141, 144).

The Son, veritable image of the Father's glory and source of light for them that walked in darkness, eternally existed as "That glorious Form, that Light unsufferable, / And that far-beaming blaze of Majesty" (8–9). When compared to this "greater Sun" (83), with its equipage of "bright Throne" and "burning Axletree" (84), the solar source "of inferior flame" (81) seems wanly pale—except, perhaps, much later when "the Sun . . . Pillows his chin upon an Orient wave" (229–31). The temptation to italicize "Orient" is strong, but withstanding it for the moment, one notices that even prior to the Bridegroom's luminous appearance, "It was no season" for Nature "To wanton with the Sun, her lusty Paramour" (35–36). And not only does the Son emerge early on as "the Prince of light" (62) as well as of peace, but toward the end, "The rays of *Bethlehem* blind . . . dusky eyn" (224).

This collocation of images from the poem and from pericopes for December 25 could be extended, but it also is important not to lose sight of the cycle of which Christmas is a part. On the day itself, as Herbert notes in "Ungratefulnesse," God opens his treasure boxes; on January 6, the Magi open theirs in return. Collop offers himself, and Milton proposes that the muse proffer a poem.

> Say Heav'nly Muse, shall not thy sacred vein
> Afford a present to the Infant God?
> Hast thou no verse, no hymn, or solemn strain,
> To welcome him to this his new abode?
>
> (15–18)

God's donation of the Son is, however, immeasurably priceless; Milton's gift in return, even at very best, can be only a "humble ode" (24), a "tedious Song" (239). The Magi were sufficiently wise to perceive royalty improbably camped out in a stable, one that Milton's muse perceives to be "Courtly" (243). To them was revealed the mystery of Theanthropos; in this poem, that particular oxymoron is surrounded by others, perhaps most plainly—if that is not a contradiction in terms—with the stupendous paradoxes of "Trinal Unity" (11) on one side, with "wedded Maid, and Virgin Mother" (3) on the other. "Everlasting Day" rhymes with "mortal Clay" (13–14) and can do so here because of the emptying process of kenosis; "that far-beaming blaze of Majesty" (9), "He laid aside . . .

And chose with us a darksome House" (12, 14). The scene is itself appropriately darkened: "Now [another tempting candidate for italics] . . . the Heav'n by the Sun's team untrod, / Hath took no print of the approaching light" (19–20). And yet much illumination can be had, and recurrently so, from two prominent sources in addition to Light Itself. More or less natural stars—as in "Star-led Wizards" (23), "The Stars" (69), and "Heav'n's youngest-teemed Star" (241)—position themselves aloft; here below, the "squadrons bright" (20) that appear early on are later identified as "helmed Cherubim / And sworded Seraphim" (112–13) in "glittering ranks" (114), and they continue to gleam in the poem's last line: "Bright-harness'd Angels sit in order serviceable" (244).

These motifs elsewhere support entire poems or major portions thereof, but the themes developed by Milton are instead the Comings, the symbolism of "Oriens," and the displacement of idolatry. True light and false gods control many of the twenty-seven stanzas of "The Hymn" (lines 28–244), and "Coming," a concept coterminous with the broadest limits of time, informs the thought of the poem as a whole, including the initial stanzas (lines 1–27). Since "coming" arises from Advent, "Oriens" from December 25, and redirected faith from Epiphany, the poem (like the Christmas cycle itself) presents an image of the entirety of time. Multiple Advents are first heralded, moreover, by the poem's title, the implications of which are worth pausing on.

"The Nativity Ode" is an undeniably handy way of referring to the poem, but this short title, however customary, is in the long run a misnomer. It can usefully apply to little more than the first stanza of "The Hymn," where Milton mentions the "Heav'n-born child . . . in the rude manger" (30–31), and the closing lines, when "the Virgin blest, / Hath laid her Babe to rest" (237–38). In between these references, and in the introductory four stanzas, the birth itself and the minutely circumstantial details of Luke's narrative for most practical purposes disappear. The many things left out from Donne's sonnet for this event in large part explain themselves since the fourteen lines of "Nativitie" simply must be quite tightly compressed. But Milton's poem, after all, runs to 244 lines, and very few of them will support the notion that it is an "ode *about* the Nativity." On the contrary, shepherds are mentioned so as to prepare for an image of Christ as "the mighty *Pan*" (89); angelic song gives way to harmony of the spheres as a symbol of perfected reality; and the sleeping babe of the final lines unmistakably reveals himself to be a king and god incomparably more powerful than pagan deities who have fled in frightened disarray.

The full title, even if entirely too fussy for everyday use, is much more helpful and is so in roughly the same way as Donne's "Goodfriday, 1613" or, better yet, Vaughan's "The Nativity. Written in the Year 1656." Since

Milton's poem times itself as being composed on the day when the subject matter of it did-does-shall take place, the time-disruptive consequence is that the celebration coincides with that which is being celebrated. A fur ther consequence of co-incidence, to quote the first of nearly innumerable instances, is the poem's opening line: "This is [as distinct from "that was"] the Month, and this the happy day." Or, to cite a situational counterpart, the Magi have not yet arrived—"See how from far upon the Eastern road / The Star-led Wizards haste with odors sweet" (22–23)—and thus must still be twelve days off. It therefore follows that the "Heav'nly Muse" (15), if it will but "run," can chronologically "prevent"—that is (as in Donne's "Nativitie") come before or precede—"them" (24). "Have thou the honor first," Milton bids, "thy Lord to greet" (26).

Vaughan, however, firmly announces the wide chronological interval between past and present in order to collapse together the disparate moments into self-perpetuating continuation: some of what happened back then is unremittingly happening, alas, even now, including ecclesiastical travail and politically imposed taxation. Milton in effect reverses the process, the import, and the appropriate response. "On" functions as the ambivalent equivalent of Latin "in" (during, in the course of) as well as "de" (concerning). Since it situates and times both poem and subject matter, only after the coincidence, not earlier, is intervallic rift opened up by "Composed 1629." The first line ("This *is*") affirms present glad tidings before "Our great redemption from above *did* bring" (4) validates the claim in terms of completed past action. In Milton, but not in Vaughan, "now" precedes and includes within itself the modes of past-present-future that are subsequently extracted, and a significant factor appears to be the correlation that Milton thus achieves between time and eternity.

Suggestive evidence for this last point is available in the passage from which some phrases have already been quoted.

> That glorious Form, that Light unsufferable,
> And that far-beaming blaze of Majesty,
> Wherewith he wont at Heav'n's high Council-Table,
> To sit the midst of Trinal Unity,
> He laid aside; and here with us to be,
>   Forsook the Courts of everlasting Day,
> And chose with us a darksome House of mortal Clay.
>   (8–14)

The *OED* indicates that "wont," in Milton's day, sometimes could be used without an auxiliary verb but that normative usage even then required an "is," a "was," or a "shall be." Milton may be clinging to the newest of the old in his own usage—he later adopts, after all, the Spenserian Chaucerism "ychain'd" (155). But he may be suppressing the auxiliary because

no one of the possible forms even begins to approximate the full truth of
the matter: this hypostasis of trinal unity is eternally existent, comes into
the world sequentially in terms of the three modes of time, and shall be
sufficiently manifested only when, the future having become the past,
the "now" of eternity begins again.

These particular ramifications need not be insisted on because even
without them it is apparent that the four stanzas prior to "The Hymn"
and the four Sundays of Advent are numerically the same (perhaps coinci-
dentally so) and have, more importantly, very similar functions. They
both introduce and establish the idea that parabolic due season is so much
more significant than mere chronology that verb tense and temporal ref-
erence need to be, as it were, both consistently and carefully inconsistent.
And in "The Hymn" itself (with a few italics added), "It *was* no season
then" for Nature "To wanton with the Sun" (35); "She woo*s* the gentle
Air" (37). Nature's Creator "*sent* down the meek-ey'd Peace" (46); "She
strike*s* a universal Peace" (52). "The Winds . . . Smoothly the waters
kiss*'t*" (64–65); "the mild Ocean, / . . . now *hath* quite forgot to rave, /
While Birds of Calm *sit* brooding on the charmed wave" (66–68).

> The Stars with deep amaze
> Stand fixt in steadfast gaze,
>   Bending one way their precious influence,
> And will not take their flight,
> For all the morning light,
>   Or *Lucifer* that often warn'd them thence;
> But in their glimmering Orbs did glow,
> Until their Lord himself bespake, and bid them go.
>   (69–76)

The concept of past-present-future com*ing* thus precedes and aug-
ments the revelation that "the mighty *Pan* / Was kindly come" (89–90),
and the musical welcome next proffered takes a remarkable but compara-
ble turn of thought of its own. According to Milton's second Prolusion,
"On the Music of the Spheres," it was "Pythagoras alone of mortals" who
"is said to have heard this harmony" (*Complete Poems*, 603). "Ring out ye
Crystal spheres," Milton now asks; "Once bless our human ears" (125–26).

> For if such holy Song
> Enwrap our fancy long,
>   Time will run back, and fetch the age of gold.
>   (133–35)

Hypothetically, musical perfection now being experienced might enable
time to race forward (*will* run) or backward (will run *back*) to anticipate
or to restore a golden age, the temporal classical myth for the spatial

symbol of paradise unlost and/or paradise regained. Here, in this case very much as in Vaughan's "Pious thoughts and Ejaculations," forward movement is retrogressive; "looking back," by moving forward, finally arrives *at* and thus returns *to* the new-old song of (re-)creation. As Job 38 and Vaughan also observe, "Such Music (as 'tis said) / Before was never made, / But when of old the sons of morning sung" (117–19).

Parabolic time arrives at the past by means of the future, when time shall be. On Christmas morning, however, January 6 is a future date, and Epiphany has not yet arrived. In liturgical time, Holy Week cannot begin until Palm Sunday rolls round (in this particular year it occurred on March 21, 1630); in terms of sacred biography, more than thirty years must first elapse; and an exact date of the final coming may not be predictable at all.

> But wisest Fate says no,
> This must not yet be so,
>   The Babe lies yet in smiling Infancy,
> That on the bitter cross
> Must redeem our loss;
>   So both himself and us to glorify:
> Yet first to those ychain'd in sleep,
> The wakeful trump of doom must thunder through the deep,
>
> With such a horrid clang
> As on mount *Sinai* rang
>   While the red fire, and smold'ring clouds outbrake:
> The aged earth aghast,
> With terror of that blast,
>   Shall from the surface to the center shake,
> When at the world's last session,
> The dreadful Judge in middle Air shall spread his throne.
>   (149–64)

These stanzas shake, if they do not uproot, the very foundations of everyday time and, indeed, of the Christmas-card-eggnog season familiarly on sale. From a past-present when Fate says no, they move forward to the past-future of the Crucifixion and then to that ultimate future when the sleep-shattering trumpet of doomsday is to sound. Having arrived at the day of wrath, the lines suddenly recede by means of a simile to that ancient time when Moses received the Law from Yahweh on Sinai and with equal suddenness vault forward again to the terrifying reappearance of the Judge. The simile compounds or implexes these violent transpositions because of possible uncertainty as to whether the referent for "that blast" is the last "wakeful trump" or the earlier "horrid clang" that on Mt. Sinai rang. If one is quick enough to think through the chronology, then "*aged* Earth" resolves the ambiguity, but if one is not, then the tense, two lines later, of "*Shall* . . . shake" makes clear the sequence. I hope, however, I am not the only one who believes that the syntactic suspension, although brief, is sufficient to suggest the folding in and the unfolding out of the future in the past and of the past in the future. In any case, four pivotal moments have been closely congregated together: the promulgation of the Law to Moses, the proclamation in Bethlehem of a new dispensation, the fulfillment in Jerusalem of the Old Law to enable institution of the New, and a final judgement by the Judge.

One of these moments is noted for glorious music and peacefulness, but others are bitter, thunderous, horrid, clangorous, ghastly, terrifying, or dreadful. All of them, nonetheless and indispensably, are not only requisite to "redeem our loss" but also, however much an oxymoron it seems, "So both himself and us to *glorify*" (153–54). Only by keeping that idea very firmly in mind can one leap up and rejoice, as Abraham is said to have done so long ago, to see this extraordinarily special "day." "This *is*" unarguably "the Month, and this the happy morn / Wherein the Son . . . our deadly forfeit should release," but on the far side of the redemptive Cross, "The dreadful Judge in middle Air *shall* spread his throne."

And not until "then," as one sees in the lines (165–67) that immediately follow, do two anomalous present tenses coincide.

> And then at last our bliss,
> Full and perfect is,
> But now begins.

The syntax defies translation, but a rough-and-ready approximation of the sense is this: perfectly full bliss, the Edenic integrity of a long since vanished place and time, is to be replicated in an ultimately future "then" which ever more shall be; and since that surely is so, "our bliss," both because of and despite its futurity, now "begins" and yet also now "is."

I introduced a spurious period after "now begins," but in actuality, of course, the words not only appear in the midst of a stanza but also are only part of a line. As placement and stanzaic form show, an extremely close corollary to what has preceded is that when our bliss begins to be, then Satan's kingdom necessarily begins to end.

> And then at last our bliss,
> Full and perfect is,
>   But now begins; for from this happy day
> Th'old Dragon under ground,
> In straiter limits bound,
>   Not half so far casts his usurped sway,
> And wroth to see his Kingdom fail,
> Swinges the scaly Horror of his folded tail.
>   (165–72)

Filling out the stanza also completes the exposition of comings. For when "the great dragon . . . the olde serpent, called the devill and Satan," begins to fail, then it also is true to say, "Now is come salvation, and strength, and the kingdome of our God, and the power of his Christ" (Revelation 12.9–10).

Milton himself does not mention "the power of . . . Christ," but the lines about the dragon clearly initiate something of their own, the catalogue and banishment of fraudulent gods. This version of the Epiphany motif resembles the one in Crashaw's "In the Glorious Epiphany" in length and ornate mythology, and the shorter, simpler treatments supply helpful commentary. With the dawning of "the sun / Of Righteousness," as Jeremy Taylor insists in "Upon the Epiphany," "Persia might then the sun adore, / It was idolatry no more." Herbert, approaching a similar conclusion in "Ungratefulnesse," but from the opposite direction, observes that with*out* the Nativity, "Gladly had man ador'd the sunne, / And thought his god most brave." In Vaughan's "The Recovery," "blind *Persians*," unable to see true Light, "bow" to a "weak *shiner*," not to the Son. And Crashaw's "cheap AEgyptian Deityes," many of them named and often grotesquely described, disappear: "MITHRA now shall be no name"; "Fatt OSYRIS now / With his fair sister cow, / Shall kick the clouds no more."

The motifs of paganism and steadfast renunciation thereof arise most directly from the turning away of the Magi from false gods to take another way, but hovering somewhere in the background is Ezekiel's vision of "about five and twenty men, with their backes toward the Temple of the Lord, and their faces toward the East, and they worshipped the Sunne toward the East" (8.16). This vision occurs inside "the chambers . . . of imagery" (8.10) wherein Ezekiel also saw "euery forme of creeping things, and abominable beasts, and all the idoles of the house of Israel pourtraied vpon the wall round about" (8.12). "In contempt of God," Matthew Poole annotates (*Commentary* 2:684B), "with an open and designed abrenunciation of God and his worship,"

> though God had prohibited this . . . yet, in imitation of the Chaldees, Persians, Egyptians, Phoenicians, and the Eastern idolaters, these . . . turn their back on God, who created the sun, and worship the creature in contempt of the Creator.

And Matthew Henry, looking at the same passage, usefully adds, "The more glorious we see God to be the more odious we shall see sin to be, especially idolatry, which turns his truth into a lie, his glory into a shame" (*Commentary* 4:792B)

Milton inverts this thinking so as to proclaim that comparisons to idolatrous lies augment the glory of truth, but pagan reflections are mirrored quite as comprehensively in the poem's chambers of imagery as they are in the prophet's. Milton's own extensiveness includes references to private or semi-public spirits in the form of Lemures, the ghosts of the dead, and Lares, gods of the hearth. There are—more accurately, until this day there *were*—Genii, public deities attached to delimited locales, but now "each peculiar power forgoes his wonted seat" (196). More widely adored deities of whole nations become enervated even as they are catalogued, including those of major pagan tribes in the Old Testament as well as those of Egypt, Greece, and Rome. These gods never approach omnipresence, however, no matter how wide their sway, and one of them was driven to "incarnate and imbrute" himself, as Satan was in *Paradise Lost* (9.166). This is "Libyc *Hammon*" (203) or Jupiter Ammon, whose oracle was located at Siwah in the Libyan desert. Ovid (*Metamorphoses*, 5.318–28) reports that the offspring of Typhon—"*Typhon* huge ending in snaky twine," as Milton here describes him (226)—once put the Olympians to flight; Jupiter himself took refuge in the horned ram, and his cohorts became, in Milton's phrasing, "the brutish gods of *Nile*" (211). Still another of these gods, Moloch—whose name means "king"—demanded that young children be sacrificed. "With Cymbals' ring / They call the grisly king" (208–9), the noise being needed (as Merritt Hughes annotates in *Complete Poems*) "to drown the cries of the suffering infants."

A recurrent idea, therefore, is not only perversion but inversion: omnipresence by localized presences, incarnation by imbruting, prefigurations of the Holy Innocents by sacrificed infants, and Christ the King by demotic and demonic kings. Less sensational than these lurid contrasts but nonetheless forceful is the verbal disjunction between "Oriens" and pagan darkness. "No nightly trance" henceforth affects Apollo's "pale-ey'd Priest" (179–80), even though "The Nymphs in twilight shade of tangled thickets mourn" (189), and "The *Lars* and *Lemures* moan with midnight plaint" (191). Peor and Baal "Forsake their Temples dim" (198); Moloch leaves behind "His burning Idol all of blackest hue" (207); and Osiris is summoned "In vain with Timbrel'd Anthems dark" (219) by "sable-stoled Sorcerers" (220).

Satan was chief among the "rulers of the darknesse of this world" (Ephesians 6.12), and most of the divinities named in the poem were famous for having strived to mask their own subservient darkness with lightsome disguises. A rapid survey uncovers Apollo, the sun-god from Greece; the lares, Roman spirits of fire and hearth; Peor, otherwise known as Priapus and, because of seminal powers, a figurative sun; Jupiter Ammon, the Egyptian sun; Moloch, the Moabian sun; and Thammuz or Adonis or Osiris, alternative names in diverse cultures for Priapus, Baal-Peor, and (yet again) the sun.[15]

15. The syncretic mythographers relied on for the identifications listed above are Alex-

"Mooned *Ashtaroth*" (200)—the noun is plural—presumably are various delusive lunar reflections of suns already false, but partly outside the imagistic pattern is "Typhon huge ending in snaky twine" (227). He is needed toward the end of the catalogue of gods so that the catalogue itself can come full circle and return to the personage with whom it began: "Th'old Dragon," Satan himself, who "Swinges the scaly Horror of his folded tail" (168, 172). This part of "The Hymn" resembles Milton's later and much longer catalogue of fallen angels in *Paradise Lost*, and it has much of the effect of a gigantic epic simile. Satan locally assumes the forms of diverse gods, characteristically concealing himself and his dark intent behind aliases; his masks are designed to seem radiantly bright but in fact are insubstantial and ostentatious reproductions of the "ignis fatuus," the fatuous fire that,

> Kindl'd through agitation to a Flame,
> Which oft, they say, some evil Spirit attends,
> Hovering and blazing with delusive Light,
> Misleads th' amaz'd Night-wanderer from his way
> To Bogs and Mires, and oft through Pond or Pool,
> There swallow'd up and lost, from succor far.
> (*Paradise Lost*, 9.637–42)

"So glister'd the dire Snake, and into fraud / Led *Eve*" (9.643–44). And so glister Satan, the Dragon, and Typhon here, but with this serpent-bruising difference: "Our Babe, to shew his Godhead true, / Can in his swaddling bands control the damned crew" (227–28). This extensive digression into paganism is thus not digressive at all. It is comparable, nonetheless, to the wakeful trump of doom heard earlier in that Luke's narrative recedes into a far-distant background until the lines just quoted foreshorten the perspective.

In the middle and transitional distance, still another compositional pattern is visible. These gods, while sometimes noisy, are bereft of speech. Since "The Oracles are dumb" (173), "No voice or hideous hum" now sounds from Delphi, merely a "hollow shriek" (174, 179). "A voice of weeping" (183), nothing more articulate, is heard as "The parting Genius is with sighing sent" (186). "*Lars* and *Lemures* moan" (191), a "drear and dying sound / Affrights the *Flamens*" (193–94), and with hideous monstrosity, the "lowings loud" (215) of Osiris diminish into silence. William Cartwright's "On the Epiphany," a poem that I have been holding back

ander Ross, *Pansebeia* [my transliteration from Ross's Greek]: *Or, A View of All Religions of the World* (London, 1653), especially 66, 181, 518–19; and the commentaries of George Sandys in his translation, *Ovids Metamorphoses* (London, 1640); see Sandys's "Index" for numerous but scattered references to the gods mentioned by Milton. Ross cites various classical authorities upon which he himself depends, but Sandys usually does not.

until now, raises the imagistic point to the surface; one of his wisemen prays that Christ's "Mouth be / A more Inspired Oracle to me," his reason being, "Since that our own are Silenc'd."

Cartwright may have been remembering Plutarch's celebrated essay, "On the Cessation of the Oracles," a source mentioned by Hughes in his headnote to Milton's poem. Pericopes for Christmas day also should be kept in mind. "God in times past, diuersely and many wayes spake vnto the Fathers by Prophets, but in these last daies he hath spoken to vs by his owne sonne" (Hebrews 1.1). "In the beginning was the Word, and the Word was with God, and God was the Word" (John 1.1). And perhaps especially,

> The heauens declare the glorie of God: and
> the firmament sheweth his handy worke.
> One day telleth another: and one night
> certifieth another.
> There is neither speach nor language: but
> their voyces are heard among them.
> Their sound is gone out into all lands: and
> their words into the endes of the world.
>
> (Psalter Psalm 19.1–4)

False gods spake oracularly in times past or at any rate pretended so to speak in order to utter an Anti-Logos, but when the Word becomes flesh, then even true prophets, not to mention fakes, are superseded by the voice of the Son, uttering speech in all the earth, in every land and in all languages. Plutarch knew nothing about the Incarnation and reported no more than that the oracles ceased when a mariner was heard to cry, "The great god Pan is dead." Cartwright improved on that situation by allowing his Magi to draw a pointed contrast between false oracles and true. Milton improved on it still more by proclaiming that "the mighty *Pan*," far from being dead, "Was kindly come" (89) on Christmas day.

Attempting to ape the Logos, deified ventriloquists produce cacophany or no sound at all; parading as gods of light, they cloak themselves with self-propagated darkness. The Day-spring from on high dawns all the more brightly by contrast, and the Word speaks with amplified articulation. "Oriens" is the more prominent of the symbols for latter lines of "The Hymn," among other reasons because of the sun billowing its chin on an orient wave in the penultimate stanza. It is the Logos, however, that has the greater dominance throughout the poem because of its pivotal interiority. The peaceful scene depicted in the opening of "The Hymn," if largely adapted from Luke, has nearly total silence as one of its principal characteristics. "No War, or Battle's sound / Was heard" (53–54); "The Trumpet spake not," at least not yet or at least "not to the armed throng"

(58). Winds engage in "Whispering" (66), nothing louder. "The Stars with deep amaze / Stand fixt . . . Until their Lord himself bespake, and bid them go" (69, 76). From the midst of this quietness, angels and spheres quite suddenly burst forth into musical speech and harmonies that are wondrously and profoundly glorious. Once before, when "the sons of morning sung," the "Creator great" (119–20) elicited comparable music; ears deafened by sin will later be unstopped by a clangorous trumpet on the day of wrath. And proleptic to that thunderous moment, dark gods, mutely or noisily, abscond in horrified terror. The progression is thus from quiet silence to perfected sound and speech and thence to speechlessness.

A final progression, made in the poem's last stanza, is to the tranquility of humble adoration. Mary, "the handmaide of the Lord" (Luke 1.38), "Hath laid her Babe to rest"; the star that led the Wizards attends "Her sleeping Lord with Handmaid Lamp." "And all about the Courtly Stable, / Bright-harness'd Angels sit"—but evidently neither speak nor sing—"in order serviceable." In this awesome silence, "Time is" indeed "our tedious Song should here have ending," for who would dare speak more? Indeed, what more could one possibly hope or even want to hear? The poem has projected the import of Christmas with fullness unmatched by other verse for the day and season. All major themes have been developed, lesser motifs have been introduced, and the implications have been pursued as they pertain to the entirety of universal redemptive history.

Two moments in that history surge forward at the end, as they did at the outset, to refold expansive time into timelessness. "But see!" So the final stanza begins, as Milton bids himself and his muse to take one final look at two Christmas mornings: the day long ago that comprehensively included the "was" of Creation and the "shall" of Judgement Day within an expansive "is"; and the day in 1629 that encompasses any and every calendar year between first Advent and last. "This day" of December 25 therefore looks back to the future and forward to the past. The repercussive effect, simultaneously spectacular and serene, is that additive process advances toward an ultimate finality that in turn reverts to the infinite moment whence all process originally began. And then, as Milton says,

> And then at last our bliss
> Full and perfect is,
> But now begins.

6 Christ Crucified

When Epiphany season ends on the day before Septuagesima, the preparation for Lent is about to begin, and one might even think about anticipating the arrival of Easter itself. Hammering away at the Christmas cycle is one thing, however, whereas driving Holy Week into the ground very likely is another. Now, therefore, may be an appropriate time to adopt a different approach, especially since I thereby can stop neglecting three significant facts.

First, despite complaints from dissenters about the substitution of empty ceremony for the preaching of Christ, sermons were regularly and, by some standards, quite lengthily included in established church services.[1] A probable cause of "puritan" disgruntlement, though mostly invisible today, was not so much that Anglicans mulishly refused to preach or be preached at but that the sermons were tied entirely too closely to "papistic" rites. George R. Potter and Evelyn M. Simpson print Donne's sermons in chronological order, but since the liturgical year supplied much of the original context, it also determined the sequence often adopted in the massive seventeenth-century folios. Hence, to recast the example by inserting Andrewes in place of Donne, the first seventeen of the *XCVI Sermons*, as first published in 1629, were preached on Christmas, the next eight on Ash Wednesday, and the following six during Lent. Not only that, but the pericopes appointed to be read were the texts usually expounded in the sermons, although more than a little latitude here has to have been inevitable. Even Andrewes, extraordinarily subtle exegete though he was, would have had to work overtime to extract (for example) his eighteen Easter sermons from the day's Communion Gospel and/or Epistle.

Anglican sermons for particular feasts and fasts certainly vary, therefore, but they share a tradition in much the same way that poems for

---

1. I should note, however, that Richard Hooker in *Of the Laws of Ecclesiastical Polity*, 5.21–22 (2:76–105), does take the position that excessive reliance on sermonizing devalues God's Word in favor of a sermonist's words. He is defending, however, the time spent by Anglican inclusion of multiple biblical lessons and also the various means of inculcating biblical values, including not only a specially prepared sermon but also catechizing and the reading aloud of a sermon from the officially appointed *Homilies*.

Christmas do. Homilies for the Passion are a collective case in point, and some of them are worth knowing about, among other reasons because of their correlation, both positive and negative, to the sermon preached by Donne to himself while riding westward on Good Friday 1613.

Crashaw's work is another and no doubt more obvious body of material the importance of which I have been minimizing when not disregarding it completely. My own notion, however, is that it may be extremely misleading and quite unfair to cite, even for merely illustrative purposes, only one version of those poems by Crashaw that exist in two or more forms. It seems entirely possible to me that Crashaw preached the same text, as it were, in more than one year and that distinguishable poems (as distinct from "textual variants" within a single poem) were the result. Comparing Donne's verse for "The Crosse" with comparable work(s) by Crashaw can amplify this point and partly compensate for shortshrifting Crashaw until now.

And third, there are the secularized rites that Vaughan complains about, rather testily, in "The True Christmas." A goodly number of these not only were not condemned but were enthusiastically celebrated by Herrick. His individual poems very frequently are miniatures, but his work as a whole is expansive in that ecclesiastical rites exist side by side with the ceremonies of love and of art, and the three somehow manage, at times quite oddly, to complement one another. Herrick stages a Passion Play at one point and erects "This Crosse-tree here" at another, and part of his world corresponds to the domains explored in the poems by Donne and Crashaw just mentioned, but since the universe in which Herrick places his own explorations is uncommonly—perhaps singularly—distinctive, a separate description of it is worth trying in (therefore) a separate chapter.

"GOODFRIDAY, 1613. RIDING WESTWARD"

"Men must imitate the Planets that go not their own motions, otherwise than they are permitted *per primum mobile.*" This proposition is advanced in a sermon by Arthur Lake (1569–1626), the immediate and specific application being that "so should all the motions of our soule conforme themselues to the good pleasure of God."[2] The occasion for these remarks definitely was Good Friday, but the date is not specified in the folio and very possibly was not 1613, a year in which Lake must have been more than ordinarily busy. He was Bishop of Bath and Wells when he died in May 1626, "having made his confession," as the *DNB* tells us, "to Bishop An-

2. *Sermons with some Religious and Divine Meditations* (London, 1629), "In the third Alphabet" [third pagination], 148. Much of the information given about Lake in the *DNB* (soon cited in the paragraph above) was taken, with minor changes in wording, from the unsigned preface to the *Sermons.*

drewes a few hours before breathing his last." Thirteen years earlier, though not yet a bishop, he may have been known for practicing what he preached since "in 1613," as we also are told, "though not a candidate for the office, he was unanimously elected warden of New College, where he established at his own cost lectureships in Hebrew and mathematics."

On Good Friday of that same year, the traveler of Donne's poem was much occupied with quite different matters, but he sounds a bit like the new Warden when he explains, to his own evident satisfaction, how he happens to be headed in precisely the wrong direction on this day. As "other Spheares" (3) are "whirld" by the "first mover" (8), so is his body "carryed towards the West," even though his "Soules forme bends toward the East" (9–10). For Lake, however, the governing factor is theistic good pleasure, whereas Donne's speaker inverts the argument: his movements, quite explicitly, are directed not by God's "Pleasure or businesse" (7) but by his own. This aggrandizement of personal vanity in terms of divine and cosmic processes indicates that self-centeredness, if not solipsism, is well to the forefront here, and the fact that this journey, in modern parlance, is an ego trip as well as a westward ride is further shown by the not quite visible shrug that next occurs: a gesture over the shoulder at what might be observed if one took the trouble to look.

The scene there is a "spectacle" (16), and if a less worldly speaker were using the word on this particular day, then one might expect it to have close resemblance to the "sight"—in the Greek text, a "theorian" ("spectacle")—depicted in St. Luke's account of the Crucifixion, when "the people . . . came together to that sight" (23.48). As it is, however, the differences are conspicuous, and one way to underline the fact is to backtrack, for a moment, to Good Friday 1605 and the sermon for that day by Andrewes, Bishop Lake's death-bed confessor.

"Saint *Luke*," Andrewes begins, "though he recount at large our SAVIOVR CHRIST'S whole storie, yet in plaine and expresse termes he calleth the *Passion* 'theorian' [my transliteration of Andrewes's Greek], a *Theorie* or *Sight*" (*XCVI Sermons*, 365). Nearing his conclusion, he says that some of those who came together "returned from it . . . as having seene a *dolefull Spectacle*" (381). Surface similarities can be seen, but in Donne's poem the Passion Play is enacted on a not quite cleared stage, and in this sermon, even more so than in the Gospels, jumbled crowd scenes (including mob action) are called for. The only personages acknowledged by Donne's rider—other, that is, than himself—are "Christ on this Crosse" (13) and "his miserable mother" (30). But Andrewes asks, "Was it a *Tragaedie* [*sic*]," truly a "*Passion*"? Yes indeed,

> A *Passion* it was: yet, by their behaviour it might seeme a *may-game*. Their *shouting* and *out-cries;* their *harrying* of him about, from *Annas* to *Caiaphas;* from him to *Pilate;* from *Pilate* to *Herod;* and from him to *Pilate*

again: One while in *purple, Pilate's* suit; another-while in *white, Herod's livery:* Nipping him by the *cheekes,* and *pulling* off his *haire; blindfolding Him* and *buffeting Him; bowing to Him* in *derision,* and then *spitting in his face. (XCVI Sermons,* 376–77)

Donne's equestrian is aware, to be sure, that "Christ on this Crosse, did rise and fall" (13), but Andrewes would have us know that "the *Crosse* is a *rack,*" that

> they ploughed His back, and made (not *stripes,* but) *long furrowes upon it.* They did not *put on* His *wreath of thornes,* and presse it downe with their hands, but *beat it on* hard with *batts,* to make it enter through *skinne, flesh, skull,* and *all.* They did not (in *Golgotha*) pierce his *hands* and *feet,* but made *wide holes* (like that of a *spade*) as if they had been *digging* in some ditch. (*XCVI Sermons,* 374)

Backtrack still another year, to 1604, and to "The Passion Sermon" preached at Paul's Cross by Joseph Hall: "Which of his senses now was not a window to let in sorrow? . . . Look up . . . look upon this precious body . . . That head . . . that face . . . those eyes . . . those ears . . . lips . . . feet . . . hands . . . that whole body" (*Works* 5:35–36). Since Hall inherited this hortative mode, for a sampling of the kind of material that fills the ellipses just made, one can look back to 1571 and the two-part Sermon for Good Friday in the second of the officially appointed *Book[s] of Homilies*:

> Call to mind, O sinful creature, and set before thine eyes Christ crucified: think thou seest his body stretched out in length upon the cross, his head crowned with sharp thorns, and his hands and his feet pierced with nails, his heart opened with a long spear, his flesh rent and torn with whips, his brows sweating and blood: think thou hearest him now crying in an intolerable agony. . . . Couldest thou behold this woful sight, or hear this mournful voice, without tears[?] . . . O my brethren, let this image of Christ crucified be always printed in our hearts. (*Homilies,* 378–79)

Donne must have been alive to details of this kind, if not from Andrewes and Hall and the *Homilies,* then from *The Golden Legend;* or the earlier (often pseudonymous) medieval meditations on which the *Legend* levies; or the Passion sermons of Church Fathers such as St. Augustine and St. Ambrose; and, of course, from the Gospels themselves and the Old Testament prefigurative types cited by the Evangelists and by St. Paul. I do not wish to be more tedious than need be, but it is important, I think, to remember that the Crucifixion customarily was displayed with an abundant wealth of detail, which invited the eye to linger.[3]

3. See the magisterial survey by J. A. W. Bennett, *Poetry of the Passion: Studies in Twelve Centuries of English Verse* (Oxford: Oxford University Press, 1982). Donne's poem is specifically considered on 151–52, but most of Bennett's earlier pages also are directly or indirectly relevant.

Indeed, as Andrewes observed in another sermon, preached at White-hall in 1604, there is insufficient time, even on Good Friday itself, to look into the Passion fully: "Thus we have *considered* and seene, not so much as in this sight we might or should, but as much as the time will give" (*XCVI Sermons*, 361). Or, as Hall put it, at Paul's Cross on that same day, "There is no branch or circumstance in this wonderful business which yields not infinite matter of discourse" (*Works* 5:25).

Donne, however, leaves almost all of it out. Admittedly, he was writing a poem, not a sermon, but so was John Davies of Hereford (or, if not a poem, then verse), and *The Holy Roode, or Christs Crosse: Containing Christ Crucified, described in Speaking-picture* (1609) puts *in* (regretta-bly, as it happens) almost everything. One can and should allow for dif-ferences on both sides of this issue: on the one hand, the contrast between verse and homiletic prose; on the other, more than twenty-five rambling pages of verse by Davies and a tight dramatic monologue by Donne. Even so, it is clear enough that one of Donne's rhetorical strategies could be thought of as significant silence.

By one kind of reckoning, in fact, Donne gives rather less than half of what the reference to "spectacle" might cause one to expect in even a brief poem. When Andrewes proposes in 1605 to "let all other *sights* goe . . . to see this great *Sight*" (*XCVI Sermons*, 367), he divides his material by saying that the "principall parts thereof are two. [1]*The sight it selfe* (that is) the *Thing* to be seen: [2]and the *Sight* of it (that is) the *Act of seeing it*, or *looking* on it." In the poem, there are a few objects (Christ, the cross, the sun, the mother) that *might* be seen if one were only facing the right way ("There I should see," 11). Others, however, are not affected by geographical place-ment since they are mental constructs dependent on invisible rather than visible reality: "all spheares" (22), for example, or "endlesse height" (23), or the "Zenith" and "our Antipodes" (24). Rabbi Akiba (sometimes Akiva) once entered Pardes ("paradise"), saw God, and safely returned to have the fact recorded in the *Talmud* (Hagigah, 14b). Gershom G. Scholem and Bauer attest to the continuing fame of that experience in some circles, both Jewish and Christian.[4] The general rule proved by that remarkable excep-tion is, however, "Thou canst not see my face: for there shall no man see me, and liue" (Exodus 33.20); one therefore will hardly quibble with Donne's assertion, "Who sees Gods face . . . must dye" (17).

And yet one of the rapidly emerging effects quite obviously is a stress on that which is *not* seen, and another, equally strong, is an emphasis on not *seeing*. This entire "spectacle" is "of too much weight" (16). "Yet dare

4. Gershom G. Scholem, *On the Kabbalah and Its Symbolism*, trans. Ralph Mannheim (New York: Schocken Books, 1965), 57–58; Bauer, 949B ("Vision of God"). (Since I cite Hagigah 14b above, I perhaps should mention that Bauer cites "77a"; the highest possible reference number in Hagigah—which regulates "festival pilgrimages"—is, however, 27.)

I'almost be glad, I do not see" (15). A question is raised: "Could I behold those hands which span the Poles . . . peirc'd with those holes?" (21–22). Since the sun itself is forced to "winke" (20), a reply is scarcely required; how could anyone perceive such piercings, after all? But the question evidently is beside the point since even upon the very human and most pitiable mother, "I durst not looke" (29).

This imagery is consistent and persistent, but other literature for the Passion points up the fact that somewhere in between "There I should see" and "I durst not looke," the argument has turned inward implosively. When the poem ends, the rider is still in England, not Jerusalem, and the year continues to be 1613. In the middle, however, planes of normal time and diametric spaces of physical geography shift in and out of discontinuous existence since, in England in 1613, daring or not daring to cast one's eye ought in one sense to be a meaningless alternative: no miserable mother is there to be seen in either case. Language also becomes chaotic since distinctions between the literal and metaphoric disappear when the rider pointlessly blinks and an eclipsed sun, with surrealistic parallelism, is said to "winke." The words blur, perhaps obliterate, the customary coordinates of macrocosmic space-time and of microcosmic thought processes so that neither supplies a meaningful referential system. One also recognizes, of course, that from the devotional point of view, which Donne's speaker at first declines to take, this destructive process is appropriate at this psychological moment of the poem and is so in more than one way. Macrocosmically, when "those hands" are "peirc'd" that "span the Poles," then the cosmos being held in and supported by the hands is likely to tilt. Microcosmically, if reviewing the past is to be followed by redemption in the future, then the personal world of sinful corruption will need a new kind of map. The literal meanings of words have to be undermined so as to be displaced by symbolic vocabulary; geography and time themselves must be translated into states of mind. Otherwise, this traveler surely will arrive, sooner or later, at whatever destination his body is moving toward, but the disparity between self-sacrificing God and self-centered humanity will be as abysmal at journey's end as it was at the outset.

Preoccupied and beguiled, this wayfarer thus begins by turning away the eyes of his body and then fastidiously tries to avert the eyes of his mind. He does manage to remain oblivious to, and thus never notices the existence of, that richness of detail so compelling to other viewers. But however egocentrically he thrusts forward his own limited ability to see some things and his self-serving aversion to seeing others, a few hard truths simply have to be faced. In effect, therefore, a heavily truncated Passion sermon is being preached unwillingly to the equally reluctant audience of the self. A parallel, but with considerable inversion, might be drawn to the last stanza of the "Hymne to God my God, in my sicknesse":

> So, in his purple wrapp'd receive mee Lord,
>   By these his thornes give me his other Crowne;
> And as to other soules I preach'd thy word,
>   Be this my Text, my Sermon to mine owne,
>   Therfore that he may raise the Lord throws down.

On Good Friday 1613, however, the homiletic text for the day (a biblical source for it will be given shortly) is this: "They *shall* looke vpon mee whom they haue pierced." Almost but not quite successfully suppressed, that statement underlies the fussiness about what one may or may not be willing and/or able to see, and it surfaces in the rhetorical question, "Could I behold those hands . . . peirc'd with those holes?" That the question goes unanswered turns out, in fact, to have been another significant omission.

The emergent text just quoted is from Zechariah 12.10, and I delayed the reference for two reasons. First, "shall" is not italicized in any of my editions, but the imperative verb regularly was emphasized, and it seemed worthwhile to underline at the outset that about this particular seeing, very little choice exists: one way or another, they *shall*. Second, the statement was conventionally understood to be prophetic of the Passion, an overwhelmingly powerful reason being that St. John interpreted it that way, and not once but twice. As a result, the words reappear in two variant forms. At the Crucifixion, "one of the Souldiers with a speare pierced his side, and foorthwith came there out blood and water. . . . For these things were done, that the Scripture should be fulfilled, . . . They shall look on him whom they pierced" (John 19.34–37). And on Patmos, years later, the apocalyptic vision begins, "Behold, he commeth with clouds, and euery eye shall see him, and they also which pearced him" (Revelation 1.7). On this third occurrence, the soldier's spear is replaced by a divine and terrifying weapon: "out of his mouth went a sharpe two edged sword" (1.16). That sword is one of the reasons, in fact, why those who pierced *shall* look.

With scissors and a little paste, one could compile from standard commentaries an anthology of comments that illuminate Donne's biblical allusion, but Andrewes obviated the need by preaching this text on Good Friday 1597. His sermon sums up a long tradition for two kinds of looking, and a paraphrase of his remarks can further support an earlier point about the liturgical context of sermons as well as advance the one now being suggested about Donne's poem.[5]

---

5. For the sermon paraphrased and quoted above, see Launcelot Andrewes, *XCVI Sermons*, 333–48. The Latin text, "Respicient in Me, quem transfixerunt," is quoted from the Bible of Junius-Tremellius-Beza. The Vulgate reads "aspicient" ("ad" [to] + "spicio"), but Andrewes prefers "re" + "spicio" because of the ambivalent value of the prefix: *re*peated seeing but also looking *back* repeatedly. What Andrewes actually preaches tends to be a

Since hermeneutic principles control interpretive practice, Andrewes's first point is that "our warrant," in understanding Zechariah's words to be prophetic of the Passion, is "the *Holy Ghost . . .* who, in *S. Iohn's Gospell* reporting the . . . last act . . . saith plainly, that in the piercing, *the very words of the Prophecie were fulfilled.*" "There is" of course, "no part of the whole course of our Saviour CHRIST'S life or death, but it is well worthy our *looking on,*"

> But, of all other parts, and above them all, this last part of his piercing, is here commended unto our view . . . this spectacle, when He was *pierced . . .* most requisite at this time; this very day, which we hold holy to the memorie of his Passion, and the *piercing* of His precious side. That, though on other dayes, we employ our eyes otherwise, this day at least, we fixe them on this object.

Syntax is another control upon meaning, and Zechariah's may *seem* to absolve post-biblical people of this duty. "For . . . he entendeth by very construction, that first and second [*They,*] are not two, but one and the *same Parties:* And that *they* that are here willed to *looke upon him,* are *they,* and none other, that were the authors of this fact, even of the mur-ther" (the square bracket is Andrewes's own). We, however, can scarcely be the "they" who were guilty since "we" were not even there; or so we would like to argue. "Our manner is, either to lay it on the *Souldiers . . .* Or if not upon them, upon *Pilate . . .* Or, if not upon him, upon the *people . . .* Or lastly, if not upon them, upon the *Elders of the Iewes.*" One of our difficul-ties, however, is that the heterogeneously plural "they" (whom we accuse) were but "Instruments" in the perpetration of the crime: "We that *looke upon,* it is we that *pierced Him:* and it is we that *pierced Him,* that are willed *to looke upon*"; "We verily, even we, are . . . the *principalls* in this *murther.*" The "they" (who in reality are "we") must therefore look and "not slightly, superficially or perfunctorily, but stedfastly. . . . And . . . with our eye to *pierce* him that was thus *pierced.*" The "effect of such a spectacle" is or at any rate should be to "*Looke*" and "be *pierced . . .* that with *looking* on Him, wee might be *pricked in our hearts.*"

Andrewes—or rather, in his view, the Holy Ghost—was well aware that looking of this kind is distasteful. God "did easily foresee, we would not readily be brought to the *sight,* . . . Indeed, to *flesh and blood* it is but a dull and *heavy spectacle.*" "Therfore is the *Verbe . . .* put into this *Coniugation* of purpose: . . . They shall procure or *cause,* or even *enioyne* or *enforce themselves to looke upon it;* or (as one would say) *looke,* that they *looke* upon it." Our inclination, quite understandably but no less wrongly, is to abuse the verb, in effect to misconjugate it.

---

composite text from Zechariah on the one hand and from John's two references on the other. Biblical commentaries, somewhat comparably, often link the passages closely together as if each represented the others with almost complete fullness.

> For some new and strange *spectacle* (though vaine and idle, and which
> shall not profit us how strange soever) we cause our selves sometimes to take
> a journey, and besides our paines, are at expenses too, to *behold* them: we
> will not only look upon, but even *cause our selves to looke upon* vanities.

And what we therefore need to do is *re*apply the grammar. "Therfore. . .
do it *willingly,* or do it *by force:* Do it, I say; for, done it must be." "Set it
before you and looke." Or, if not that, then "*Respice, Looke backe upon it*
with some *paine:* for, one way or other, looke upon it we must." St. John's
apocalyptic vision of Christ coming in judgement with the two-edged
sword puts this last matter beyond doubt. "Either here, or some where
els; either now or then, *looke upon Him* you shall. And, they which put
this spectacle farre from them heere, and cannot endure to *look* . . . shall
be enforced to *looke* . . . whether they will or no."

In consequence, the better question to ask is not *whether* but rather
"how long we shall continue" to look "and when we may give over?"
Strict observance would necessitate that we continue to look until Christ
be as firmly fixed in our hearts as he was to the cross. "Or, if that be too
much or too hard, yet *saltem* at the least, *Respice in Illum, donec Ille te
respexerit.* Looke upon him, till He looke upon you againe." "By *looking
on Him* first, we provoke ["pro-voco"—"call forth," "elicit"] him in a
sort to a second *looking on us* againe."

Another good question to ask is, "How shall we know when CHRIST
doth thus *respect* [with deliberate pun] us?" "Then truely, when fixing
both the eyes of our meditation *upon Him that was pierced* . . . we find
. . . some motion of *grace* arise within our *hearts* . . . and so grow into
delight of this *looking.*"

Because of the heritage that Donne and Andrewes shared, the sermon
can gloss the poem without being a source for it. Some of Andrewes's
characters travel in search of new sights not worth the seeing; others
know full well what they ought to be looking at but maintain that the
spectacle on view is too heavy for them to behold. Donne's character
presumably would have felt at ease with either group, but since he as-
sumes the role of preacher as well as congregation, he also approaches the
perspective from which Andrewes is looking even while facing westward
in the wrong direction. For Andrewes, the urgent need is to fix "both eyes
of our meditation" upon Christ; for Donne,

> Though these things, as I ride, be from mine eye,
> They'are present yet unto my memory,
> For that looks towards them.

(33–35)

Donne's lines affirm an oxymoron—away "from" but "present yet un-
to"—that, in abstract terms, conjoins absence-presence. That particular

simultaneity inheres in Good Friday because of a careful distinction to be drawn on this specific day. Liturgical events and poems, as Christmas forcefully exemplifies, almost always "are" happening rather than "were," and Eucharist is no exception since Christ is sacrificed anew whenever Communion occurs. Herbert, in "The Agonie," thus validates the doctrine of The Real Presence of Christ by twofold personal experience, Christ's and his own: "Love is that liquour sweet and most divine, / Which my God feels as bloud; but I, as wine" (17–18, the last lines). Oxymoron is present, but it consists of "blood-wine," not "was-is." Minds accustomed to thinking with theological precision (Herbert's mind, for example, or Donne's) nonetheless will often want to remember that while the birth and coming and sacrifice of Christ are perpetual, his death, far from being repeatable, was instead unique. "Was ever grief like mine" is the rhetorical question repeatedly asked by Christ in Herbert's "The Sacrifice," and the charge implicitly but unanswerably being laid against us is, "Never before nor since."

The question asked by Augustine is, "Does Christ die as often as the celebration of Easter comes round?" The text being expounded is sometimes called "the Psalme of the Passion" (as Andrewes refers to it in a sermon for Good Friday 1597), partly because this psalm includes the verse, "They pierced my hands and feet."[6] Augustine answers his own question with a vigorous no, but "the yearly remembrance brings before our eyes, in a way, what once happened long ago and stirs in us the same emotions as if we beheld our Lord hanging on the cross." Similar thinking underlies language already quoted from the *Homilies* ("Call to mind . . . think thou hearest") and from Andrewes ("this very day, which we hold holy to the memorie of his Passion"). And indeed, the Eucharistic statement itself powerfully asserts (though cold print may need the italics and the bracket I have added) that Christ

> vpon the Crosse . . . made there (by his *one* oblation of himselfe *once* offered) a full, perfect, and sufficient Sacrifice . . . and did . . . commaund vs to continue a perpetuall *memorie* of that [*not* "this"] his precious death, vntill his comming againe.

These careful discriminations need not always be insisted upon and deeply pondered; pectoral crosses and those genuflected to in church mutely testify to the spiritual value sometimes accrued from the devotionally motivated supposition that Christ is everywhere crucified and ceaselessly dies in sinful hearts. But if Donne's rider was offhandedly

6. Augustine, *On the Psalms* [1–37], trans. Dame Scholastica Hebgin and Dame Felicias Corrigan, 2 vols. (Westminster, MD: The Newman Press, 1960), 1:207. Vulgate (and Septuagint) Psalm 21 = Authorized Version (and Hebrew) Psalm 22; verse numbers also vary. For Augustine, the verse quoted above is 21.17; for Andrewes, it is 22.16.

cavalier about his devotion at the outset, he is attempting to be exact about his theology now, and in terms of that which is far off and yet also present unto, the "memory" must indeed be that which "looks," and it is in terms of visual memory, not present-time reality, that "thou"—Christ— "hang'*st* upon the tree" (36).

In terms of dramatic monologue, moreover, changes in attitude can be broadly attributed to the tumultuous mental transpositions of space and time that enable the scene to be visible at all. More specifically, what has triggered awareness of the memory itself (as separable from what is "present yet unto it") may be the piercing that Zechariah foresaw, and one reason for thinking so is the meaning of that prophet's name. The etymology of "Zechariah" is, in fact, "God" (Jah or Yah) is "renowned," but at one time the import of "renown" was thought to be of a kind that may not be obvious today. Isidore of Seville translates "Zecharias" with "memoria Dei" ("memory of God"); John Stockton (citing Isidore) retranslates with "*Zacharias*, The remembrance of the Lord."[7] What is signified, as both writers immediately add, is that the Lord remembered his people when, thanks in part to Zechariah's preaching, they were moved to become mindful of him. The "populus" consequently was "reversus," as Isidore puts it—"turned back," that is—for the rebuilding of Jerusalem and the temple ("reversus est Dei populus, et reaedificandum est urbs et templum").

Whatever the specific cause, Donne's traveler has become aware that his memory actually *is* looking east. And that realization immediately leads to the further awareness that Christ has been looking west toward him: (my) memory "looks towards them; and thou look'st towards mee, / O Saviour, as thou hang'st upon the tree" (35–36). Joseph Hall's "The Christian's Crucifixion with Christ" supplies a useful parallel (although the sermon dates from 1628 and, despite the title, was not preached on Good Friday):

> Those that have searched into the monuments of Jerusalem write that our Saviour was crucified with his face to the west; which howsoever spitefully meant of the Jews, as not allowing him worthy to look on the holy city and temple, yet was not without a mystery, *Oculi ejus super Gentes respiciunt, His eyes look to the Gentiles,* &c saith the Psalmist [Psalm 66.7]. As Christ therefore on his cross looked [past tense] towards us sinners of the Gentiles, so let us look [present-future] up to him. (*Works* 5:382)

---

7. Isidore, *Etymologiarum libri XX*, 7.8 ("De prophetis"), ed. W. M. Lindsay (Oxford: Oxford University Press, 1911); John Stockton, *A Fruitfull Commentarie upon the Twelve Small Prophets* (Cambridge, 1594), 84. (Stockton says his work is an amplification of a Latin commentary by Lambertus Danaeus; I have not seen Danau's original.) Cornelius à Lapide, *Commentaria in duodecim Prophetas minores*, 634B, also translates the name with "memoria Dei."

Christ looked to the Gentiles from the Cross, and he thereby made it possible for those who believe to look back at him; the eyes of the redeemer and of the redeemed regard one another across the centuries.

Hall cites Psalm 66.7, and a slightly later verse also is closely relevant: "For thou (O God) hast proued vs: thou also hast tried vs, like as siluer is tried" (Psalter Psalm 66.9). In this instance, the point of intersection is that Donne clearly assumes that his own metal has not yet been sufficiently tried, that he ought to pray first for punishment of his errant ways. On this day of the Passion, however, Christ "gave [his] back to the smiters," as Isaiah (50.6) prophetically foresaw and as the Evangelists confirmed. He did so that he, unlike those who smote him, might be merciful to those whom he himself smites. And since Christian "faith is the substance of things hoped for, the evidence of things not seen" (Hebrews 11.1), the motion anticipated in the poem's last lines is a turning not of the back but of the face.

> I turne my backe to thee, but to receive
> Corrections, till thy mercies bid thee leave.
> O thinke mee worth thine anger, punish mee,
> Burne off my rusts, and my deformity,
> Restore thine Image, so much, by thy grace,
> That thou may'st know mee, and I'll turne my face.

Spiritual purifying is a process coterminous with the finitudes of time, and the words of Christ on the Cross, "It is accomplished," cannot be fully repeated until the eschatological reappearance of him who "is like a refiners fire" (Malachi 3.2). This may be especially true for sinners who are "like metals," as Matthew Poole puts it (*Commentary* 2:1025), "which nothing but a fierce fire can purge." Donne's rider, when contemplating his own not yet redeemed and unpurged condition, at length succeeds in re*seeing* the Crucifixion scene, but what never is *heard* at all—and this may be the most significant silence of the entire poem—is the redemptive promise to the thief, "To day shalt thou be with me in Paradise" (Luke 23.43). This traveler has been dangerously like the one who appears in Zechariah six verses before the piercing: "In that day, sayth the Lord, I will smite euery horse with astonishment, and his rider with madnesse" (12.4). In the future he certainly hopes to be on a horse like those seen two chapters later in Zechariah's own penultimate verse: "In that day shall there be vpon the belles [margin: *Or, bridles*] of the horses, HOLINES VNTO THE LORD" (14.20). At present, however, the best that can be done is to renounce metaphoric westward riding so as to make a pilgrimage.

With considerable hesitation, I follow the argument one further step, recalling but not trusting the fact that Donne himself sometimes inexorably pursues the logic of his own images. This pilgrim apparently imagines himself standing at the westernmost gates of life and turning round, just prior to passing through, so as to face his Saviour on the eastern elevation of the Cross. And if he does indeed back through the western doors of death in hope of an eastern resurrection, then presumably he will want and need to turn round yet again. And yet when (or *if*) he does, then he would have to be looking, not at the front, but rather at the *back* of Christ, who would still be facing the other way. Admittedly, that sight would itself be an astonishing spectacle and consistent with the idea that not even Moses saw more: "Thou shalt see my backe parts, but my face shall not be seene" (Exodus 33.23). Vaughan remembered that pronouncement in "Looking back" and thereby unwittingly elicited (as noted in the preceding chapter) a modern jibe. And John Davies of Hereford, no more provident in 1609 than Vaughan was later on, echoed the idea in the last two lines of *The Holy Roode:* "But if I be vnmeet thy Face to ken, / Shew me thy back-parts; kind Lord! say, *Amen."*

Perhaps, however, it is we who are now to do the imagining by supposing that the ultimate response of Christ to human turning is one last turning of himself. If so, then the prayer of Jeremiah 31.18 (echoed in Lamentations 5.21) has been significantly modified: not, "Turne thou me, and I shalbe turned" (as the prophet has it) but rather, "Turn thou, when I have been *re*-turned." For God's perspective on this matter, Donne's eye could have been on the beginning of Zechariah: "Turne yee vnto me, saith the Lord of hostes, and I will turn vnto you" (1.3). And to see both turnings from both points of view, though not simultaneously, one more sermon may be helpful. Since Donne's concluding tone is penitential, there is propriety to be found in the occasion, though not the date, of Andrewes's homily for Ash Wednesday 1619.[8]

The text announced is from Joel 2.12–13, "Turne you vnto Me . . . turne vnto the Lord your God," and one of the points heavily stressed is that Joel's words draw "a circle . . . which circle consists of *two turnings* . . . for, twise he repeats this word." Repentance, metaphorically, also "is nothing else, but . . . a kind of circling." "First, a *turne* wherein we look forward to GOD, . . . Then, a *turne* again, wherein we look backward to our *sinnes."* Each of these, by itself, is "but the *halfe-turne,"* and given that truth, the common preference for looking forward will not serve. Past sin must also be recalled: "the *Hemisphaere* of our *sinnes* (not to be under the *Horizon,* cleare out of sight) must ascend up." When both half turns are made, however, "the two between them, make up a compleate *repentance,* or (to keepe the word of the text) a *perfect revolution."* "And when our *turne* is done, GOD shall begin His."

8. In the paragraph that follows, I paraphrase and quote from Andrewes, *XCVI Sermons,* 204–13.

Donne was fully capable of taking metaphors with dedicated literalness, a notable example being the conflation of micro- and macrocosmic geographies in the "Hymne to God my God, in my sicknesse." But whether a similar process is ongoing for the final turns of this poem remains problematic. "Goodfriday, 1613," after all, is complete but nonetheless is not finished; the tense of the last line establishes future expectation but does not and cannot affirm a present certainty. The most that might be proposed, therefore, is this: double reversal of double retrospection in lines, which no one alive could ever actually write, would be spectacular verification of the vision of St. Paul: "For now wee see," and can only see, "through a glasse, darkly: but then face to face" (1 Corinthians 13.12).

Whatever the (de)merits of these speculations, looking beyond the poem's last line necessarily is to peer into unchartable territory. Retreating to safer ground, I want to take notice of Andrewes on Good Friday in 1604 one final time. The conclusion at which Andrewes himself arrived, while devout rather than dramatic in tone, proclaims the message that Donne's volatile rider, by traveling forward and looking back, has introspectively perceived to be deeply inscribed within himself.

> It is kindly to consider . . . The worke of the Day, in the Day it was wrought: and this Day it was wrought. This Day therfore, whatsoever businesse be, to lay them aside a little; whatsoever our haste, yet to stay a little, and to spend a few thoughts in calling to minde and taking to *regard*, what this Day the SONNE *of* GOD did and suffered for us: and all for this end, that what he was then, we might not be; and what he is now, we might be for ever. (*XCVI Sermons*, 364)

CROOKED CROSSES IN DONNE AND CRASHAW

Renaissance authors often claim that the poet, etymologically a "maker," creates a world even as God created a universe and authored the Book. At one time, the analogy at least *seemed* to work fairly well in terms of words and the Word, but if one begins to think of nonverbal art, then God had the enormous advantage of being able to call into existence not only the image desired but also the material in which the image was to be found; the image, in fact, must always have been intrinsic to the material or the material for it would never have been made. Human artifice, even at very best, cannot possibly duplicate those conditions, partly because the material already exists, partly because human fashioning requires either adding something or taking it away.

Donne's sermons are a convenient source for some illustrations of this kind of aesthetic theory.

To make representations of men, or of other creatures, we finde two wayes; Statuaries have one way, and Painters have another: Statuaries doe it by Substraction [*sic*]; They take away, they pare off some parts of that stone, or that timber, which they work upon, and then that which they leave, becomes like that man, whom they would represent: Painters doe it by Addition; Whereas the cloth, or table presented nothing before, they adde colours, and lights, and shadowes, and so there arises a representation. (*Sermons* 8:54)

"In a rough stone," somewhat comparably, "a cunning Lapidary will easily foresee, what his cutting, and his polishing, and his art will bring that stone to. A cunning Statuarie discerns in a Marble-stone . . . where there will arise an Eye, and an Eare, and a Hand, and other lineaments to make it a perfect Statue" (*Sermons* 2:276). And, of course, the right rough stone must be chosen for its suitability to the intended design: "A Jeweller, if he would make a jewell to answer the form of any flower, or any other figure, his minde goes along with his hand, nay prevents [anticipates] his hand, and he thinks in himself, a Ruby will conduce best to the expressing of this, and an Emeraud [*sic*] of this" (*Sermons* 9:101). Quite wonderful achievements may result from these processes, but the "perfect Statue" to which Donne refers must be homiletic hyperbole with merely verbal existence since artifacts can scarcely be any more perfect than the artists themselves. Human imperfection, moreover, implies that the product of God's own image making has become faulty, but God has an enormous advantage in this case too: "The children of God, are the *Marble*, and the *Ivory*, upon which he workes; In them his purpose is, to reengrave, and restore his Image" (*Sermons* 3:193).

Donne's "The Crosse" includes less diffuse presentation of comparable ideas, often in mind-teasing form. Anticipating the Fall, God created a universe that intrinsically contains in the original engraving the means for subsequent reengravement. As a result, one can "Looke downe" (21) or "Looke up" (22) or, indeed, look inside or outside the self and quickly perceive that crosses are well-nigh ubiquitous: a swimmer's breast stroke (19), a ship's mast (20), the wings of birds in flight (22), the very earth itself: "All the Globes frame, and spheares, is nothing else / But the Meridians crossing Parallels" (23–24). Dull-eyed sinners can see this fact for themselves wherever they happen to look, but they are likely to see it crookedly in one way or another because postlapsarian sense impression is so often unreliable. "Crosse thy senses" (43), Donne therefore urges, especially the eye: "But most the eye needs crossing" (49). Minds and hearts, however, also need to be reformed and/or reshaped: "Crosse and correct concupiscence of witt" (58), "And crosse thy heart" (51). Make right use of corrected concupiscence so as to "Be covetous of Crosses"; "let none fall" (59). "For when that Crosse . . . unto you stickes, / Then are you to your selfe, a Crucifixe" (31–32).

Donne professes certainty on all those matters, but there is some room for doubt about this one:

> As perchance, Carvers do not faces make,
> But that away, which hid them there, do take:
> Let Crosses, soe, take what hid Christ in thee,
> And be his image, or not his, but hee.
>
> (33–36)

I usually quote Donne from Gardner's edition(s), but A. J. Smith (648n) has a helpful note here: "in a celebrated sonnet, *Non ha l'ottimo artista*, Michelangelo says that even the finest sculptor has no conceit which is not already hidden in the block of marble waiting to be uncovered." Creighton Gilbert's translation of Michelangelo is worth quoting too since Smith's annotation breaks off just a little too soon.[9] Michelangelo does indeed say, "The best of artists never has a concept / A single marble block does not contain / Inside its husk." He adds, however, that an artist succeeds in uncovering the hidden form "only if hand follows the intellect," and in his own case, he claims, "skill works *against* the wished effect" (italics added). The sonnet, or this part of it at any rate, certainly was well known. Clements supplies a variety of references to document his statement that "no four lines of Michelangelo's were more famous," even though they are but one instance (to quote the title of Cambon's essay) of "Sculptural Forms as Metaphysical Conceits in Michelangelo's Verse."[10] Noteworthy for my purposes is a further example from the madrigal "Sìcome per levar": "we put . . . by subtraction, / Into the rough hard stone / A living figure, grown / Largest wherever rock has grown most small."

Michelangelo's remarks certainly resemble Donne's, but both authors may be dependent, ultimately, on Aristotle's remark (*Metaphysics*, 1048) that a statue of Hermes was *potentially* present within the marble from which it was carved. In any case, "perchance" is a complicating word in Donne's poem since it indicates that the image may *not* have been waiting to be found. A further complication is the idea that external crosses presumably become internalized so as to remove that which internally hides; that which is hidden, moreover, is not a cross but Christ. Perhaps the suggestion is that revelation of true images ("be his image") precedes restoration of reality itself ("or not his, but hee"). Donne also supposes that spiritual artifice requires not only sculpture, which subtracts, but also

9. The quotations that immediately follow are from Michelangelo, *Complete Poems and Selected Letters*, trans. Creighton Gilbert, ed. Robert N. Linscott (Princeton: Princeton University Press, 1963).

10. Robert J. Clements, "Art as Thematic in the Poetry," in *The Poetry of Michelangelo* (New York: New York University Press, 1965), 64; Glauco Cambon, *Sewanee Review* 70 (1962): 155–65.

painting, which adds: "Then doth the Crosse of Christ work . . . Within our hearts, when wee love . . . That Crosses pictures much."

These various statements make good sense, of course, but it is of the kind most tersely presented in the line, "No Crosse is so extreme, as to have none" (14). That line may be the place to pause in order to note that Donne was by no means the first to trace out crosses that "might appear far-fetched conceits," as Bennett puts it, "if we did not know that they had all been neatly packed together, and illustrated, in the *De Cruce* of the learned [Justus] Lipsius."[11] Closer to home, William Drummond of Hawthornden also saw "Masts of ships crost with their yards," observed "a Microcosm to swim, At every stroake a *crucifixe*," and noticed that "pyed Butterflies . . . their wings do raise a Crosse" ("Of the Booke," *Poems* 2:168). John Davies of Hereford remarks that Christ, though "unkindly Crost," was "crost least in his Crosse, that crost him most" (*The Holy Roode*, 15). And Donne himself repeated the argument, "There cannot be so great a crosse as to have none" (*Sermons* 3:166). In the poem, however, statements of this kind, while undeniably traditional and not "far-fetched," also are undeniably set forth in support of an argument that is overtly circular. Indeed, the illogical procedures, far from being disguised, are underlined in various ways: the self-conscious wit of crossing concupiscence with covetousness for crosses, the crossing out of cross-eyed vision, the multiple significations of *crosses* (lowercase plurals in a modernized text) that in this context seem slippery and unstable, and the recognizable differences between statues or pictures or even crucifixes on the one hand and, on the other, the uppercase singular Cross of which they are the necessarily imperfect images.

From a devotional point of view, however, these strategies triumphantly affirm the presence of rectalinearity within the circular arguments of the microcosmic poem as well as behind the curvatures of macrocosmic space-time, and they thereby vindicate the poem's status as a process, a "making" of that which the title names as having already been made. An ongoing argument, sometimes slightly beneath the surface texture of the poem, is that all images, including the poem itself and the multiple crosses to which it refers, are individually inadequate to the reality that they nonetheless collectively attempt to signify; single imperfections in effect are crossed out by self-canceling replication so that cross-eyed vision is doubly crossed and an uncrossed Cross is revealed.

Some of Crashaw's crosses function in much the same way, even though their external appearance is quite different. Christ crucified is celebrated in the verses I have in mind, but naming them poses a problem. There is a Latin version in the 1634 *Epigrammata sacra;* for the English that corre-

---

11. Bennett, *Poetry of the Passion*, 152, 225 n. 12.

sponds to the Latin, there are three different titles for three sets of lines (closely parallel but not identical) that may or then again may not represent successively revised versions of one and only one poem. A long-standard assumption was that Crashaw tried to improve many of the poems first published in 1646 by reworking them twice, first for republication in 1648 and again for their final form as given in 1652. Evidently, however, the assumption is editorially unsafe, if not demonstrably wrong. What *is* demonstrable, as George Williams explained, is that there are two lines of transmission for the revised poems, one in England (for the 1648 edition), the other in France (for the 1652). 1646, however, differs much more from both of the later editions than 1648 and 1652 do from one another. Williams therefore printed facing texts—1646 and 1648/52—of "Sacred Poems in Two English Versions." For the verse on Christ crucified, even better— but hopelessly uneconomical—would be a poetic counterpart to the famous Stavelot triptych, in this case with one panel each for 1646, 1648, and 1652. I want to call attention to filigree work on all three, in fact, and glance also at some fine-edged detail that can be seen only in the Latin, but the first *English* version (1646) is the obvious choice to give at the outset. (I have numbered the stanzas, parenthetically, for purposes of later reference.)

ON THE BLEEDING WOUNDS OF OUR CRUCIFIED LORD

(1) Iesu, no more, it is full tide
　　From thy hands and from thy feet,
　From thy head, and from thy side,
　　All thy *Purple Rivers* meet.

(2) Thy restlesse feet they cannot goe,
　　For us and our eternall good
　As they are wont; what though?
　　They swim, alas! in their owne flood.

(3) Thy hand to give thou canst not lift;
　　Yet will thy hand still giving bee;
　It gives, but ô it self's the Guift,
　　It drops though bound, though bound 'tis free.

(4) But ô thy side! thy deepe dig'd side
　　That hath a double *Nilus* going,
　Nor ever was the *Pharian* tide
　　Halfe so fruitfull, halfe so flowing.

(5) What need thy faire head beare a part
　　In Teares? as if thine eyes had none?
　What need they helpe to drowne thine heart,
　　That strives in Torrents of its owne?

(6) Water'd by the showres they bring,
    The thornes that thy blest browes encloses
(A cruell and a costly spring)
    Conceive proud hopes of proving Roses.

(7) Not a haire but payes his River
    To this *Red Sea* of thy blood,
Their little channels can deliver
    Something to the generall flood.

(8) But while I speake, whither are run
    All the Rivers nam'd before?
I counted wrong; there is but one,
    But ô that one is one all o're.

(9) Raine-swolne Rivers may rise proud
    Threatning all to overflow,
But when indeed all's overflow'd
    They themselves are drowned too.

(10) This thy Bloods deluge (a dire chance
    Deare Lord to thee) to us is found
A deluge of deliverance,
    A deluge least we should be drown'd.

Nere was't thou in a sence so sadly true,
    The well of living Waters, Lord, till now.

The "wounds" mentioned in this version of the title lead immediately, in stanza 1, to the locations of those wounds. Crashaw adopts chiastic placement:

hands X feet / head X side

And so the structure is of two different kinds: one dependent on the rhetorical scheme just diagrammed for lines 2–3, the other arising from the alternating rhyme scheme that governs the stanza as a whole. Succeeding stanzas refer to each of the four wounded places in turn, but not in the same order in which they were introduced nor at equal length. Instead, stanzas 2–3–4 dilate feet-hands-side while stanzas 5–6–7 expand from the head (5), thorns (6), and hair (7), and the initial chiasm thus shifts round so as to become

feet X hands / side X head-thorns-hair.

One of the diagonals, as in the first scheme, links two elements, but the other now places three against one; the further numerical suggestion being made is that feet-hands-side (three wounded places) are balanced by head-thorns-hair (one wounding with three parts). As a result, another diagram perhaps needs to be drawn so as to indicate the double structure in stanzas 2–7 collectively considered:

feet-hands-side (X)
(X) head-thorns-hair.

Having arrived at the hair's "little channels" in the seventh stanza, Crashaw next claims to discover unity within numerical multiplicity, but the line in which plurals are resolutely disclaimed ("I counted wrong; there is but one") is, after all, in an eighth stanza that is followed by a ninth and a tenth and then by two more lines that refer to living waters. To continue wrong counting even as one refers to the error of so doing is surely perverse, but a possible explanation is that all unredeemed activity, including counting, necessarily is of that kind: doubleness and duplicity are intrinsic to it. Extreme counter-measures come into play in the tenth stanza as human self-contradiction is overwhelmed by divine oxymoron: *d*eluge-*d*eluge-*d*eliverance, in alliteratively triple climax, results in *d*eluge-(not)-*d*rowned.

The conclusion is a pentameter couplet set off against the tetrameter quatrains, but there are oddities in it. "True" and "Now," despite terminal position, are not eye-rhymes and also may not be aural rhymes except to the ears of a "Caedmon" ("*Nu* sculon herigean [/] heofonrices Weard") or, possibly, a Scot. Mis- or off-rhyming is audible and visible earlier, of course, perhaps most noticeably in stanza 9 (proud-overflow-overflowed-too), but this fact intensifies rather than obviates the problem in the "couplet" because of the intervening sequence of closer rhymes in stanza 10 (chance-found-deliverance-drowned). The image of the well is watery, to be sure, but its depth abruptly replaces length on the one hand (rivers, channels) and breadth as well as depth on the other (flood, deluge). Another diagonal can be drawn:

Nere
now.

And this is an exceptionally strong one, in fact, since it links alliterated words, placed in emphatic initial and terminal positions, that contrast denial (*N*ever) and affirmation (*n*ow). Only half, however, of a "chi" is there. The ten syllables of either of the pentameters might be thought to balance the ten quatrains, and the twenty syllables of both could correspond, by means of poetic division, to the preceding forty lines. And yet multiples of four and five are still being counted despite the claim for focal oneness, and it is not probable that the age-old dichotomy of the One and the Many can be resolved in this way.

"*All* thy Purple River*s*," "a *double* Nilus," "*Halfe* so fruitfull, *halfe* so flowing," "Not *a* haire," "their little channel*s*," "I counted wrong": the poem invites observation of its numerical inconsistency, and a comparison to the Latin version indicates how very explicit that invitation is. Thousands ("mille & mille") of drops ("guttis") of blood are there to be counted, and each "capillus" ("small hair" but with pun on "capillary") is as if a river from a red ocean ("*quasi de* rubro *rivulus* oceano" [this typography, reproduced from L. C. Martin, *reversed* italics]). The numerical discrepancy, if anything, is thus exaggerated, but one cannot find any Latin equivalent for "I counted wrong."

Another phrase for which no corresponding Latin can be found is "in a sence." I call attention to the fact in an effort to be scrupulously fair about the next point. The phrase is medially placed in what is only the penultimate line, and since the position is not emphatic, "in a sence" could be passed over as rather casual, perhaps even metrical "filler" rather perfunctorily tossed in. Comparison of the two couplets as wholes may support this view. The Latin,

> *O nimium* vivae *pretiosis amnibus* undae!
> Fons vitae *nunquam verior ille fuit*,

roughly translated, means, "O superabundance of vital water in costly streams! never more truly was that one the fountain source of life." Since the English adaptation omits the first line of the Latin, the second of them has to be stretched into two: "Nere was't thou in a sence so sadly true, / The well of living Waters, Lord, till now." Notice, however, that "precious stream" (to invent only one obvious alternative) easily could have been derived from "pretiosis amnibus" (as "costly spring" may already have been in stanza 6); and that "Nere was't thou, precious stream, so sadly true" meets metrical, verbal, and alliterative needs. Crashaw, no doubt, could have contrived something much better, but the point is the ease with which one readily turns up a substitute for "in a sence." I therefore think it fair to observe that these words deny the literal truth of the "sadly true" statement that follows and implicitly call into question the accuracy of that which previously has been said. Reverting for a moment to Donne's metaphors, one could say that the lines of this poem's picture turn out to be skewed; the image, though at first glance so painstakingly engraved, is revealed to be flawed. For Crashaw, however, this fact may represent no more than an admission of foregone failure. In terms of Crashaw's own metaphors, the Latin gives "fons vitae," and "fons" (in this case, "wellhead" might be a suitable translation) is especially apt for language that earlier has permitted Crashaw to stress the "frons" or face of Christ. But it is "the well" itself with which the English concludes, and this particular one proves to be far too deep, infinitely so, to be fully fathomed.

The inevitable corollary is that revision, at the most fundamental level, is hopeless. Incidental flaws, perceived at some later time, certainly might be correctable by further subtraction and/or addition, but the primary problem simply cannot be solved by merely human art. It thus is no accident, I think, that while Crashaw reworked various details in the main body of the poem, he never changed, apparently, its conclusion; presumably he continued to think that "in a sence" was the very best to be hoped for no matter how many revisions he made. What was possible, however, was to look again at the deep truth in somewhat different ways, not necessarily to expose more of it, and certainly not all of it, but to allow one part of it to emerge with greater clarity even if that which earlier was clear becomes less visible as a result. At this point, if not earlier, we want the 1648 text. (Since Martin usually copies 1652, but not always, what follows is a reconstruction from his text and textual apparatus; Martin supplies stanzaic numbers in this case, but I have moved them from the center of the page to the margin.)

ON THE BLEEDING BODY OF OUR CRUCIFIED LORD.

I. Iesu, no more! It is full tide.
      From thy head & from thy feet,
   From thy hands & from thy side
      All the purple Riuers meet.

II. What need thy fair head bear a part
      In showres, as if thine eyes had none?
   What need They help to drown thy heart,
      That streames in torrents of it's own?

III. Thy restlesse feet now cannot goe
      For vs & our eternall good,
   As they were euer wont. What though?
      They swim, Alas, in their own blood.

IV. Thy hands to giue, thou canst not lift;
      Yet will thy hand still giuing be.
   It giues, But ô it self's the gift.
      It giues though bound; though bound 'tis free.

V. But ô thy side, thy deep-digg'd side!
      That hath a double Nilus going.
   Nor euer was the *Pharian* tide
      Half so fruitfull, half so flowing.

VI. No hair so small, but payes his riuer
      To this red sea of thy blood
   Their little channells can deliuer
      Somthing to the Generall floud.

VII. But while I speak, whither are run
    All the riuers nam'd before?
    I counted wrong. There is but one;
        But ô that one is one all ore.

VIII. Rain-swoln riuers may rise proud,
    Bent all to drown & ouerflow.
    But when indeed all's ouerflow'd
        They themselues are drowned too.

IX. This thy blood's deluge, a dire chance
    Dear LORD to thee, to vs is found
    A deluge of Deliuerance;
        A deluge least we should be drown'd.

N'ere wast thou in a sense so sadly true,
    The WELL of liuing WATERS, Lord, till now.

The effect of the changes in 1648 is felt first of all in the title. The only substantive difference is that "Body" replaces "Wounds," but in a poem that counts and miscounts, a shift from plural to singular is not trivial. In 1646, Crashaw extracts—more accurately, indicates a need to extract—oneness from multiplicity, but in 1648 that process is first reversed before being repeated. The eye first sees "Body"; then a division of that body into its parts and their several wounds becomes evident. In this version, therefore, it is reunification, not unification, that would result from a successful effort to reassemble the wounded parts into "one." Lack of success continues to be acknowledged, but in this case divine self-division compensates in advance for human miscounting.

Crashaw also rearranges the four wounded places of the crucified body by transposing lines 2–3 of the first stanza. Instead of hands-feet-head-side, the stanza now gives

head   feet
hands   side.

Paraphrasable meaning is the same, but no diagonals can now be drawn. I earlier elided the fact that a "chi" is a skewed cross, partly to arrive at the idea of skewed lines first, partly to notice now that if a crooked cross was especially suitable for 1646, then subtracting it from 1648 at first seems indeed to be a loss rather than a gain, and partly to observe that what Crashaw has done is to replace the rhetorical scheme with a specifically Christian gesture. The four repositioned nouns "parallel," as Williams points out in his headnote, the movement of a hand making the sign of the cross. Since the moving hand cannot be Christ's (his own are crucified and therefore "bound"), a further result is that Christ remains crossed on the cross, the poem is recrossed, and the reader is self-crossed. "Then," to requote Donne, "are you to your selfe a Crucifixe."

(I also elided another fact that may be dealt with parenthetically, namely that the Latin poem, so far as I can see, is built on a partly different base. It begins, chiastically, with "O Frontis, lateris, manuúmque pedúmque"—or, in diagram form, with

frons (face) — laterus (side)
(crossing)
manus (hand) — pes (foot).

The next verses amplify each of these nouns but do so in bottom-to-top order: foot-hand-side-face. Since point-by-point inversion thus occurs, perhaps one is to conclude that upside-down symmetry necessarily is crooked since it is not straight and/or what is displayed is an invertedness finely appropriate to human redemption from the perverse downward progress of the Fall. The point, in any case, is that because of what the Latin does and does not do, the chance of two casual and yet distinguishably different crossings in the English verses seems remote. Latin stanzaic order, in theory, ought also to be considered in the next paragraph, but since the English probably is enough to make the next point clear, I would now like to leave the Latin behind lest the tunnel-vision effect of all this be even worse.)

Having transposed lines 2–3 in 1648, Crashaw next transposes the stanzas that immediately follow. Facing texts would be especially helpful here, but a comparative table may be a workable substitute.

Stanza	1646	1648
2	feet	head
3	hand	feet
4	side	hand
5	head	side

The two columns plainly show that feet and head are upside down in 1646 but right side up in 1648. Inversion and reversion may be equally appropriate, but in 1648 the order now corresponds to the noun positions in lines 2–3. As a result, the parallel to cross-making movement of the hand is repeated in elongated and slower form. "Addition" thus has occurred, but so has "subtraction": the 1646 balancing of feet-side-hands against head-thorns-hair has been lost because repositioning the "head" has necessitated separating it from "hair" and "thorns." The two subparts have become structurally superfluous. Crashaw can and does omit the thorns; an inevitable side effect is, of course, the reduction of the total number of quatrains from ten to nine. But he simply cannot leave out the hair. He needs "their little channels" in order to arrive at "all the rivers" that he "counted wrong," and to omit miscounting would be to subtract entirely too much. One whole stanza has been lost as it is. A weekend number symbolist like me can be happy with either the "totality" of 10 (1646) or the "divine perfection" of 9 (1648), but the 10s and 20s of the concluding pentameters are less flexible. One could cheerfully entertain the possibility that a crossover from 9 to 10 is taking place in the last two lines of 1648, but even if that is true, the crosses of 1646 do not look the same in 1648. Remaking the image results in a different picture.

Both 1646 and 1648, moreover, are and can only be pictures or images no matter how cruciform they are in their differing ways: *crosses* but not the *Cross*. This point leads directly to the third title, the one in 1652: "Vpon the Bleeding Crucifix A Song." Williams, quoting and abridging his own earlier work (the ellipsis that follows momentarily is his own), remarks, "The progressive change of name is significant. The emphasis has been shifted from the wounds [1646] through the body [1648] to the crucifix [1652], and . . . the poem has been made consciously cruciform in the later version [1648/52]." I would want to reword the latter part of this statement to allow for the chiastic structure in 1646, and I think the earlier part of it might usefully be expanded. First, the subject now announced, a crucifix, is an image of the Cross but is neither the Cross itself nor Christ crucified. Second, while all versions might be suitable for singing, to call the third one "A Song" is to give, at the very outset, a second emphasis on art and image making. Third, the intensification of *"Upon"* just conceivably underlines the already implicit idea that the poem could be placed on an icon in much the same way that Milton's "On Time" was to be placed, as Merritt Y. Hughes tells us, on "a clock-case." Better yet, of course, for comparative purposes, is the Ruthwell cross in Dumfriesshire on which part of the Old English *Dream of the Rood* is carved in runes. In Crashaw, moreover, music is being closely associated, though not indistinguishably fused, with verbal and iconic arts as a triple sign of the underlying reality by which they are informed—that is, given shape and significance.

The 1652 poem fulfills its own iconographical demands by being a verbal cross that needs no picture, but whether that fulfillment would be as evident without 1646 and 1648 as it is with them is necessarily moot. Much of the emblem in 1652 is drawn by cross-making movement, a movement also present, of course, in 1648, and yet 1648 meets the demands of its own different title by tracing out the one body's distinguishable parts before gesturing toward reunification of them. 1646, moreover, enacts the discrepancy between singular and plural, brought to the surface by "I counted wrong" (words found, however, in 1648 and 1652 as well), and does so with lines that are fittingly skewed and chiastic. The poetic body as given in 1648 and 1652 may seem to have more weight than the one given only in 1646 because it was twice printed and at later dates, but since that same substantive body has two different titles, perhaps the weight should be reduced, if not halved. Quantity alone, in any case, can hardly be the only point; if it were, then arguing that 1646 is "weightier" because it has four more lines would not be inane or frivolous.

The source of these quandaries is, of course, the customary and reasonable presumption that one or another of a poem's various versions must be the final form, but here it may be preferable to suppose that Crashaw carved this stone three times precisely because finality would itself be a distorted image of truth. Instead of referring to one poem twice revised, I suggest that we acknowledge a fact that to some extent has long been abundantly clear: Three alternate texts exist, each possessed of (limited) claims to intrinsic authority; they differ among themselves in significantly different ways, one of them being that the differences themselves are of different kinds. At this point, we could even hypothecate other alternative texts—up to and including a symbolic ninth or tenth, perhaps—that would continue to indicate that each poem, while complete in itself, can never be the final word for the profound but extraordinarily simple reason that only the Word could speak it. Or, rather, in these poems the reason is that only within the sacred amplitude of the Cross, not crosses, can its own divine image and meaning quite perfectly coincide.

From this point of view, each of Crashaw's English crosses had to be crooked, though only one of them is chiastic, but in this particular case, addition actually subtracts since three are less crooked than one.

7 Herrick and the Ceremonies of Art

The second edition of Crashaw's double volume, *Steps to the Temple* with *Delights of the Muses*, appeared in 1648, the same year in which Herrick published his poetry for the first and only time. That Herrick wanted his own work divided into "Hesperides" on the one hand and "Noble Numbers" on the other is clear enough, but the second of the two title pages in the book, the one for "Noble Numbers," is dated 1647, and since Herrick was on hand in London (as Crashaw, self-exiled to the continent, was not), the discrepancy in dates may indicate a change in plan about which of the work's two sections was to have been placed first.[1]

Perhaps, therefore, an advantage was originally proposed (though subsequently conceded) in adopting the same design as in Crashaw: begin with the avowedly religious verse of "Noble Numbers" and postpone the more secular pieces of "Hesperides." In Herrick's case, either order is theoretically tenable because the two parts of the book prove to be complementary and even reversible. What largely obscures the close relationship is that there are 1,130 poems to encounter in "Hesperides" before getting to "Noble Numbers" at all, but since that problem is basically quantitative, it could be quickly solved by the simple expedient of turning the two parts around.

Reversal tactics, as I hope momentarily to show, merely accelerate, therefore, the process of comparison that Herrick's split volume more leisurely demands of its readers no matter which part is printed first. Far more problematic, precisely because it is essentially unquantifiable, is the difference actually effected in 1647/48 by the decision (regardless of whether it was made at the very outset or later) to defer "Noble Numbers" in favor of "Hesperides." My own inference is that the consequence was and is enormous. The social and religious tumult that drove Crashaw abroad also expelled Herrick from Dean Prior, the country parish where

---

1. L. C. Martin, *The Poetical Works of Robert Herrick*, 568, heavily discounted the possibility that "Herrick intended either to publish the *Noble Numbers* separately or to let them precede *Hesperides* in one volume"; such "suppositions," he says, "appear to overlook the fact that the signatures in the *Noble Numbers* run Aa-Ee not A-E." My own suppositions, however, will shortly be seen to rest on a different kind of base, including the fact that the contents obviously could have been rearranged before the compositor began work.

he served as priest. Since Herrick returned there when allowed to in 1660 and was buried in its churchyard in 1674, it is reasonable to suppose that in calmer moments he would not have been resident in London in 1647/48 and that the timing of the publication of his book is inextricable from the turbulent history of the times themselves. If so, then the volume's arrangement (and just possibly its rearrangement) can be construed as a reaction to and a comment on what was happening outside the printshop as well as merely the result of what went on inside it.

I think I see vast irony in the fact that "Noble Numbers" is literally outnumbered, and decisively so, by "Hesperides": the ratio is more than four to one in countable items (272 poems vis-à-vis 1,130) and more than five to one in readable length (84 of J. Max Patrick's pages compared to 432). Since, however, terminal position itself counts for much, also to be reckoned with are the delayed positioning of the religious poems as a group and the placement of Passion poems at the end of that group. In 1647/48, rather more than in some years, the Cross may have been looming as a last court of appeal; it was, after all, quite soon to be the only one apparently left for Charles I as he mounted the scaffold to be executed in January of 1649.

I am not, of course, in any way proposing that the published format of Herrick's book turned it into a tract for the times. Indeed, since no reprint was demanded until long after Herrick's own burial in an unmarked grave, the better conclusion may be that Herrick and his book are far more notable now than they ever were then. In any case, supportive details, while always in order, very likely are especially so here.

ANGLICAN PRIEST AND SON OF BEN

The second title page, the one dated 1647, announces "His Noble Numbers: or, His Pious Pieces, Wherein (amongst other things) he sings the Birth of his CHRIST: and sighes for his *Saviours* suffering on the Crosse." Herrick lives up to this promise with "*An Ode of the Birth of our Saviour*" (N-33), "*A Christmas* Caroll" (N-96), and a series of Passion poems (N-263 through 271) that begins with "*Good Friday:* Rex Tragicus" and ends with "*His coming to the Sepulcher.*" There also are four poems for the Circumcision (N-60, N-97 and 98, N-125) and at least one (N-102) for Epiphany. ("*To his Saviour, a Child, a Present, by a child,*" N-59, may be another example, but the Epiphany motif of an exchange of gifts is suggested more by the elaborate title than by the lines themselves.) Sacred epigrams—among them, "*Christs twofold coming*" (N-257) and "*Christs words on the Crosse*" (N-167)—fill in some chinks here and there, and the wider liturgical framework is established by starting off this part of the work with *"His Confession"* and *"His Prayer for Absolution"* (N-1 and 2) and then adding poems such as *"His Letanie, to the Holy Spirit"* (N-41), *"His Creed"* (N-78), *"The Eucharist"* (N-155), and *"To keep a true Lent"* (N-228).

These titles and subjects are much in accord, of course, with the vocation of a priest, but Herrick seems to have seen no reason to conceal his allegiance and deep devotion to Jonson and to the classicism that Jonson had anglicized. Full membership in the Tribe of Ben scarcely fell into the same heinous category as being "a secret papist," and classical materials, far from being rigorously suppressed, find their way into "Noble Numbers" with conspicuous regularity.

Anticipating this fact in advance may not, however, completely forestall occasional surprise at some of the results. Patrick footnotes Pausanius's report concerning the existence in Athens of a statue to the goddess Mercy. Herrick's adaptation is, "Mercy, the wise Athenians held to be / Not an Affection, but a *Deitie*" (N-148). Nestor was an ancient (specifically, Homeric) prototype for venerable old age. Herrick turns the fact into a moral comment: "Nor makes it matter, *Nestors* yeers to tell, / If man lives long, and if he live not well" (N-230). *"Good men afflicted most"* (N-108) is the pious and aphoristic title of a poem that begins with a generalized scene of Christian warfare; "GOD" brings "good men"

> to the field, and, there, to skirmishing;
> With trialls those, with terrors these He proves,
> And hazards those most, whom the most He loves.

Details of martial action emerge by means of a roll-call of examples, but these figures most definitely are *not* the saints and martyrs invoked in church litanies.

> For *Sceva*, darts; for *Cocles*, dangers; thus
> He finds a fire for mighty *Mutius;*
> Death for stout *Cato*; and besides all these,
> A poyson too He has for *Socrates;*
> Torments for high *Attilius;* and, with want,
> Brings in *Fabricius* for a Combatant.

The entire poem, moreover, takes its cue from Seneca and not only that, but from a comment being made, not about divine Providence, but about blind Chance. In Seneca, it is "fortune" (not God) that "attempteth the most confident and couragious sort of men . . . tryeth her fire upon *Mutius*, povertie in *Fabricius*, . . . poyson in *Socrates*, death in *Cato*" (quoted from Patrick's note).

Stoicism and Christianity share a sometime contempt for the world and for that reason at times can be combined, but the mixture given in

"*Good men afflicted most*" is neither traditional nor conventional. Much stranger, however, is the equivocal commitment that Herrick makes in "*Good Friday: Rex Tragicus*" (N-263). Launcelot Andrewes rhetorically asked himself and his congregation whether the Passion was "a *Tragaedy*" (quoting, as in the preceding chapter, from *XCVI Sermons*, 376), but he did not suppose that it was of the kind wherein Aristotelian unities or "Lawes of Action," as Herrick refers to them, were to be observed. Nor does the classicism of Milton's *Samson Agonistes* retrospectively prepare one for the ironies of Herrick's Passion play. The "Crosse" is here a "Stage"; the "spacious field" where it is reared, a "*Theater*"; and Herrick (this is where oddity sets in), a stage manager busily ordering actors about and keeping an eye on the house out front, especially impatient groundlings. The "rude . . . Multitude," bored by the wait, "Yawne for" the catastrophe: "How He deferres, how loath He is to die." "Why then begin, great King!" (Herrick commands); "ascend Thy Throne, / And thence proceed, to act Thy Passion."

Roscius Gallus, the famous Roman actor, was unavailable for the lead (Herrick doesn't explain why, but a plausible guess is that his fees were too high). In consequence, "Thou"—Christ—"art that *Roscius*. . . . That must this day act the Tragedian." Cicero once inquired whether anyone could be so savage of heart and hardened of soul as not to have been moved by the feigned death of Roscius.[2] The answer expected was no, but at this theater, by and large, it is yes, though there are some, including Herrick himself, who "will both sigh, and weep." No matter how the audience reacts on Good Friday, the ending of this day's play will prove to be indecisive. It requires a sequel that is to be staged elsewhere and later, and Hell, when the harrowing of it is enacted on Saturday, "may stand amaz'd." Herrick evidently has no time now to start worrying about Sunday's uncomfortably early matinee, but on Easter, of course, the third installment is to be a comedy in which the original Roscius—though "supreme" in that dramatic genre—will at best have a walk-on part.

"Noble Numbers" is decidedly a mixed (one may be tempted to say mixed-*up*) affair. It might be the work of a priest who frequently flouts decorum and sometimes cuts a slightly ludicrous figure by toting round the baggage of an elegant education. The author of "Hesperides" is approximately the same person or, if not that, his alter ego, but in retreating to the first part of Herrick's volume one also needs to turn the description upside down: the Hesperidean verse is that of a latter-day classicist whose well-thumbed copies of Roman poets and, at least as importantly, of Old

2. Cicero, *Pro Archia*, 8.17. See also *The Oxford Classical Dictionary*, 2d ed. (Oxford: Oxford University Press, 1970), 937 ("Roscius Gallus"): "Supreme in comedy, he also played tragic parts. . . . His name became typical for a consummate artist . . . his popularity being prodigious. . . . His earnings were enormous."

Ben have somehow become interleaved with pages from the Bible and Prayer Book.

Consider, for example, the recurrent motif that "Poetry perpetuates the Poet" (the title of H-794). This aesthetic faith could not possibly have been introduced any earlier in "Hesperides" than it actually was since it appears in the form of an epigraph on the 1648 title page, "Effugient avidos Carmina nostra Rogos," my songs shall escape the eager funeral flames. Patrick points out that the source is Ovid (*Amores*, 3.9.28), and this is a clearly announced point of departure for the 1,130 poems that follow. But before arriving at the stopping point, one definitely will want to supplement Ovid with the formula that Horace (*Carmina*, 3.30) devised: "exegi monumentum," I have built a monument more enduring than bronze. The reason why is the monument Herrick himself reared in "*The pillar of Fame*" (H-1129), the penultimate verse in the book's first part.

> Fames pillar here, at last, we set,
> Out-during *Marble, Brasse*, or *Jet*,
> Charm'd and enchanted so,
> As to withstand the blow
> Of   overthrow:
> Nor shall the seas,
> Or   OUTRAGES
> Of storms orebear
> What we up-rear,
> Tho Kingdoms fal,
> This   pillar   never   shall
> Decline or waste at all;
> But stand forever by his owne
> Firme and well fixt foundation.

And yet Herrick's "The pillar," however classical in theme, looks very much like Herbert's "The Altar," and the resemblance, even if coincidental, is not without meaning, for Herrick's enduring monument often is inscribed in a religious alphabet. "A Psalme or Hymne to the Graces" (H-777) propitiates the protective divinities of verse, but Herrick indicates his willingness, if need be, "to suffer in the Muses *Martyrdome*" (H-1128). To perpetuate the fame of others, a calendar of "saints" is constructed. "Late you come in; but you a Saint shall be, / In Chiefe, in this Poetick Liturgie" ("*To his Kinswoman, Mistresse* Penelope Wheeler," H-510). "Sprightly *Soame*" is to be among "A stock of Saints," all sealed in an "eternall Calender" ("*To his worthy Kinsman, Master* Stephen Soame," H-545). Herrick also has, as it were, a patron saint, who is, of course, none other than Ben Jonson.

> When I a Verse shall make,
> Know I have praid thee,

> For old *Religions* sake,
> Saint *Ben* to aide me.
>
> . . . .
>
> Candles Ile give to thee,
> And a new Altar;
> And thou Saint *Ben*, shalt be
> Writ in my *Psalter.*
>
> ("*His Prayer to* Ben. Johnson," H-604)

That Herrick feels more than a bit inane in reaching for hyperbole is shown, among other ways, by stretching for the foolish altar-psalter rhyme. And yet from one point of view (this one inverts the perspective that allowed Herrick to play stage manager in "Rex Tragicus"), to invoke Jonson as St. Ben is entirely reasonable and eminently appropriate.

"*To* Julia" (H-584) unfolds one reason why Herrick adopts this kind of vocabulary for this kind of subject. "The Saints-bell calls" him to read "The Proper Lessons for the Saints now dead." Julia lends "grace" to the "Service" or, as it turns out, what does so is the singing of "One *Holy Collect*" for her, anticipating a time when "A *Trentall*" shall be "sung by Virgins" over Julia's "Grave." "Meane time we two will sing the Dirge of these; / Who dead, deserve our best remembrances." However worthy (or unworthy) Herrick's own kinfolk actually were, and totally apart from the autobiographical identity (if any) of Julia, there can be no question at all about whether Jonson merited Herrick's very best remembrances, nor did Herrick hesitate to downplay himself in order to magnify Jonson all the more.

Herrick frequently pokes fun at all sorts of things, and some of his jokes, as in the routines of many a stand-up comic, can be at his own expense; Jonson, however, by no means is subject to ridicule. "Rex Tragicus" plays out a sardonic farce, but it is we who are the farceurs, not Christ. These two poems and others just mentioned could be tagged as "parodies," but they represent a two-edged response to the otherwise terrifying mutability of all human affairs, including human endeavor to prevail by transcending that mutability. Herrick's Hesperidean universe, lovely though it often is, repeatedly threatens to collapse into vacuity unless vigorous counteraction is taken by bringing to bear enduring materials from whatever sources may be available. This particular theme will have to be returned to because it is pervasive and takes many forms, but for the moment one can begin by noticing that it too is started up at nearly the very outset. In the programmatic first poem of "Hesperides," Herrick accurately announces, "I sing of *Times trans-shifting.*" "All things decay and die" (H-69), as a soon encountered title rather mildly asserts. A parallel epigram (H-432) is both succinct and devastating:

> *PUTREFACTION*
> Putrefaction is the end
> Of all that Nature doth entend.

Searching out preservatives and buttresses wherever they may be found, Herrick shores up a title page with Ovid and a nearly final poem with Horace, for the goal at which those poets aimed was an enduring poetic monument to their own effort and to the subjects they hoped to immortalize.

The epigraph from Roman Ovid is balanced on the second title page by one in Greek from Hesiod, who once asserted, "We know how to say many things that bear the guise of truth, and we also know when we intend to state the truth" (Patrick's translation). Nothing could possibly be more classical than the *Theogony*, but to say that it differs markedly from Ovid's *Amores* is, if anything, to understate. A similar observation arises from the fact that the clear counterpart to H-1129, "The pillar of Fame," has to be the untitled N-268 since it is the only other typographically shaped poem. Almost all of Herrick's poems, even the two-line distichs, have separate titles, but it may be fair to say that H-1129 benefits from having "The pillar" as a heading to identify, quite precisely, the form traced out by the lines and to intensify by announcing in advance the defense against mutability that those lines enunciate. The parallel poem, however, could be left nameless because the typography unmistakably exhibits an image that had long been the most potent reminder ever devised that it is mutability itself that shall not endure. (I shorten the poem because I am primarily interested in the symbolic shape; Herrick's greater length, however, may lend additional force to the symbol and certainly does not diminish it.)

> *This Crosse-Tree here*
> *Doth JESUS beare,*
> . . . .
> . . . .
> . . . .
> Here all things ready are, make hast, make hast away;
> For, long this work wil be, & very short this Day.
> Why then, go on to act: Here's wonders to be done,
> Before the last least sand of Thy ninth houre be run;
> Or e're dark Clouds do dull, or dead the Mid-dayes Sun.
> Act when Thou wilt,
> Bloud will be spilt;
> Pure Balm, that shall
> Bring Health to All.
> . . . .
> . . . .
> Meane while, let mee,
> Beneath this Tree,
> This Honour have,
> To make thy grave.

Cross-referencing Roman monuments and monumental Christian occasions can deepen the resonance of a classical heritage or finely attune an application of the ecclesiastical to intensely felt personal needs. There is no mistaking, however, the direction of the major thrusts being made in each case. The liturgy of the saints in "Hesperides," as Herrick himself remarks, is of the "poetic" sort, a clerical mode whereby to render homage in a basically classical way, and adulation for Jonson, while quite rightly and hugely hyperbolic, stays on this side of fatuous idolatry because of self-deprecatory tone. In "Noble Numbers," Herrick partly undermines Seneca's system of values from beneath and superimposes a different contour on the names that Seneca himself supplied. He sweeps up Roscius so as to observe that the human condition is not sufficiently perfected, at least not yet, for Roman drama itself to be swept aside. And Horace's pillar, though it looks like an altar that is itself overshadowed by a towering cross, is possessed of an independent and substantial reality of its own.

There are, however, a number of poems in "Hesperides" that generate approximately equal force in antithetical directions from an ambivalent center. In the two sections that next follow, I suggest that "The Transfiguration" and the much better known "*To Daffadills*" are examples worth looking at in their own right and that they also can serve as focal points for clusters of poems that in turn are representative of topics to which Herrick regularly returned. "Corinna's *going a Maying*" is similarly ambivalent but must be placed in a separate section since it is entirely too famous to be lumped with anything else, including the verse by Catullus on which Herrick directly relied.

MODIFIED RITES

Since The Transfiguration of Christ falls on August 6 in Roman and Anglican calendars, a fact of which Herrick can scarcely have been unaware, one might momentarily suppose that "The Transfiguration" (H-819) has somehow escaped from the "religious" part of Herrick's book and strayed into the "secular" part by mistake. More than a few titles of this kind are to be found in "Hesperides," and in some instances the poems that they head actually could be placed among the "Noble Numbers" with little or no impropriety. "Julia's *Churching, or Purification*" (H-898) and "*To* Julia *in the Temple*" (H-445) and, for that matter, "*To* Julia" (H-584, the poem quoted a few paragraphs back) evidently are religious poems. The only serious cause for dubiety is the name of the person to whom they are addressed, and for that misgiving to arise, one would need to recall other poems to Julia that confess a decidedly amorous interest priests are not commonly encouraged by their bishops to take.

There are Hesperidean poems, however, that probably *would* be mis-placed in "Noble Numbers" despite their religious titles. *"Ceremonies for Christmasse"* and *"Christmasse-Eve, another Ceremonie"* (H-784 and H-785), *"Ceremonies for Candlemasse Eve"* (H-892, and see H-980, *"Ceremony upon Candlemas Eve"*), *"The Ceremonies for Candlemasse day"* (H-893 and H-894), *"Twelfe night"* (H-1035), *"Saint Distaffs day, or the morrow after Twelfth day"* (H-1026)—language of this kind (and I break off the list well before Herrick does) frequently introduces verse that explores the realms of folklore and secular custom. Also frequently visible, however, is a yoking together of activities going on both inside and outside church on whatever "ceremonial" day it may be.

> The Holly hitherto did sway;
>   Let Box now domineere;
> Untill the dancing Easter-day,
>   Or Easters Eve appeare.
>
> When Yew is out, then Birch comes in,
>   And many Flowers beside;
> Both of a fresh, and fragrant kinne
>   To honour Whitsontide.
> ("*Ceremonies for Candlemasse Eve*," H-892)

In this instance, natural growth and decay keep pace with the litur-gical year and thereby enable two rituals to be simultaneous. Both meth-ods of marking out time are predicated on cycles of seasonal change, those of nature on the one hand and of the church calendar on the other. "Thus times do shift" (as Herrick remarks, concluding the poem from which the eight lines above are quoted); "each thing his turne do's hold; / *New things succeed, as former things grow old.*" Both time schemes fur-ther assume that calendrical recurrence carries the year around so that what was old—whether Box and Birch or Easter and Whitsunday—once again becomes new. "Kindle the Christmas Brand, and then / Till Sunne-set, let it burne; . . . then lay it up agen, / Till Christmas next returne" ("*The Ceremonies for Candlemasse day*," H-893). In both rituals the "returne" is of critical importance, and the ceremonies are designed to be protective of those who properly observe them. Part of the Christmas brand, Herrick says, must be kept to enkindle "The Christmas Log next yeare; / And where 'tis safely kept, the Fiend, / Can do no mischiefe (there)." I have no notion at all as to where around the house the brand actually was to be laid up, but I also doubt that Herrick thought the specific place greatly mattered so long as part of the tinder was safely preserved within the hearts of the inhabitants.

"Mattens, or morning Prayer" (H-320) and *"Evensong"* (H-321) com-panion one another but not quite in the same way as those poems (noticed

in an earlier chapter) with closely similar titles by Herbert, Vaughan, and others. For one thing, these services are to be conducted in high-church fashion, and Herrick firmly expects the congregation to shape up accordingly. "When with the Virgin morning thou do'st rise, / Crossing thy selfe; come thus to sacrifice: / . . . Give up thy soule in clouds of frankinsence. / Thy golden Censors fil'd with odours sweet, / Shall make thy actions with their ends to meet." A second thing Herrick will tolerate no nonsense about is ending the day, as well as beginning it, with solemn prayers; they are to be addressed, however, to Jove.

> Beginne with *Jove;* then is the worke halfe done;
> And runnes most smoothly when tis well begunne.
> *Jove's* is the first and last: The Morn's his due,
> The midst is thine; But *Joves* the Evening too;
> As sure a[s] *Mattins* do's to him belong,
> So sure he layes claime to the *Evensong.*

Substituting a monosyllabic (and also monotheistic) "God" for the one-syllable "Jove" would be easy enough for author and reader alike. Herrick, in fact, invites the substitution, or appears to do so, partly by pointing to Mattins and Evensong, but also by echoing a statement attributed by St. John to God himself, "I am . . . the first and last" (Revelation 22.13). And indeed, a translation, as it were, into biblical language would be exactly to the point, though also totally beside it. One automatically assumes that God is the unnamed deity addressed in *"Mattens,"* especially because "Crossing thy selfe" is or can be a specifically Christian gesture. This morning prayer has been preceded, however, by 319 Hesperidean poems, and *"Evensong,"* coming next, looks back as well as moves on by being classical, biblical, and ecclesiastical all at the same time.

"The Transfiguration" is an exceptionally striking poem of this kind. The biblical story is recorded in the synoptic Gospels (Matthew 17, Mark 9, Luke 9) and is especially reserved for August 6, as already noted, in Anglican and Roman calendars alike. No proper pericopes or prayers are appointed by the Prayer Book, but the Breviary is a useful index to the recurrent meaning of the event.[3]

The narrative from Matthew (Jesus was "transfigured," "his face did shine as the sun," and "his garments became white as snow") is supplemented with brief lessons from the Epistles. The first "capitulum" or little chapter is Philippians 3.20–21, "we look for the Saviour . . . who will reform the body of our lowness, made like to the body of his glory"; the second is from 2 Corinthians 3.18, "we beholding the glory of the Lord with open face, are transformed into the same image from glory to

---

3. Quotations are from *The Roman Breviary in English.*

glory." 2 Peter 1.10–21 is sectioned into three "lectiones" or readings that, taken as a whole, show Peter awaiting "the laying away of this . . . tabernacle" and anticipating the "excellent glory" of the everlasting kingdom. The pericopes, when thus assembled together on this day, direct one toward the belief that the "body of glory" that was momentarily manifested at the Transfiguration prefigures the far greater glory of Christ's (and all other) resurrected and immortal bodies. The image emphasized is "claritas" (glory, brightness, splendor), one of the "dotes" or qualities attributed to the glorified bodies of the Resurrection, and the process at work is change: the body is to be transformed, reformed, transfigured, or—as the Greek text of Matthew has it—"metamorphosed" from corruptible darkness into transcendent radiance.[4]

Given this context, the surface piety of Herrick's first stanza,

> Immortall clothing I put on,
> So soone as *Julia* I am gon
> To mine eternall Mansion,

may be ruffled by the fact that it is Julia who is at the very dead—or rather, the vivacious—center of the middle line. (Italics, whether Herrick's or the printer's, underline the fact, but positioning alone makes it fully apparent.) The remaining two stanzas, at any rate, reveal that it is the sight of a transfigured Julia that has caused Herrick, both like and yet very *un*like Peter, to anticipate his own changed body. He supposes, moreover, that if Julia's body is transfigured now into momentary glory, then its future radiance will be far more admirable.

> Thou, thou art here, to humane sight
> Cloth'd all with incorrupted light;
> But yet how more admir'dly bright

> Wilt thou appear, when thou art set
> In thy refulgent Thronelet,
> That shin'st thus in thy counterfeit?

From a purely Hesperidean point of view, these stanzas merely engage in a metamorphosis of their own by adapting the ceremonial language of August 6 to the celebration of Julia's beauty. "Counterfeit," however, is a

---

4. Bauer's entry ("Transfiguration," 923–25) assembles the same passages that supplied the Breviary pericopes but usually is too modern in its orientation to be of much help here: "A theory in which every individual element in the story falls into place convincingly and without strain has yet to be discovered" (924A); it does, however, refer to "features which are characteristic and definitive of the heavenly mode of existence" (925A). For earlier discussion of the "dotes" of glorified bodies of the Resurrection, see Aquinas, *Summa theologica*, 3 (Supplement), Qq. 82–85, and Donne, *The Sermons of John Donne*, ed. George R. Potter and Evelyn M. Simpson, 3:114–33.

disquieting word with which to end, a fact that may dictate some second thoughts. Herrick, after all, does invert the Transfiguration about as completely as possible by having Julia fill in for Jesus, and the clothing metaphor, therefore, may not be entirely metaphoric. Instead, the splendors on view in *"Upon* Julia's *Clothes"* (H-779) hover in the background as an attractive alternative to the vision of St. Peter.

> When as in silks my *Julia* goes,
> Then, then (me thinks) how sweetly flowes
> That liquefaction of her clothes.
>
> Next, when I cast mine eyes and see
> That brave Vibration each way free;
> O how that glittering taketh me!

Since comparable glitter is envisaged in *"The Transfiguration,"* a strong possibility is that Herrick expresses enormous admiration for a clothed Julia but suggests that unclothed beauty would be much more admirably bright. If so, then he no doubt would welcome being changed by the sight—better yet, the intimate experiencing—of a Julia so refulgently revealed.

Imagery of "claritas" is as fundamental for the poem as it is for the rite, and the process that both emphasize is change. In church, however, bodies are working up to souls whereas in this poem, as in Donne's "The Exstasie," souls "are to bodies gone." The reversal of direction is accompanied by a lowering of tone from moral gravity in the first stanza (a masquerade, as it turns out) to a burlesque in the third. The nadir may not be apparent until "counterfeit" directs attention back, but it actually occurs in the preceding rhyme-word "Thronelet," a ludicrous diminutive that presumably means, by analogy to its Greek equivalent ("thronion"), "a little elevated seat." The preposterous distance opened up between the two transfigurations is evident, and so also is the comment offered on the absurd lengths to which an infatuated lover will sometimes go. Julia's body, clothed or unclothed, seems so glorious that only outrageous exaggeration could possibly convey suitable reaction to it, but the flagrancy itself threatens to lapse into bathos, and the ambivalent result is that Herrick's speaker—though surely not Julia herself—becomes a figure of ardent absurdity.

This transfigured ritual for August 6 could have been, at least conceivably, another straightforward example of "the religion of love," or it might easily have been nudged further in the direction of satire on amorous folly. But as it is, the poem is neither the one nor the other but something of both.

THE BLOSSOMS OF TIME

Time, so busily trans-shifting everything else in the world of "Hesperides," becomes especially inexorable whenever Herrick contemplates flowers.

His daisies close up shop with unseemly haste ("*To* Daisies, *not to shut so soone,*" H-441); primroses shed dewy tears even as they first begin to bloom ("*To Primroses fill'd with morning-dew,*" H-257); petals show themselves as "Leaves" of a book in which one

> May read how soon things have
> Their end, though ne'r so brave:
> And after they have shown their pride,
> Like you a while: They glide
>   Into the Grave.
>   ("*To Blossoms,*" H-467)

Botanical distinctions aside, these various flowers in effect have been transplanted from "De rosis nascentibus," the famous poem long attributed to Ausonius.[5] Dismayed by the destruction caused by fleeting time, "Ausonius" marvelled that roses should perish nearly as soon as they bloom: "quam longa una dies, aetas tam longa rosarum," only so long as a single day is the time span of the rose. Floral mutability cannot be effectively remedied, but Herrick discovers several sources of consolation, among them Ausonius's own, that the rose, most especially the rose of love, both can and should be plucked. "Collige . . . rosas . . . et memor esto aevum sic proparare tuum," gather roses and be mindful that your time also hastens away. Herrick's well-known "translation" is "*To the Virgins, to make much of Time*" (H-208).

> 1   Gather ye Rose-buds while ye may,
> 2   Old Time is still a flying:
>
> 5   The glorious Lamp of Heaven, the Sun,
> 6   The higher he's a getting.

Buoyant rhythms temporarily exempt rose-gathering virgins from fleeting time, but the exemption begins to be hedged even in the quatrains that grant it:

> 3   And this same flower that smiles today,
> 4   To morrow will be dying
>
> 7   The sooner will his Race be run,
> 8   And neerer he's to Setting.

And the third quatrain, with nonchalant rhymes, which in this case look rather bizarre, takes away much more than it gives:

> That Age is best, which is the first,
>   When Youth and Blood are warmer;

5. The poem is included in an appendix to the second volume of the Loeb edition of Ausonius but is now thought to be pseudonymous.

> But being spent, the worse, and worst
> Times, still succeed the former.

The final stanza urges marriage as a preferable alternative to tarrying, but a question left unasked is whether connubial bliss can long continue if worse times lead only to worst.

Enduring monuments, however, can sometimes be built, as in *"The Lilly in a Christal"* (H-193), a flower preserved with augmented beauty by art. "Tomb'd" (and thus undeniably dead) "in a *Christal* stone," it thereby is made "More faire in this transparent case, / Then when it grew alone; / And had but single grace." In *"The Funerall Rites of the Rose"* (H-686), the "Rose was sick," but it "smiling di'd" because its moment of final expiration (with implicit pun on the "breathing out" of perfume) is also the instant of greatest self-fulfillment. When "prayers for the dead, / And Rites were all accomplished," the rose's "sweets smelt every where" as if "Heaven had spent all perfumes there." What has been "accomplished" powerfully contrasts to deprivation, but if the evidence of other poems can be trusted, then gain does not outweigh loss, for even when blooms give way to fruit, the metamorphosis appears to be at best a lamentable blessing. Hence, for example, *"To Cherry-blossomes"* (H-189):

> Ye may simper, blush, and smile,
> And perfume the aire a while:
> But (sweet things) ye must be gone;
> Fruit, ye know, is comming on:
> Then, Ah! Then, where is your grace,
> When as Cherries come in place?

"Subsumed into gratifying fruitfulness" is a response that the question invites, but Herrick himself declines to give it, perhaps because cherries merely postpone evanescence by subsuming grace into that which is itself to be consumed. And not only does melancholy cause flowery consolation to be tinted with grief; in addition, as achievement apparently mounts, sadness increases all the more. Fruit may be—indeed, indisputably *is*—on its way, but Herrick's sympathies lie almost exclusively with the blossoms soon to depart.

The distance between fulfillment and forfeiture accordingly becomes greatest when Herrick invokes the assurance of liturgical time. The poem, long familiar but short enough to be quoted in full, is *"To Daffadills"* (H-316).

> Faire Daffadills, we weep to see
> You haste away so soone:
> As yet the early-rising Sun
> Has not attain'd his Noone.
> Stay, stay,

> Untill the hasting day
>   Has run
> But to the Even-song;
> And, having pray'd together, we
>   Will goe with you along.
>
> We have short time to stay, as you,
>   We have as short a Spring;
> As quick a growth to meet Decay,
>   As you, or any thing.
>   We die,
> As your hours doe, and drie
>   Away,
> Like to the Summers raine;
> Or as the pearles of Mornings dew
>   Ne'r to be found againe.

Since Herrick's flowers often appear to be horticulturally interchangeable, these daffodils may be mistaken for exaggerated versions of Ausonian roses, their existence far shorter than that of a single day, hasting away even as the early-rising sun quite briefly awakens them into life. With roses, long since associated with fragility, this situation is cause for lament. With daffodils, however, although they are fully as classical in their provenance, it ought to be cause for astonishment. The *OED* entry under "asphodel" ("earlier affodil, whence daffodil") is instructive: "by the poets made an immortal flower." Also worth knowing, however, is a paramount instance of this poetic making. It is Homer's "asphodelos leimon," the daffodilly mead or meadow, descriptive of Elysium, the Hesperides or western isles of departed shades. One of the places where this phrasing occurs is toward the opening of the final book of the *Odyssey.* In Pope's translation:

> CYLLENIUS now to *Pluto*'s dreary reign
> Conveys the dead, a lamentable train!
> . . . .
> Trembling the Spectres glide, and plaintive vent
> Thin hollow screams, along the deep descent.
> . . . .
> And now they reach'd the *Earth*'s remotest ends,
> And now the gates where ev'ning *Sol* descends,
> And *Leucas*' rock, and *Ocean*'s utmost streams,
> And now pervade the dusky land of *Dreams*,
> And rest at last, where souls unbodied dwell
> In ever-flow[r]ing meads of *Asphodel.*[6]

6. The bracket in the last line enables me to change "everflowing" (the reading in the Twickenham edition) to "everflowring," the reading in earlier editions, including *The*

The scene thus unveiled is curiously mixed: the realm itself is one of meadows forever new, but the shades lament their own lost transience. Herrick adopts a similar attitude but complicates matters at the very outset by supposing that daffodilly meads, however unchanging the poetic landscape presumably should be, are trans-shifting at least as rapidly as everything else. Indeed, unlike the roses of love, they cannot even be plucked: they fade at the very moment of first perceiving them.

In this context, "We weep to see / You haste away so soon" carefully understates matters, but when immortal flowers begin to be mutable, then the strong counterthrust to bring into play is Evensong, that time of day when one is "content" (requoting, as in an earlier chapter, Sir Thomas Browne) to take one's "leave of the sun and sleep unto the Resurrection." This symbolism is not obvious in Herrick's "*Evensong*," the poem addressed to Jove, but its presence certainly is felt here. Wait, Herrick urges, wait for the due time of departing in peace, that hour when time transshifts itself out of existence, when eternity is about to begin. And then, having prayed together, we too will go with you along. If these flowers could survive but a single day—merely as long, that is, as the frail roses of poetic tradition—then they would be, as daffodils should be, images of permanence, not decay.

Were that the case, other modifications necessarily would follow. In lines 12–13, "Spring," "growth," and possibly "quick" (as in "the quick and the dead") could be stressed, and "pearls of morning dew" (19) might assume new meaning for which the old theory that pearls were a hardened form of dew would be directly or indirectly relevant. And if that kind of emphasis were appropriate, then the last lines of Marvell's "On a Drop of Dew" would be an illuminating analogue.

> Such did the Manna's sacred Dew destil;
> White, and intire, though congeal'd and chill.
> Congeal'd on Earth: but does, dissolving, run
> Into the Glories of th'Almighty Sun.[7]

Making any of these changes, however, much less all of them, would not merely retouch the details but fundamentally rewrite the very substance of Herrick's poem. The language actually used merely gestures toward veiled images—the better word might be mirages—of solace, and Even-

---

Odyssey, ed. Gilbert Wakefield (London, 1806). George Chapman's translation, the more obvious one to use, abridges this scene too heavily to be useful here.

7. Quoted from *The Poems and Letters*, ed. H. M. Margoliouth, 2d ed. (Oxford: Clarendon Press, 1952). For the "unnatural" natural science of pearls as hardened dew, an appropriate authority to cite here is the encyclopedic Gerard Jan Vossius, *De theologia gentili, et physiologia Christiana* [Of pagan theology and Christian physiology] (Amsterdam, 1641), 1463.

song in this instance brings cold comfort, for when Herrick contemplates the gardens of Hesperides, he is no less moved than the shades in Homer's Elysium to lament the passing of the blossoms of time.

CATULLUS AND THE ARITHMETIC OF LOVE

"Corinna's *going a Maying*" is Herrick's bountiful expression of "carpe diem," seize the day, and since poem and theme alike are exceptionally well known both separately and together, it sometimes is easy to underestimate, if not completely overlook, the ignobling numbers of destructive time that verse within the tradition, including Herrick's, normally attempts to manipulate. A classical antecedent manifestly not overlooked by Herrick himself is Catullus, but I temporarily delay reproducing his fifth song, among other reasons because a prime instance of "carpe diem" is or presumably should be the ode in which Horace included those words to articulate the thought for which they became and still are the shorthand reference:

> dum loquimur fugerit invida
> aetas. carpe diem quam minimus credula postero.[8]

Even as we speak, Horace warns, begrudging time will have taken flight. "Seize the day," putting minimal trust in tomorrow.

The brevity of Horace's poem, a mere eight verses, makes a concise comment of its own, and several compressed and finely wrought ironies are to be observed as the ode concludes: The perfect tense of "fugerit" to express the suddenness of long time's quickly completed past action; the rough violence of seize; and a terminal line that begins with "aetas" (possible meanings include youth, or old age, or the whole time of life) and ends with "postero" ("later in time" but often "secondary in importance"), words that squeeze "diem" into the middle and thus threaten to squeeze it out unless one grips fast and holds on hard. Horace tightly binds all this up with astrology by having already urged Leuconoe to eschew the predictive fortune-telling of idiotic "Babylonios . . . numeros"; these are barbaric numbers not only to be contemptuously dismissed but also in markedly plural contrast to "die*m*" (not "dies"), a pointedly singular day. And since "aetas" (the cumulative result of taking more than one day at a time) is perniciously "invida" and hence inevitably subtractive as a whole, each day is indeed best seized upon as singularly as possible.

Horace advocates straining some wine, a recommendation elucidated

---

8. *Carmina*, 1.11.7–8, in *Carminum libri IV [et] Epodon liber*, ed. T. E. Page (London: Macmillan & Co., 1952; first issued in 1883, revised in 1895, subsequently and frequently reprinted "with additions and corrections").

for young scholars (or elderly amateurs) by Page's note: "Wine was strained through linen or snow." An additional point, I take it, has to do with quality of a different sort; the advice is not to drink life down to the lees but rather to filter out its dregs beforehand. The ode says nothing about lovemaking, nor does it mention Catullus, but by means of its telling restraint, Horace—intentionally or not—sets the earlier poet quite firmly to one side. Lack of restraint, after all, was one of the things Catullus was famous for, the celebrated example being the incredibly large numbers of kisses he demanded from Lesbia. Two classical witnesses to this fact can suitably lead up to the testimony of Catullus himself.

Ovid (*Amores*, 1.8) happens to overhear and would much like to strangle a hag giving sage counsel to a young maid (never named, any more than Catullus is, but the identity is clear): forget all those thousands of kisses from what's-his-name, that poet of yours. Time's too precious; fleece some rich lovers instead. Martial (12.59), finally getting back to dear old Rome after long absence, is quite properly welcomed, as he himself modestly points out, by many more kisses than Catullus ever ranted about; since, however, they come from a cobbler's lips wiped off with leathery hides, from the owner of a filthy beard, and from a foul-mouthed wretch of questionable alcoholic (not to mention sexual) preferences, on the whole it was hardly worthwhile to return. Elsewhere, Martial is momentarily convinced (6.34) that Catullus must have been a mere piker (if you can count the kisses, there can't be nearly enough of them) and also is persuaded (11.6) that since his own wine-flown excellence equals that of any fifteen sober poets, he has every right to demand as many kisses as Catullus did.

Martial's parodic satires, whatever the topic may be, usually refuse to obey laws other than their own, and it can be risky business to draw fixed conclusions from them about what the balloon looked like to others before Martial punctured it. These particular epigrams do suggest, however, the potential presence in Catullus of more than one profitably exploitable line of thought, a possibility that Ovid's ebullient outrage and Horace's restrained ironies further support. The poet to whom these Roman authors responded appears to have been considerably more interesting than the one with the same name who is mentioned in handbooks, and my own notion is that several English writers saw greater complexity in the relationship between Catullus and Lesbia than can be suggested by an editor's note. Herrick could be idiosyncratic or, from a hostile perspective, downright peculiar at times—but not, I think, when he perceived a profoundly deep and quite fascinating ambivalence in the work of his illustrious predecessor that he proceeded to carry over into his own.

Catullus opens his fifth song with "Viuamus," let us live, and closes it with "basiorum," kisses. There are so many other plurals in between these two that Catullus, despite Martial's joke, actually does lose count and fervently hopes that others will do the same.

> Viuamus, mea Lesbia, atque amemus,
> Rumoresque senum seueriorum
> Omnes unius aestimemus assis.
> Soles occidere et redire possunt;
> 5   Nobis, cum semel occidit breuis lux,
> Nox est perpetua una dormienda.
> Da mi basia mille, deinde centum,
> Dein mille altera, dein secunda centum,
> Deinde usque altera mille, deinde centum,
> 10   Dein, cum milia multa fecerimus,
> Conturbamimus illa, ne sciamus,
> Aut ne quis malus inuidere possit,
> Cum tantum sciat esse basiorum.

(Let us live, my Lesbia, and love, and value at one farthing all the talk of crabbed old men. Suns may set and rise again. For us, when the short light has once set, remains to be slept the sleep of one unbroken night. Give me a thousand kisses, then a hundred, then another thousand, then a second hundred, then yet another thousand, then a hundred. Then, when we have made up many thousands, we will confuse our counting that we may not know the reckoning, nor any malicious person blight them with an evil eye, when he knows that our kisses are so many.)[9]

Impetuosity of language is designed to speed over and thus temporarily blur without obliterating the by no means seamless joints between structural units: live and love whatever others say (1–3), for short is the day of love and long is the night of oblivion (4–6); stockpile the kisses in a self-satisfyingly bewildering profusion (7–11) that will confuse and frustrate malignant hostility (12–13). This outline, despite the apparent disservice of its bluntness, does expose the existence of a two-part poem (1–6, 7–13) each "half" of which is further subdivisible. Several verses are knitted together by "Da . . . deinde . . . dein . . . deinde . . . deinde . . . dein," but the knots themselves are numerous, and completion of syntax at the end of verses 3 and 6 plus the disjunctive "Aut" at the beginning of verse 12 open up space on either side of their locations.

Structure, therefore, looks to be inherently dependent on multiplicity and was subsequently perceived as constituted from substructures that are sufficiently extractable to take on independent existence of their own. Martial plays with the idea of enormous numbers of kisses, and Ovid's

---

9. *Catullus,* ed. Elmer T. Merrill (Cambridge: Harvard University Press, 1951; first issued in 1893). The translation is by F. W. Cornish, *The Poems of Catullus* (Cambridge: Harvard University Press, 1913; repr. 1968). The translation of Catullus's seventh song, quoted later, also is Cornish's.

despicable old crone blatantly steals the phrase "milia multa" to advance the greater attraction of a rich lover's "many thousands." The much later English adaptations go so far as to turn various parts of Catullus's song into separate poems. "My deerest mistresse, let us live and love," an eight-line song doubtfully attributed to Campion, dilates (and thus dilutes) verses 1–3 for contrasts between the lovers and "old doting fools": "youthful dalliance" vis-à-vis "Old ages critticke and censorious brow."[10] Ralegh, dispensing with what comes before and after, lifts out verses 4–6 for a self-subsistent epigram.

> The sunne may set and rise:
> But we contrariwise
> Sleepe after our short light
> One everlasting night.

In "My sweetest Lesbia," the authenticity of which is not in doubt, Campion reattaches verses 1–3 to 4–6 but omits 7–13 entirely, the result being a version of Catullus's first "half."

> My sweetest Lesbia, let us live and love,
> And though the sager sort our deedes reprove,
> Let us not way [weigh] them: heav'ns great lamps do dive
> Into their west, and strait againe revive,
> But, soone as once set is our little light,
> Then must we sleepe one ever-during night.

With some assistance from Propertius (as Walter Davis shows in his annotation), Campion replaces Catullus's second "half" with two stanzas of his own invention, each of which closes, however, with "ever-during night." Donne, in "The Computation," omits verses 1–6 but recalculates the numbers of 7–11 to make them appropriate for separation rather than togetherness. And Jonson retains 1–6 for "Come my Celia" (*Forest* 5: "To Celia") while performing some recalculation of his own in the companion poem, "Kiss me, sweet" (*Forest* 6: "To the Same").

Catullus, however, appears to be working with several additional multiplicities that were not suited for the purposes of Ovid and Martial nor readily rendered in English adaptation. The sententious sayings of old censors are worth no more than an "as" (the smallest unit of measurement) and thus worth nearly nothing at all. Scarcely more valuable, evidently, is the grammatically and numerically singular "brevis lux," the short light of mortal existence, especially when unfavorably contrasted not merely to the sun but to a plural "soles," suns. "Lux," though it cer-

10. *The Works of Thomas Campion*, ed. Walter R. Davis (New York: W. W. Norton, 1970), 478. Ralegh, cited next, is quoted from *The Poems of Sir Walter Ralegh*, ed. Agnes M. C. Latham (Cambridge: Harvard University Press, 1951).

tainly means light and occupies emphatic terminal position in verse 5, is immediately followed by "Nox," the baneful night at the start of verse 6, and these antithetical words are separated by no more than a comma (which may, in fact, have been added by an editor). The hundreds of thousands of kisses confuse evil-eyed detractors but also stupify the lovers, and while Lesbia can offer many more things to count than can single-minded old censors, her charms are not in fact infinite but can merely seem to be so, partly because one repetitively stretches out "then" after "then" after "then" to lengthen artificially the inordinately short time in which love may be enjoyed.

And even if kisses were in reality uncountable by the lovers, rather than deliberately confused by them, there is another number to be reckoned with. Huge numbers of individual kisses amass themselves into "basiorum," the final plural word, but presumably they also lead retrogressively back not only to "Viuamus," let us live, but especially to "amemus," let us love, in the first verse. In the meantime, "let us live" has been conclusively shown to be a delusive subjunctive verb; the collocation of "lux-nox," of light-night, punctures that balloon far more devastatingly than Martial ever did. Since Latin verbs are inflected, a fact exemplified at the very outset by "viuamus," the second subjunctive, "amemus," may at first appear to be like any other instance of a single word in which two subjects come together in joined activity. "Amemus," however, reflects the activity inherent in lovemaking itself and in this particular case turns out to have done so with insidious irony. For if the sexually climactic point of countless kisses is the contraction of expanded multiplicity back down to duality and thence to a shared oneness, then the only "una" specifically mentioned in this poem looms even larger in its overshadowing importance, and that explicitly irreducible and unavoidable "one" is the "nox . . . perpetua una dormienda," the one endless night that must be slept.

Manipulate or computate them how you will, there simply can be no escape for Catullus and Lesbia from the numbers of time. The question, therefore, is not how to elude but rather how to react to the dark "one," the number from and to which plurals initially replicate and then reduce themselves. For Catullus, intolerable bleakness drives compulsive desire toward an insatiableness almost certainly not satisfiable in the course of "brief light" no matter how intensely one lives and loves. The reaction against time, however vigorously unrestrained, must be ultimately unavailing, therefore, but at least the activity is *self*-defeating and *not* a subjugation passively suffered and/or imposed from without. Since the quatrain extracted by Ralegh cannot by itself admit of even that much solace, the English turns out to be darker hued than the Latin, and this is true of Campion's English as well. Catullus, in brushing old censors aside, necessarily acknowledges their admonitory presence even as he dismisses their moralistic arithmetic. The song doubtfully attributed to Campion derides "old doting fools," but "My sweetest Lesbia" goes beyond Catullus when it indicates that censorious views, were there time enough to heed them, might actually carry considerable weight; those who reprove, after all, are of "the *sager* sort."

In Jonson's companion poems, first mentioned three paragraphs earlier, additional complications are visible, some of them arising from the fact that Jonson levies upon the seventh song of Catullus, "Quaeris quot," as well as the fifth. Lesbia, perhaps not so bemused by amorous numbers as Catullus hoped, evidently requested further elucidation:

> You ask how many kissings of you, Lesbia, are enough for me. . . . As great as is the number of Libyan sand that lies on silphium-bearing Cyrene, between the oracle of sultry Jove and the sacred tomb of old Battus; or as many as are the stars, when night is silent, that see the stolen loves of men . . . kisses, which neither curious eyes shall count up nor an evil tongue bewitch.

The two Latin poems, although not quite consecutive, keep nearly as close company as Jonson's *Forest* 5 and 6, but straightforward equations among the four songs cannot be made. "Come, my Celia," firmly attaches itself to "Viuamus, mea Lesbia" with the lines,

> Suns, that set, may rise again:
> But if once we lose this light.
> 'Tis with us perpetual night.

In Catullus, however, the (mis)counting of kisses immediately follows, whereas in Jonson this is not the case. He reserves the arithmetic for *Forest* 6, "Kiss me, sweet," in order to combine it with anglicized details from "Quaeris quot":

> First give a hundred,
> Then a thousand, then another
> Hundred, then unto the tother
> Add a thousand, and so more:
> Till you equall with the store
> All the grass that Romney yields,
> Or the sands in Chelsea fields,
> Or the drops in silver Thames,
> Or the stars that gild his streams
> In the silent summer nights,
> When youths ply their stol'n delights:
> That the curious may not know
> How to tell 'em as they flow,

> And the envious, when they find
> What their number is, be pined.

Also worth attention is that Jonson had been anticipated by Joannes Secundus (Jan Everaerts, 1511–1532), who expanded outward from Catullus to create nineteen Latin lyrics, the collective title being *Basia* ("Kisses"). The seventh of them is the song to take note of here, if only in translation, since its opening lines also rework parts of Catullus 5 and 7:

> First a hundred hundred kisses,
> Then a hundred thousand more,
> Then a million, till my bliss is
> By the millions of the score.
> Limitless as drops of rain
> Or waves upon the ocean main
> Or stars in heaven's floor. [11]

Redivision and recombination of Catullus's two poems allowed Joannes and Jonson to follow up boundless kisses with nature's bounty, but Jonson's reference to a grassy marshland in Kent ("All the grass that Romney yields") considerably reduces the aura of "laserpiciferis . . . Cyrenis," silphium-bearing Cyrene. This diminishment occurs, moreover, even if (thanks to Elmer T. Merrill's annotation) one has the prosaic botany ready to hand: "The plant was doubtless the *ferula asafoetida*, the exuded juice of which is still widely used as an antispasmodic." Merrill adds a quotation from Pliny, who reported that Cyrenaica no longer produced the plant, and the unscientific point to be inferred is that Catullus was instancing, as Jonson is not, a commodity both precious and rare. "The sands in Chelsea fields" is a line that similarly familiarizes and thus deflates something which in the Latin is strangely and mysteriously remote. Catullus, moreover, in this case sheds some somber light of his own by elongating Libyan sand from Jove's oracle to a distant locale that, however exotic it may be, is geographically pinpointed by a *tomb*.

Additionally significant is that Jonson not only renders "furtivos . . . amores" of the seventh Catullus with "stol'n delights" in "Kiss me, sweet" but also transfers the idea back into "Come my Celia," his own prior poem. The original reason, presumably, is that *Forest* 5 first appeared in *Volpone* as a song of seduction to a chaste Celia from the evil-eyed Fox. One can ignore the play, of course, when reading or hearing the poem, but echoes from Catullus are likely to be more audible, not less, when heard offstage than on, the reason being that one has more time to notice

11. *The Love Poems of Joannes Secundus*, ed. and trans. F. A. Wright (New York: E. P. Dutton, 1930), 57.

them. If so, then even in the absence of dramatized corruption, it will be difficult not to be aware of revisions and additions that tilt Jonson's poem in the direction of illicit—as distinct from self-defeating—sexuality: "Fame and rumour are but toys."

> 'Tis no sin, love's fruit to steal,
> But the sweet theft to reveal:
> To be taken, to be seen,
> These have crimes accounted been.

Joannes Secundus, despite his own death at the age of twenty-one, somehow managed to exclude perpetual night from his *Basia*. Apart from that wonderfully lyric exception, these several poems interject realistically uncomfortable details that continually remind one that links to a world larger than the self remain unseverably in place even as proposals are being made to sever them. Jonson's adaptations, arguably the finest ever made, simply are not "romantic" in the (admittedly, now largely old-fashioned) Hollywood-movie sense. Neither are the other English versions, nor did these writers suppose Catullus to be. What is more, the various under- (and cross-) currents of language and thought in no sense reduce but magnify all the more the insistent urgency of immediate human action and reaction in the face of implacable time, and for that very reason these also are not simplistic poems of "joie de vivre." Blending extraordinary vehemence with great clarity of vision, they stare at, though they do not and cannot possibly stare down, the limitations of human existence, and they decline to ignore the realities that cause passion to seem a bare minimum if life, however briefly, is to be worth living at all. Crashaw, while not famous for poetry of this kind, did write "Out of Catullus," and it may be this version of "Viuamus . . . atque amemus" in which powerful ambivalence most particularly is blazoned forth. "Come and let us live my Deare, / Let us love." For

> Brightest *Sol* that dyes to day
> Lives againe as blith to morrow,
> But if we darke sons of sorrow
> Set; ô then, how long a Night
> Shuts the Eyes of our short light!
> . . . .
> Thus at last when we have numbred
> Many a Thousand, many a Hundred;
> Wee'l confound the reckoning quite,
> And lose our selves in wild delight.

But there is, of course, no "if" about it. We dark sons of sorrow must most certainly set, and with equal certainty, at least in these poems, the emotional imperative therefore must be to "confound the reckoning quite,

/ And lose"—though very probably we cannot *find*—"our selves in wild delight."

MAY DAY IN HESPERIDES

The spectral images of Catullus and Lesbia, standing closely behind Herrick and Corinna throughout most of "Corinna's *going a Maying*," briefly step forward toward heavily shaded frontlights in Herrick's fifth stanza before disappearing back into their dark, unending sleep. "Our life is short; and our dayes run / As fast away as do's the Sunne." "All love, all liking, all delight / Lies drown'd with us in endlesse night." These remarks might be applied to all four lovers, not merely the two at the forefront of Herrick's attention, but if Herrick and Catullus apparently speak from approximately the same position, Corinna differs markedly from Lesbia in having a strong personality of her own. Her principal trait, of course, is a procrastination so pronounced that very likely she will still be abed at sunset, never notice the swift running away of time, and in fact not get round to going a Maying (if indeed she ever does) until long after May day itself has long since finished going. "Get up, sweet-Slug-a-bed," Herrick implores; "Come, my *Corinna*, come"; "Rise"; "Come, let us goe." "Come, we'll abroad; and let's obay / The Proclamation made for May." But Corinna lazily insists (even though that may be a contradiction in terms) on being at least as slow as the sun is fast.

The first irony thus proves to be the inaccuracy of the title since "going a Maying" is exactly what Corinna adamantly refuses to do. Of greater consequence, no doubt, is the cause behind the initial discrepancy, namely that Herrick and Corinna themselves are at odds in their response (or lack thereof) to the passing of time. Herrick is altogether positive, as lovers tend to be, that the arguments are entirely on his side; in his view, Corinna not only disregards broadly applicable amorous proclamations and his own personal needs but disobeys natural laws and ignores ecclesiastical injunctions. She does so, moreover, at a time when Nature and the Church agree with one another and mutually accommodate their own seemingly conflicting demands. Normally, if the poem "*Mattens*" is indicative, one must not merely "with the Virgin morning . . . rise" but also "Crossing thy selfe . . . Give up thy soule in clouds of frankinsence." On May day, however, prayers may be short, or—as Herrick puts it, in apparently high Anglo-Catholic fashion—"Be briefe in praying: / Few Beads are best, when once we goe a Maying." And that easement can be allowed because Nature reciprocates by holding church services out of doors: "Each Flower has . . . bow'd toward the East"; "all the Birds have Mattens seyd, / And sung their thankfull Hymnes."

Further erasure of demarcating boundaries results from the devotional practices of May day worshippers, practices that mediate between—by being simultaneously directed to—the ecclesiastical and the natural.

> Devotion gives each House a Bough,
> Or Branch: Each Porch, each doore, ere this
> An Arke a Tabernacle is
> Made up of white-thorn neatly enterwove.

"Each field" thus "turns a street; each street a Parke / Made green." Every "Boy" and "Girle" may be naturalistically described as "budding"; "a thousand Virgins on this day, / Spring, sooner then the Lark, to fetch in May." Corinna herself thus is urged,

> Rise; and put on your Foliage, and be seene
> To come forth, like the Spring-time, fresh and greene;
> And sweet as *Flora*. Take no care
> For Jewels for your Gowne, or Haire:
> Feare not; the leaves will strew
> Gemms in abundance upon you.

In these circumstances, "'Tis sin, / Nay, profanation to keep in." "Let's . . . sin no more, as we have done, by staying." And lest it be thought that the values here invoked are those of an exclusively natural and purely amorous religion, "some have wept, and woo'd, and plighted Troth, / And chose their Priest, ere we can cast off sloth."

Somewhere in the course of all this—it would be difficult, I think, to stipulate the exact line or phrase—two additional lovers have arrived on the scene, the pair more usually to be found in Canticles or The Song of Solomon. "Come, my beloued, let vs goe foorth into the field: let vs lodge in the villages. Let vs get vp early to the Vineyards . . . there will I giue thee my loues" (7.11–12).

> Rise vp, my loue, my faire one, & come away. For loe, the winter is past, the raine is ouer, and gone. The flowers appeare on the earth, the time of the singing of birds is come, and the voice of the Turtle[-dove] is heard in our land. The fig tree putteth forth her greene figges, and the Vines with the tender grape give a good smell. Arise, my loue, my faire one, and come away. (2.10–13)

The language is immensely sensual, but thanks to a tradition so venerable that it was incorporated in the chapter headings of the Authorized Version, the speaker here is the mystical Bridegroom, and the figure being addressed is the mystical Bride. The former is identifiable most specifically as Christ; the latter (depending on what is being emphasized by whom) is the Church and/or the Soul. Herrick is not Christ nor was he meant to be, and Corinna (whether in or out of her plumage) is no allegorical figure, but there is a curious parallelism here nonetheless, especially when one comes to matters such as slothful delay and obdurate refusals to heed the voice of a would-be lover.

In Canticles, however, the conflict emerges through internal dialogue since the Bride, unlike Corinna, is herself heard from. What is more, although she does belatedly respond, her delay might have been perilous.

> I sleepe, but my heart waketh: it is the voyce of my beloued that knocketh, saying, Open to mee, my sister, my love, my doue, my vndefiled: for my head is filled with dew, and my lockes with the drops of the night.
> I haue put off my coat, how shall I put it on? I haue washed my feete; how shall I defile them? . . .
> I rose vp to open to my beloued, and my hands dropped with myrrh . . . vpon the handles of the locke.
> I opened to my beloued, but my beloued had withdrawen himselfe, and was gone: my soule failed when hee spake: I sought him, but I could not finde him, I called him, but he gaue me no answere. (5.2–6)

The Bridegroom stands at the door and knocks, prepared to enter unto those who respond to his voice; offering the dew of grace, the locks well-oiled with the myrrh of God's blessing, he asks merely that the key of the heart be turned from within. So runs the traditional gloss, and as for the Bride, she certainly ought to have answered and to have done so in haste. She should have had "her *loynes girded about*," Ainsworth tells us (*Solomons Song*, 39):

> her selfe waiting for his returne; that when he came and knocked, she might *open to him immediately.* . . . But she had not only ungirded, but put off her coat, and washed her feet, so composing her selfe to a setled rest in her bed; and in stead of watching, sleepeth; in stead [of] opening the doore, driveth him away through her neglect and sloth.

Or, as Matthew Henry puts it (*Commentary* 3:1082), "She did not open to him at his first knock, and now she came too late." "Christ will sought when he may be found; if we let slip our time, we may lose our passage."

The biblical scene is simulated by Herrick in that "sin," "profanation," and "sloth" are words and concepts that readily come to his lips and mind, but high seriousness is uniformly transposed down to a lower key. "Get up, get up for shame," out of context, might be part of Ainsworth's harsh reproof, but "Sweet slug-a-bed," and "Wash, dresse, be briefe in praying" could not possibly be. Sexual comedy diverts the parallelism still more, especially in the mild ribaldry that closes the fourth stanza.

> Many a green-gown has been given;
> Many a kisse, both odde and even:
> Many a glance too has been sent

> From out the eye, Loves Firmament:
> Many a jest told of the Keyes betraying
> This night, and Locks pickt, and yet w'are not a Maying.

And back in the second stanza, it is "*Titan*," not the mystical Bride-groom, who "on the Eastern hill / Retires himselfe, or else stands still / Till you come forth." Corinna is as slothful as the Bride, but her dilato-riness seems less culpable when seen through the eyes of an impatient but no more than mildly exasperated lover.

This lover, however, has himself been a bit tardy, if in nothing else, then in coming to a full realization of his predicament. Or perhaps it is Corinna's prolonged and apparently inexplicable sluggishness that, by causing the difficulty, at length arouses him, though she herself is still abed. Four stanzas, filled with vibrancy but also repose, relax the often taut lines between fertility rites and morning prayer, folk custom and religious observance, the ceremonies of Nature and those of the Church, but there has been little or no sense of the peril invited by letting slip the proper time and thus losing one's passage. It is the fifth stanza, the last one, in which time dangerously accelerates, threatening to leave Herrick and Corinna lagging irremediably far behind. This is where the ghosts of Catullus and Lesbia glide forward from the penumbra, and in doing so, they appear to be accompanied by a whole host of other wraiths, nebu-lously present as summoned forth from the pages of biblical and classical antiquity.

> Come, let us goe, while we are in our prime;
> And take the harmlesse follie of the time.
>> We shall grow old apace, and die
>> Before we know our liberty.
>> Our life is short; and our dayes run
>> As fast away as do's the Sunne:
> And as a vapour, or a drop of raine
> Once lost, can ne'r be found againe:
>> So when or you or I are made
>> A fable, song, or fleeting shade;
>> All love, all liking, all delight
>> Lies drown'd with us in endlesse night.
> Then while time serves, and we are but decaying;
> Come, my *Corinna*, come, let's goe a Maying.

One of the allusions here may be to Tibullus (*Elegies*, 3.2), a poet who foresaw his own change into a slender shade ("cum tenuem fuero mutatus in umbram"). Alternatively, one recollects the somber conviction of Job, "Man . . . fleeth also as a shadow" (14.1–2). The New Testament admo-nition of James's Epistle surely is sounded: "Ye know not what shall be on the morrow: for what is your life? It is euen a vapor that appeareth for a little time, and then vanisheth away" (James 4.14). Or so, at any rate, one supposes until noticing that Cornelius à Lapide annotates this passage by quoting similar phrasing from Martial, Seneca, Menander, Horace, and others.[12] Lapide also adds Wisdom 2 as a significant analogue, an interesting fact since Martin considers that biblical chapter to be a principal source for Herrick, and the first eight verses of it are quoted, with minor abridgement, in Patrick's notes.

> Our life is short . . . our life shall passe away as the trace of a cloud: and shall be dispersed as a mist that is driuen away with the beames of the Sunne. . . . For our time is a very shadow . . . Come on therefore, . . . Let vs crowne our selues with Rose buds, before they be withered.

I reproduce rather less of the passage than Patrick does because it is not, I think, the only inherited text of major proportions that Herrick evokes, but however many ellipses one chooses to make, Wisdom's prefatory and austere *de*valuation of this kind of thinking simply must not be omitted: "For the vngodly said, reasoning with themselues, but not aright: Our life is short" (Wisdom 2.1).

Whether all of these analogues or only some of them or even others like them are specifically audible may be an unanswerable question, but it is not probable that the hearing of echoes can be one-sidedly selective. The sensuous language of Canticles cannot be wholly divorced from moral and spiritual interpretations incorporated in the Authorized Version in which one presumably encounters that language. The remark in James's Epistle reminded Lapide of many classical variations on the biblical idea. Wisdom reports an argument for "carpe diem," but not until after a stern warning is posted that the case being made is wrongheadedly advanced by the ungodly. And the language of the poem itself, even though addressed to an unhearing Corinna, is far too sophisticated for eavesdroppers deaf in one ear.

And besides all that, there is Catullus, whose passion was all the more vehement because its fire so quickly would be surrounded and then nullified by endless night. In a pagan world, fully effective remedies for that situation are not easily come by. Clarifying out impurities from the wine of life and heeding advice to take the money and run, though greatly different in terms of what is honorable and dishonorable, pertain to living with, not altering, the inescapable realities of human time. And if anachronism and cultural disparities are not one's primary considerations, then Catullus and Job can be allowed to speak nearly together.

> To draw then to a close, let us looke alwayes upon this *Day-Lilie* of life, as if the *Sun* were already *set*. Though we *blossome* and *open* many *mornings*,

12. Cornelius à Lapide, *Commentaria in Acta Apostolorum, Epistolas canonicas, et Apocalypsin*, 159.

we shall not do so always, *Soles occidere & redire possunt* [quoting Catullus]; but *man* cannot. *He hath his time appointed him upon earth, which he shall not passe, and his days are like the days of an hireling* [quoting Job 7.1].

This is how Vaughan prepares for his concluding remarks in *The Mount of Olives* (*Works*, 186); two paragraphs away is his recommendation, "Live a *Christian*, and die a *Saint*."

Once that kind of territory is entered, then sooner or later Job will be heard to testify, "I know that my redeemer liueth" (19.25), and Catullus will be thought to have gone wrong, whether or not he had much choice about it, in attempting to find his way in the total absence of light wherewith to see.

> When once the Soule has lost her way,
> O then, how restlesse do's she stray!
> And having not her God for light,
> How do's she erre in endlesse night!

The pious pilferer in this case is Herrick himself ("The Soule," N-233), but there probably is nothing stealthy about the theft. Vaughan, after all, names neither one of the authors whom he quotes so familiarly. In any event, "The Gentils, and their Poets," as Donne told a funeral gathering in 1626, "describe the sad state of Death so, *Nox una obeunda*, That it is one everlasting Night; To them, a Night; But to a Christian, it is *Dies Mortis*, and *Dies Resurrectionis*, The day of Death, and The day of Resurrection" (*Sermons* 7:272).[13] Jeremy Taylor, preaching at a funeral in 1663, quoted a bit more of Catullus and for much the same purpose.

> We so converse every night with the image of death, that every morning we find an argument of the resurrection. Sleep and death have but one mother, and they have one name in common.

> Soles occidere et redire possunt;
> Nobis cum semel occidit brevis lux,
> Nox est perpetua una dormienda.

> Charnel-houses are but "koimeteria" [my transliteration of a Greek word which means "bed chambers" or "burial sites"], cemeteries or sleeping-places, and they that die are fallen asleep, and the resurrection is but an awakening. (*Works* 8:402)

For Taylor, there definitely remains a night to be slept, but equally definite is that it by no means is unending. Quite the contrary, in fact,

---

13. I cannot tell whether Donne misquoted Catullus by mistake or by intent; "obeunda" (from "obeo"—meet face to face and, specifically, meet with death) could be a deliberate substitute for "dormienda."

since darkness is to be annihilated by light when the narrow confines of
the tomb expand toward infinity. "O Yeares! and Age! farewell," Herrick
exclaims ("Eternitie," N-58),

> O Yeares! and Age! Farewell:
>   Behold I go,
>   Where I do know
> Infinitie to dwell.
> And these mine eyes shall see
>   All times, how they
>   Are lost i'th'Sea
> Of vast Eternitie.
> Where never Moone shall sway
>   The Starres; but she,
>   And Night, shall be
> Drown'd in one endlesse Day.

By this point, it is Herrick himself who insists on turning his own line,
"Lies drown'd with us in endlesse night," completely upside down or
inside out, but before doing so he has first retuned his lyre for "Noble
Numbers." Within the realms of "Hesperides," some couples on this day
"have . . . chose their Priest," and since the ceremony there is to be a
wedding, one trusts that the rector will refrain from funereal remarks. A
text from Canticles might, however, make for a suitable short homily
before the nuptial Eucharist. Other couples on this day are entirely too
much hurried to have any time at all for that sort of thing. They cannot be
bothered about being brides and bridegrooms in lowercase lettering,
much less the capitalized variety, for there are pressing occasions when
some go a Maying on whatever terms they can. Herrick, so far as I can
tell, would cheerfully swell the numbers of either group with an addi-
tional pair if Corinna would but arise.

And yet for Herrick, the plea is *not*, after all, "Viuamus . . . atque
amemus," but rather, "Come, let us goe, while we are in our prime; / And
take the harmlesse follie of the time." The rhyming of "time" with "prime"
sounds ominous, but on May day "prime" does, at least, take precedence;
in between the rhymes is "follie," but "harmlesse" partly disarms the
noun before foolishness can be acknowledged. Far more threatening is
the poem's final couplet: "Then while time serves, and we are but decay-
ing; / Come, my *Corinna*, come, let's goe a Maying." Time, however, as
we already know from this poem alone, will never be subservient; it can
be used but never mastered. Indeed, it has even now initiated the destruc-
tion, the "nox dormienda *et* obeunda," as it were, of these lovers whether
they sleep face to face or not. True, they are merely "decaying" instead of
having decayed, but May day is "a going" fast, and "All love, all liking, all

delight," at least for this pair, will soon have been gone. Even as we speak, to recollect Horace, envious time will have taken flight.

On the other hand, "Many waters cannot quench loue, neither can the floods drowne it"; "for loue is strong as death" (Canticles 8.7, 8.6). For Catullus, those statements might not have made any sense at all. For a priest, one assumes, the statements have to be true, no matter how often that truth is disregarded by parishioners or abused through secular and sexual misapplication. The sad note sounded here is that since Corinna refuses to go a Maying on any terms whatsoever, she and Herrick will never find out whether love is strong or weak. Neither a spouse, nor an *un*wedded but bedded "bride," nor yet a mystical Bride-to-be, Corinna slothfully wastes the day that is wasting both her and her suitor away. From either perspective from which Herrick chooses to look, whether classical or Christian, or from both of them more or less simultaneously, on May day 'tis sin, nay profanation, to keep in.

There may, however, be still a third position to be inferred from what Corinna herself does or rather declines to do. It is Herrick, after all, who often is the classicist-priest, but over and beyond that (or possibly beneath and behind it) he is in this poem a hopelessly enamored male. If an initial irony is the one between the title and what does not, in fact, actually happen in the poem, then a final one may be Corinna's good sense in turning over and going back to sleep instead of going a Maying when her slumber is disturbed by masculine caterwauling at the crack of dawn. One of Herrick's favorite roles, one recalls, is that of a comic figure, frequently more than a little absurd, and on Good Friday he goes so far as to play God's fool. Genuine seriousness can be seen and deep sympathy be felt for him here without being fully persuaded that the imminent drowning of *all* love is not an excessively absolutist and premature conclusion. Herrick apparently soars aloft in the final lines, transfiguring himself into a towering protagonist of tragic dimensions afflicted by classical Christian despair, but the earlier voice of exasperated impatience is not totally drowned out, nor has that speaker yet vanished into either endless night or endless day. Bounded by time within the context of eternity, the poem as a whole is a prism that refracts both Canticles and Catullus into a magical and luminous image of ambivalent disparities discoverable within existence itself, especially on May day in Hesperides.

"NOBLE NUMBERS" AND "HESPERIDES"

Since Herrick is frequently a miniaturist, his book includes large numbers of tiny poems that simply have to be as completely straightforward as language can ever be. At times, in fact, there is barely sufficient length for a proposition to be advanced, much less for complications to be explored. Unless, however, one ruthlessly excises surrounding context, then few cut-and-dried views remain unchallenged for long because the miniatures habitually comment on and hence entangle one another, often disconcertingly so. This does not mean that one needs to approach everything in "Hesperides" with Bible and Prayer Book in hand or bring along a *Corpus poetarum Latinorum* when advancing into "Noble Numbers." "*A Country life: To his Brother*" (H-106), although not a short poem, especially by Herrick's standards, nicely illustrates half of this fact; generally Horatian and specifically a cento of Jonsonianisms, it would profit from being set off against a backdrop consisting of Jonson's verse epistles. Sacred epigrams, with upside down similarity, ought to have biblical passages or a handbook of theology placed behind them to make even more apparent their compact brevity. One could o'erleap the great divide between "*To his Brother*" and, for example, "To his . . . Saviour" (N-77), but comparing these two, despite the similar titles, would reveal nothing more than a fact that is already self-evident, namely that Herrick is capable of great range and diversity.

Some poems, however, do clamor aloud that the space intervening between them be temporarily closed up. "The pillar of Fame" and "*This Cross-Tree here*," the two examples of typographically shaped verse, are a notable but also singular instance. More typical are widely separated poems called "The Bell-man," and since the very fact of encountering the second poem reveals that the first poem was *only* the first, it seems fair to me to do some jumping back and forth from one to the other.

> Along the dark, and silent night,
> With my Lantern, and my Light,
> And the tinkling of my Bell,
> Thus I walk, and this I tell.

These lines might introduce either poem, though in fact they begin the one in "Noble Numbers" (N-121), which takes a bit longer to get under way; it also is slower to finish. The comparatively greater length (and the sound thereby prolonged) of the second "Bellman" produces a significant effect, but to expose parallelism more clearly I omit some of the middle lines of N-121.

H-299	N-121
From noise of Scare-fires rest ye free	Death and dreadfulnesse call on,
From Murders *Benedicitie*.	To the gen'rall Session;
From all mischances, that may fright	To whose dismall barre we there
Your pleasing slumbers in the night:	All accompts must come to cleere:
Mercie secure ye all, and keep	Rise ye Debters then, and fall

The Goblin from ye, while ye sleep.　　To make paiment, while I call.
Past one aclock, and almost two,　　　Ponder this, when I am gone;
My Masters all, *Good day to you.*　　　By the clock 'tis almost *One.*

H-299 is scarcely a cameo shot of the charming-scenes-of-olde-London variety but in itself does not at first glance display the terrors of N-121. Indeed, since the second bellman with great clarity tolls his listeners on to Judgement Day, "the *tinkling* of my Bell" as heard in the opening four lines may seem too high in pitch and entirely too low in volume to be a fitting prelude for what ensues. But except in terms of alarming understatement the tinkling would sound scarcely better if transferred back to the earlier poem. The sardonic humor of Murder's "bless you," the malevolence of the Goblin, the sudden conflagrations of "Scare-fires," and the self-evident great need for "Mercie"—coming on the heels of all this, "*Good* day to you" now becomes distinctly lacking in its customary cheerfulness, even though—since it is "almost two"—the dreaded time of "almost one" is safely past for, presumably, another twenty-four hours. Because of the second bellman, the first one retrospectively looks uncomfortably like the Grim Reaper taking an infrequent night off. Those to whom he speaks of "pleasing slumbers" might well be advised to commend body and soul to sleep in preparation for the final sudden conflagration of them all, and if so then a third bellman, the one addressed in "*Cock-crow*" (N-43), will be usefully heard, and "My Masters all," the plurals in the last line of H-299, will be elevated to "my Master" Christ.

> BELL-man of Night, if I about shall go
> For to denie my Master, do thou crow.
> Thou stop'st S. *Peter* in the midst of sin;
> Stay me, by crowing, ere I do begin.

These bellmen, individually considered, seem merely cardboard silhouettes when compared to the full-bodied Corinna, but their composite substance is not inconsiderable. For an approximation of three-dimensional verisimilitude, other poems could reasonably be asked to deepen the perspective. N-230, "*His Meditation upon Death*" (I quote only the opening lines) and H-549, "*Upon himselfe being buried*" might be allowed to complement the Bellmen by running far apart but also side by side.

H-549	N-230
Let me sleep this night away,	When sleep shall bath his body in mine eyes
Till the Dawning of the day:	I will believe, that then my body dies:
Then at th'opening of mine eyes,	And if I chance to wake, and rise thereon
I, and all the world shall rise.	I'le have in mind my Resurrection.

Herrick, I think, would not have been scandalized (though others may be) by a further effort to round out the picture by putting into it frankly erotic verse such as "*The Night-piece, to* Julia" (H-619), then stepping back to gauge the overall effect of adding the mildly risqué "*In the darke none dainty*" (H-586), and next making use of one's bifocals to include "*To his sweet Saviour*" (N-77):

> Let me Thy voice betimes i'th morning heare;
> Call, and I'le come; say Thou, the when, and where:
> Draw me, but first, and after Thee I'le run,
> And make no one stop, till my race be run.

Looking for "companion" poems might work up into a full-time job, but perhaps a bare handful of further examples, different from the preceding and from one another, will be enough to illustrate a strong tendency that is visible in Herrick's book as a whole. "*To the Virgins, to make much of Time*" (H-208), a poem mentioned earlier, is echoed by "*Upon Time*" (N-38) and "*No time in Eternitie*" (N-229). In N-38, "Time was upon / The wing, to flie away," and in H-208 (though a prior poem), "Old Time is still a flying." In one case Herrick discovers that his "end near was," and in the other, maidens are instructed to cease being maids by marrying while they may. The situations and conclusions to be drawn differ markedly, but in each the cause and perhaps even a remedy is the same; as N-229 points out, "By hours we all live here, in Heaven is known / No spring of Time, or Times succession."

"*To finde God*" (N-3) turns out, strictly speaking, to be an impossibility, an idea illustrated by Herrick's directives to those who would vainly try. "Weigh me the fire," he says, or "find / A way to measure out the Wind." "Then shew me Him / That rides the glorious *Cherubim*." The title "*Impossibilities to his friend*" (H-198) apparently gives away much of the argument in advance: "If you can see, that drop of raine / Lost in the wild sea, once againe"—but it cannot, of course, be done; the hypothetical "if" is founded on an obvious impossibility. There is, however, a painful impossibility that is not given away in advance but rather is reserved for the second half of the "If . . . then" construction: "Then there is hope that you may see / Her love me once, who now hates me."

"The work(e) is done," Herrick announces—twice, in fact, once with a final "e" and once without: at the outset of "*To God*" (N-262) and also to begin "*On Himselfe*" (H-1128). One poem requests a "*Lawrell*" to be conferred by God; the other, a "*Mirtle Coronet*" from "young men, and maidens." On the one hand, "The Muses will weare blackes, when I am dead," but on the other, "Thou"—God—"dost me create / Thy *Poet*, and thy *Prophet Lawreat*."

In these several pairs of poems it is the divine side, or so one would think, that is of incomparably greater significance. And yet to renounce the lesser half implies, for Herrick at least, not merely the giving up of human loving, including sexuality though not limited to it, but also an abdication from human living. The quatrain next quoted insists that, while Love and Life can be walled off into separate couplets, writing off the one requires writing off the other as well.

> Il'e write no more of Love; but now repent
> Of all those times that I in it have spent.
> Ile write no more of life; but wish twas ended,
> And that my dust was to the earth commended.

These two couplets are not, moreover, a sacred poem—for Ash Wednesday, say—but instead appear toward the end of "Hesperides" (H-1124, *"On Himselfe"*).

Two other couplets that Herrick's placement invites one to compare and contrast are separated by 271 intervening poems. The last lines of "Noble Numbers" are,

> Of all the good things whatsoe're we do,
> God is the ΑΡΧΗ, and the ΤΕΛΟΣ too.

271 poems earlier, "Hesperides" closed with,

> To his Book's end this last line he'd have plac't,
> *Jocond his Muse was; but his Life was chast.*

Herrick repeatedly directed his attention toward both the first Beginning and the final or telic End. In between, however, he regularly found space and time to keep an eye on poetry and life, neither of them negated but rather made possible by ultimates on either side. A probable source for N-272 is Revelation 1.8, "I am Alpha and Omega, the beginning and the ending, saith the Lord." For H-1130, a strong possibility (the one cited by L. C. Martin) is Ovid, *Tristia*, 2.354: "Vita verocunda est, Musa iocosa mea" (with a little context added, "I assure you my person differs from my verse: my life is moral; my muse, gay"). Also fairly close is Martial, *Epigrams*, 1.4.8: "Lasciva est nobis pagina, vita proba" (moral laxity characterizes my page; probitude, my life). Regardless of whether it is Ovid or Martial who is to be paired with St. John and the Book of Revelation, Herrick evidently did not find these ancient authorities so totally incompatible to one another for only one of their positions to have been reaffirmed.

In effect, then, the two parts of Herrick's book make an implicit request that one somehow reconcile "Noble Numbers" with "Hesperides" by taking them on their own terms, both separately and together, and in attempting to honor that request, one might do worse than to remember

Milton's "L'Allegro" and "Il Penseroso." Mirth and Melancholy also demand an elasticity of mind sufficiently great to embrace antitheses, which in themselves are manifestly incomplete, even though topographical features of their shared common ground are not readily described, perhaps not even by Milton. He gives elaborately parallel explorations of highly visible dichotomies but does not verbalize a synthesis. George Frideric Handel and Charles Jennens (1700–1773), the librettist behind the music, managed to supplement Milton and thus came up with *L'Allegro, il Penseroso ed il Moderato,* but the purely verbal (as distinct from musical) pleasures of the newly devised third part are decidedly inferior to the preceding two. For example,

> Keep, as of old, the middle way,
> Nor deeply sad, not idly gay
> But still the same in look and gait,
> Easy, cheerful, and sedate.
> . . . .
> Thy pleasures, Moderation, give,
> In them alone we truly live.[14]

Giving Handel cause to compose more music must surely be laudable, and Jennens, to be sure, must be credited for supplying the texts of *Saul* (1735) and *Messiah* (1742), but I prefer not to think what he would have done to Herrick.

If, however, there probably can be no satisfactory blueprint for the mental construct that informs the two parts of Herrick's book, it might nevertheless be safe to suggest that "Noble Numbers" and "Hesperides" initially radiate from and then circumscribe a center at which there exists a serio-comic affirmation of the value of timely pursuits in the here and now with a further regard for an untimable hereafter, the consequence being a celebration of this immensely variegated world as it spins its way both out of and back to ineffable endlessness.

"HESPERIDES" AND "NOBLE NUMBERS"

Since abundant plenitude is an irreducible and undeniable quality of Herrick's work, the suggestion made in the preceding sentence looks equitable to me. I would have fewer qualms, however, about having inflated the sentence into a paragraph if "To his Book's end this last line he'd have plac't" really were half of the very last couplet at the very end of Herrick's book. As it is, however, the next line—"*Jocond his Muse was; but his Life*

14. Quoted from the libretto supplied with a recording of the Handel with the Monteverdi Choir and English Baroque Soloists directed by John Eliot Gardner (Editions Costallat, 1981).

was chast"—completes the couplet and is placed last with respect to "Hesperides" but *not* with respect to the book as a whole. There are 272 "Noble Numbers," after all, remaining to be read. Instead, therefore, of ending with a jocund muse and a chaste life, Herrick concludes with the definitive Beginning and End. Since this strategy presents the ultimates of religious faith with the full rhetorical force of terminal position, the sense of finality is well-nigh absolute. It seems to me, to rephrase matters from the other side, that if the 1,130 poems of "Hesperides" were placed *second* (rather than first), then they might more readily be seen as supplementing divine absolutes by means of a complementary framework for flexible human values. The uncompromising stance taken in N-272 would more nearly be balanced, though by no means outweighed, by the cumulative number of Hesperidean poems—by their composite length, as it were, and additive substance. The very considerable force of Hesperidean thought continues to be felt, of course, in the volume as Herrick chose to publish it, but the strength nonetheless was diminished, I think, when he decided to place "Hesperides" first and "Noble Numbers" last.

Another issue here is that, while poems far apart frequently afford mutual support, those contiguous to one another often are mutually destructive. Successive poems in "Hesperides" can shift their ground as rapidly and unpredictably as Proteus changed his shape, and when they do, the apparently rock-solid position adopted in one poem disintegrates in a second that then is detonated by a third. Since prior normative standards have not been established, as they would have been had "Noble Numbers" been first, a frequent result is self-canceling indeterminacy. Almost any group of contiguous poems perhaps would exemplify in small compass this ongoing process, but the short series from H-496 through H-499 is not a totally arbitrary choice because the verse encapsulates a number of characteristic themes and does permit artificial boundary lines to be temporarily drawn on either side.

"*To his Honoured Kinsman*" introduces Sir Richard Stone into a "*white Temple of . . . Heroes,*" the nave being filled with "stately Figures" and "rare *Saint-ships.*" There also is room to raise Horace's lofty monument even higher.

> High are These Statues here, besides no lesse
> Strong then the Heavens for everlastingnesse:
> Where build aloft; and being fixt by These,
> Set up Thine owne *eternall Images.*

"*Upon a Flie,*" the next poem, elaborates Martial's verse (*Epigrams*, 4.331, "De ape electro inclusa") about a bee preserved in amber and thereby sets forth a radically different image of that which can be made to outlast change.

> A Golden Flie one shew'd to me,
> Clos'd in a Box of Yvorie:
> Where both seem'd proud; the Flie to have
> His buriall in an yvory grave:
> The yvory tooke State to hold
> A Corps as bright as burnisht gold.

In a rapidly trans-shifting world, endurance of any kind evidently is much to be admired, but one of the functions of art often is said to be the transmutation of that which is ugly and grotesque (the corpse of a dead fly, say) into the aesthetically beautiful (ivory and burnished gold, for example). The claim is both validated and exploded by "*Upon* Jack *and* Jill," the epigram that follows.

> When *Jill* complaines to *Jack* for want of meate;
> *Jack* kisses *Jill*, and bids her freely eate:
> *Jill* sayes, of what? sayes *Jack*, on that sweet kisse,
> Which full of Nectar and Ambrosia is,
> The food of Poets; so I thought sayes *Jill*,
> That makes them looke so lanke, so Ghost-like still.
> Let Poets feed on aire, or what they will;
> Let me feed full, till that I fart, sayes *Jill*.

And next there is "*To* Julia," also concerned with air.

> *Julia*, when thy *Herrick* dies,
> Close thou up thy Poets eyes:
> And his last breath, let it be
> Taken in by none but Thee.

But unless Julia herself is to "expire" posthaste, this exquisitely touching scene disappears when she next breathes out what is Herrick's, but scarcely her own, last breath.

A pattern of sorts can be traced out, but it is less an association of ideas than a jumbled concatenation of poetic conventions and hard-headed realities. Rare saintships and golden flies, although defensive images against instability, sap one another's strength instead of reinforcing it and become fugitive visions almost as quickly as glimpsed. One wonders whether their visibility can possibly outlast the closing up of the poet's eyes, especially in view of Jill's windy retort to Jack's airy poeticisms.

Instability can be further intensified by the miniaturization of poems and positions therein taken, even though brevity in and of itself does not necessarily erode certainty. Shortness never jeopardizes the amplitude of subject matter in "Noble Numbers"; there, as in Crashaw's sacred epigrams, paring down often reveals rather than reduces the stupendous magnitudes being considered. But in "Hesperides," the cumulative effect of tininess is a sense of fragmented bits and pieces colliding and veering off again in much the same fashion as the atoms of Epicurus and Lucretius. Sooner or later, chaos never seems far off, even though it is never yet quite come again. H-565, the numerical midpoint of the 1,130 Hesperidean poems, turns out to be *"Upon the losse of his Finger."*

> One of the five straight branches of my hand
> Is lopt already; and the rest but stand
> Expecting when to fall: which soon will be;
> First dyes the Leafe, the Bough next, next the Tree.

The placement itself need not be symbolically exact for one to notice that the writer's hand itself is being dismembered and felled and that much of what it has written and is to write is disjointed in appearance. Looked at from this particular center, *"Delight in Disorder"* (H-83) is prototypical in the sense that if delight is to be taken, then disorder will have to be the usual place wherein to find it since order itself very seldom is on view.

Also significant, surely, is that extreme brevity becomes increasingly the norm toward the end of "Hesperides," often in the form of harsh distichs that ruthlessly satirize and contemptuously minimize their subject matter. The hundred poems from H-1030 to H-1130 stuff themselves into not quite twenty-six congested pages, and many of the last fifty items—including *"Upon* Grubs" (1077), *"Upon* Gut" (1085), and *"Upon* Pimpe"* (1113)—are among Herrick's coarsest epigrams. *"Upon* Rush" (1116) and *"The Hagg"* (1122) are final instances of this kind of coarseness, and in between them is the reserve and restraint of *"Abstinence"* (1117), a poem anticipatory of the upward change of direction that allows Herrick to make an elegant finish. By that point, however, celebration is collapsing inward on hollowness, and fame's sturdy pillar, for all its poetic reality, appears to have been built on shifting sand.

Disillusionment not merely threatens but at length dispels enchantment, and the western isles of Hesperides reveal themselves to have been reminiscent of the Photae, those Floating Islands of equally ancient antiquity that unfixedly drifted on a dark and alien sea. Whether or not an exact midpoint worth locating actually is H-535, *"Upon the losse of his Finger,"* it is not so much that the center of "Hesperides" simply will not hold nor that poems career wildly off as if impelled by centrifugal force. The metaphysical horror is when the outmost barricades have crumpled and the underlying veneer been stripped away, then the nightmarish vision is of minuscule particles, some of them momentarily but surrealistically beautiful, swirling their way though a centerless void.

And that may indeed have been what Herrick thought he saw round about him in England in the late 1640s. In these terms, "Noble Numbers," though much shorter than "Hesperides," is a lengthy palinode that supplements what comes before and also largely contravenes it. The grandest irony may be, not that "Hesperides" outnumbers its counterpart, but that the discarded numbers of senseless time recede into eternity when God's fool acknowledges this world's defeat and unfurls aloft the towering banners of the Cross. In these terms, the biggest miniaturization of them all is that Herrick left behind him no more than a single book but two distinguishably different volumes, exactly identical in length, made up of precisely the same poems, and taking up the shelf space of only one not notably large publication, but nonetheless ambivalent not only from first to last but also from last to first.

Postscript: 1674–1974

The year 1674 marked the deaths of Herrick and of Milton but did not signal the passing away of liturgical verse of the kind so prominent in earlier years of the seventeenth century. Wentworth Dillon, Earl of Roscommon, who died in 1684, paraphrastically translated the "Dies irae," as William Drummond did toward the beginning of the century and as Sir Walter Scott, in "The Lay of the Last Minstrel," was later to do. Isaac Watts, born in 1674, included various liturgical occasions in *Horae Lyricae*, especially in the first book, "Sacred to Devotion and Piety." Among the work's successors in various ways were Christopher Smart's *Hymns and Spiritual Songs for the Fasts and Festivals of the Church of England*, John Keble's *The Christian Year*, and Christina Rossetti's *Some Feasts and Fasts*, not to mention William Cowper's *Olney Hymns* or the work of Victorian hymnodists. John Pomfret, born three years after Milton and Herrick died but prematurely dead himself in 1703, wrote a poem for the Christmas cycle with a title as ponderous as the subject: "*Dies novissima; or, The Last Epiphany. A Pindaric Ode, on Christ's second Appearance, to judge the World.*" Robert Browning's simpler heading for a more latitudinarian work was "Christmas Eve." Dr. Samuel Johnson's "Upon the Feast of St. Simon and St. Jude," Alfred Tennyson's "Saint Simeon Stylites," and Gerard Manley Hopkins's "St. Thecla" are part of the evidence that the legends of the saints could still be possible subjects for verse.

And yet merely to list these authors and titles is to indicate that liturgical verse was not cultivated in the eighteenth and nineteenth centuries as it had been earlier. The poems named in the preceding paragraph, while not especially obscure, are not works of major significance, and in most cases the subject matter evidently was of merely minor interest even for the authors themselves. William Wordsworth is a partial exception in that he did write a large number of "Ecclesiastical Sonnets," and one of them, "The Liturgy," is too convenient for my needs to pass it by. The verse describes the liturgical year as "a zodiac" or "circle," one which begins with the "mild advent" of "the King of Glory" and ends when that king's "countenance / Shall dissipate the seas and mountains hoary." Wordsworth's sonnet is traditionally and accurately descriptive, but in addition to verse that at best is of indifferent quality, a serious problem here is that it gives *merely* a description, nothing more; as Wordsworth himself observes, upon this "circle traced from sacred story / We only dare to cast a glance."[1]

David Jones, born in 1895, was much aware of the trend begun about three hundred years earlier than his own death in 1974, and in "Religion and the Muses" (first published in 1941) he enumerated the factors to be reckoned with in accounting for it. "It is clear," Jones wrote,

> that we have *three* rather than two elements—the problem is triangular, but not permanent—it belongs to our kind of time, even if such times are recurrent. I attempt to name those elements roughly as follows:
> (1) The symbolic life of the Church,
> (2) The preoccupations and tradition of contemporary art,
> (3) The world of technics and utility (alien alike to [1] and [2]) into which we are born, and which informs and conditions us all, whether we like it or not.[2]

As Jones makes clear, he was primarily addressing himself to a twentieth-century problem, one most prominent in "our kind of time," but his "elements" also are helpful in understanding the changing relationship between poetry and liturgy in times that by now are long past.

In the seventeenth century, possibly because the world of technics and utility was not quite so very much with us, the elements were largely favorable, and when it came to writing liturgical verse, the dividing line between poets and priests was not always worth drawing. Liturgy, it is true, became a subject of bitter dispute in Hooker's time and in Milton's, and yet major liturgical patterns and many details nonetheless managed to endure and for that matter are largely recognizable even today. The "preoccupations and tradition" of art, however, repeatedly and regularly have been affected by revolution as well as evolution, and at some point there occurred "The Break" (as Jones calls it) between culture as it was and as it came to be. Jones saw active service in World War I and was profoundly affected, perhaps as deeply as anyone who actually survived. The fact is abundantly clear from *In Parenthesis*, his first book-length poem, and probably is further underlined by the agonies that delayed publication of that work until 1937. Jones, however, also could take a very long view indeed, up to "fifty milleniums," as he remarks in the preface to *The Anathemata*, the book-length liturgical poem published in 1952, and he dated "The Break," not from 1914 or so, but from somewhere in

1. *The Ecclesiastical Sonnets: A Critical Edition*, ed. Abbie F. Potts (New Haven: Yale University Press, 1922), 171. The sonnet was revised several times; in some versions of it, Wordsworth hoped to "cast a more than transient glance" (201).

2. *Epoch and Artist: Selected Writings by David Jones*, ed. Harmon Grisewood (London: Faber & Faber, 1959), 101.

the latter eighteenth century, when assumptions about human existence and the experiencing of it took, in Jones's view, an aberrant and, he hoped, impermanent turn for the worse.

For Jones, this turn was disastrous, among other reasons, because the creation of liturgical art, the highest and best kind in his opinion, became extraordinarily difficult. In the preface to *The Anathemata* and in "Art and Sacrament," an essay from 1955, Jones starts from the premise that art primarily depends on the "making" of "signs" that signify something other and beyond themselves. He further supposes that sign-making is very probably inherent since mankind—this is the context for the long view referred to in the preceding paragraph—"has, for about fifty milleniums [*sic*] (perhaps immeasurably longer) made works, handled material, in a fashion that can only be described as having the nature of a sign" (*Epoch and Artist*, 155). More specifically to the point, "the Lord" was one of those who employed "art-forms" and established "a tradition commanding the continued employment of these forms" (163). A very clear corollary to this view is that liturgy is itself a form of art.

> The Notices for the week may read: Sunday within the Octave of Corpus Christi, Sung Mass, 11 A.M. or they may read: Lord's Day next, Breaking of Bread at 11 o'clock. In both cases we are notified of an intention to represent [Jones's hyphenization presumably signifies double meaning], recall or show-forth something under certain signs and by manual acts, so an "art-work" is notified. (163)

Two conclusions necessarily follow. First, although Jones formally embraced Roman Catholicism in 1921, the truth or falsity of specific rites is immaterial to their artistic validity. Since people are sign-making creatures and since liturgy is a form of this activity, the ritual of art and the art of ritual are fundamental to what it means to be human, even for those who are, in Jones's phrasing, "antipathetic to the signs" (170). Second, as Jones immediately adds, for those who *are* sympathetic, Christian art is or at any rate may be "an abstract art *par excellence*" because "sign and thing signified are regarded as having a true identity." An aesthetic difficulty, of course, is that an artist of any given period may assent to the truth of the signs but be more or less prevented from using them because of the preoccupations of art at that time. Jones does not mention Swift and Pope in this connection, but one might want to recall the one as an exiled Dean of the Anglican Cathedral in Dublin and the other as a disenfranchised Roman Catholic in London.

And, of course, an artist may be born into a world or be nurtured by a largely personal environment in which the signs, however artistic, no longer seem true. A. E. Housman began *More Poems*, published posthumously in 1936, with "Easter Hymn" and followed it up with "When

Israel out of Egypt came" (derived from Psalm 114, appointed for Easter day).[3] The "hymn" sets forth two hypothetical and mutually contradictory conditions. On the one hand, "If in that Syrian garden, ages slain, / You sleep, and know not you are dead in vain," then "Sleep well and see no morning, son of man." "But if," on the other hand, "the grave rent and the stone rolled by, / At the right hand of majesty on high / You sit," then "Bow hither out of heaven and see and save." Since the antecedents of the "if" clauses are neither affirmed nor denied, no logically valid conclusion can be drawn, but Housman nonetheless arrives at a position of firm conviction in the course of the "psalm" that follows. It begins conventionally:

> When Israel out of Egypt came
> Safe in the sea they trod;
> By day in cloud, by night in flame,
> Went on before them God.

Housman does not call into question the biblical history; for all he knows, it might even be true. Also true, however, is the irrelevance of that history for Housman himself. "The tokens that to Israel came, / To me they have not come."

> I never over Horeb heard
> The blast of advent blow;
> No fire-faced prophet brought me word
> Which way behoved to go.

Housman's own exodus journey accordingly leads to an unpromised land of nothingness of which death affords the Pisgah view.

> But I will go where they are hid
> That never were begot
> To my inheritance amid
> The nation that is not.

Housman's liturgy has not been the only kind produced, to requote Jones, in "our kind of time." Jones's *The Anathemata* is a remarkable liturgical poem, and it may not be entirely coincidental that its appearance was greeted with an acclamatory review from T. S. Eliot, whose "Journey of the Magi" and "Ash Wednesday" had seen print some years earlier. A postscript cannot possibly be the place to venture remarks about those poems, but since this study began by considering psalms and litanies, it may be permissible to cite here the litany that Anthony Burgess incorporated into *The Doctor Is Sick*, the wonderfully inventive comic novel first published in 1960.

---

3. A. E. Housman, *Complete Poems* (New York: Henry Holt, 1959 [the "Centennial Edition"]), 157–59.

Edwin Spindrift, the book's principal character, is a linguist by train-
ing who has been far more fascinated by words than by those who use
them. Through a series of wildly bizarre incidents he begins for the first
time to enter into communication with someone other than himself, but
as in other rites de passage, there are treacherous pitfalls on all sides
round. At one point, walking through London's streets, Edwin "com-
posed a litany to himself":

> Ineffectual fornicator,
> Purge of poor publicans,
> Kettle-mob catamite,
> Cheater of Chasper,
> Furniture-fracturer,
> Light-hearted liar,
> Counterfeit-cashman,
> Free meal filcher
> > Prey on us.[4]

Burgess does not say so, but Edwin's litany probably takes its origins from
a slightly earlier experience (172–74) in an after-hours drinking club. "A
lank young man with glasses, turtle-neck sweater and hair geometrically
straight, was sitting on a stool in the middle of the floor, tuning unhand-
ily a Spanish guitar" and "emphasising his cadences in the supposed man-
ner of the Psalmist."

> For them that looked for the way out and found it:
> This.
> There were holes that grew as doors with looking for them,
> And for those that walked through with their heads high as kites,
> This.
> Where were the holes?
> In man, in woman, in bottles, in the tattered book picked up from
> > the mud on the rainy day by the railroad junction.
> But the whole of wholes, the holy of holies, where was,
> > where is
> This?
> . . . .
> Through the ultimate hole is reached
> This:
> What mouselike becomes lionlike when the hole is seen not
> > just as a door in but a door out,
> A door out of
> This:

4. Quoted from a reprint, *The Doctor Is Sick* (New York: W. W. Norton, 1907), 188.

> Cage. Cage.
>
> . . . .
> The holy, the whole, when seen through the hole
> Not seen wholly, but only whole holy deliverer
>   from
> This.

As it happens, "No Exit" is *not* posted anywhere in this novel as an existential sign, but "this" does keep coming persistently round until one finally and quite conclusively discovers, as the novel's last line so pointedly states, "This is the end, that's what it is, the end."

Bibliography

I do not duplicate here those items that are fully footnoted, nor do I include works such as *The Oxford English Dictionary*, *The Oxford Latin Dictionary*, *The Dictionary of National Biography*, or individual volumes in the Loeb Classical Library. As a matter of convenience, however, I do include those works previously mentioned in the Note on Abbreviations and Short Titles.

For some authors, the work of two different editors needed to be cited, but quoting the text itself from only one edition was desirable to reduce confusion. In Herbert's case, for example, Patrides's explanatory and textual notes are indispensable, but Hutchinson's have not been entirely superseded, and Hutchinson's volume, like others in the series of Oxford English Texts, to some extent continues to be "standard." Where necessary, therefore, an asterisk (*) below identifies the edition from which all quotations, unless otherwise specified, are taken. I have annotated a few items with material placed inside square brackets; in each case, the reason is self-explanatory.

ABCP: *The Annotated Book of Common Prayer; being an Historical, Ritual, and Theological Commentary on the Devotional System of the Church of England*. Edited by Rev. John Henry Blunt. London: Gilbert and Rivington, 1866.

Alabaster, William. *The Sonnets of William Alabaster.* Edited by G. M. Story and Helen Gardner. London: Oxford University Press, 1959.

Andrewes, Lancelot. *XCVI Sermons*. London: Richard Badger, 1629.

Aquinas, Thomas, St. *Summa theologica*. 6 vols. Turin: Ex Officina Libraria Marietti, 1937.

Bauer, Johannes B., ed. *Encyclopedia of Biblical Theology: The Complete "Sacramentum Verbi."* New York: The Crossroad Publishing Company, 1981. (A translation from *Bibeltheologisches Wörterbuch*, Graz: Verlag Styria, 1959.)

Beaumont, John, Sir. *The Poems of Sir John Beaumont*. Edited by Alexander B. Grosart. [Edinburgh:] Printed for Private Circulation, 1869.

Beaumont, Joseph. *The Complete Poems of Dr. Joseph Beaumont*. Edited by Alexander B. Grosart. 2 vols. [Edinburgh:] Printed for Private Circulation, 1880.

———. *The Minor Poems of Joseph Beaumont*. Edited by Eloise Robinson. Boston: Houghton Mifflin Company, 1914. [From a previously unpublished manuscript not available to Grosart.]

[Bible.] *Biblia sacra*, sive Testamentum vetus ab Im. Tremellio et Fr. Junio . . . et Testamentum novum à Theo. Beza. London: Apud Nathaniel Parker, 1680.

[Bible, Douai-Rheims.] The Holy Bible Translated from the Latin Vulgate. Baltimore: John Murphy Company, 1914.

[Bible, Greek.] The New Testament in the Original Greek. Edited by Brooke F. Westcott and Fenton J. A. Hort. London: Macmillan & Co., 1904.

[Bible, Hebrew.] The Hebrew-English Old Testament. From the Bagster Polyglot Bible [with the Authorized Version]. London: Samuel Bagster and Sons Limited, 1971.

[Bible, Vulgate.] Biblia sacra juxta vulgatam. Rome: Desclée et Socii, 1956.

Boys, John. *An Exposition of the Dominical Epistles and Gospels vsed in our English Liturgie*. London: Printed by Edward Griffin for William Aspley, 1614–1616. [In four parts, separately paginated; where necessary I specify which part is being cited.]

———. *An Exposition of the Festivall Epistles and Gospels vsed in our English Liturgie*. London: Printed by Edward Griffin for William Aspley, 1614–1615. [In three parts separately paginated; again, where necessary, I specify which part.]

Browne, Thomas. *The Works of Sir Thomas Browne*. Edited by Charles Sayle. 3 vols. Edinburgh: John Grant, 1927.

Carey, Patrick. See Saintsbury.

Cartwright, William. *The Plays and Poems of William Cartwright*. Edited by G. Blakemore Evans. Madison: University of Wisconsin Press, 1951.

Collop, John. *The Poems of John Collop*. Edited by Conrad Hilberry. Madison: University of Wisconsin Press, 1962.

Constable, Henry. *Poems*. Edited by Joan Grundy. Liverpool: Liverpool University Press, 1960.

Crashaw, Richard. *The Complete Poetry of Richard Crashaw*. Edited by George Williams. Garden City, N.Y.: Anchor Books, 1970.

*———. *The Poems . . . of Richard Crashaw*. 2d. ed. Edited by L. C. Martin. Oxford: Clarendon Press, 1957.

Davies, John, of Hereford. *The Complete Works of John Davies of Hereford*. Edited by Alexander B. Grosart. [Edinburgh:] Privately printed, 1871.

Diodati, John. *Pious and Learned Annotations*. 4th ed. London: Printed by Tho. Roycroft for Nicholas Fussell, 1661.

Donne, John. *The Anniversaries*. Edited by Frank Manley. Baltimore: Johns Hopkins University Press, 1963.

———. *Biathanatos*. London, n.d. Reproduced from the first edition with a bibliographical note by J. William Hebel. New York: The Facsimile Text Society, 1930.

———. *The Complete English Poems of John Donne*. Edited by C. A. Patrides. London: J. M. Dent and Sons Ltd., 1985.

———. *The Complete English Poems of John Donne*. Edited by A. J. Smith. Harmondsworth: Penguin Books, 1971; repr. with corr. 1976.

————. *The Complete Poetry of John Donne*. Edited by John Shawcross. Garden City, N.Y.: Anchor Books, 1967.

————. *Devotions Upon Emergent Occasions*. Edited by Anthony Raspa. Montreal: McGill-Queen's University Press, 1975.

*————. *The Divine Poems*. Edited by Helen Gardner. Oxford: Clarendon Press, 1952.

*————. *The Elegies and the Songs and Sonnets*. Edited by Helen Gardner. Oxford: Clarendon Press, 1965.

————. *Essays in Divinity*. Edited by Evelyn M. Simpson. Oxford: Oxford University Press, 1952.

————. *Letters to Severall Persons of Honour (1651)*. Fasc. repr. with introduction by Thomas Hester. Delmar, N.Y.: Scholars' Facsimiles and Reprints, 1977.

————. *The Sermons of John Donne*. Edited by George R. Potter and Evelyn M. Simpson. 10 vols. Berkeley and Los Angeles: University of California Press, 1953–1962.

Drummond, William, of Hawthornden. *Poetical Works*. Edited by L. E. Kastner. 2 vols. Manchester: Manchester University Press, 1913.

Flatman, Thomas. See Saintsbury.

Gascoigne, George. *A Hundreth Sundrie Flowres*. Edited by C. T. Prouty. Columbia: University of Missouri Press, 1942; repr. 1970.

Hall, John. *The Court of Virtue*. Edited by Russell A. Fraser. London: Routledge and Kegan Paul, 1961.

Hall, Joseph. *The Works . . . of Joseph Hall*. Edited by Philip Wynter. 10 vols. Oxford: At the University Press, 1863.

Hammond, William. See Saintsbury.

Harvey, Christopher. *The Complete Poems of Christopher Harvey*. Edited by Alexander B. Grosart. London: Printed for Private Circulation, 1874.

Henry, Matthew [1662–1714]. *Commentary on the Whole Bible*. 6 vols. Scottdale, Penn.: Herald Press, [c. 1935].

Herbert, George. *The English Poems of George Herbert*. Edited by C. A. Patrides. London and Tottowa, N.J.: J. M. Dent and Sons Ltd., 1974; repr. 1975.

*————. *The Works of George Herbert*. Edited by F. E. Hutchinson. Oxford: Clarendon Press, 1953.

*Herrick, Robert. *The Complete Poetry of Robert Herrick*. Edited by J. Max Patrick. Garden City, N.Y.: Anchor Books, 1963.

————. *The Poetical Works of Robert Herrick*. Edited by L. C. Martin. Oxford: Clarendon Press, 1956.

[Homilies.] *Certain Sermons or Homilies Appointed to be read in Churches in the Time of the late Queen Elizabeth . . . And now . . . Reprinted . . . Anno MDCIII*. Oxford: Oxford University Press, 1840.

Hooker, Richard. *Of the Laws of Ecclesiastical Polity*. 2 vols. London: J. M. Dent and Sons Ltd., 1907; repr. 1954.

Jonson, Ben. *Poems*. Edited by Ian Donaldson. London: Oxford University Press, 1975.

Lapide, Cornelius à. *Commentaria in Acta Apostolorum, Epistolas canonicas, et Apocalypsin.* Antwerp: Apud Joannis et Jacopus Meursius, 1647.

––––––. *Commentaria in duodecim Prophetas minores.* Antwerp: Apud Joannis et Jacopus Meursius, 1655.

––––––. *Commentaria in Ecclesiasten . . . Canticum canticorum . . . [et] librum Sapientiae.* Antwerp: Apud Joannis et Jacopus Meursius, 1638.

––––––. *Commentaria in . . . Pauli Epistolas.* Antwerp: Apud Joannis et Jacopus Meursius, 1637.

––––––. *Commentaria in quatuor Evangelia.* Antwerp: Apud Joannis et Jacopus Meursius, 1639.

Leigh, Edward. *Critica Sacra . . . Observations On all the Radices, or Primitive Hebrew Words of the Old Testament . . . [and] Philologicall and Theologicall Observations upon All the Greek Words of the New Testament,* 3d. ed. [combining the two parts from earlier publication]. London: Printed by Abraham Miller and Roger Daniel for Thomas Underhill, 1650.

Milton, John. *Complete Poems and Major Prose.* Edited by Merritt Y. Hughes. New York: The Odyssey Press, 1957.

More, Henry. *The Philosophical Poems of Henry More.* Edited by Geoffrey Bullough. Manchester: Manchester University Press, 1931.

Nashe, Thomas. *The Works of Thomas Nashe.* Edited by Ronald B. McKerrow. Reprinted from the original edition with corrections and supplementary notes. Edited by F. P. Wilson. 5 vols. Oxford: Basil Blackwell, 1958.

Nelson, Rt. Rev. Msgr. Joseph A., ed. *The Roman Breviary in English.* 4 vols. New York: Benizinger, 1950.

OCEL: The Oxford Companion to English Literature. 5th ed. Edited by Margaret Drabble. Oxford: Oxford University Press, 1985.

ODCC: The Oxford Dictionary of the Christian Church. Edited by F. L. Cross. London: Oxford University Press, 1958.

PBD: The Prayer Book Dictionary. Edited by George Harford and Morley Stevenson. New York: Longmans, Green, and Company, 1912.

Pearson, John. *An Exposition of the Creed.* 21st ed. London: Thomas Tegg, 1839.

Poole, Matthew [1624–1679]. *A Commentary on the Holy Bible.* 2 vols. London, 1685. Reprint in 3 vols. London: The Banner of Truth Trust, 1962.

Pope, Alexander. *The Poems of Alexander Pope.* Edited by John Butt et al. 11 vols. London: Methuen and Co.; and New Haven: Yale University Press, 1940–1969.

Quarles, Francis. *Hosanna or Divine Poems on the Life of Christ* [and] *Threnodes.* Edited by John Horden. Liverpool: Liverpool University Press, 1960.

Saintsbury, George., ed. *Minor Poets of the Caroline Period.* 3 vols. Oxford: Clarendon Press, 1905–1921.

Sidney, Philip, Sir. *The Poems of Sir Philip Sidney.* Edited by William A. Ringler. Oxford: Clarendon Press, 1962.

Southwell, Robert. *The Poems of Robert Southwell, S.J.* Edited by James H. McDonald and Nancy Pollard Brown. Oxford: Clarendon Press, 1967.

Sparrow, Anthony. *A Rationale vpon the Book of Common Prayer.* London: Printed for T. Garthwait, 1688.

Taylor, Jeremy. *The Whole Works of the Right Rev. Jeremy Taylor.* Edited by Reginald Heber, revised by Charles P. Eden. 10 vols. London: Longmans, Green, and Company, 1883.

Toal, M. F., ed. *The Sunday Sermons of the Great Fathers.* 4 vols. Chicago: Henry Regnery Company, 1955.

Traherne, Thomas. *Poems, Centuries, and Three Thanksgivings.* Edited by Anne Ridler. London: Oxford University Press, 1966.

Vaughan, Henry. *The Complete Poems.* Edited by Alan Rudrum. New Haven: Yale University Press, 1981.

*———. *The Works of Henry Vaughan.* 2d ed. Edited by L. C. Martin. Oxford: Clarendon Press, 1957.

Wilson, Thomas. *A Christian Dictionary.* 3d ed. London: Printed by William Jaggard, 1623.

Wither, George. *HALELVIAH: or Britains second Remembrancer.* Manchester: Printed for the Spenser Society, 1879.

Wogan, William. *An Essay on the Proper Lessons Appointed by the Liturgy of the Church of England.* 4 vols. 2d ed. London: Printed for John and Charles Rivington, 1764.

Wyatt, Thomas, Sir. *The Complete Poems.* Edited by R. A. Rebholz. New Haven: Yale University Press, 1978.

Index

Taylor, Jeremy, 49–50, 112, 151, 153, 162, 187, 247
Tennyson, Alfred, 259
Teresa of Avila, St., 14–16, 120
Tibullus, 245
Time: biblical time versus western time, 125–41; "carpe diem" approach to, 234–42; in Herrick's poetry, 229–34. *See also* Calendar of the Church
Traherne, Thomas: compared with Herbert, 56; numbers and quantitative patterns in, 54–55; and paradox of the fortunate Fall, 53; sense of filiation, 52, 54; timelessness of, 54
—works: "The Approach," 56; "Bells," 56; *Centuries of Meditations*, 50–51, 54–56; *Christian Ethicks*, 56; "The Designe," 56; "The Evidence," 56; "For Man to Act," 56; "The Improvement," 56; "An Infant-Ey," 56; "The Inference," 57; "Innocence," 56; "Insatiableness," 57–58; "My Spirit," 57; "Nature," 57; "The Preparative," 57; "Sight," 56; "Silence," 50; "Solitude," 50; "The Vision," 56, 57
Transfiguration, 227–29

Vaughan, Henry: importance of sequential proximity in, 163, 166, 170–71; internal flintiness of, 52; poem on Mary Magdalene, 113; sequence in poetry of, 42–45
—works: "Abels blood," 45n; "Affliction," 170, 172; "The Ass," 46; "The Bee," 174; "Buriall," 44; "Childe-hood," 44–45, 47–48; "Christs Nativity," 164–66, 167, 168, 170; "Come, come, what doe I here?" 41–42, 43, 44; "Content," 44; "Corruption," 166, 167–68; "The Dayspring," 170, 171, 175; "De Salmone," 174; "Discipline," 170, 172; "Distraction," 43, 44; "The Ecclipse," 170, 172; "The Evening Watch," 106, 109–10; "Faith," 40; "H. Scriptures," 166, 167,

168; "*Isaacs* Marriage," 43; "Jordanis," 174; *The Life of Holy Paulinus*, 37, 38; "Looking Back," 44, 170, 172, 176, 203; "Midnight," 41, 42, 43, 44; "Misery," 164; "The Morning Watch," 109–10; *The Mount of Olives*, 106, 247; "The Nativity, Written in the Year 1656," 44, 169–70, 171, 173–74, 182, 183; "The Night," 37, 45–48, 57; "Pious thoughts and Ejaculations," 173, 174, 185; "The Pursuit," 43, 44; "The Recovery," 170–71, 187; "Regeneration," 43; "Repentance," 37, 38–39; "The Request," 174; "Retirement," 170, 172; "The Retreate," 37, 40–41, 42, 43, 44; "The Revival," 170, 172; "The Search," 43; "Servilii Fatum, *sive* Vindicta divina," 174; "The Shephards," 163–64; "The Shower," 43, 44, 170, 172; *Silex Scintillans*, 37, 43, 49, 163, 170; "The Stone," 44; *Thalia Rediviva*, 44, 163, 168–69, 170; "The Throne," 45n; "To Christian Religion," 174, 176–77; "To his Books," 173; "The true Christmas," 193; "Unprofitablenes," 166–67, 168; "The World," 174
Vaughan, William, 42
Virgil, 134, 135, 135n

Washbourne, Thomas, 153n
Watkyns, Rowland, 142, 151–52, 156
Watts, Isaac, 259
Williams, George, 14, 15, 27, 30, 31, 209, 216
Wilson, Thomas, 87–88, 98
Wither, George: on the Circumcision, 79–80; hymn for Easter, 72; poetry on Christmas, 142
—works: "An Evening Hymn," 108; "For the Advent Sundays," 145, 151, 162; *Halelviah*, 70; "A Morning Hymn," 108
Wordsworth, William, 259–60
Wyatt, Thomas, 72